P9-CFC-074

THE PARTING OF THE ROADS

THE PARTING OF
THE ROADS

STUDIES IN THE DEVELOPMENT OF
JUDAISM AND EARLY CHRISTIANITY

BY

MEMBERS OF JESUS COLLEGE, CAMBRIDGE

WITH AN INTRODUCTION BY

W. R. INGE, D.D.

LATE PROFESSORIAL FELLOW, NOW HONORARY FELLOW OF
THE COLLEGE AND DEAN OF ST. PAUL'S

EDITED BY

F. J. FOAKES JACKSON, D.D.

FELLOW AND DEAN OF THE COLLEGE

LONDON
EDWARD ARNOLD
1912

TO THE

MASTERS, FELLOWS, AND SCHOLARS,

PAST, PRESENT, AND FUTURE

OF THE COLLEGE

OF THE BLESSED VIRGIN MARY, ST. JOHN THE EVANGELIST,

AND THE GLORIOUS VIRGIN ST. RADEGUND,

COMMONLY CALLED JESUS COLLEGE,

IN THE UNIVERSITY OF CAMBRIDGE,

AND ESPECIALLY TO

HENRY ARTHUR MORGAN, D.D.,

MASTER OF THE COLLEGE,

THIS VOLUME IS DEDICATED.

EDITOR'S PREFACE

THIS volume of essays differs from its predecessors in being essentially a young man's book, and the work of a single college, instead of representing the opinion of an English University.

Jesus College, Cambridge, has been singularly fortunate as regards Theology in recent years in having secured for its professorial Fellows two occupants of the Chair of the Lady Margaret's Reader in Divinity, the present Master of Pembroke (Dr. Mason), and Dean of St. Paul's (Dr. Inge). It has been further helped by the late Lord Justice Kay's generous and discriminating benefaction in memory of Lady Kay, herself a daughter of Dr. French, Master of the College (1820–1849). This has enabled men who have obtained honours in a Tripos to stay up after taking the B.A. degree to study Theology in the College, with a view of taking Holy Orders in the Church of England. Not that the study of Theology has been pursued solely by members of the National Church. Jesus College boasts of Nonconformists who have won distinction in the subject, and one of the essayists is of the Jewish faith.

With the exception of the Introduction by the Dean of St. Paul's and the first essay by the editor, the volume is the work of men, every one of whom, except Dr. Oesterley, took his degree within the present century; and all the writers of Essays III. to X. were pupils of the editor.

It must not be supposed, however, that, though the plan of the volume was sketched by the editor, there has been any attempt to make it a mere echo of his opinions. The essayists are of very different schools of thought, and have always been encouraged at Cambridge to give full play to their individuality; and the editor has met with a gratifying determination on the part of his fellow-workers to express their own opinions in their own words. The book, therefore, is not in any sense a manifesto of any particular opinions; and any unity it may possess is to be found in its general plan, and in the desire to place the facts historically before the reader.

Of the introductory essay, it is sufficient for the editor to express his thanks to Dr. Inge—whose abandonment of the Lady Margaret Chair his college still deplores—for his kind words, and for the brilliant exposition of his conception of the history of the Church.

The second essay is by the editor. The third, by Mr. R. T. Howard, chaplain of the College, will be interesting owing to the standpoint of the writer. Brought up in what may be described as the old-fashioned Evangelical school, Mr. Howard, who obtained first-classes in Mathematics and Theology, has endeavoured to present the beliefs in which he was educated in the light of one who has accepted many of the results of modern criticism. It will be evident that these have not prevented him from continuing to be a devotional student of the Old Testament.

Of Dr. Oesterley's work in the fourth essay commendation is superfluous. He has won his place among experts on questions affecting Early Judaism, and needs no introduction to scholars.

Mr. H. G. Wood, late Fellow and Lecturer in History, is one of the most distinguished Nonconformist students of the College. To the great regret of his friends at Cambridge he abandoned the work of teaching history, in order to devote himself to the study of theology at the Woodbrooke Settlement, and the fifth essay is one of the earliest outcomes of labours which promise to be of the highest service to theological thought.

Mr. W. K. Lowther Clarke, Rector of Cavendish, and formerly Fellow, was a contemporary of Mr. Wood, and gained identical honours with him in both Classics and Theology. His essay on Apostolic Christianity represents the views of moderate Anglicanism, and gives reason to hope that the English Church will in him provide one more strenuous worker in the field of New Testament study.

The difficult subject of Pauline Theology has been entrusted to Mr. G. B. Redman, formerly Scholar of the College, whose career in Classics and Theology has been virtually identical with that of Mr. Clarke and Mr. Wood. Mr. Redman, who is at present at Ridley Hall, would, presumably, have no hesitation in enrolling himself with the Evangelical party.

Mr. B. T. D. Smith, the author of the essay on the Johannine Theology, and now Vice-Principal of the Cambridge Clergy Training School, is not like most of the essayists a product of our English public schools. Leaving school at an early age, he joined the staff of the Northamptonshire County Council, and prepared in his leisure hours for the University. After taking the Historical Tripos, he joined Jesus College as a Lady Kay Scholar, and was distinguished both in Old and New Testament in the Theological Tripos. His scholarly work shows the importance of encouraging young Churchmen, who may have embraced other careers, to study Theology if they show a decided bent in that direction. Mr. Smith may be described as of the High Anglican school.

Mr. Ephraim Levine, formerly Scholar of the College, took a first-class in Oriental languages, and afterwards in the Hebrew section of the Theological Tripos. He is an orthodox Jew, and seems to be drawn towards the ministry of the Synagogue. His contribution to the *Parting of the Roads* is valuable as giving the Jewish view of the matter.

Mr. P. Gardner-Smith, the youngest contributor, has made a special study of the Philosophy of Religion for the Theological Tripos. The subject he has been asked to undertake, that of Revelation, is a most difficult one; and it is a matter for congratulation that the editor has been able to secure two essays from such different standpoints as the third and the tenth. In Mr. Howard we have the Conservative position represented, whilst Mr. Gardner-Smith represents the side of Liberalism.

The editor greatly regrets that his most distinguished pupil, whom he now regards as his most sympathetic teacher and adviser, Professor Alexander Nairne of King's College,

London, late Fellow of the College, has not been able to contribute to this volume; but, though his name does not appear, his influence is to be recognised throughout the book. His letters of advice and criticism of the work submitted to him in themselves almost extend to the limits of an essay; and his unstinting labours on its behalf deserve hearty recognition. Thanks are also due to Dr. Mason, Master of Pembroke, Dr. Lukyn Williams, Mr. A. C. Jennings, and Mr. G. G. Morris, Fellow of the College, for reading essays in proof, and to Miss Helen Maud Slee for preparing the Index.

It is with no ordinary feelings that the editor presents this volume to the public, now that he has almost completed thirty years of service to the College, which gave so kindly a welcome to him as a stranger from Trinity in October 1882; in the furtherance of whose interests he has found an unfailing source of happiness.

CONTENTS

ESSAY I

INTRODUCTORY₁

BY

W. R. INGE, D.D.

Dean of St. Paul's, Honorary Fellow of Jesus College

ESSAY I

INTRODUCTORY

IT is a rare pleasure to me to be asked to contribute to a volume of Essays by members of Jesus College. My connection with that foundation—the third College, of which I have had the honour to be a Fellow—has been a pure delight to me. The place has a charm and fascination which are quite unique. Standing in an isolated position, withdrawn from the chaos of pale yellow bricks which make the streets of Cambridge so unromantic, and surrounded by spacious lawns and green fields, it preserves, in its peaceful cloisters and venerable chapel, the quiet dignity and grace of the mediæval convent which it superseded. That such a College should be the home of vigorous athleticism, respected in the University for its prowess on the river and cricket-field, does not appear strange to the Englishman, but the combination is not without piquancy. The buildings seem more adapted for a body of theological students, such as have, in fact, been frequently collected at Jesus, where interest in religious and theological questions has never been suffered to flag. The contributors to the present volume are only a few of many who, in recent years, have gone forth from this College into the ministry of Christ's Church. They have not belonged to any one school of thought, or been confined to one denomination; but have found their mutual advantage in cultivating that friendly and brotherly spirit which has made the College one of the most united in either University. How much this spirit of friendliness and loyalty is due to the example of the venerable Master and his family is known to all members of the College. To me, therefore, whose official connection with the University has lately ceased, it is no small satisfaction to join in a co-operative volume with my friends, colleagues, and former pupils.

* * * * * * *

The subject of Christian origins, with various aspects of which these Essays deal, is one of perennial interest, and is probably inexhaustible. Fresh light is thrown upon its problems in each generation, and the light is to a large extent that of present experience, both inner and external. For the Christian revelation is (to use Eucken's convenient phrase) not merely a phenomenon, but a *fact*. It was not an isolated event, which now belongs to past history. On the contrary, it was the inauguration of a grand historical drama, which is yet far from completion, and the meaning of which will only be fully understood when the *dénouement* is known. As each page in the story is turned, the significance of the first chapter becomes a little clearer. There is a true sense in which we may be said to know much more about the Incarnation than the first Christians did.

The well-known saying of Clement of Alexandria, that Christianity is like a river which receives tributaries from all sides, is full of truth to the modern student of Church history. But we should now say that Catholic Christianity was the result of the confluence of two great streams, which differed in their origin and in the colour of their water more widely than the Rhone and the Saône, or than the White and Blue Niles. These two streams, the Semitic and the European, the Jewish and the Greek, still mingle their waters in the turbid flood which constitutes the institutional religion of civilised humanity; but to this day the waters flow side by side in the same bed, perfectly recognisable—so alien are the two types to each other. And yet the attempts that have been made from time to time to purge Christianity of Hellenism, or of Hebraism, have never come near success. Christianity is and must remain a composite creed, an amalgamation of opposite types of belief. This is its weakness, and also its strength.

In speaking of the Jewish element in Christianity, it must be remembered that the cradle of our faith was not Judæa but Galilee, and that the Galileans had probably hardly a drop of Jewish blood in their veins. They were tolerated by the Jews, in consideration of their strict and almost fanatical orthodoxy, while the heretical Samaritans, who were probably nearer to them in race, were detested; but the Jew never looked upon the Galilean as a member of his own tribe. Judæa itself was perhaps the last place in the world from which the religion of the Græco-Roman Empire could have sprung.

It has been asserted so often as to be almost a commonplace, that the Jews have had an unique genius for religion. But this judgement can only be accepted with many qualifications. The priests who manipulated the records of the national history in the interests of the hierarchy have succeeded only too well in obscuring the real facts. The religion of the most ancient Hebrews was neither monotheistic nor pre-eminently moral; it much resembled the cults of the surrounding nations. And when Judaism assumed the form under which we recognise it, it was not, if we judge it by its effects on the national character, a religion of a very elevated type. The main interests of the Jew were secular and materialistic, and were raised into a purer atmosphere almost entirely by intense racial feeling. Fanatical, indeed almost insane, patriotism was the dominant passion of the average Jew. Jehovah was, for the majority, the only real God, because He was the God of the Jewish people, and the Jew, as Philo says, is "the only real man." Patriotism, which involves self-sacrifice, and requires a historical imagination, is an ennobling sentiment, and it lifted the Jew into a kind of idealism. But the close identification of religion with the national fortunes had another result of far-reaching importance. For the Jew, faith always clothed itself in a historical dress. For him, every idea must be squeezed into the form of time. The truth is not something which is there all the while, if we could see it. It is that which was, or (more decidedly) that which will be. There is nothing illusory about the goods and ills of the material world. They are real enough. But the time has not yet come, as come it surely will, when the chosen people

will achieve their destiny, which is to bruise all other nations
with a rod of iron, or break them in pieces like a potter's
vessel. So salvation is not "the knowledge of God"; it is
"the good time coming."

This fierce and passionate nationalism consumed the heart
of the Jew, and filled his whole horizon. This people had no
art, no science, no secular literature. It knew nothing of
natural law, and was therefore unacquainted with the idea
of miracle, in the modern sense of the word. Arbitrary will
ruled in heaven, the irresistible but reversible decrees of
an absolute personal ruler. And on earth, too, the victory
would ultimately fall to that race which possesses the most
indomitable will, the most stubborn tenacity and patience,
whether in doing or suffering.

Judaism was a religion of law, never of redemption; in
saying which, we touch one of the main lines of cleavage in
the classification of religions. The Jewish doctrine of repentance was, and is, quite unlike that of Catholicism. As a
learned Jew once told me, persons of his faith are never
encouraged to "worry about their sins" (in Sir Oliver
Lodge's phrase); with them the one and only requisite is
to "turn to the Lord." In other words, conversion of the
will is enough; bygones may be bygones. The Jewish
consciousness of sin was generally awakened by consciousness of personal or national misfortune, which, in accordance with his presuppositions, could only be interpreted
as a proof that the "covenant" with his God had been
broken. When the political horizon looked very black
indeed, it behoved every patriotic Jew to omit no precaution, no minutest detail of pious observance, if so be
that the wrath of God might be turned away. Even the
pedantries of the Rabbis were inspired by love of country
and race; they are not purely contemptible, for this reason
only. And there were never lacking teachers to insist that
the only sacrifice acceptable to God is moral reformation.

Side by side with the learned legal religion of Pharisees
and "lawyers," we find a rich growth of apocalyptic fancies
among the common people. No consistent beliefs, no "eschatology," can be constructed out of the wild welter of

pictorial imagery in which these hopes took shape. But one thing is clear to the unbiassed reader of this strange literature. The same ardent nationalism, the same concreteness of religious hopes, which characterise the mental outlook of the Jewish race throughout, are the controlling elements in the apocalyptic books. In one form or another, the theocratic empire of the God of the Jews is to be established over the whole earth, and the chosen race is to trample the Gentiles underfoot.

It would indeed be unjust to emphasise these unlovely elements in Judaism without remembering the glorious religious poetry of the Psalms and Prophetical Books, which constitutes for us nearly the whole of the strictly religious value of the Old Testament, and enables us still to venerate the Jewish Scriptures as an uniquely inspired literature. Religion in its purest form is strangely independent of race, time, and creed. Religious genius is even more universal and independent in its appeal than artistic genius; the mystics all the world over understand each other without interpreters. A nation so gifted as the Jews could not fail to produce examples of supreme excellence in the one creative and imaginative field from which it was not debarred by its intense self-concentration. Even when the provincialism of Jewish politics is the proximate inspirer of these meditations, the fire of pure devotion frequently bursts through, and turns "Jerusalem" from a second-rate hill-fortress into the ideal city of God, and "Israel" into the symbolic name of elect humanity. This part of our legacy from the Jews is happily more indestructible than the plastic art of the Hellenes. It will live and be loved as long as Homer and Plato, and by a far larger number of the sons of men. It was indeed *God* who, at sundry times and in divers manners, spake in times past to this people, as He never spoke to the other nations of the world.

There was a time when it seemed likely that this indomitable race would succumb, like the rest of the Near East, to the seductive influence of Hellenic culture. Contact with Greek ideas leaves no race and no man quite where they were before; and even the Jews were bent a little, for a time. But the instinct of self-preservation asserted itself. The race sacrificed all that Greece had to give it—and who can measure that sacrifice?—in order to keep its national type pure. It was magnificent, and rather terrible.

The contrast between the Hellenic and Hebraic views of life has been drawn out by many since Matthew Arnold. The difference is indeed striking between the narrow and fierce absorption of the Jew in the fortunes of his nation, his indifference to all but concrete, tangible marks of Divine favour, his intense will-power and defective æsthetic sensibility, and (on the other side) the genial, open-minded mentality of the Greek, full of curiosity and enjoyment of nature, an artist to his finger-tips, as the Japanese, and no other nation, are to-day; whose religion was a poetical and symbolical mythology; who lived in a present which he loved to enjoy and ardently desired to understand; who, like a child, craved only to *see* all that is to be seen of this wonderful world and the spiritual mysteries which may lie behind it; whose intellect was so much more developed than his will, that he sincerely believed that to see the truth was to possess it, vice being only ignorance and virtue knowledge; and whose sense of the finer values of life was so keen that he frankly despised unnecessary apparatus, and lived a hardier and healthier life than any civilised race has lived before or since.

But there were (speaking broadly) no Greeks left in the time of Christ. The race was all but extinct, or swamped in the mongrel horde with which the Roman Empire was filling its Eastern provinces. It was a grand tradition, not a living race, which did battle with the Jews for the spiritual tuition of Europe during the next two thousand years, and who can say how much longer? The Greek race had died in giving birth to Hellenism, a mode of thinking and feeling—a view of life—which is still very much alive. It has been said that almost all that lives and moves in the world, outside the blind forces of nature, is Greek in its origin. The Jewish race, on the contrary, survived. It had determined to survive at all costs. Judaism was the desperate expedient whereby a subjugated or homeless race might hope to exist for an indefinite period without losing its national characteristics.

The contribution of Greece to Christianity—if we may regard the Hellenistic age as in any true sense the heir of the Hellenic—has probably been much larger than that of Judaism. In one very important domain, that of eschatology, Christianity had before the end of the first century definitely made its choice in the direction pointed out by the heathen rather than in the direction pointed out by the Jew. The home of beatified spirits was not to be on earth. Moreover, the late Greek conception of religion, as a complex of three parts—ritualism, ethics, and mysticism—has passed into Christianity, though Catholicism has welded the three together in a manner never attempted by Paganism. For the " Greek " (using the name as St. Paul used it) religion included a symbolical mythology, which he never thought of turning into history, connected with a sacramental system which gathered round the temples where votaries were "initiated " ; and a philosophy which tended more and more to become a strict ethical and devotional discipline, conducting the soul, as was believed, through purification to illumination, and through illumination to the beatific vision of God. This conception of religion, which might have satisfied Plato, made for the conservation of the classical tradition. The art and literature of the great period were valued, though the brighter and more genial side of the tradition was in danger of being lost. The Attic salt had wholly disappeared from the Greek-speaking provinces in the second and third centuries ; and with the decay of art and science came up a crop of Oriental superstitions, magic, theurgy, and theosophy, which were rampant in those two centuries, when Christianity was contending with other syncretistic cults for the favour of the populace.

This kind of superstition had never taken root among the Jews. They were indeed too stubborn materialists to be superstitious. Catholicism, with its *ex opere operato* theory of sacramental grace, its worship of Isis, renamed as the Virgin Mary, its cult of relics, its Neoplatonic theology and mysticism, is no child of the synagogue, from which it only borrowed its war-cry, "*extra Ecclesiam nulla salus.*"

The weakest side of Hellenism corresponds exactly to the strongest side of Hebraism. The Jews, as I have said, had an inveterate habit of forcing all ideas into the form of time. The real as opposed to the apparent, the divine as opposed to the human, was envisaged by them as the future opposed to the present. "*Non si male nunc, et olim sic erit,*" is the spirit of their religious hope. But Hellenism, so far as it was a religion of hope at all, offered only a hope of redemption for the individual from the mists of error and the "muddy vesture of decay." Its real-ideal world was exalted above time, and therefore had no history. And since time is the form of the will, while the intellect is timeless, there was in Greek thought an undoubted tendency to an will-less intellectualism, though this has been often exaggerated. The mysteries promised the initiated a blessed immortality in which the soul, exempt henceforth from the "grievous wheel" (ἀργαλέος κύκλος) of reincarnation, should enjoy for ever the bliss of contemplating the eternal antitypes of all that is good and fair on earth. How different from the Jewish dream of universal sovereignty over a transfigured earth, with Jerusalem as the world's capital!

So "thy sons, O Zion," stood confronted with "thy sons, O Greece." Two racial types utterly unlike each other; two histories equally dissimilar; two philosophies of life, and two religions, were now to unite in begetting that strangest product of time, Catholic Christianity. How was it possible that fire and water could thus coalesce?

συνώμοσαν γὰρ, ὄντες ἔχθιστοι τὸ πρίν,
πῦρ καὶ θάλασσα.

The deepest and truest explanation is surely this, that the Divine Founder of Christianity was above the antithesis. His character and view of life were unlike those of the typical Jew; but we can hardly call them Hellenic. He loved His nation, but neither hated nor despised the foreigner; He obeyed the Law, but showed a marked favour to the Samaritan schismatic; He proclaimed the approaching King-

dom of God, but foresaw with perfect certainty that Jerusalem
would soon be levelled with the ground, and the apocalyptic
political dreams of its inhabitants dispelled for ever. He
knew God to be one, personal, omnipotent, all-seeing; in this
He confirmed the faith of His countrymen; but He knew
Him also as His Father and the Father of all men, Jew and
Gentile. Like the Greek, He loved all unspoilt nature—the
flowers of the field and the cool breeze of the mountain top;
but He has no direct message to the artist. His heaven is
neither purely in the present nor in the future, neither "here"
nor "yonder." He brings heaven down to earth, and exalts
earth to heaven. Of Him, as of no other, the famous lines
of Jacob Böhme might seem to have been written:—

> "Weme ist Zeit wie Ewigkeit
> Und Ewigkeit wie diese Zeit,
> Der ist befreit von allem Streit."

His God has His centre everywhere, His circumference nowhere. All barriers fall before His teaching, like the walls of
Jericho at the blast of Joshua's trumpets. He taught mankind the religion of pure inwardness, of true spirituality;
and by elevating love, or sympathy, to the throne in the
world of spiritual realities, He revealed a principle of inexhaustible ethical and philosophical value. It is idle to pretend that this Teacher, and this teaching, can be explained
within the lines of Jewish pietism. Christ bursts these
cramping fetters at every movement. It was a new faith
which He brought, a new view of time and eternity. Judaism
could no more imprison the soul of this revelation than the
tomb at Jerusalem could retain the body of its Founder.
The universality of Christianity is based upon, and explained
by, the universality of Christ.

In the Epistles of St. Paul we see the true meaning of
the new revelation grasped by the intuition of a man of
genius, and expounded with ever-increasing clearness and
confidence. The rupture with Judaism is reluctant, but
decisive. "In Christ there is no more Jew nor Gentile, bar-
barian, Scythian, bond nor free." So vanish all the barriers
at once, national, cultural, and social. A wholly new hierarchy
of human values is established, the charter for all time of

"the liberty of the Christian man." In the Fourth Gospel we see that the conflict with Judaism, within the Church, is already over. The European has won his footing, and the first and greatest of Christian philosophic mystics has soldered the Pauline religion of the Spirit into the historical framework of the Gospel. In this treatise we have, if we may dare so to speak, an absolutely true interpretation of the Christian revelation, of its intention, meaning, and universal value.

When we leave the age of the inspired writings, we have the less pleasing spectacle of Christianity as a competitor with other popular religions for the empire of souls. It did not come out of the conflict unscathed, for it borrowed not a little that was alien to its real essence. Throughout the struggle the Judaic ingredient was a stiffening element which perhaps determined the issue of the strife. Religious exclusiveness, which appears already within the circle of the twelve Apostles while Christ was still alive, differentiated the Christians completely from the tolerant worshippers of Isis and Mithra. The hope of an early deliverance, at the expected return of Christ to earth, was another element of strength derived from Judaism, though it rested on a pure illusion. These ideas, while they made the Christians aliens to their fellow-subjects, and detached them too much from interest in the welfare of the Empire, gave them a cohesion, tenacity, and confidence which were not be found in any other religious body.

But the controversy with Paganism was not allowed to work itself out to its inevitable end. The old religion was not suffered to die a natural death. The Christians, after the failure of the last persecution, were able to force a concordat upon the Empire. The strong arm of the State before long exerted itself to establish religious uniformity. An era of forced conversions began again, this time in the interests of the Catholic Church. The result was a "settlement" as illogical, and as dexterous, as the Elizabethan settlement of the differences between Catholics and Puritans. By a rough and ready amalgamation of Jewish and Hellenic ideas, myth was mixed with history, poetry with science, and belief in this conglomerate was enforced in the only possible form, namely, that of acceptance and obedience. Most of our present difficulties are the result of this heavy-handed State intervention, whereby discussions were closed before difficulties had been solved, and a vast quantity of crude Pagan superstition was incorporated in Catholicism, from which it has never yet been dislodged. The Church was allowed to settle its internal disputes, not without secular dictation and occasional violence from the Government, but on the whole in accordance with the wisest counsel available, and with no undue haste. But the suppression of Paganism was effected by making conformity easy and dissent dangerous; and as usually happens when this policy is adopted, much of the good which lurked in the defeated system was destroyed, and much of the evil smuggled in.

Christianity had to build its house out of the traditions of ruined and embittered Jewish nationalism and a degenerate and barbarised Hellenism. Neither stock was able to contribute its best to the new building. In these circumstances, the marvel is not that our religion retains some evil legacies from that miserable time, when "two expiring civilisations were drawing their last sighs," but that an institution so splendid in achievement and so rich in promise as the Christian Church should have arisen out of such foundations. The only explanation (so at least it seems to the present writer) is to be found in the personality of the Founder. In the New Testament the historical Christ is for ever enshrined and preserved. From Him the Church has always been able to draw fresh springs of living water. Incomparably greater than His disciples, even when they were still under His personal influence, He was able to impress upon them enough of His message to stereotype for all time the main outlines of the highest religion which mankind is capable of understanding. This message constitutes an unattainable, but not an unintelligible, ideal. For all succeeding generations down to our own time, for ourselves, and for the long series of Christian centuries which lie before us, the task has been, is, and will be, "to grow up into Him in all things, which is the Head, even Christ."

The very discords and contradictions which distress the thoughtful mind when it attempts to analyse the Christian creed are the price which we have to pay for its unique comprehensiveness. No scheme which makes religion either purely historical, or purely ideal, can satisfy the needs and intuitions of the human race. Christianity does justice to both claims. The *anima naturaliter Judaica* and the Neoplatonic mystic are both at home in the Church, though each finds a great part of her teachings alien and distasteful. To reconcile these two views of life probably passes the wit of man; it has certainly passed the wit of Christian theologians and philosophers.

Meanwhile, we Northern Europeans of Teutonic race have our own contribution to make to the evolution of the Christian religion. We are a young people; we hardly yet know ourselves, or stand firmly on our feet; but there is probably no other race which surpasses ours in natural aptitude for a deep and pure spiritual religion. We are far less entangled in the relics of debased Pagan superstition than the Latin races, and this gives us an immense advantage in attempting to understand the religion of Christ, which was wholly untouched by these influences. We have learned much from the Greeks, but there is not the slightest danger that we shall follow them in making a religion of art or beauty. We are idealists by nature, as is proved by the magnificent literature of England and Germany; but our restless energy seeks an outlet in works of practical utility—

"Not for the gain of the gold, for the getting, the hoarding, the having,
  But for the joy of the deed, but for the duty to do."

Such a race must have something of its own to offer to the great Master Builder. Let us not be so timid as to trammel ourselves by the traditions of earlier Church history, the deposit of nations weaker than our own, and of periods of exhaustion or decadence. The one Divine Model is enough for us. Our Church—the Teutonic Catholic Church —is an ideal of the distant future. But an ideal is an idea which is in process of being realised.

ESSAY II

HOW THE OLD TESTAMENT CAME INTO BEING

BY

F. J. FOAKES JACKSON, D.D.

Fellow and Dean of Jesus College, Cambridge

ANALYSIS

I. THE REFORMS OF EZEKIEL.

The Fall of Jerusalem causes a revision of the ancient religion of Israel.
Highest aspirations of Israel before the Captivity.
Work of Jeremiah and Ezekiel.
Danger of idolatry during and even after the Captivity.
The priestly scheme a prophylactic against idolatry.
Ezekiel's fitness for the task.
The reformed Temple and priesthood.
The importance of the growth of Apocalyptic.

II. JEWISH SCRIPTURES UNDER BABYLONIAN INFLUENCE.

Why the Jewish law-book begins with a Babylonian chronology.
Polemic against idolatry in Isaiah ii.   Deuteronomy.
Feeling of the need of purification from sin.
Contest with Babylonian idolatry in Daniel.
The Psalms.   The sufferings of the righteous remnant.
Affection for the Law.
The lessons of Israelite history.
The Bible in existence before our present Old Testament.

HOW THE OLD TESTAMENT CAME INTO BEING

I.—THE REFORMS OF EZEKIEL

EVERY great religion or philosophy of life is founded on early beliefs, readapted to the growth of the human mind and the development of its consciousness.[1] Speaking generally, a religion only dies when it becomes unalterable; for whenever it seems incapable of change it is so because it has been abandoned by thinking men. A living religion, in fact, can never completely satisfy mankind, because it necessarily instils into the heart a craving for better things. Herein lies the great hope of the future of religion in our own days, when no single form of faith can be said completely to satisfy those who hold it. The study of the rise and fall, the progress and decay of the religions of the past shows almost uniformly that the beliefs of one age arise from the doubts and dissatisfaction of preceding times; and that even when a particular faith dies it gives birth to another which, however unlike it may appear to be, is really its legitimate offspring.

The subject of which this essay treats is one of exceptional interest in the study of religious development. So obscure an event as the destruction of an unimportant city and its sanctuary in Syria by Nebuchadrezzar's generals to punish

---

[1] *Cf.* Réville, *Prolegomena of the Hist. of Religions*, pp. 98 ff. : "It is a law of religious history that every new and higher principle is established only on the condition of accepting more or less completely the heritage of the past still existing under other forms." Robertson Smith, *The Religion of the Semites* (2nd ed.), p. 2 : "The positive Semitic religions had to establish themselves on ground already occupied by . . . older beliefs and usages ; they had to displace what they could not assimilate. . . . No positive religion that has moved men has been able to start with a *tabula rasa*, and express itself as if religion were beginning for the first time."

B

the rebellion of a petty Syrian kinglet is really a turning-point in the religious history of the world, since the fall of Jerusalem in B.C. 586 led to the remodelling of the ancient religion of Israel. Not that a new movement was really inaugurated at the time; for the process of reformation had been in progress at least since the appearance of the great prophets who heralded the fall of the Northern Kingdom in B.C. 722. But the calamity which overtook Jerusalem made the necessity of revising earlier religious ideas and practices imperative; and two great leaders appeared in the prophets Jeremiah and Ezekiel, the former imparting to the new movement its spirit, and the latter clothing it in definite shape. In the prophecies which bear their names we must find the origins of post-captivity Judaism.

The appearance of this form of religion was not, however, a unique phenomenon; for in the sixth century it seems probable that Sakya Muni first preached the tenets of Buddhism in India, and the spread of Zoroastrianism in Persia belongs to the same period. If, moreover, the collection of the Homeric poems belongs to the age of Peisistratus, what may be called the sacred scripture of Greece was being compiled contemporaneously with the rise of Israel from the ruin of the Captivity, with the Old Testament in its hands.

The interest in the history of early Israel is centred in the fact that we are able to see the efforts of the great national teachers to raise a primitive traditional religion to the level of a faith inspiring the lives and actions of men. One result of criticism and the study of comparative religion seems to be to make it tolerably certain that the beliefs of the ancient Israelites were practically the same as those of the other Semitic tribes in a similar state of civilisation and enlightenment.[1] But however close the external resemblance may be, there was in Israel a spirit which distinguished it from all the surrounding nations. The Old

---

[1] This has been further substantiated by the results of archæological research in Palestine; the spade of the excavator has shown that the beliefs and practices of the Israelites were in many respects identical with those of the Canaanites. *Cf. e.g.* Sellin, *Tell Ta'anek* (Vienna, 1904); Macalister, *The Excavation of Gezer* (1911).

Testament reveals, even in the most barbarous age, a striving after a higher ideal than the mass of the people had in contemplation. A Moses, a Samuel, a David, if behind the ideas of modern times, were far ahead of those of their day, and their appearance marks an advance in the religious conceptions of the nation. In the form in which we possess it the history of Israel is one of religious development, of an increasing knowledge of the true God, a rising ethical standard, and a growing perception of the demands of duty. Judged by the best products of the nation, not by the mass of the people, there is manifested a continuous advance in the religious conscience. Samuel is very different from the Gideons and Jephthahs who preceded him. Amos and Hosea proclaim a message alike more true and comprehensive than that of Elijah and the fierce prophets of Northern Israel. The first Isaiah supplements his predecessors and bears witness to the truth of a progressive revelation.

In order to develop our subject it may be well to endeavour to ascertain to what a stage the highest religious aspirations of Israel had attained at the time of the Captivity. In doing this we may safely ignore the popular conceptions of religion, which, as we see from the writings of the prophets, were often almost inconceivably degraded, and confine ourself to those ideals, which the best teachers of Israel laboured to set before their countrymen; our object being to ascertain not what the religious condition of the people actually was at this time, but that of its true leaders.

Starting with Amos, who is presumably the earliest literary prophet, we see that he had reached a comparatively high idea of the nature of the Deity. To him Jehovah was no local or national god, but the supreme judge of the world.[1] The nations surrounding Israel are arraigned before Him and condemned for their misdeeds.[2] He is not confined to any place; He does not "come forth from Seir or march from the fields of Edom," as others had described him;[3] He does not even ride upon the Cherubim and fly and swoop like an eagle upon the wings of the

---

[1] Amos iv. 13; v. 8; ix. 5–7.   [2] Amos i.–ii.   [3] Judg. v. 4.

wind.[1] He is represented as transcending all, to adopt Isaiah's words, "as sitting upon the circle of the earth, and the inhabitants thereof are but as locusts."[2] But this transcendence does not imply indifference; Jehovah is keenly interested in man's moral state, and judges the nations not by arbitrary standards which He has devised and concealed from all but His own people, but by those laws which Amos conceives to be inherent in the human breast. Edom, Syria, Ammon are condemned, not because they know not the Law, not even because they worship false gods, but because they are false, treacherous, cruel, and vindictive, not merely to Israel, Jehovah's people, but to one another. Thus in the opening chapters Amos vindicates the principle so strongly insisted upon in the Old Testament of the Divine Government of the world, and makes all nations morally responsible before God. In this we have the foundation of the claim that in Israel were the seeds of a true and universal religion, because it was recognised that in Jehovah there was a great power making for righteousness to whom the whole of mankind is accountable.

Joined, however, to this conception of Jehovah was a belief which may at first sight appear to be in contradiction to it. "You only," says God in Amos to Israel, "have I known of all the families of the earth."[3] Israel is the favoured nation to whom alone Jehovah has deigned to reveal Himself. It is certain that this idea led to much that we justly blame in the nation; that particularism, which led to the arrogant assumption that, as a Chosen People, Israel stood in isolated superiority to the rest of humanity. There is, however, another side which had a most salutary effect on the religious development of the nation. In accepting the position of a peculiar people,[4] Israel, through its teachers, realised that it had a special destiny fraught, not so much with valuable privileges, as with grave responsibility. For this reason Israel has hitherto proved inherently indestructible; nations may rise and fall, but as long as God has a providential purpose to work out by His people, Israel

---

[1] Ps. xviii. 10. [2] Is. xl. 22.
[3] Amos iii. 2. [4] *Cf*. Ex. xix. 5.

must continue to remain. However crudely this idea may
have presented itself to different generations, God's people
have never lost sight of the hope that a great and glorious
destiny is in store for them, and that in its realisation the
whole world will ultimately benefit.[1] "In thee," as God said
to Abraham, "all the nations of the world shall bless themselves." In view, however, of the unsatisfactory condition
of the nation in the days of Amos and his successors, the
indestructible character of the nation was confined to what
Isaiah styles "the remnant." In the coming judgment of
the Assyrian invasion the main part of Israel will perish,
but there will always be left a small remnant to carry on its
destiny. "The holy seed shall be the substance thereof." [2]

This belief in the survival of a remnant and the providential destiny of the nation led to two important consequences. It emphasised the importance of individual rather
than national or even family righteousness. The remnant
were to be the good men in Israel, the "seven thousand who
had not bowed the knee to Baal." [3] It was no longer the
nation, but the best of the nation, which God is conceived
as desiring to preserve; and each man felt that to be of the
remnant depended upon his own conduct. Further, it tended
towards what became the Messianic hope. The righteous
Israelites, destined to become the regenerated nation, were to
the imagination personified as a single righteous man by
whom the redemption was to be accomplished. In addition
to this, the virtuous minority was naturally persecuted and
despised by the more prosperous majority. Hence the important part which "the poor," the afflicted, the despised are
given in the devotional literature of Israel; and here, again,

---

[1] As Mr. Hart truly says (*The Hope of Catholick Judaism*, p. 31): "It is
clear that the Hope of Catholick Judaism is primarily a state of confidence in
God, and as far as it is legitimately and really an expectation of anything at
all, it is always the expectation of the Sovereignty or Reign of God, which
can only be set up by a Prophet, and necessarily results in public and private
peace."

[2] Is. vi. 13, *cf.* x. 20–23. I am naturally aware that many critics deny the
antiquity of these "remnant passages." I cannot, however, believe that mere
predictions of disaster, not always literally fulfilled, unrelieved by future hopes,
should have been carefully preserved.

[3] 1 KINGS xix. 18.

there must have been a tendency, as we see in Isaiah xl.–liii., to personify Israel in the suffering but faithful servant of Jehovah.

A belief, therefore, in the unity, justice, and supremacy of Jehovah, and of a high destiny in store for His people, appears to be the most enduring result of the prophetic dispensation. It was this twofold assurance which made the restoration of the nation after the captivity possible, and forms the keynote of the preaching of two reformers, Jeremiah and Ezekiel, otherwise totally different in aims and character.

Of the former it is here sufficient to remark that he was rather a precursor of reform than an actual reformer. Jeremiah supplied the ideas which others carried into practice, but his work can hardly be described as constructive. This prophet and his school are the idealists of the Old Testament. To him religion is a spiritual matter; the covenant between God and His people needs no symbolical ark;[1] circumcision is demanded for the heart alone;[2] the Law is to be written there, not engraven on stones.[3] Yet in Jeremiah the belief that Israel was indestructible was as firm as in any of the prophets, and in after days it was his prophecy which was regarded as being fulfilled in the decree of Cyrus[4] permitting the return.[5]

Ezekiel demands more careful attention. His prophecy is very widely regarded as almost unique in the Old Testament in being, not like many other books a collection of utterances on various occasions, and the work of an editor or compiler, but as the contemporary work of a single author.[6] There is in Ezekiel a unity lacking in most books of the

---

[1] JER. iii. 16.   [2] JER. iv. 4; ix. 25, 26.   [3] JER. xxxi. 33; *cf.* xxiv. 7.
[4] "Though he (Cyrus) might not be aware of it, we can perceive that all his thoughts are coloured by the religious relation to God of which he was himself conscious" (A. B. Davidson, in *Hastings' D.B.*, ii. 576).
[5] EZRA i. 1.
[6] "No critical question arises in connection with the authorship of the book, the whole from beginning to end bearing unmistakably the stamp of a single mind" (Driver, *Introduction*, p. 261 [1891]). Cornill (*Einleitung in das A.T.*, p. 176) likewise says: "Kein anderes [Buch] ist eine so grossartig angelegte und so klar durchgeführte planvolle Einheit, kein anderes zeigt so vom ersten bis zum letzten Buchstaben dieselbe Hand, denselben Geist, dieselbe scharf ausgeprägte Individualität."

Old, and even of the New Testament, and it is generally admitted that it has come down to us, even if corrupt in text,[1] much as the author left it, without either alteration or adaptation to the needs of a later age. Ezekiel, as he himself tells us, was a priest of the Temple at Jerusalem who had been carried into captivity,[2] and his prophetic ministry was fulfilled in a foreign land, from which he watched the fall of the Holy City and sanctuary, and, ultimately, planned their restoration. The important point to be noticed is that Ezekiel was evidently acquainted with the conditions of life and worship in Jerusalem before the fall of the city and Temple, when he sketched the provisions for a national polity under a totally new state of things, which did not come into being in his lifetime.

In so doing Ezekiel lies open to the criticism of an influential school of religion. In him the prophetic element is seen to be decaying and making way for an hierarchic development of religion. He begins as a prophet and concludes as a priest, the moral reformer becomes the organiser of a cultus. Is he for this reason liable to the charge of undoing the work of his predecessors, and teaching men to substitute external for spiritual religion?

It may be considered almost as a law in religious history that no sooner has a principle become generally accepted, than, as if to show the impossibility of satisfying the cravings of the heart, a reaction occurs in the opposite direction. The early prophets had contended with all their might against the religious externalism which had set in after the overthrow of the Baal worship by Jehu in Israel and Joash in Judah, and culminated in the Northern Kingdom in the days of Amos, and in the Southern in the time of Isaiah. These prophets had appreciated the magnitude of the danger, and had combated it with all their might. Jehovah had, through Amos, declared that He hated and abhorred the

---

[1] Cornill (*Das Buch des Propheten Ezechiel*, p. 4) says : " Der Satz dass der Text Ezechiel's in besonders schlechtem und verderbtem Zustande auf uns gekommen sei, geht durch alle Einleitungen ins Alte Testament und durch alle Schriften, welche sich mit dem alttestamentlichen Texte beschäftigen."

[2] EZEK. i. 3 ; 2 KINGS xxiv. 14–16.

splendid sacrifices offered at Bethel in the days of Jeroboam II.,[1] and Isaiah had pronounced the Divine displeasure at the elaborate worship of the Temple services under Uzziah and Jotham.[2] These protests culminated in the time of Jeremiah. The reaction which came with the Captivity under the guidance of Ezekiel was as necessary as it had been inevitable. Those forms of worship, which in earlier days had been in danger of sapping the spiritual life of Israel, now became requisite for its very existence. Absolute spirituality, as practical experience proves, is as incompatible with the continuance of a religion on earth as the attempt to realise a soul without a body. A faith needs something tangible and visible to secure its permanence. In the days of the monarchy, the nation, the king, the sanctuaries, the land had combined to supply the religion of Israel with form and substance. All these had disappeared in the appalling catastrophe when Nebuchadrezzar destroyed the Temple. Bereft of all earthly supports, the faith of Israel was now the only bond of union, and, unless this were provided with some definite organisation, it could not, at any rate humanly speaking, have continued to exist. A mere sentiment could not have ensured the permanence of a nation overwhelmed by calamity, and hourly threatened with being engulfed by the nations of the world. Unless the worship of Jehovah became a concrete reality it must have perished, and the small southern portion of ancient Israel, which had continued it in Judah and Jerusalem, have been as irrecoverably lost as the ten northern tribes. It is to the credit of Ezekiel and his friends that they recognised this fact and sought to find a remedy. Idolatry, it must be remembered, was an ever present danger at and even after the Captivity. The assumption that the Jews completely abandoned idolatry is absolutely without foundation; the fact being that it was only after vigorous efforts on the part of the religious teachers in the sixth century B.C. that Judaism became once and for all a non-idolatrous religion.[3] It has been truly said by

---

[1] Amos iii. 4 ; iv. 4, 5 ; v. 4–6, 21–23 ; vii. 10–17.   [2] Is. i. 11–15.

[3] As illustrating the tenacious grasp upon the Semite of traditional modes of worship, *cf.* Curtiss' *Primitive Semitic Religion To-day*, chaps. vi.–viii.

Cornill that the tendency of the legislation subsequently embodied in the Priestly Code was to encourage all that the earlier prophets had previously denounced; but this was the necessary price at which the complete abandonment of idolatry had to be purchased.[1] It was only by giving the people religion organised under ritualistic forms that the vast majority could be brought to consent to abandon the attractions of the old sensuous worship. To condemn the priestly legislators as unspiritual is totally to misapprehend the situation.

The essence of idolatry may be said to be making the symbol, rather than that which is symbolised, the object of worship; or allowing that which is intended as an aid to devotion to receive the adoration due to God alone. The danger inherent in it is the complete loss of spirituality in religion by the mind becoming accustomed to connect worship only with visible and tangible objects, and to attribute to them a sort of magical efficacy. Though not the same as polytheism, idolatry inevitably tends to lead men in that direction, inasmuch as the symbols themselves become separate objects of worship; and even the same God is worshipped under different aspects in the various emblems by which he is represented. Thus in the Middle Ages the local virgin or saint became almost distinct from those who were worshipped under the same name in a different spot.

Among the early Israelites there was not only a danger of polytheism but of idolatry being continued even when the worship was monotheistic. It is always a difficult task to ascertain the popular religion at any particular time; but from the Old Testament we are able to gather that the general standard of the people was far below that of the great prophets. At its worst it was polytheistic as well as idolatrous, at its best monotheistic with a marked tendency towards idolatry. The former was unhesitatingly condemned, not only by the prophets, but by the awakened conscience of Israel; the latter was condoned and even partly encouraged by many of the recognised teachers of the nation.

Israelite tradition says that the demand in the desert,

---

[1] Cornill, *Einleitung in das Alte Testament*, E. T., p. 115.

" Make us gods (or a god) to go before us," was answered by
Aaron making the Golden Calf; and his words show that
neither he nor the people were consciously deserting Jehovah,
but that the image represented Him who had brought
Israel out of Egypt. The worship which accompanied the
making of the calf is described as idolatry, but not necessarily apostasy. Gideon's ephod, Micah's and David's teraphim, Jeroboam's calves at Bethel and Dan, Solomon's
images in the temple were not incompatible with the
worship of Jehovah, and, though some are condemned, others
are mentioned without comment by the sacred writers.

But idolatry, according to our definition, had assumed
far more insidious forms in the worship of Jehovah. The
popular conception both of priest and prophet most
distinctly savoured of a materialism closely akin to it.
It is often assumed that in ancient Israel prophet and
priest were in antagonism, the one representing the spiritual
and the other the hierarchic conception of religion. But
the estimation in which the prophets are held in the prophetical books of the Old Testament hardly warrants this.
Jeremiah who, though a priest, is entirely free from sacer-
dotalism, regards the prophets of his time with anything
but a friendly eye, and notes the closeness of their alliance
for evil with the priests of Jerusalem. "The prophets
prophesy falsely and the priests bear rule by their means." [1]
To Zechariah the disappearance of the prophets in their
" hairy garments " is a blessing to be hoped for in the better
age in store for Israel.[2] The hundreds of prophets, headed
by Zedekiah the son of Chenaanah, who urged Ahab to go
against Syria, and the one true prophet Micaiah, who told
the truth, represent possibly a by no means unusual state
of things.[3] The average prophet was often a charlatan and
an impostor; and the great prophets from Samuel to
Malachi were exceptions to the general rule. The popular
explanation, that the people regarded a prophet as a *forth
teller* rather than as a *foreteller*, is founded on a misconception, since a prophet was, as a rule, considered less as a preacher
of righteousness than as a useful person who knew what was

---

[1] JER. v. 31.   [2] ZECH. xii. 4.   [3] 1 KINGS xxii. 6–28 ; 1 CHR. xviii. 5–27.

going to happen. He was believed to be a person inspired by his God whose presence was manifested in ecstasy or mental derangement.[1] In Deuteronomy there is an injunction coupled with a promise, which has received a spiritual interpretation in the New Testament, forbidding Israelites to resort to sorcerers and diviners, and promising that Jehovah will raise up prophets.[2] The prophet is, therefore, the lawful person to consult as opposed to the magician; and it is hardly to be wondered at that many prophets supplied that which would otherwise have been demanded of the diviner. In the story of Saul's going to the witch of Endor, the conduct of the King is explained by Jehovah's refusal to answer him by prophets.[3] The real objection to the wizards and sorcerers is that they were often connected with the worship of the spirits of the dead and the ancient Canaanitish and local gods.[4] The prophet, as a pledged champion of Jehovah, was not likely to persuade his clients to go to other gods, but he was not in most cases averse to giving oracles according to his own interest or at the instigation of his employers. At any rate only the very best of the prophets can be said to have been above magical or theurgic arts.

The average priest fulfilled much the same function of an authorised diviner.[5] Saul's priest accompanies his army much as the augurs did that of a Roman Consul.[6] Inquiring of Jehovah by means of an ephod was really equivalent to consulting an oracle.[7] The whole point of the story of Micah and his Levite is that the young man knew his business as a diviner, and skilfully led the Danites to undertake a successful expedition. That he was self-seeking, cowardly, and ungrateful to his benefactor mattered little—

---

[1] *Cf. e.g.* Cornill, *Der Israelitische Prophetismus*, pp. 9–16; Robertson Smith, *The Prophets of Israel* (2nd ed.), pp. 390 ff.; Stade, *Biblische Theologie des Alten Testamentes*, i. pp. 131 f.

[2] DEUT. xviii. 13–15. [3] See 1 SAM. xxviii. 6. [4] *Cf.* Is. viii. 19; xix. 3.

[5] For details see Foote, *The Ephod, its Form and Use* (Baltimore, 1902); *cf.* also an important article on the recent discovery of what is believed to be an Ephod in the *Bulletin* of the Boston Museum (vol. ii. No. 2), and articles on "Ephod" and "Urim and Thummim," in *Church and Synagogue*, v. pp. 50–53 (1903), also Nowack, *Hebräische Archäologie*, ii. pp. 22, 93 f.

[6] *Cf.* 1 SAM. xiii. 8 ff.; xiv. 36.

[7] See for exhaustive details Stade, *Biblische Theologie des Alten Testamentes*, i. pp. 122–130.

he knew how to manage the ephod and rightly to discern the future.[1] As it is a mistake to consider the majority of prophets preachers of righteousness, so is it to regard the law of the priests as a moral code. *Torah* has its primary meaning—that of guidance or instruction; and when a man sought *torah* he wanted to know what he should do in a particular emergency. To the priest, therefore, he resorted, as he did to the prophet, in order to be instructed as to the best course of action. Thus Saul seeks the advice of the prophet in order to discover the lost asses of his father,[2] of the priest as to who is guilty of violating his command that all should abstain from food,[3] and of the witch of Endor, when priest and prophet alike failed him.[4]

When we recollect the habitual use of teraphim or household images, the sacred stones, wells, trees scattered throughout the land, the sacrificial feasts, the worship on the mountains, the devotion of an enemy and every living thing he possessed to destruction, the way in which human sacrifice is alluded to, if without approval at least without censure, we are able to judge how closely the popular religion of the ancient Hebrews, even if its monotheism be granted, approximated to that of other Semitic nations.[5] Its distinguishing feature is the steady protest of the few men who from time to time were raised up to lead the nation onward to higher and purer ideals.

But down to the very end of the exile the attraction of alien religions seems to have been almost irresistible. The ancient Hebrew, like the modern Jew, was not unsusceptible to the influence of contemporary thought, and showed a disposition to adapt himself to the world in which he lived. On his entrance into Canaan, his religious practices tended to conform with those of the older inhabitants. No sooner had the King of Israel entered into an alliance with the Zidonians than the Baal worship became popular, and at the time of the captivity the attraction of the Assyrian-Babylonian deities is clearly seen. During the period of the

---

[1] JUDG. xvii. 18.   [2] 1 SAM. ix. 6 ff.
[3] 1 SAM. xiv. 36.   [4] 1 SAM. xxviii. 6.
[5] See *e.g.* Stade, *op. cit.*, passim ; and Lagrange, *Études sur les Religions Sémitiques*, chaps i.–vii.

exile the prophets inaugurated a campaign against foreign religions, and their success is the striking feature of the period.

To understand the strength of alien cults and the character of the popular religion of the seventh and sixth centuries B.C. it is advisable to gather from notices in the Old Testament the condition of the Temple at Jerusalem. Whenever we read of a reformation of religion in Judah there are allusions to a thorough purification of the Temple. In the days of Asa, in the ninth century B.C., the queen-mother had set up an Asherah or sacred pole within the precincts, and religious prostitutes of both sexes practised their rites in the sanctuary.[1] In Josiah's time the drastic purification of the Temple[2] resulted in the removal of innumerable idolatrous objects of worship, among them altars made by Ahaz, which presumably remained undisturbed under the sway of his pious son Hezekiah. This alone is sufficient to show that idolatry and polytheism were not considered incompatible in the pre-exilic temple. Even the reformation of Josiah did not extirpate the evil, for in Ezekiel's visions of what was being done in the Temple just before its overthrow, secret but shameless idolatry was practised by those high in authority.[3] The fact that the Temple was used by the Kings of Judah for any form of religion which they desired to encourage is beyond dispute, and is only emphasised by the attempt of the orthodox chronicler to pass in silence over the reformation of Josiah so fully related in the Book of Kings. And if all this happened at Jerusalem under the eyes of the prophets and reforming kings and priests, what must have gone on in the local sanctuaries and high places?

It has been necessary to dwell on these sufficiently obvious facts in order to understand the problem before the reformers of the age of the Exile, and to do justice to their motives. To the spiritually minded Hebrews of the prophetic age religion consisted in the service of one only God, Jehovah, who had as yet revealed Himself to Israel alone, but governed the whole world in righteousness. Truly

---

[1] 1 KINGS xv. 11.   [2] 2 KINGS xxii.   [3] EZEK. viii. 6 ff.

to serve Him was to yield obedience to His moral law. But to the popular mind Jehovah was the God Who favoured Israel if properly propitiated by sacrifices, and, when duly served, guided His people to victory and prosperity. Other gods, however, existed and possessed power to help and harm, and these it was advisable to conciliate, especially when Jehovah was not ready to assist His Chosen Race.

The reformers desired to make the central teaching of the prophets universal among God's people, and, in order to do this, they had to take into consideration the weakness of the people's faith and to wean them by gradual means from the degraded forms of religion to which they had been hitherto accustomed. With this object they revised and codified the vast amount of law and of tradition which had come down to them.

No one was better qualified to inaugurate such a work than the priest-prophet Ezekiel, combining as he did the qualifications of both offices. The function of the priest is to ensure the permanence of a religion, whilst the prophet imparts to it the spirit necessary to its life. In times of crisis the prophet's voice makes itself heard, but in the long periods of comparative torpor the priest continues his less stirring work of witnessing to the truth of his religion and the duty of worship. It is for the prophet to touch the heart and conscience, for the priest to regulate the lives of his people. His book leaves us no doubt that Ezekiel was full of the spirit of prophecy. In elevation of spirit and sublimity of thought he attains to the level of the greatest seers of ancient Israel. His prophecy concerning the Prince of Tyre,[1] and his vision of the Valley of the Dry Bones,[2] are surpassed by no utterances in the Old Testament. But he possessed that constructive power which characterises a true priest, and was able not merely to foretell but to shape future events. As a moral teacher he gave the ethics of Judaism a momentous impulse by his insistence on personal responsibility; and he laboured so to revise the laws of the worship of his people as to make idolatry henceforward impossible in any professing member of the Jewish community.

[1] Ezek. xxvii.   [2] Ezek. xxxvii. 1–14.

He makes this attempt in the latter part of his book in chapters which, if they do not interest the general reader of to-day, had a profound influence on the religious development of his age.

Ezekiel's ideas are brought before us in a series of visions which represent the restored worship of Jehovah in a new and purified Temple. It is not necessary to take his words too literally or to attempt exactly to reproduce what the prophet describes. It is sufficient for us to consider the general purport of his utterances and the object he had in view. It is unimportant for our purpose that much of his prophecy has remained unfulfilled, and that some of his projects proved entirely impracticable. The great fact to bear in mind is that his general objects were secured.

Of these the first may be said to be that the distinguishing feature of restored Israel is that it should no longer be a people with secular aims and ambitions, but a purely religious nation wholly occupied in the service of God. In ancient Israel secular interests had had an important part, but in the new state they were to be practically non-existent. In place of the old king a prince was to preside over the nation, and the choice of the title may have been deliberate. In the first place the prophet saw that restoration could only be permitted by some powerful nation, which would be ready to sanction a colony of religionists re-occupying the deserted cities of Palestine, provided they made no attempt to become politically independent. A king who would, as the Israelites once desired, go before them and fight their battles was out of the question; and the only possible ruler was a peaceful prince, a delegate of the ruling power, whose only duty was to preserve order. But the prophet had doubtless a deeper motive than that of not arousing the suspicion of Israel's masters. All the devouter spirits in Israel had recognised that its ruin was attributable to the secularity of its rulers and the part they had tried to play in the politics of their age.[1] The remonstrances which Samuel is represented as making when Israel desired a king were

---

[1] *Cf. e.g.* Is. xxx. 1–5, and the Isaianic principle, " In quietness and in confidence shall be your strength " (Is. xxv. 15).

only the first of a long series of protests against the seculari-
sation of the nation. Ezekiel is willing to sacrifice all idea of
a restored kingdom to secure his object. Israel is not to be
as other nations. With this end in view he groups the tribes
round the sanctuary with a total disregard of historical or
geographical conditions. The territory east of Jordan is
abandoned ; Jerusalem becomes the centre of the land, and,
after assigning land to the prince and to the priests, the
tribes have their territory six on one side and six on the
other. Literalism is out of the question in interpreting
this. We must remember we are within the visionary
sphere.[1]

But the fact remains that this ideal of a religious and
utterly unsecularised Israel had an abiding hold on the
nation. We see it in the reforms of Ezra, in the curious
history of the Chronicler, in the attitude of the Chassidim, the
Essenes, the primitive Christians. The politicians among
the Jews were never without earnest and often fanatical
upholders of the spiritual ideal of a Church-state.

The new conditions demanded a reorganised priesthood.
The history of priesthood in early Israel is extremely obscure,
and it is largely a matter of conjecture by what stages it
reached the form in which we know it. Following the
analogy of other peoples, the priest appears to have been
in early times the ruler of the family tribe or nation, and
afterwards a person skilled in the arts of the office. From
perhaps a remote period the Israelitish priests went under
the generic name of Levite, and, as among ancient nations,
all professions tended to become hereditary ; the families of
priests were enrolled as the tribe called after the old secular
tribe of Levi. At any rate, the Levitical priests were pre-
ferred to all others, though it is certain that members of
other tribes often acted in the same capacity, especially in
the northern Kingdom. It may even be conjectured from
the tradition that Moses, a Levite, was an Egyptian priest,
that the Levites, as the name Levi (associate) implies, were

---

[1] By the time of Ezekiel the vision had become "a literary and poetical form
consciously employed to embody and communicate truths that have become
clear to the inner consciousness" (W. Morgan).

not originally Israelites, but an alien tribe peculiarly skilled in the business of divination.[1] In the prosperous days of Israel the priesthoods—for every sanctuary had its hereditary hierarchy—were numerous; and in the days of Josiah, when an attempt was made to centralise the cultus at Jerusalem, the ancient local priesthoods received a certain amount of recognition. As each high place or local sanctuary must have had its own praxis, it is evident that the priestly traditions as to how Jehovah was to be served must have varied greatly; and one of the chief desiderata in the new Temple was a uniform and disciplined tradition of worship. With this end in view Ezekiel limits the priesthood of the restored Temple to a single family—that of Zadok—and relegates the other Levites to a secondary rank, depriving them of the right to offer sacrifice. A single priestly house, even though numerous, which had ministered in the Temple at Jerusalem since its foundation, was more likely to remain true to the reformed worship as prescribed for the new Temple, than a variety of priestly septs brought from different sanctuaries; and discipline would be more easy to maintain. Ezekiel's policy made the tendency towards an hereditary priesthood a permanent reality, resulting in the creation of a powerful aristocracy in Judah, which ultimately monopolised the political power. Throughout the history of Judah the fact must never be lost sight of that the priest was essentially an aristocrat, and that he exercised his authority as a nobleman rather than as a cleric in the modern sense of the word.

For some centuries the religion of Judah became, in a sense which it had never been before, sacerdotal; and under the organised hierarchy of the priestly families not only the king and priest but even the prophet disappeared. In Ezekiel's time the ruler of the restored nation was thought of as a

---

[1] *Cf.*, above all, the Maccabæan leaders during the second century B.C. On the whole subject see, among others, Wellhausen's *Prolegomena to the History of Israel*, pp. 121–151 (1885); Stade, *Geschichte des Volkes Israel*, i. pp. 152–157; Budde, *Die Religion des Volkes Israel*, pp. 73–102; Steuernagel, *Die Einwanderung der Israelitischen Stämme in Kanaan*, which is full of interesting and suggestive matter.

prince—that is, the king shorn of much of his former importance—but in about two centuries the High Priest became the recognised head of the Jewish people.

The worship of the Temple was naturally a subject of the prophet's care. To secure the adherence of the majority it was necessary to have the ritual service dignified and impressive; and at the same time to guard against the idolatry which had disgraced the first Temple. With the misfortunes of the Captivity the sense of national and personal sin had deepened, and the need of pardon was keenly felt. Consequently, a sacrificial system involving continual atonement with God for sin receives much attention. This craving of the human heart for pardon is met in the sublime vision of the cleansing waters issuing from Jerusalem.[1] A regular round of sacrifices offered exclusively to Jehovah and recurring festivals in His sole honour are prominent in the ritual legislation of Ezekiel's vision.

A few points, however, remain to be noticed. We cannot help distinguishing Ezekiel from his predecessors in the importance attached to visions. In him we seem to pass from the prophetic to the apocalyptic age. He is, it is true, the successor of Amos, Isaiah, and Jeremiah, but he is also the forerunner of Daniel, of Enoch, and of John.

In a sense the apocalyptic vision is a manifestation of God inferior to the revelation of the true prophet, in the fact that it is more of an appeal to the bodily senses than to the spiritual side of man. The seer beholds God's glory with his eyes, the prophet's heart understands His will. St. Paul had, we may believe, a truer revelation of God when he was inspired to write his description of charity, than when caught up into heaven he saw things which it is not lawful for man to utter. The Sermon on the Mount reveals God to us in a manner which the Apocalypse of John is unable to do, in that it makes His will as to what we ought to be clearer to us than any vision of the glories of His dwelling-place. But the age of visions had a most important part in the development of Israel. It brought God nearer to the people. If they might have no visible representation of Him, nothing

[1] EZEK. xlvii. 1-12.

to make Him realisable to the mind, as the image did the gods of the Gentiles, at least an Ezekiel or a Daniel would tell them what they had seen. The Apocalypses helped to bring God closer to the earth, and made the people feel a little less dependent upon sensuous representations of His attributes. Those whom the preaching of the prophets could not touch felt comfort in the vision of the seer.

The insistence on the ritual and sacrificial aspect of religion is condemned in our age as a retrogression upon the spiritual teaching of the prophets. If it is so, it is nevertheless one of those backward steps which are at times necessary to a real advance. Ezekiel's message conveyed in the vision of the Temple has no appeal to us; the words of an Amos or an Isaiah still speak to even the modern man with compelling force. But had not the work of an Ezekiel been done, the words of his predecessors would have been irreclaimably lost. They influenced but a chosen few. He carried the whole nation forward by showing them something that could be understood and appreciated, and not demanding a spirituality which was beyond their comprehension. The reforms he sketched in exile resulted in a great advance on the Temple worship of the days of the Kings, and ultimately brought Judaism into being as a reformed religion in which idolatry, at any rate in its grosser forms, was henceforward an impossibility.

Ezekiel's prophecies gave an impulse to a movement inaugurated perhaps as early as Hezekiah, which culminated first in the publication of the Priestly Code, and finally in that combination of Priests' Law and primitive history which is known to us as the Pentateuch. At Ezekiel's death the materials were all to hand. Primitive law, traces of which are to be found in Amos (B.C. 770): Deuteronomic legislation, the influence of which is plain in the books of Joshua, Kings, and Jeremiah: southern Israelitish tradition embodied in J: northern tradition in E: the Priests' Code sketched by Ezekiel, developed in the "Law of Holiness" (H), and taking form in P. Of the precise date of these materials it is difficult to speak authoritatively. Perhaps those which are assigned to the latest period take us back to very early traditions, whilst those pronounced most ancient contain quite recent additions. But probably before the close of the fifth century B.C., we may assume that the most sacred books of Judaism took their final form, and began to be guarded, in place of the Ark of the Covenant, as the true " Palladium " of Israel.

II.—The Jewish Scriptures under Babylonian Influence

A people so intelligent and receptive of external influences as the Jewish could not fail to be profoundly affected in captivity in Babylonia. Tradition, with every appearance of truth, describes them as Bedawins in Egypt, reduced to slavery by a nation far more advanced in civilisation, and pining to return to their old freedom of the life of wandering shepherds. But in Babylonia the exiles were not treated as slaves but as valuable settlers, a proof that the Babylonians recognised that they had to deal with an educated people ; and the Jews must have joined in the pursuits of their new neighbours and adopted their manner of life, and even in a measure partaken of their ideas. But in exile the strength of the instinct of nationality asserted itself by means of religion. The Babylonian Jews recognised that the real distinction between their cultus and that of the Gentiles was that theirs was not idolatrous, and that its maintenance away from their native land depended upon an unhesitating rejection of all forms of image worship. Henceforward their literature is filled with arguments against idolatry ; and the vehemence of the polemic found in the contemporary prophets testifies alike to its fascination and their deter-mination to destroy it. But the Babylonian religion was much more than an idolatry. It busied itself with the deepest problems of existence and recognised the cravings of the human heart, not only after the supernatural, but also for a knowledge of the visible universe. I do not for a moment deny the possibility of the Jewish story of creation, &c., being known to the Hebrews from remote antiquity. My thesis here is that the condition of the Jews in Babylon explains the presence of the creation story at the beginning of their law book. It is most significant, therefore, that when the Jewish legislation was codified it began with an unmistakably Babylonian cosmogony; and whereas in early Israel the initial reference usually is to the choice of Jacob-Israel, in the great law book attention is directed to the origin of the world and the relation of God, not to Israel, but to humanity.[1] It appears to be an initial mistake, often made in studying the book of Genesis, to ignore the fact that, however important it may be to determine from what sources it is derived, the really crucial point is to discover the object of whoever reduced it, at any rate approximately, to its present form. The Priestly Editor is often regarded as a somewhat clumsy interpolator, instead of being, in the modern sense of the word, the author of the book. In one sense the book of Genesis is a highly artificially constructed history with its materials drawn from the most varied sources; in another it reveals the purpose of perhaps a single mind, who pressed the different narratives into his service in order to produce a distinct impression on his readers and to convey special lessons. Genesis is not of course an isolated book, but part of a great scheme of legislation intended to mould the character of the religion of God's people. Now it may for our purpose be premised that this scheme was outlined, if not completed, during the Babylonian Captivity; and that Genesis, as its preface, reflects the intention of those unknown men who conceived it. Nor can it be denied that the first book of the Law has succeeded in basing the subsequent legislation on a noble survey of the work of God and His relation to the world. It is not easy to imagine that this work was other than the outcome of national experience, and the conditions of the captivity appear to satisfy this requirement. The teachers, people expatriated, scattered and ruined, without country or sanctuary, but still firmly possessed by the idea that to them alone of all the nations of the world the true God had revealed Himself, finding it necessary to reconstitute its

[1] See the Introduction to Gunkel's *Genesis*.

ancient laws and practices, strove to impress upon the nation the character of their God and of His dealings with them. The first chapter of Genesis vindicates the claim of Jehovah to the obedience of Israel against the hierarchy of deities whose temples filled Babylonia. Standing as they do at the beginning of the Law, the first two chapters of Genesis are a challenge to the idol-worshipping and polytheistic world. The opening words declaring that "In the beginning God created the heaven and earth," proclaim that Israel rejected all cosmogonies which ascribed creation to chance or to a conflict of discordant elements. God (*Elohim*) stands forth in solitary majesty, and creates by the power of His word. "He speaks and it is done, He commands and they stand fast." But that there may be no misconception as to the identity of *Elohim* with the God of Israel, the writer has introduced a second creation narrative in which God with the double name *Jehovah-Elohim* is the Maker of the world. I repeat that it is a mistake to regard the books of the Hexateuch as a mere patchwork of documents, some early and some later till the age of the Priestly Compiler. The last named had a distinct object in view to which he subordinated the materials at his disposal; and the creation story, though in a sense twofold, has the single object of declaring Jehovah the God of Israel, the source of all existence. So too in the Fall and the Flood narratives the Babylonian influence is evident, and in each the story is used to show the fundamentals of Israel's faith—namely, that God as Creator demands the obedience of His creatures, that sin is rebellion against Him, and that the punishment which follows proceeds from Him. Babylonian tradition, science, and even mythology have been pressed into the service of the writer; but the one object which he appears to have in view is to vindicate the honour of Jehovah against the claims of the pantheon of Babylon. In the tenth chapter we are given a survey of the human race, descended from Noah, and peopling the earth from the mountains of Ararat, the source of the great Babylonian rivers. It can hardly be an accident that the only personal hero whose name appears in the catalogue of nations is that

of Nimrod, the founder of the great Mesopotamian cities;
nor that in the following chapter, before man went forth
to fill the earth, the cradle city of humanity is called
Babylon or Babel. At the risk of repetition it may be
mentioned that the important question of the date of
Hebrew tradition is here subsidiary to the theory, now
widely accepted, that *Genesis* is intended to be the prelude
of a scheme of legislation developed during the period of
the Captivity; and that the importance of the association
of the great teachers and prophets with Babylonia is seen
in the arrangement of the book. In any case the remodelled
Law of Israel, with its avowed object to suppress idolatry,
is based on this account of the primitive world and the
origin of the nation. Even where it is probable that the
writer or compiler has borrowed from Babylonian tradition,
he has done so with the intention of vindicating the sole
majesty of Jehovah. The Flood and Creation stories may
well be designed as correctives to the study of the legends
current in Babylonia, which, embracing as they did the best
science as well as the religion of their captors, were eagerly
perused by the Jewish exiles. This polemical aspect of the
book of Genesis seems to have been somewhat overlooked
in the interest which recent criticism of its early narratives
has aroused regarding the scientific and historical problems
which it has raised; but it appears of service in enabling
us to understand the purport of the work *in its present
form*.

Equally significant is the insistence on the Divine command to the father of the Hebrew nation to leave the land
in which his exiled descendants were in bondage. That
Abraham was originally a native of Ur Chasdim (Ur of the
Chaldees) may well be a historical fact; but at the same
time the prominence given to the circumstances that he
left the country never to return, and that this was the proof
of his obedience to the Divine call, suggests that, when the
prelude to the Law was compiled, the ancestral home of
the patriarch was the centre of idolatry, which he forsook
because the true God could not rightly be served there.
The way in which Abraham enjoined his servant Eliezer

never to permit his son to go back to Mesopotamia, lends additional plausibility to this theory. I am disposed, therefore, to believe that the compilation of the book of Genesis is part of the great polemic against idolatry, which resulted in the promulgation of the Priestly Law.

This view seems to be borne out by utterances of the so-called "Evangelical Prophet," which are embodied in our present book of Isaiah [1]; and I also venture to suggest that the legend of Abraham being the son of Terah, a maker of idols, and being persecuted by Nimrod, expresses the meaning of the story of his call in the canonical Genesis.

Deutero-Isaiah was certainly addressed to Jews under the fascination of Babylonian idolatry, with the object of weaning them from it by demonstrating that the worship of images was contrary to the plain dictates of reason. We often read the prophets' diatribes as though they were a defiance of heathenism; but their purport evidently was to dissuade the exiles from lapsing into the religion of their neighbours. The Jews, on the whole, were not unhappy in their new country, nor did they find themselves amid uncongenial surroundings. The pious exile sighed for his ruined temple and longed to see the Holy Mount once more. The ardent patriot thought of his captive king and the glories of the house of David. But those who sat down and wept beside the waters of Babylon were the few, whereas the many bought and sold and built and planted and prospered in a rich land and an active trading community. They were not bondsmen as their fathers had been in Egypt, but rather privileged colonists, inclined to sink their nationality in the country of their enforced adoption. This was the peril their teachers sought to avert, especially Deutero-Isaiah in the prophecy of the divinely planned victories of Cyrus leading up to the work of the servant of Jehovah. It is noticeable that here, side by side with the denunciations of idolatry, we meet with a declaration of the creative power of Jehovah, showing that herein lay His unique position in the mind of both this teacher and the compiler of the book of Genesis. The fortieth chapter is of itself sufficient to show

[1] Is. xl.–lxvi.

this. Verse 12, "Who hath measured the waters in the hollow of His hand, and meted out heaven with the span, and comprehended the dust of the earth in a measure, and weighed the mountains with scales and the hills in a balance?" is followed by verses 18–20: "To whom then will ye liken God? or what likeness will ye compare unto Him? The graven image, a workman melteth it, and the goldsmith spreadeth it over with gold, and casteth for it silver chains. He that is too impoverished for such an oblation chooseth a tree that will not rot; he seeketh unto him a cunning workman to set up a graven image that shall not be moved." In the forty-second chapter we find that in verse 5, "Thus saith God the Lord, He that created the heavens and stretched them forth; He that spread abroad the earth and that which cometh out of it" is the prologue to the declaration, "Thus saith Jehovah, that is My name, and My glory will I not give to another neither My praise to graven images." Thus it is that idolatry is combated, not only by an appeal to reason, as in the splendid satire of Isaiah xliv. 10–17,[1] but by dwelling on the transcendence of the God of Israel. As is seen from xlvi. 1–2, the idolatry aimed at is not that of Canaan but of Babylon.

It must not, however, be supposed that the conflict with idolatry was confined to Babylonia. The Captivity was only part of a general dispersion of the Chosen People, and there

---

[1] "Who hath fashioned a god, or molten a graven image that is profitable for nothing? Behold, all his fellows shall be ashamed: and the workmen, they are of men: let them all be gathered together, let them stand up; they shall fear, they shall be ashamed together. The smith maketh an axe and worketh in the coals, and fashioneth it with hammers, and worketh it with his strong arm; yea, he is hungry, and his strength faileth; he drinketh no water, and is faint. . . . He (the carpenter) heweth him down cedars, and taketh the holm tree and the oak, and strengtheneth for himself one among the trees of the forest: he planteth a fir tree and the rain doth nourish it. Then it shall be for a man to burn; and he taketh thereof, and warmeth himself; yea, he kindleth it, and baketh bread; yea, he maketh it a god, and worshippeth it; he maketh it a graven image, and falleth down thereto. He turneth part thereof in the fire; with part thereof he eateth flesh; he roasteth roast, and is satisfied; yea, he warmeth himself, and saith, Aha, I am warm, I have seen the fire. And the residue thereof he maketh a god, even his graven image: he falleth down unto it and worshippeth, and prayeth unto it, and saith, Deliver me, for thou art my god."

seems to be evidence that it already extended from the banks of the Euphrates to the cataracts of the Nile.[1]   Palestine had been by no means depleted of its Hebrew inhabitants, and communication between the scattered portions of the nation may well have been maintained.   What happened must be guessed at rather than asserted : we are in the realm of conjecture rather than fact ; and, unless further evidence is forthcoming, our theories must be at the best no more than plausible.   Still it may be said with some confidence that if Isaiah xl.–xlviii. and the preamble to the Law in *Genesis* shows Babylonian influence, the fifth book of the Law is Palestinian.   It has been considered probable by many critics that our book of Deuteronomy was the result rather than the effect of the reforming movement in the days of Josiah, and that it began to assume its present form in Palestine during the obscure days of the desolation of the land when Jerusalem and the Temple were in ruins, but Judah and part at any rate of Israel were occupied by the descendants of the race which had once been predominant.   These, as well as their brethren of Babylonia, were stirred by the movement in favour of rigid monotheism, and, like them, were striving to make it the necessary badge of every Israelite.   The Deuteronomic law may have served for the remnant as the plan of restored Temple worship as Ezekiel did for those of the Captivity.   Deuteronomy, like the book of Ezekiel, is a mixture of legal and prophetical elements.   The Deuteronomic spirit permeates the Bible and is revealed under historical, prophetical, and legal forms. From Jeremiah [2] we learn that the ancient Temple continued to be frequented even in its ruins by worshippers, and doubtless the other sanctuaries still had their votaries. The Levitical priesthood, even in its poverty and degradation, found a home in the families of pious Israelites, and the consciousness of a religious unity grew among the people, expressing itself in a desire to carry out the idea of Josiah's

---

[1] The Mond and Sachau papyri show that before the reign of Cambyses, B.C. 529, the Jews had a temple at Teb on the First Cataract.

[2] See the description of Hezekiah's Passover in 2 CHRONICLES xxix.–xxx. Evidently describing a much later state of things.

age of worshipping Jehovah in a single sanctuary, though whether it was to be on Mount Zion or Mount Gerizim was long an open question.

The past history of the nation was pressed into the service of religion as the feeling that Jehovah had a special mission for His people grew deeper and stronger. From Amos and Hosea, whose prophecies are earlier, as well as Deuteronomy, it would appear that the story began with Jacob and was continued down to the Captivity, the main object being to show that fidelity to God by avoidance of idolatry certainly resulted in prosperity to His people; whilst all their misfortunes must be attributed to the worship of false gods. The prophetic spirit was evidently alive at the time, since even Moses the lawgiver is here, as in Hosea, spoken of as a prophet.[1] Obedience to Jehovah is insisted upon in the prophetic manner by appealing to the many evidences of the love of God for His people, whose gratitude is demanded in the form of a ready obedience to His commands and loyalty to His service. The prime mover of this movement seems to have been Jeremiah. The difference in the treatment of the Fourth Commandment in the books of Deuteronomy and Exodus shows a difference of spirit which may mark the distinction between the Palestinian and Babylonian movement in the days of the Captivity. In Deuteronomy the Sabbath is to be kept because rest is necessary to man and beast alike, and the master is to allow his slaves and his cattle to rest on the seventh day.[2] In Exodus xx., on the contrary, the reason for observing this day is connected with the worship of Jehovah, the one and only God, who on the seventh day "rested" from the work of Creation. In the Old Testament the Sabbatical legislation seems to have been influenced by Babylonia, where the "Sabatu" was scrupulously observed. In order that there might be no possible mistake about the worshippers of the God of Israel keeping a Babylonian day from the same motive as the idolators, the command to observe it is deliberately connected with the work of Creation, which separated Jehovah from all other gods.

[1] Hos. xii. 13.   [2] Deut. v. 14, 15.

But where the Babylonian religion seems to have had the greatest influence on Israel was in the importance it attached to the removal of guilt. The Babylonian rituals are marked by confessions of sin and prayers for pardon. It is as yet impossible to prove that the story of the Fall has its counterpart in the Babylonian religion; but joined as it is to the Creation and Flood narratives, it seems probable that it at any rate was considered worthy of an important place at the commencement of the Law, because of a growing desire to solve the problem of sin in such a way as to account for the increasing prevalence of purificatory sacrifices and rites in the reformed Judaism of the Priests' Code. We may repeat what has already been urged, that for our present purpose it matters little how long the Israelites had known what is related in Genesis i.–ix. It is quite possible that these traditions belong to a much earlier connection with Babylonia, which had had intimate relations with Palestine from immemorial antiquity. But the Fall narrative plays no part in the theology of the earlier prophets, nor was its full significance realised, so far as we are able to judge, by the earliest readers of *Genesis*. The question is why was it retained or inserted in the Jewish law book? And the answer appears to be that it was in order to account for the legislation about sins and trespasses. It teaches that all the human race, including Israel, stands in a wrong relation to God, and that the nation needed constant purificatory rites to reconcile itself to Jehovah. This is not the teaching of the earlier prophets or of such an historian as the compiler of Judges. With them repentance and a renewal of the true worship of God obtains pardon; and though, as we see in Micah, even pious Israelites desired to approach Jehovah with thousands of sacrifices and "rivers of oil," to give "their first-born for their transgression—the fruit of their body for the sin of their soul,"[1] the prophet regards all this as a mere species of God-compelling magic, and exhorted his disciples to do righteousness and walk humbly with God. Moreover, even in Deuteronomy there is no inherent impossibility implied in a man living in such a way as to please God without

[1] MICAH vi. 7.

purificatory rites. The highly elaborated religion of Babylon insisted on these, and Israel, in the days of its degradation, keenly felt their need; consequently they play an important part in the scheme of legislation which appears to have been gradually in the making during the Captivity. The danger, of course, of this side of religion, as the early prophets saw clearly, lies in attributing a magical rather than a sacramental efficacy to these rites; and the insistence upon them, divested however of all appearance of idolatry, is characteristic of the Babylonian period and the influence of the Captivity.

Although the book of Daniel bears every appearance of being a later work, it may contain a genuine tradition that the contest with idolatry was carried on with great ardour in Babylon. This view is supported by Isaiah xl.–lxvi. as well as by the book of Ezekiel. From the absence of denunciation of idolatry in Haggai, Zechariah, and Malachi, and the silence in the personal memoirs of both Ezra and Nehemiah as to this sin, it may be reasonably inferred that, by the time of the restoration of Jerusalem the Jews had accepted the Law, and that no professor of their religion could serve strange gods or worship Jehovah in an idolatrous manner, as was certainly the case in the days of Ezekiel. There must, however, have been a very bitter struggle against idolatry in Babylon, and not a few of the Israelite nation must have abandoned their people, and, perhaps, even have joined the heathen in persecuting the faithful. It seems, therefore, at least possible that we find echoes of this struggle in the Psalms, and that, long before the Maccabæan age, the devotees or *Chassidim* made their appearance. It is difficult to believe that the Law, as we now have it, had already come into being, though the movement in that direction had assuredly commenced; but the advocates of an uncompromising service of Jehovah were gaining influence despite many adverse circumstances. Their progress amid persecution and difficulties may possibly be seen in the earlier Psalms.

It has been generally held by modern interpreters that the personal note in many Psalms must be regarded as representing the nation rather than the individual; but it seems more reasonable to suppose that the speaker, in giving vent to his own experience, is endeavouring to express the collective utterances of the pious remnant who scorned to conform to heathen customs, and suffered persecution on this account.   All attempts to date different Psalms must be based largely on conjecture; but the influence of Jeremiah, Deutero-Isaiah, and Deuteronomy upon the language of some cannot be denied, and many appear to answer to the struggles of the pious and half-despairing portion of the Jewish people during the Captivity.   The early collection of Psalms ascribed to David seems to be peculiarly applicable to this period.[1] The concluding verses of the book of Kings are a testimony to the pathetic interest taken in the ruined dynasty of Judah, and its great ancestor came to be regarded as a type of the national fortunes.   His youth, spent amid persecution when expatriated by the jealousy of Saul, exposed to the perils of the enmity of men like Doeg and Cush the Benjamite, and the perfidy of the Ziphites, may well have been regarded as typical of the fortunes of pious Israel, whose very existence in the dark days of the Captivity seemed precarious.   The ultimate triumph of the shepherd-king over all his enemies would prove a strong encouragement to those in Israel who, amid all the afflictions of the time, looked forward to the vindication of the nation's fidelity to Jehovah.   With scarcely an exception the Psalms in the first book, from iii.–xli., are ascribed to David, and in most cases the main theme of each is the sufferings of the writer, the malice of his enemies, and his confidence in God.   The Psalmist, though his adversaries increase, though men say "there is no salvation for him in his God,"[2] is yet a favoured person, one set apart by Jehovah.[3]   His enemies are on all sides, and he prays to God for guidance.[4]   He is afflicted like one in grievous sickness; yet Jehovah has heard the voice of his supplication.[5]   He is an innocent person whose enemies are constantly on the watch for his destruction, "travailing with iniquity," "digging a pit" for the unwary; yet surely to be

---

[1] Sellin, in his recent *Einleitung in das Alte Testament*, regards Psalms iii.–xli. as containing "Davidic material," pp. 107–113 (1910).

[2] Ps. iii.   [3] Ps. iv.   [4] Ps. v.   [5] Ps. vi.

recompensed by God.[1] Even when he glorifies God for His work of creation, he makes mention of his "adversaries."[2] He glorifies God for his goodness to "the poor," whose cry He "forgets not." Man will not prevail, but the nations will be judged in Jehovah's sight.[3] He is advised to flee from his enemies; but Jehovah hates the wicked and loves the righteous.[4] The faithful are diminished, the sons of men prevail in their arrogance, but God will arise to help.[5] God seems to have forgotten him; but the Psalmist will sing His praise.[6] The impious deny God; but He will bring back the Captivity of Zion.[7] God is the sole trust of His servant; those who go after other gods shall have great trouble; but because the Psalmist has set Jehovah before His eyes he is sure to be shown "the path of life."[8] He prays to Jehovah, assured of his innocency, and begs to be protected against his "deadly enemy."[9] Thus one Psalm after another is occupied by the same theme as we find in Jeremiah's expostulations with Jehovah, the unmerited sufferings of the righteous, and often [10] the sufferer is mocked and ill-treated because he is doing God's special work in declaring His glory. In Deutero-Isaiah the deliverance of Israel from the oppression of Babylonian idolatry is intimately connected with the work of the servant, representing in the first instance suffering Israel, the remnant true to Jehovah, the success of whose mission is seen in the worldwide recognition of His worship, as it is also in Psalm xxii. Thus we see that side by side with the legalistic movement is an outburst of devotional literature absolutely unique in the poetry of the world, based on a firm trust in God in the midst of suffering. The Hebrew Psalter has many attractions; but the chief is the expression of a personal relation towards God; for the Psalmist, whether he speaks in his own name or that of the nation, seems to echo the desire of every afflicted spirit for that consolation which God alone can give.

Not that the whole Psalter or even the Davidic collection

---

[1] Ps. vii.   [2] Ps. viii.   [3] Ps. ix. x.   [4] Ps. xi.
[5] Ps. xii.   [6] Ps. xiii.   [7] Ex. x. 4.   [8] Ps. xvi.
[9] Ps. xvii.   [10] *E.g.* Ps. 40.

in Book I. is solely occupied by one theme. Psalms viii., xix., xxix., for example, deal with the wonders of the natural world and the power of God as displayed in creation, whilst part of Psalm xix. speaks of the Law in language which reminds us of Psalms in later collections. We shall never understand the affection of the Jews for the Law,[1] nor the great movement which led to the acceptance of the Priestly Code, unless we keep in mind the fact that to the Jew it was the expressed will of God, and that happiness was only to be found in conformity with this. Apart from devotion to God the minute precepts of the Law must always be intolerable, and, even regarded as a national bond, the many inconveniences attending its observance must have outweighed the advantage of keeping it. But when men are convinced that the Law was given by God with the object of bringing human life into conformity with His will, obedience to its regulations must be their glory and their delight, and they can say from the heart: "Lord, what love have I unto Thy law, all the day long is my meditation therein."

The books of Kings concludes with the notice that Evil-Merodach showed some mercy to Jehoiachin, who, from his early years, had been a captive in Babylon, and, though the date of the work in its present form is disputed, it appears possible that its composition in the decidedly Deuteronomic dress in which it is cast may belong to the age of the Captivity. If so, the feeling that the worship of Jehovah is an historic religion had evidently gained ground, and the Jews had begun the attempt to give the story of their nation from Abraham to the fall of Jerusalem, a continuity very rare among Orientals. One of the most interesting problems which modern scholars have to solve is the precise value of the Old Testament story of ancient Israel regarded as a relation of what actually occurred. Here we must be content with the fact that the Jews believed that the period closed by the Captivity, or at any rate by the rehabilitation of Jerusalem and the Temple, was of supreme importance as illustrating the providential dealing of Jehovah with His

[1] See p. 87, below.

people, and that the subsequent history of the nation had less religious importance. With the single exception of the memoirs of Ezra and Nehemiah, we find no attempt to write a continuous history till we come to 1 Maccabees and Josephus; and Jewish literature, when aspiring to rank as Scripture, or even to convey fresh religious truth, is almost always dated back to a period anterior to the Return. The work of Jesus the son of Sirach is an exception; but then the translator, in the Prologue to Ecclesiasticus, denies that his grandfather, who wrote the book, could be ranked with the inspired authors.

The object of the books of Judges and 1 and 2 Kings, for 1 and 2 Samuel, though part of the series seem to stand apart, is to show from history the fatal effects of idolatry. Everything seems to be subordinated by the compilers to this object; though in most respects they show commendable honesty in recording facts to the detriment of national heroes, and in giving the reader long extracts from the ancient documents before them. They even allow it to be seen that their forefathers did not attain to the standard of monotheism which they themselves inculcated. They did not even hesitate to tell us that after the extirpation of Baalism by Jehu, so far from a revival of national prosperity taking place, "Jehovah began to cut Israel short." Nevertheless, their object is clearly enough to show us that from the time of the entry into the Promised Land idolatry was always visited by Divine displeasure, and that the final overthrow, first of Israel and then of Judah, was due to the refusal of the two peoples to fulfil their destiny in absolute fidelity to their God. The effect of this was so to arouse the national conscience against idolatry that the Judaism of the Return was above all things, if not yet a pure monotheism, at any rate a monolatry, differing in many respects from that which prevailed as long as the old Temple remained standing. When, however, we compare the ancient method of writing history with that employed two or more centuries later by the Chronicler when legalism was at its height, we can judge of its superiority in the matter of fairness and a desire to relate as far as possible the facts. It is impossible to understand

D

the work of the Biblical historians without giving due weight to its religious purpose and influence.

At the risk of seeming paradoxical we may venture upon the assertion that Judaism was becoming the religion of a book, though the book itself was as yet hardly in existence. Strictly speaking, though there was no lack of literature, there was no "Scripture" in existence in the age of the Captivity. No book of the Old Testament probably existed in its present form, with the single exception of Ezekiel, and perhaps some short prophecies. Yet the materials were there and, in a sense, ready to hand. If Judaism had put forth but tender shoots as yet, it was firmly rooted in the past. Already its ceremonial law was taking shape, based on the priestly *praxis* of the first Temple; its ancient traditional law perhaps already in existence in writing; and the great Deuteronomic movement in Palestine had based its observance on the love of Jehovah and fear of His displeasure. The story of the nation beginning with a theory of the origin of the universe—monotheistic as contrasted with that of Babylonian polytheism—was being set forward; and a devotional literature of unusual beauty, destined to culminate in the Psalter, had commenced. Judaism had under these influences begun to be a religion rather of personal conviction than a matter of heredity. God's favourites, the *Chassidim,* were not only so because they were Jews by birth, but because they were personally devoted to His service. Not only so, but a Judaism of a non-political character, capable, that is to say, of existing independent of country, government, and external circumstances, had come into being, and Ezekiel had shown how in captivity and exile the Jews could hold their faith as in their own land.

But beyond this Judaism had shown itself capable of borrowing from another civilisation, and even from an alien religion, without losing its essential characteristic. The uncompromising monotheism, which had in early days been the glory of the prophets and teachers of Israel, had now become the mark of every Jew; but, saving this, external influence seems to have been potent in shaping the course of religious development. Before the exile any approach to other religions had led to apostasy and idolatry. Now, safe-guarded by the confession of the unique majesty of Jehovah, Israel could safely take of the riches of the Gentiles. Not only Babylon, but also Persia and Greece, were destined to have their part in the development of the worship of the One and only God.

ESSAY III

THE DEVOTIONAL VALUE OF THE OLD TESTAMENT

BY

RICHARD THOMAS HOWARD, M.A.

Chaplain of the College

ANALYSIS

I. THE PRESENT SITUATION.

 The situation described and accounted for.
   Due to mistaken connection between Verbal Infallibility and Inspiration.
   Due to extreme methods of criticism.
 The effect of criticism on the general public.
 The effect of criticism on the devout reader.
 The effect of criticism on the ultra-conservative.

II. HISTORICAL DEVELOPMENT OF DEVOTIONAL READING.

 As an introduction to the subject.
  1. The original readers.
  2. The Rabbis.
  3. Jesus Christ.
  4. The Apostles and the sub-Apostolic age.
  5. Allegorical interpretation.
  6. The Middle Ages.
  7. The Reformation—two misconceptions.

III. THE NATURE OF THE OLD TESTAMENT.

 A record of religious experience.
 God's gracious dealings with nations and individuals by action produced History.
 God's gracious dealings with nations and individuals by message produced Prophecy.
 God's gracious dealings with nations and individuals by communion produced Psalms.
 Man's response—character studies of Old Testament saints.
 Man's response—language of communion with God.

IV. DEVOTIONAL USES TO WHICH THE OLD TESTAMENT MAY BE PUT.

  1. Learning the character of God.
  2. Appropriating to ourselves the religious experiences of the saints.
  3. For bringing us into communion with God, and hence for moulding the language of devotion.
  4. As a practical guide to life and morals.
  5. For the instruction of children and the ignorant.
  6. To lead men to Christ (rare).
   To teach Christian people more about Christ (common).

V. IMPORTANT SUBSIDIARY QUESTIONS.

  1 How does non-historicity affect devotional reading ?
   The necessity of an open mind.
   Two general results of criticism.
    (a) Discovery of development of religious ideas in the Old Testament. This enhances the spiritual value of the religious experience of the saints.
    (b) Discovery of date of authorship of Old Testament books. This does not affect their value for devotional reading.
   Complications with regard to teaching of children and ignorant people.
  2. How far we may use allegory and typology in devotional reading.
   Criticism has shown the real use of those apparently unedifying portions of the Old Testament which once gave rise to fanciful allegorisation.
   Legitimate methods of allegorisation and use of types.

CONCLUSION.

THE DEVOTIONAL VALUE OF THE OLD TESTAMENT

I.—The Present Situation

THE situation with regard to the devotional reading of the Old Testament, which has arisen from its critical study during the past two generations, is perhaps easier to account for than to remedy.

When the critics began their work in earnest, devout Christians had not only long been accustomed to use the Old Testament (if not literally, at least mystically) as a spiritual treasure and guide, but had also connected this devotional value inseparably with its verbal accuracy and infallibility. It gave them the deepest spiritual pleasure to read it as the message of God to the soul. They found in it a moral standard and example, the study of which produced a character at once robust and gentle. It supplied comfort in time of spiritual and physical depression. The pleasure was enhanced by its infallibility. It was inspired because it was helpful; it was helpful because it was inspired.

But jealously as the pious reader asserted the infallibility of Scripture, he, nevertheless, unconsciously acted as a critic. Broadly speaking, he distinguished two kinds of Scripture. He recognised those bright gems of peculiar devotional worth which sparkle brightly under the gaze of the spiritually minded Christian, those words of God which prove themselves "sweeter than honey to the mouth" of him who will "taste and see," not because of their verbal infallibility, but because of their intrinsic value. On the other hand, he acknowledged that there were Scriptures less obviously fit for devotional reading. Many passages did not appear to be of much practical use for edification. These he found often in large sections of history or prophecy, sometimes as short passages in the midst of otherwise edifying reading. In these cases either the words were passed over as having a meaning at present altogether hidden from human understanding, or a meaning was read *into* the words, and pronounced the infallible Word of God. Thus the method of mystical interpretation and allegorism was adopted to defend the spirituality of these Scriptures, and make them useful for the edification of the soul. How far was this justifiable?

Whatever may have been the *essential* connection between the devotional worth and the inerrancy of Holy Scripture in the mind of the pious reader, it is unquestionable that they *seemed* to him to be inseparable. And when the new criticism began to proclaim their fallibility the devotional reader felt at once that he was thereby deprived of his greatest means of assistance, and that the foundations of his spiritual life were being shaken. It appeared to him at first that the chief exponents of the new views were rationalists and atheists. It was only another attack from outside by the ancient foes of the Faith. They were relentless in their criticism, careless of the effect upon delicate souls, wholly indifferent to the shock to devout minds. But the attack was from *outside*, the enemy was outside, and therefore there was no unusual surprise.

But by degrees Christian theologians themselves adopted the new methods of criticism, and, while their attitude was generally sympathetic, yet their criticism was extreme, and often led them to similar results. The attack had begun from *within*. Grief was succeeded by feelings of indignation and dismay.

The general effect of Old Testament criticism on the devotional reading of the Old Testament may be considered under three classes—the general public, the devotional reader who has accepted the results of modern criticism, and the devotional reader who cleaves to the traditional view of inspiration. The impression conveyed to the mind of the general public by criticism from within and without is that the Bible has been somewhat discredited as a *true* book, and is therefore not so worthy of attention and study as formerly. It is impossible to compare the extent to which it was read intelligently two generations ago and to-day. But, on the whole, it is greatly to be feared that much damage has been done, and that the Old Testament is not read now as it was. We are not at present concerned with the effect of criticism on the *Faith* of the Church in general, but as to whether the Old Testament is still a *vital force* in the life of the Church. There always has been a large section of people within the Church who, while content to listen to the exposition of Scripture from the pulpit, and its public reading from the lectern, make very little use of it for private religious meditation. And there has always been a still larger number outside the Church to whom the Bible is little more than a name, whose knowledge of its contents is confined to a few well-known texts and familiar narratives. Criticism has not decreased devotional reading of the Scriptures among these classes, because it was already non-existent; but it has deterred many from devotional reading of the Scriptures by raising the suspicion that its foundations have been undermined.

Then there are those who have accepted intelligently the results of modern criticism, and still find help from the Old Testament. The universal testimony of such is that, so far from spoiling the Bible for them, the new light thrown upon the writings by the deeper knowledge of the circumstances under which they were written has brought fresh illumination and increased their spiritual teaching tenfold.

It is the third class of readers who have felt most keenly the "attack" on the Bible. The number of people who still cling to the old position is much larger than is sometimes supposed. Their feelings are the more sensitive, because the words of Scripture are so dear to them. The experience of hearing in the words of the Scriptures the living voice of God to their souls has been so real, the connection of this experience with the infallibility of those words has been so close, that certain suggestions of modern criticism seem absolutely blasphemous. We may suppose a person of this type asking, if the Bible is the Word of God, how can there

be absolute errors in fact? If there are mistakes in the
history and the geography and the science, how can I read
the devotional parts without being tormented by the suspicion that there are mistakes here too? If there is no
ground for believing that the Acts of God in the Old Testament ever took place, what ground have I for believing that
similar works may be wrought by God in my own life?
Such is the cry; and it is natural, logical, and worthy of
our sympathy. Our purpose is to answer it by saying
that there can be a devotional spiritual reading of the Old
Testament outside the old traditional method.

II.—HISTORICAL DEVELOPMENT OF DEVOTIONAL READING

So far an attempt has been made to describe and account
for the present situation. The object of this essay is to add
one more to the many efforts that have been made to recover
the Old Testament for devotional reading, by showing how
little has been lost and how much has been gained by criticism.

The best introduction to a successful solution of the question will be to trace the history and development of the way
in which the Old Testament has been used devotionally in
the successive ages since it was compiled. It is most
important to realise that there has naturally been a development in its use. Each age has had its own method of drawing help and inspiration from the Scriptures, and we who,
from our own point of view, stand at the end of the ages are
most likely to arrive at the true spiritual value of the sacred
writings for our age, not by totally disregarding all previous
experience and attempting to discover an entirely new way
for ourselves, but by seeking to make use of all that was
best in the methods of our forefathers, and by adding all the
benefits acquired by modern research.

1. The natural starting-point for our inquiry is the age of
those to whom the words were first addressed. The legislation was at first probably handed down by word of mouth.
The prophetical writings were originally spoken sermons;
the Psalms were hymns; only the history and the Hagio-

grapha existed from the beginning as writings, and the substance of most of these was known long before it was committed to writing. What, then, was the devotional value of these sermons and hymns and living traditions? We have little or no contemporary literature to guide us. But the words themselves give their own answer. "Such a prophet as Amos or Isaiah used writing precisely as he used speech; his writing was but a condensation or an expansion, as the case might be, of his speech. To what objects, then, did he direct his speech? His objects were to enable men to live unto God in their day, and to show them from God how to live. The Word of God was at all times practical, and at all times relating to life and conduct. If we go back to any one of the religious teachers from God, do we see him pursuing any other end than religious ones? Does he seek to correct men's notions of nature or history, or any other subject on which they had the opinions of their day? Does it not appear that the men to whom he spoke were left by him to think on every subject as they thought before, except in regard to living and living unto God?" [1]

If it is a prophetical sermon, the object of the prophet's words is to raise men from their grovelling worldliness, to awaken them to a sense of their sin and its inevitable consequences upon individual character and national prosperity, with gentle pleadings to woo them back to fellowship with God. Wherever there were hearts responsive to the operation of God's spirit, ears sensitive to the voice of God through His prophets, the desired results were achieved. Men listened, were touched, turned, repented, and lived again unto God.

Or was it a hymn of plaintive prayer or joyous thanksgiving? In many cases we do not know whether it was written to express the feelings of an individual or to give utterance to the desire for united worship. But the Psalms betray their own effects. The cadences of religious feeling, of repentance and hope, deep depression and sweet exaltation, consciousness of alienation from and close fellowship

---

[1] A. B. Davidson, *The Expositor*, January 1900.

with God, express not only the feelings of the first writer, but the effect of the words on those who sung them—

> "And lo, with that leap of my spirit,—heart, hand, harp, and voice,
> Each lifting Saul's name out of sorrow, each bidding rejoice
> Saul's fame in the light it was made for—as when, dare I say,
> The Lord's army, in rapture of service, strains through its array,
> And upsoareth the cherubim-chariot." [1]

Again, the writers of the historical and legal literature were essentially religious men, dominated by religious feelings and principles. They showed how from the very beginning God was in the history of their nation. In the lives of the patriarchs, in the formation of the nation, in the history of the kingdom, God was ruling and working out His purpose. And all who had access to these writings would find in this history of God's dealing with their nation a replica of what His dealings with themselves might be and ought to be.

2. The form which religion tended to assume under the Rabbis up to the time of Christ was reflected in their use of the Scriptures. The chief characteristic of their religious life was a strict adherence to the Law, sometimes degenerating into the coldest formalism, less often maintaining itself as true devotion and piety. Hence the reading of the Scriptures for devotional help, in the true sense of the word, was largely superseded by a study of the Law in order to discover its exact meaning. Thus, while we may recognise with true gratitude the debt we owe to the Rabbis in the careful preservation of the text of the Hebrew Bible, and in some exegetical work of considerable value, yet, on the whole, the reading of it was religious rather than devotional, commentative rather than expository.

3. Although Jesus lived and taught in the middle of the Rabbinical age, His use of the Old Testament for devotional purposes presents a striking contrast to the use of the Rabbis. We must leave on one side as beyond the scope of the essay the wider question of the general interpretation of the Old Testament adopted by Our Lord. What we are at present concerned with is the narrower question of the way in which He read the Scriptures for His own spiritual benefit. His

---

[1] Browning, *Saul.*

example will be guide and inspiration to us as far as He as
"very man" found the Bible of His day helpful to Himself;
and the light that He threw upon the sacred pages as the
result of His self-consciousness of Messiahship will show us
how to "find Christ in the Old Testament."

Naturally we cannot expect to find many instances in the
Gospels which reveal Our Lord's inner devotional life. But
on those rare occasions when we are allowed a glimpse into
the mysterious depths of His lonely self-consciousness, we do
find Him making use of the words of the Old Testament for
the definite comfort and inspiration that they brought to
His human soul. In the hour of fierce temptation He
repelled the Tempter's insidious solicitations to evil by cast-
ing Himself on the authority of the Word of God written in
the *Law,* "It is written." [1] At the moment when He first
stood publicly before the Synagogue, at the outset of His
life-work of teaching and preaching, the words of *Prophecy*
came naturally to His lips as applying to Himself on that
occasion. [2] And during the utter loneliness of the hour
when, because He did not shrink from sharing the bitterest
but most universal experience of man, He was tasting death
upon the Cross, out of the three occasions when He addressed
His soul to God, twice He expressed the cry of depression
and resignation in the words of the *Psalms.* [3]

This is quite enough to show that Jesus did not think it
wrong to take the experiences portrayed in the sacred writings
as applying to Himself as an ordinary man, and freely use
their language to express the deep feelings of His soul.

But the great work which Jesus did in establishing a
more "devotional" reading of the Old Testament was the
rescue of the Law and the Prophets from the formal interpretation of the Rabbis and Scribes. Brushing aside the
traditions and legal intricacies of the accepted methods as of
little or no value, He showed how a deeper meaning underlay
the teaching of the Old Testament, how many of the incidents
of Jewish History were a type and a figure of His own work
and personality, how He Himself "fulfilled the law," and how
the writings, when read with eyes open to see spiritual truths,

[1] LUKE iv. 4, 8.   [2] LUKE iv. 18, 19.   [3] MARK xv. 34 ; LUKE xxiii. 46.

would lead men to Himself. In the course of this weaning of His disciples from the formal to the spiritual and Messianic interpretation, our Lord frequently quoted texts from the Scriptures and pointed out their true meaning, using definite incidents to illustrate His own work.

4. In the Apostolic and sub-Apostolic age this method of interpretation was carried on, sometimes a great deal farther than the point reached by Jesus. Having seen the real force of those verses and incidents which were genuinely capable of a spiritual interpretation, the tendency was to apply the same method to other passages which really lay outside this category. They sought to find references to Christ on every page. They used the Old Testament to learn of Christ in lieu of a New. Even at the expense of a wrong translation or a violently forced interpretation they read their teaching about Christ out of all the Scriptures.

5. The process was carried to its utmost limit in the allegorical methods of interpretation used by Origen, Augustine, Ambrose, and all the Fathers after the close of the second century. Not that their method exhausted their use of the Old Testament. It was mainly applied only to those parts which were found to be trivial and uninteresting. From the very first the Old Testament proved a stumbling-block in many of its parts, and this method was adopted to justify its existence as the uniformly inspired Word of God.

6. This method lasted on through the Middle Ages, a period when the main use of the Old and New Testament was as proof text for dogma.

"Up to the time of the Reformation the only kind of theological study which was thought worthy of serious attention was the study of dogma. People's daily spiritual life was supposed to be nourished, not by Scripture, but by the Sacraments. The experimental use of Scripture, so dear to Protestants, was not recognised as one of the main purposes for which God has given us the Bible. The use of the Bible was to furnish proof texts for the theologians of the Church, and the doctrine of the Church as expressed in the Creeds was the necessary and sufficient object of faith. The believer had indeed need of Christ as well as of a creed, but Christ was held forth to him, not in the Bible, but in the Mass. The Bible was the source of theological knowledge as to the mysterious doctrine of revelation, but the Sacraments were the means of grace." [1]

7. An entirely new era in the devotional reading of the Bible was ushered in by the Protestant Reformation, not so much because it increased the dissemination of actual copies of the printed Bible, nor even because it removed the dangers in the way of private reading, but chiefly because the new doctrine of personal salvation, individual grace, and private judgement carried with it as an essential corollary or rather as a twin doctrine a new idea as to the character, purpose, and use of the Scriptures. The Bible became "a book of Experimental Religion," as containing the free message of God's love and redemption to the individual soul. It is the history of God's gracious dealings with the saints of old. The great use of the Bible is for personal help, individual spiritual growth. It is the permanent written Word of God, the complete standard of faith and morals. Men must read it for themselves, following the lives of the characters depicted and the teaching of the writers.

But although the work of the Reformers in this direction can never be too highly praised, or ever be a cause for too much thankfulness, we must recognise that the general use and theory of Scripture represented by the ages begun by the Reformation and following upon it, was not free from a certain misconception which greatly influenced the devotional reading of the Bible. The weight of authority, having been somewhat violently shifted from an infallible Church as its proper seat, found its resting-place in the conception of an infallible Book.[2] This desire for a particular kind of inerrancy and absolute final infallibility was very real and very natural. Attaching itself to the new-found treasure of an open Bible it begat the sturdy belief in the Verbal Accuracy of Holy Scripture—that is to say, the belief that every word of the *original* writings is true historically, scientifically, geographically, theologically, and of course spiritually, and

[1] Professor W. Robertson Smith, *The Old Testament in the Jewish Church*, chap. i.

[2] See Foakes Jackson on Hooker, *Camb. Hist. of Eng. Lit.*, vol. ii. chap. xviii.

that there can be no possibility of mistake in any sense of the word or in any direction.

We ought never to deplore this belief. Unquestionably for a long time it defended and stimulated that devotional reading of the Scriptures which has had such measureless results in the depth and purity of the religious life of the Protestant Christian Churches. It would be ungenerous to speak evil of it. But we need not for that reason deny that the influence of this belief was unsatisfactory in at least two ways. In the first place, as we have already noticed, it led to a very forced method of exegesis, borrowing largely from the allegorising methods dear to the early Fathers. Often, especially in the less edifying portions of the Old Testament, a meaning was sought out of difficult passages entirely apart from the context. The other tendency has been still more disastrous. Though the pioneer of Protestantism was Martin Luther, a fearless and original critic, the position soon assumed by the adoption of a theory of the inerrancy of Scripture led to an intolerant attitude towards all criticism as a matter of life and death.

We have thus come back to the point from which we started, viz. the present situation in the age when criticism has achieved its best, or done its worst, according to the point of view adopted. We are now confronted with the real problem which this essay is attempting to solve, the vital question for all reverent minds to answer. What is now the devotional value of the Old Testament? How can a reverently minded critic study the Scriptures for the benefit of his soul? How much has criticism left the devout reader, how much has criticism contributed to the spiritual edification to be obtained from reading the Bible? Or, more important still, how can one who has hitherto believed in the infallibility of the Old Testament readjust his methods of devotional reading to the wider view without spiritual loss, and how can one whose faith has been shaken re-discover the immense spiritual worth of the Old Testament?

The best answer that can be given is an inquiry into the exact nature of the Old Testament which we have before us to-day.

III.—THE NATURE OF THE OLD TESTAMENT

The Old Testament contains the record of the religious experience of a nation, and of specially inspired individuals within that nation. Now in all such experience there are two sides, God's and man's. Religion is the infinitely varied relation between the Creating and Preserving Father of all mankind and the manifold life of humanity in all its complex spheres of existence, so that religious experience can be as varied as the nature of God, and as complex as the nature of humanity. Thus the Old Testament is a history in epitome of many varied relations between God and man, treated sometimes from the standpoint of God, sometimes from the standpoint of man. On God's side it is Revelation, on man's side it is religious experience.

While it is manifestly impossible to draw any clear distinction between these two spheres of religion, each being impossible without the other, or to analyse the Old Testament records under these two headings, yet it will be a help to our study if we look at these devotional writings first from the Divine and then from the human standpoint.

1. When we say that the Old Testament is the revelation of God we do not mean that the character of God lies revealed there in abstract definitions, but that it contains the written record of His dealings with the nation and with individuals. It records God's approach to man. God was working in the history of the nation from beginning to end, but His dealings with the nation were so often mediated through saints and heroes that the larger part of Old Testament narrative is taken up with God's personal dealing with the individual. Only it must always be remembered that His dealings had always the wider purpose of proving a benefit to mankind at large. " I will bless thee . . . and in thee shall all nations of the earth be blessed."

But when we come to examine the methods of God's approach to nation or individual we find that they fall into three divisions corresponding roughly to the three great kinds of Old Testament literature.

Sometimes, or rather at all times, God was approaching

E

the children of Israel through His ordering of their national
life. God came down into the life of the nation to direct
it and mould it by His gracious deeds of love, by those great
Redemptive Acts which were familiar to every Israelitish
household, or by the ordering of the ordinary course of
events. Thus He made Himself known to the nation. "He
showed His ways unto Moses, His acts unto the children of
Israel." This produced those writings which may be styled
"the prophetical *History* of Israel." Mention has already
been made of the fact that the prophets were religious
historians who could interpret the history of their nation
in terms of divine love and guidance. Holy men of old,
inspired by the Holy Ghost, could see what less inspired
men could not see. Under the Inspiration of God—and it
does not matter in the least *how* that inspiration worked—
they realised the purpose of God's dealings with the nation ;
they grasped the true significance of ordinary events. They
illustrated the character of God by this record of His dealings. But never let it be forgotten that they could thus
interpret God's dealing to His people only because they
had first received that revelation into their own souls.

"The history is not a mere chronicle of supernatural
deeds and revelations. It is the inner history of the converse of God with man that gives the Bible its peculiar
worth. The story of God's grace is expounded to us by
psalmists, prophets, and apostles, as they realised it in their
own lives. For the progress of revelation was not determined arbitrarily. No man can learn anything aright about
God and His love, unless the new truth come home to his
heart and grow into his life. . . . Inspired men were able to
receive and set down new truths of revelation as a sure rule
for our guidance, because these truths took hold of them
with a personal grasp, and supplied heartfelt needs." [1]

What is true of God's dealings with the nation is true of
His dealings with the saints. How He ordered the lives
of the patriarchs, "delivering them out of all their troubles" ;
how He gave strength to Moses and Joshua and Gideon and
Elijah and Nehemiah for the work He gave them to do, is

[1] Robertson Smith, *The Old Testament in the Jewish Church*, chap. i.

the theme of these Old Testament stories which will never fail to inspire their readers.

But, again, God at other times revealed Himself to the nation and the saints by those messages, delivered to the prophets, which we call "*Prophecy.*" "The word of the Lord came unto me, saying, 'Thus saith the Lord.'" It is useless and profitless to attempt to explain too minutely the psychological process by which this communication was made. What really matters is the Message. The prophets were conscious of thoughts and inspirations which came from God. Living so near to Him, in a plane of spiritual life above their contemporaries, they were able to grasp ideas about God beyond the apprehension of unspiritual men. These they delivered first in sermons, which were afterwards committed to writing. Or it may have been the codifying of laws which they realised had the Divine sanction and authority. Their communications were Messages from God to men mediated through the power of spiritual apprehension.

Again, God sometimes revealed Himself in a way almost too deep for words by drawing near to the soul of man, not for the purpose of giving him a message direct to His people, but for communion and fellowship. In the *Psalms* and in many other parts of the Old Testament we have the record of that spiritual experience which we describe by the expression "Communion with God," but which none but those who have experienced it can understand. They give us the language in which God speaks to the heart of man when he is alone before Him, the messages of love from the Father to His child, from the Husband to His spouse, from the Master to His servant, from the Saviour to the sinner.

2. Turning now to man's side, there is little left to be said, since the consideration of God's side has inevitably led us to trespass upon that of man. Quite briefly, the Old Testament describes the response of man to the approach of God. When the nation responded to the Voice of God through loving acts interpreted to them by the prophets, or through their direct exhortations, then the nation prospered, if not always in temporal matters, at any rate in its spiritual

life; but when the nation disobeyed, the gradual process of corruption and disintegration set in which led ultimately to defeat and exile. We have also here portraits of the life and character of the saints and prophets to whom God drew near. We see the developing faith of Abraham, his obedience to the heavenly call, his life of pilgrimage, and his frequent communion with God. We see Elijah on Mount Carmel passionately defending, with amazing moral courage, the unworldliness of Jehovah-worship against the inroad of foreign influences, because he has learned some of the deep things of the God before whom he stands. And the Psalms reveal the human side of the language of communion with God. Here are the breathings of the Mystics in their intercourse with Him, the cries and complaints of sin-stricken souls who struggle upward to the sanctuary of the Lord, the peaceful sighs of relief from those whose sin is forgiven and conquered, the hymn of praise from those whose foes have been set at nought.

IV.—Devotional Uses to which the Old Testament
may be put

Such then is the Bible which we hold in our hands, and open to read for our devotional profit. To what legitimate uses may we put these sacred writings for spiritual edification?

1. In the first place we learn deeply of the Person and Character of God. Through the supreme Revelation of God through His Son we have advanced far beyond the prophets in our conception of God, but nevertheless He did speak " in ancient days . . . to our forefathers in many distinct messages and by various methods through the prophets." [1] The prophets did not interpret His loving acts and gracious-messages amiss. Reading the Old Testament we gain a conception of Him without which the knowledge we gain from the New Testament would be incomplete; for the New assumes the Old. For example, we gain an insight into the Immanence of God in History. We see a model of His guiding hand in

---

[1] Heb. ii. 1 ; Weymouth, *New Testament in Modern Speech.*

the development of the events of the world ; His purpose for mankind is unfolded. It has been said with great force and no irreverence that " you cannot think of God without thinking of Him as a missionary God." The God of the Old Testament has a purpose for the redemption of all mankind. The day of the Lord will see all nations worshipping at His Temple. It is towards the final perfection of all mankind that God was directing the development of Israel's life as its consummation. Reverent criticism has done much to bring into prominence this idea of a God who reveals Himself gradually in the evolution of mankind, and orders the course of national life for the achievement of His purpose. It has given us the book of Jonah as the missionary story of the Old Testament.

It is rarely that we find the knowledge of God as a God of awful purity and jealous holiness apart from the influence of the Old Testament. From the first crude ideas of physical sanctity associated with primitive notion of taboo, we may trace the development of the revelation to its final issue, where God is known in experience and preached by word to be "Holy, Holy, Holy, the Lord of hosts, the whole earth is full of His glory." If shallow views of sin are prevalent in our day, if there is a general lowering of the standard of perfect moral purity, may it not be because we have too much neglected our Old Testament reading and partially lost the knowledge of the fact that God in His holiness is a consuming fire ?

Again, the tender love and forbearance of God is the constant theme of Prophet and Psalmist alike. Who has read through the book of Hosea without being drawn into an atmosphere charged with the tender yearnings of a loving God for His wayward and faithless people ? The passionate pleadings, the *"abandon"* of God in seeking Israel "His bride," the readiness to accept the smallest signs of returning love, may be anthropomorphic, but they cannot fail to teach us the Love of God for His wayward children in all ages.

We may learn the character of God in our devotional reading from isolated passages, or the general trend of a whole book or set of books. We cannot afford to do without the Old Testament in either private or Church life, if we wish to understand and know God.

2. The greatest value of the Old Testament lies in the fact that the religious experiences described there were not unique and isolated revelations, but typical methods of God's dealings with man. They were part of the religious history of mankind. So that we may be perfectly sure that they may be repeated in our own case, and that we may appropriate to ourselves the experiences which the saints of old passed through, and may make them our own. The way in which God approached man in those days is not different from the way in which He will approach him now. Man has changed very little in his essential nature. Knowledge and civilisation have advanced, but man still goes through the same mental and spiritual processes. We may, therefore, so to speak, place ourselves on the same stream of religious experience and be carried along with the saints towards the ocean of perfect communion with God. We can take all the promises of God through His messengers as applying definitely to ourselves in so far as we put ourselves into the same receptive attitude. Every religious experience recorded may have its counterpart in the lives of modern saints. God's deliverance, salvation, guidance, correction, and encouragement may become as actual realities in our own lives as they were to those for whom the acts and words were first given.

"God has no message to the believing soul which the Bible does not set forth, and set forth not in bare formula but in living and experimental form, but giving the actual history of the need which the message supplies, and by showing how holy men of old received the message as light to their own darkness, a comfort and a stay to their own souls. And so, *to appropriate the divine message for our wants* . . . all we need is to put ourselves by the side of the psalmist and the prophet, *to enter by spiritual sympathy into his experience*, to feel our sin and need as he felt them, and to take home to us, as he took them, the precious words of divine love. This it is which make the Bible perspicuous and precious to every one who is taught of the Spirit." [1]

This appropriation of experience, this launching out into the stream of the spiritual life of mankind, can only be effected where there is a humble faith in the Spirit of God, whose work it is to unite us to God.

3. Closely akin to the use described above is the common everyday use which devout Christians make of those precious messages which come instinctively from God to man. Isolated texts or short passages of Scripture have the mysterious power, explain it as we will, of drawing the soul into converse and communion with God. We draw aside from the world to enter into the Presence of God, and as we read the Bible we find that God is speaking to our souls in words that we can understand. The words are food to our spiritual natures. We are consciously strengthened, and inspired, and "helped." We freely admit that such usage may be unsystematic. As we have seen in an earlier part of the essay, it is fraught with grave danger in the direction of fancifulness and forced interpretation. But where these dangers are recognised and guarded against this is a legitimate source of fruitful communion with God.

This is the reason why the Psalms and other devotional parts of Scripture have always been used to mould the language of devotion in church services, in meditation, and in prayer. The soul naturally expresses itself in these exquisite tones of Old Testament utterances. It is quite natural that such should be the case. Originally utterances of high and holy-minded men who enjoyed communion with God to a peculiar degree, it is not surprising that at those times when we draw nearest to God we should fall back for expression on the same words, and that conversely we should find those words as we use them exercising that elevating power on our spiritual feelings and desires.

4. Yet, again, we still find in much of the Old Testament a practical guide to life and morals. The principles which governed the lives of the Old Testament saints will, in spite of the complete difference of circumstances and environment,

[1] Robertson Smith, *The Old Testament in the Jewish Church*, chap. i.

produce a character alike strong, and humble, and trustful, and successful. The Seventh Article has laid it down that "no Christian man whatsoever is free from the obedience of the commandments which are called moral."

This use of the Old Testament is all the more necessary, because the present generation still lags far behind the standard of social ethics preached by many of the prophets. The code tolerated by society sorely needs to be reinforced by the moral and social obligations enjoined in the Scriptures. It cannot be said that we are not bound by this high standard of purity and honesty because we have passed into a New Dispensation. If it was binding in that early age of social and moral development, how much more must it bind us in our enlightened age ?

5. Nothing appeals to a child so much as the Old Testament Stories. The graphic details, the homeliness, the touching pathos, all go to create a living interest in the characters themselves which never fails to move and stimulate the childlike heart. The stories of Abraham and Jacob and Joseph and Moses and Elisha cannot be dispensed with in any scheme of instruction of children or less educated people in home or church or school. They rank second only to the Gospel Stories themselves. How far the preacher may employ "allegorism" in his teaching, and how far this form of instruction is complicated by the question of the historical "truth" of these stories, are questions of such importance that they may better be left for separate discussion.

6. Finally, the Old Testament may be said to lead men to Christ. In the Bible is depicted "the converse of God with His people in all its stages up to the full and abiding manifestations of saving love in the person of Jesus Christ." No one realised this more fully than Christ Himself. "The Scriptures . . . are they which bear witness of Me." The reading of the Old Testament awakens a sense of spiritual need which can only be perfectly satisfied by Christ, and arouses hopes of salvation which can only be realised in Him. The life of Jesus was the Personal Manifestation of the indirect revelation of God which was continually being made

in the Old Testament, wherein we find germs to be fully developed in the New. Many of the Old Testament stories beautifully illustrate the way in which the human soul comes to Jesus Christ. Once the likeness is seen it cannot be erased from the memory.

It is not, however, often that a man would find Christ, in the sense of being led for the first time to see in Him the Personal Saviour and Redeemer, by reading the Old Testament without instruction. This discovery of Christ in the sacred pages is rather a help to the Christian in the deepening of his knowledge and appreciation of Christ's work, than a guide to the unconverted seeker after truth.

The Seventh Article is again suggestive. "Modern criticism may affect the interpretation of particular passages. It may show us that texts which were relied on by the older expositors as prophecies of the Messiah can no longer be appealed to with the same confidence as formerly. It may even involve a rewriting of the whole history of the Messianic Hope. But the broad truth stated in the Article will remain untouched by this, for the undeniable fact that, before the Incarnation, the fathers who lived under the Old Covenant had come to look for the 'redemption of Israel,' and were expecting a personal Messiah of the house of David is sufficient to justify the general statement that 'both in the Old and New Testament everlasting life is offered to mankind by Christ, who is the only Mediator between God and man, being both God and man.'"[1]

To carry this question further into the meaning and scope of Old Testament Prophecy would be to forsake the devotional for the theological side of the subject. It is a question rather of Christian Evidences than of devotional reading.

V.—IMPORTANT SUBSIDIARY QUESTIONS

Before bringing this essay to a conclusion there are several subsidiary questions which cannot possibly be passed over in silence if the devotional reading of the Old Testament is to be reinstated in a new position.

[1] Bishop Gibson on the Thirty-nine Articles.

1. The first and most pressing is the question as to what change the surrender of the belief in the verbal infallibility and historical accuracy of the Scriptures need make in our devotional reading. The question is indeed a vital one, because of the situation which has already been described. At first sight it might seem quite obvious that if we ceased to believe that the Bible is infallible it would cease to be to us a message from the God of Truth. For if doubt is thrown upon the historicity of the records of religious experience of patriarchs and prophets, how can we be sure that the same experiences may be repeated in our case? If there was no such person as Abraham, and the stories of his life are traditional legends, can they reasonably be regarded as an authoritative guide to our spiritual life?

In the first place this important question must be approached with an open mind. God has given us powers of reason as well as the Holy Spirit, and the Christian who takes up his study with a prayer that his intellectual powers may be guided and sanctified by the Spirit of Truth is not doing wrong in accepting the clear dictates of a reason thus sanctified by Him.

There are, however, those who refuse to do this, and are not prepared to accept any argument against Verbal Infallibility. Although these may enjoy the spiritual reading of the Bible, they not only will lose that richer and wider view which the light of criticism reveals, but they stand in danger of leading others into a perilous position tending to unbelief.

There are also those who do approach the Bible with an open mind, and yet can conscientiously say that the Bible can be proved to be historically infallible. But whilst continuing themselves to derive spiritual benefit from the Word of God, they can only justify their position by arguments which too frequently appear somewhat far-fetched.

But the majority of thoughtful readers in the present day who have come to the Old Testament in the reverent attitude have found it impossible to avoid the conclusion that the Old Testament cannot claim complete verbal and historical accuracy. These see the vista of new possibilities for the better and safer interpretation of the Scriptures opening out before them. How do these explain the effect of criticism on their devotional reading?

(*a*) Roughly speaking, there are two general results of criticism. It is maintained by many students that the recorded history of the people of Israel was committed to writing many years, in some cases many centuries, after the actual events occurred. In the course of the interval between the original event and the writing of its history there occurred a development of religious ideas which coloured the original story with new tints as the religious experience of mankind developed from age to age. The prophets assimilated to the needs of their own time stories and traditions dating back to an early period in the religious history of man, interpreting them in the light of experience born of intercourse with God, and thus left the impress of their own fellowship with God upon the stories as they related them. They endorsed the truth of the religious experience recorded in the stories they found, and supplemented it with their own. Hence if we come to the scriptural narrative, expecting to find an accurate historical chronicle of facts in the exact order in which they are described as happening, we shall be disappointed, but if we are seeking the history of religious experience, we find more than we expected. We find the experience of two ages wrought into one, or rather the experience of God's Church stretching over a long period wrought into a single story. The "historicity" in the narrow sense matters little. The stories are histories of religious experience, and are for that reason as helpful and spiritual and devotional as before. Nothing is lost. Much is gained. And we have been able to use our highest faculties of enlightened judgement and reverent scholarship. "That the early history of Israel is a perfect accurate record of bare facts need not be supposed. The body is more than the raiment, the idea more than the fact. Nevertheless, it was the fact or event that suggested the idea, though the idea, once born, with vital energy once transformed details in order perfectly to express itself." [1]

Take, for example, the early narratives of mankind in the

[1] A. B. Davidson, *The Expositor*, Jan. 1900.

opening chapter of Genesis. They teach us truths about God and man that do not in the least depend upon their historicity for their value. God the Origin, the Creator, the Illuminator, the Orderer of all. Man, the consummation of nature, made in the image of God, created to enjoy the divine blessing, approval, and communion. The stories of the Fall, of Cain and Abel contain a wealth of suggestive teaching about the nature and consequences of temptation and sin.

Or take the life of Abraham—his call to a life of separation and blessing and purposefulness and usefulness under the Divine direction, the promises of inexhaustible wealth on all sides for him to appropriate through faith, his pleading for Lot, his supreme devotion and faith and his willingness to offer up his only son—these are things which bear the hallmark of truth upon them. They are true in religious experience. We might almost argue back from their agreement with what we discover to be true in our experience when we try to follow Abraham, to the historical existence of some person in whom these experiences were first realised. Even if it were to be proved that there was no such actually historic personage as Abraham, the writer of the story had met such an Abraham, or was perhaps an Abraham himself. He had seen the experience of Abraham in the saints of his day, or felt it in his own life, and under the inspiration of the Spirit expressed that rich experience in the story of Abraham's life in its present form.

(b) The second part of criticism has been to discover the dates of authorship of the Prophets and Psalms. In this case criticism cannot affect the message enshrined in prophecy or psalm. The words speak for themselves. And as far as devotional reading is concerned, we are no worse off in appropriating to ourselves the messages and experience and in holding communion with God, if the originals were written somewhat later than, and in different circumstances from, the date and circumstances allotted to them by the traditional view.

" Of this I am sure at the outset that the Bible does speak to the heart of man in words that only come from God— that no historical research can deprive me of this conviction, or make less precious the Divine utterances that speak straight to the heart. For the language of these words is so clear that no readjustment of their historical setting can conceivably change the substance of them. . . . The plain, central, heartful truths that speak for themselves and rest on their own indefeasible worth will assuredly remain to us." [1]

The question of the teaching of children and uneducated people is difficult. It may appear hard to enforce the lesson to be drawn from an Old Testament story if we are unable to guarantee that it actually happened as set forth. But the difficulty is not as great as it seems. The child can be made to feel that the story embodies a truth which comes with all the authority of the God Who inspired the writer, whoever he was, as he wrote it down. The impressiveness of the story depends chiefly upon the personality of the teacher who, himself under the inspiration of the same Spirit of God, conveys the message to the child. As a matter of fact the question is not often raised as a serious difficulty, but rather as a question of curiosity. If from the beginning of mental development the child understands that the message can be authoritative without being crudely historical, no mishap will occur. On the other hand, it is far better that the child should be thus informed than that he should have his faith built up upon an unsafe foundation because it is an easier one to build upon. It is not fair to lay at the door of reverent criticism the many shipwrecks of faith that have occurred in the modern age of criticism. The fault has been not criticism but lack of instruction or warning.

2. There is one last question that needs elucidation. As we traced the history of the development of devotional reading of the Old Testament through the ages, we saw how often an exaggerated use of allegorism led even some of the greatest Early Fathers into a field of interpretation where we feel unable to follow them. The two reasons which prompted this method were the worthy desire to do justice to the superficially trivial and uninteresting portions of Holy Scripture by reading some deeper meaning into every text, and

---

[1] Professor W. Robertson Smith, *The Old Testament in the Jewish Church*, chap. i.

the misunderstanding as to the nature of inspiration. Now intelligent criticism has taken away the need for fanciful allegorisation by pointing out the real use of these apparently unedifying passages. They serve the purpose of bringing us closer into touch with the Bible era by revealing under the searchlight of criticism the circumstances and environment of those saints whose religious experience it is so important for us to appropriate. We cannot put ourselves side by side with these Fathers of the Old Covenant and enter by spiritual sympathy into their experiences unless we understand something of their daily life and ideas, their aspirations and limitations, their grasp of truth and their ignorance of it. But by a careful study of the literature of the Old Testament, as literature, we can do this ; and then trivial passages are not to be regarded as wasted, but as throwing light on those passages that *are* devotional.

But when we have said this we may still ask whether there was not a great deal of truth underlying the allegorical method which undoubtedly gave such spiritual pleasure to those who adopted it, and whether we too may not to a certain legitimate degree use allegory and typology in devotional reading.

In the first place Christ Himself taught us to see in many of the Old Testament stories a type of His own life and work, and we may follow Him so long as we keep within the limits which He observed. Since the long development of religious experience in the Old Testament age had its perfect realisation in the experience of the Son of Man, we may expect to find the life of Jesus reflected in the former, and the Old Testament to be in a certain sense an epitome of the work of Christ. Nor are we disappointed. When we take the cardinal examples of God's dealings with the national life of Israel, *e.g.* the uplifting of the serpent in the wilderness, or with individual Israelites, such as the life of Joseph, we often find the most remarkable foreshadowings of the life of Christ. These are perfectly legitimate subjects of typology, if the details are not forcibly pressed into a service which they cannot be expected to render to the analogy, and much real help for personal spiritual life or for the instruction of believers may be derived from them.

In the second place, much of the Old Testament may be used as a type of Christian experience. This is closely allied to, though slightly different from, the usage described as appropriation of religious experience. For example, the command of Elijah to the widow woman at Zarephath to make a cake of bread for himself first and *then* for herself and her son, may be regarded as a type of the way in which the Christian is called upon to place the claims of God in the first place as the condition of receiving his daily bread from God. "Mystical interpretation, as applied by its real masters, was no mere play of poetic fancy, no arbitrary reading into history or prophecy of a meaning which it did not contain. It rested upon the principle that all true spiritual utterances, or spiritually circumstanced events, are manifestations of a law which is eternal, and may therefore be regarded as symbolic or descriptive of every subsequent operation of that law ; while since history deepens as it develops, deepens in complexity and scope, its later phrases express more fully what its earlier did but indicate, and in this sense are realities of which the latter were the types." [1]

But there is a place where the line must be drawn in this use of typology. There are certain cases where we may use Old Testament stories and facts as an *illustration* of a truth which we may wish to emphasise, but where we must not invest that illustration with the Divine authority of the Bible, as though it *proved* the truth. The story must be used only as an illustration, not as a proof. There is a great danger in some modern exegesis of drawing fanciful illustration from the Bible, and then using the Bible as an umpire to decide the truth which the story illustrates. But provided the distinction between proof and illustration is maintained, and the illustrations are not far-fetched, much really devotional help may be derived from such comparisons.

There is yet a third kind of legitimate typology which may be applied to most of the ritual of the Temple or Tabernacle worship. There is a great deal of spiritual teaching underlying some of the laws of sacrifices and offerings and purifications. The ritual enshrined within it a deeper truth

[1] Illingworth, *Personality, Human and Divine*, chap. vii.

than was conveyed to the formal worshipper. We do not know how far the Israelites saw through the ritual into the spiritual realities which were foreshadowed. But although the ritual has now been discarded, and the truth embodied in it stands clear as an entity apart from its corresponding ceremonial, yet we do well to look back and study the truth as it was in its concrete form. A great deal of suggestive teaching is yielded by the observation of the form of the truth in the ritual stage, before it issued out into the spiritual sphere of its evidence. Reading these laws in the light of the Christian era, they come to us with all the weight of Divine authority at the back of their spiritual counterparts.

The results of criticism can, in fact, if they are reverently employed, make the Old Testament even more alive than it was before. In it we begin to hear the prophet not merely uttering "dark sentences," but speaking his message to living men and women like ourselves. In the customs, ritual, and laws we recognise what people actually did and why they so acted. Archæology is making the Palestine of the prophets a land more and more alive to our imagination, and sound methods of criticism are transforming the Old Testament once more into a living book. We have certainly to abandon something, but we are as certainly finding that the gain outweighs the loss. If we have to modify traditional methods of interpretation, we need not for that reason see no longer in the Old Testament the preparation of Israel for the coming of the Light of the World, nor cease to look for profit in the teachers of the nation. Minute details, once neglected, are becoming once more significant. Portions which seem to our forefathers almost without meaning are fraught with a new life. We can still learn with Israel, pray with its saints and join in its praises; and we can still find in the Law, the Prophets, and the Psalms our treasury of devotion.

ESSAY IV

JUDAISM IN THE DAYS OF THE CHRIST

BY

W. O. E. OESTERLEY, D.D.

Examining Chaplain to the Lord Bishop of London

ANALYSIS

I. JUDAISM AND HELLENISM.

Two thought-tendencies which, though in process of development previously, came into existence as definite "schools" of thought and teaching during the two centuries immediately preceding the beginning of the Christian era.

These two "schools" of thought represent respectively two aspects of Judaism :—

> *Palestinian Judaism, a religion of Law;*
> *Hellenistic Judaism, a religion of Hope.*

II. JUDAISM AS A LAW.

The place that the "Law of Moses" occupied among the Jews of Palestine ; the evidence of Philo, Josephus, and the Books of the Maccabees. The Oral Law and its origin ; its binding character ; its authority equal to that of the Written Law ; evidence of the Talmud ; of Maimonides. The meaning of *Torah;* its observance not a burden ; illustrated from the Mishnah and Midrash. Some dangers involved in the Jewish attitude towards the Law, viz. dangers owing to the exalted character assigned to the Oral Law, the danger of Legalism, the danger of Spiritual Pride ; while these dangers were real, and many succumbed to them, they must not be exaggerated ; the Jews were the people of the Law because they were first the people of Jehovah.

III. CHRIST AND THE LAW.

Christ's acceptation of the Law illustrated from the Gospels. His attitude towards the Law : while normally accepting it as a whole, He is often critical and, in some cases, directly antagonistic towards it. His "fulfilling" of the Law. His opposition to the Oral Law. The consideration of Christ's attitude towards some special points of the Law—Adultery ; Murder ; Love towards one's neighbour ; the Washing of Hands ; the Dietary Laws ; the Sabbath ; Divorce.

F

IV. JUDAISM AS A RELIGION OF HOPE.

The prophetic literature of the Old Testament formed the basis of the *Apocalyptic Literature,* which was the outward expression of Judaism as a religion of Hope. Some characteristics of this literature: the essence of its teaching centres round the Kingdom of God and the Righteous Ruler. Its popular character. The Apocalyptists and their followers were not antagonistic to the Law; it was by them merely subordinated.

V. THE ESCHATOLOGY OF THE GOSPELS GENERALLY.

Christ accepted, as a basis for His teaching, the Eschatology of the Apocalyptic Literature as a whole, whatever more exalted and spiritualised direction it may have taken in His hands. The need of realising that the Eschatology of the Gospels is based on that of the Apocalyptic Literature; this is illustrated by adducing evidence from this literature on some salient points, with references to the Gospels: the signs of the end; the Kingdom; the Messiah; His Judgeship; the Advent. The need, for the sake of His hearers, for Christ to utilise the Eschatology of the Apocalyptic Literature as a whole. The consideration of some special points in Christ's eschatological teaching —the *Kingdom ;* varying elements in Christ's conception of this; it is sometimes spoken of as present, sometimes as future; sometimes as something inward, sometimes as something outward; this teaching differs from that of the Apocalyptic Literature on the subject. Further consideration of the same subject: the Parables of the Kingdom; some special sayings of Christ concerning the Kingdom. The *Parousia.* Christ's teaching concerning the Kingdom is apparently variable and inconsistent; how is this to be accounted for?

VI. CHRIST AND ESCHATOLOGY.

The problem not to be explained along any *one* line of thought; various points considered: (*a*) Misunderstandings on the part of some of the witnesses; (*b*) clearer discernment on the part of others. The course of the development of the Gospel records; two opposing theories; the content of " Q." The variations in the Gospel records of Christ's eschatological teaching is largely owing to the fact that they represent two modes of envisaging things among the followers of Christ; (*c*) a further consideration is the fact of Christ's gradual Self-revelation to His followers; (*d*) Christ taught to a large extent a "transmuted Eschatology." In spite of all that has been said, it is difficult, with the evidence before us, to regard the whole of Jewish Apocalyptic as requiring " transmutation "; the Second Advent of Christ the Judge cannot be explained away. The prime lesson of Gospel Eschatology for modern times is contained in its other-worldliness.

VII. CONCLUSION.

The need of due proportion in estimating the respective spheres of Ethics and Eschatology in Christ's teaching. Because the latter transcends human understanding, that is no reason for refusing to accept it in its essence. Religion is supernatural, and therefore Reason must sometimes give way to Faith.

JUDAISM IN THE DAYS OF THE CHRIST

I.—Judaism and Hellenism

" Ezra had set his heart to seek the Law of the Lord, and to do it, and to teach in Israel statutes and judgements."[1] The movement initiated by Ezra, which these words express, was destined to be of profound and lasting influence upon the Jews. In order to make the Law of the Lord the dominating factor in the national life it was necessary that all intercourse between the Jews and their Gentile neighbours should be rigidly curtailed. This was brought about by the efforts of Ezra and Nehemiah. As long as they lived these efforts were entirely successful. But after they had passed away the isolation of the nation gradually ceased. That which, above all, tended to break down the barriers between Jew and Gentile was the rise of Greek civilisation, to the fascination of which the bulk of the nation soon succumbed. Nevertheless, the work of Ezra and Nehemiah had not been in vain; a small minority of the people remained true, in spite of all temptations, to their love for and practice of the Law which these two leaders had inculcated. This minority soon formed itself into a party which had for its twofold object the strenuous upholding of the Law and the combating of all Hellenistic influences. It was owing to these upholders of the Law, who were known as the " pious ones " (*Chassidim*), that the Maccabæan revolt became possible. This revolt marked the climax, therefore, of a movement which had been in the working long previously. As we shall see presently, the champions of the Law, who were characterised by their nationalistic and particularistic attitude, were opposed to those who, being also Jews, were

[1] Ezra vii. 10.

dominated by the Hellenistic spirit, and who wished to obliterate national barriers by a frank acceptance of the higher culture and freer intellectual atmosphere of the Greeks.

For Judaism this Hellenistic movement contained within itself profound good, as well as great evil; the universalistic tendency which it engendered being absolutely indispensable if Judaism, in issuing into Christianity, was to become a world-religion; on the other hand, the particularistic attitude which the reaction against it ultimately called forth, hardened into a stereotyped form of Judaism which became the bitter and lasting enemy of Christianity. Yet each form had its necessary part to play in the Divine economy; if Universalism was the herald of great things to come, Particularism stood forth as the champion of great things past; if Universalism, in its all-embracing character, was prepared to welcome some things that were dangerous, Particularism, with zealous scrutiny, rejected much that was incompatible with true religion. Universalism betrayed a tendency to accept too much, Particularism erred in retaining too much; the danger lurking in each could only be avoided by balancing one against the other. The true equipoise thus gained reached abiding perfection in Him who came "not to destroy, but to fulfil." [1]

The existence of these opposing parties is graphically illustrated by some passages in the first book of the Maccabees, the author of which, a zealous adherent of the orthodox party, says that "In those days (*i.e.* of Antiochus Epiphanes) came there forth out of Israel transgressors of the Law, and persuaded many, saying, Let us go and make a covenant with the Gentiles that are round about us; for since we parted from them many evils have befallen us. And the saying was good in their eyes. And certain of the people were forward herein, and went to the king, and he gave them licence to do after the ordinances of the Gentiles. And they built a place of exercise (γυμνάσιον) in Jerusalem according to the laws of the Gentiles; and they

---

[1] MATT. v. 17. The spirit of these words is most forcibly expressed by St. Paul when he says that in Christ "there is neither Jew nor Greek" (GAL. iii. 28).

made themselves uncircumcised, and forsook the holy covenant, and joined themselves to the Gentiles, and sold themselves to do evil." [1]   It must have been largely owing to the encouragement derived from the existence of this Jewish Hellenistic party that Antiochus Epiphanes determined to assay the impossible task, as the sequel proved, of obliterating Judaism altogether.   He wrote, we are told, "to his whole kingdom, that all should be one people, and that each should forsake his own laws." [2]   The grasp which the Hellenistic spirit had gained upon the Jews is grimly evidenced by the fact that "many of Israel consented to his worship, and sacrificed to the idols, and profaned the Sabbath." [3]   Antiochus followed this up by a special decree for Jerusalem and the cities of Judah, according to which every distinctive Jewish rite was to be abrogated; [4] the carrying-out of this decree began in December 168 B.C. with the desecration of the altar in Jerusalem. [5]

The policy of Antiochus was supported by many Jews; "from the people were gathered together unto them many, every one that had forsaken the Law." [6]   Their action seems traitorous, unpatriotic, and rebellious against the God of their fathers; but while there were doubtless many who were renegades and time-servers, it is impossible to believe that there were none who were actuated by nobler motives. There must have been those who were convinced that the Jewish religion was doomed if divorced from progressive thought, and cut off from the possibility of development; thinkers who realised that a religion which does not advance becomes stagnant; was there not in the past history of the religion of Israel ample precedent for upholding the cause of progress which they were championing?   How had the pure monotheistic worship of Jehovah been attained?   Certainly not by retaining the ancient crude conceptions of Him characteristic of earlier ages.   How had the Law become what it

---

[1] 1 Macc. i. 11–15. [2] 1 Macc. i. 41.
[3] Ver. 43 ; *cf.* ver. 42. [4] See verses 44–51.
[5] See ver. 54. The building of "an abomination of desolation upon the altar" refers to the building of a heathen altar upon the altar of Jehovah and offering sacrifice upon it to a heathen idol ; *cf.* ver. 59.
[6] Ver. 52.

was? Certainly not by refusing to welcome periodic re-formation. And what an irony it was that the orthodox party itself gloried in that Law which at its hands was constantly being developed![1] There must have been among the Jewish Hellenists many persons firmly convinced that they were the truest representatives of the religion of Jehovah, and who, therefore, as a matter of conscience, felt bound to act upon their convictions, bitter as it was to be opposed to their countrymen. But while the first book of Maccabees witnesses to the strength of the Hellenistic party in Palestine, the book is the most eloquent testimony we possess regarding the existence of the orthodox party and the indomitable perseverance and fanatical courage which preserved it from annihilation; this might be illustrated by almost endless quotations from the book; one will, however, suffice. Nothing could better express the firm determination to cling unswervingly to the ancient traditions than the words of Mattathias, the first of the great Maccabæan leaders: "If all the nations that are in the house of the king's dominion hearken unto him, to fall away each one from the worship of his fathers, and have made choice to follow his commandments, yet will I and my sons and my brethren walk in the covenant of our fathers. Heaven forbid that we should forsake the Law and the ordinances. We will not hearken to the king's words, to go aside from our worship, on the right hand nor the left."[2] This spirit was typical of thousands of Jews, who willingly laid down their lives rather than swerve from what they believed to be the right path. These represented the orthodox party in Palestine.

Long before the commencement of the Christian era, therefore, we find these two opposing parties in existence among the Jews of Palestine. It is supremely important to remember this fact; the history of the beginnings of Christianity cannot be adequately understood without bearing it in mind. Broadly speaking, the Gospels and the Acts present us with two aspects of Judaism (as distinct from Christ's specific teaching), representing, in the main, the characteristic of each of the two parties referred to. While,

[1] See below, p. 89.   [2] 1 MACC. ii. 19-22.

doubtless, either party was influenced by the teaching of the other, it may be said that the distinguishing feature of the Hellenistic faction was its presentation of Judaism as a religion of Hope, while to the orthodox party Judaism was, above all things, a religion of Law.

It is these two fundamental aspects of Judaism which we must now briefly examine.

II.—JUDAISM AS A LAW

For the bulk of the Jewish nation in Palestine, at the time of Christ, the Law was the foundation of all religion; it was the supreme guide of life; and, as being for the Jew the articulate expression of the Divine will, it was the final appeal in all matters of religious life and practice. Christ accepted the Law, with all its inadequacies, in order to "fulfil" it. As the Law represented the essence of orthodox Judaism in the time of Christ, and as it formed part of the background and one of the bases of the newer teaching which was to come, it is important that some insight into the Jewish conceptions of it, and of the individual attitude of the Jew towards it, should be illustrated by citations from contemporary writers, as well as from the literature belonging to the ages immediately preceding the beginning of the Christian era.

The influence and power of the Law were largely due to the fact that from earliest childhood its practical carrying-out was witnessed in the home;[1] the husband taught his wife, the father his children, the master his servants the precepts of the Law and the need of observing them (Philo, in Eusebius, *Praep. Evangel.* VIII. vii. [Migne]); *cf.* also 4 Macc. xviii. 10, where the mother, in speaking to her children of their martyred father, Eleazar, says: "It was his wont moreover, when he was still with us, to teach you the Law and the Prophets"; and see the concluding sentence of the Prologue to *Ecclesiasticus.* The result of this is well illustrated by the words of Josephus (*Contra Apion.,*

---

[1] *Cf.* LUKE i. 59 ; ii. 21–24, 39, 41.

II. § 18): "But, as for our people, if any do but ask one of them concerning our laws, he will tell them all more readily than his own name, and this because of our having learned them at once, as soon as we could understand anything, and because they were, as it were, graven upon our souls." The love and veneration for the Law which had thus been instilled in the Jews from childhood became passionate, and even fanatic, when assailed by outside enemies; indeed, every true Jew was always ready to suffer martyrdom rather than be unfaithful to the Law. During the Maccabæan struggle this was often exemplified, *e.g.* 1 Macc. i. 62, 63: "And many in Israel were fully resolved and confirmed in themselves not to eat unclean things; and they chose to die, that they might not be defiled with the meats, and that they might not profane the holy covenant; and they died" (*cf.* 2 Macc. vi. 19; vii. 1, 6, 37). In 1 Macc. ii. 32–38 there is a description of how a thousand Jews died rather than profane the Sabbath (*cf.* Josephus, *Antiq.*, XII. vi. 2). The words of Eleazar in 4 Macc. v. 27–30 express what were undoubtedly the feelings and resolutions of numberless Jews in actual life: ". . . nor will I, in truth, break the glorious vows which my forefathers made to keep the Law, yea, even though thou shouldest tear out mine eyes and melt my very entrails!" Men evidently wondered at this excessive loyalty to the Law; but to the Jew to die for his Law rather than to be unfaithful to it lay in the ordinary course of things. Josephus (*Contra Apion.*, II. § 32) says: "Nor ought men to wonder at us, if we are more courageous in dying for our laws than are all other men; for other men do not easily submit to the easier things such as those to which we are accustomed . . . whereas our being accustomed willingly to submit to laws in these instances, renders us fit to show our fortitude upon other occasions also" (see further, Philo, *Ad Gaium*, XVI. §§ 29, 32). Quotations could be greatly multiplied in order to show how intense were the love and loyalty of the Jew for the Law.

While it is, of course, true to say that by the Law is meant the "Five Books of Moses," this does not by any means sufficiently describe the content of the word as used and understood in the Gospels. From the time of Ezra [1] onwards there existed not only a theory of the Law, but, above all things, its practical observance; the theory, as will be seen, and to a large extent the practice, was based upon the existence of the Written Law (*i.e.* the Pentateuch); but with the march of time and the rise of changing conditions new problems arose as to the practical application of the Law, and cases were constantly arising which called for new decisions because the Written Law provided neither solution nor guidance. How, then, were these to be met? Since the Law was of a wholly divine character,[2] there could be no sort of doubt that every conceivable case was in reality provided for, if only the Law were properly understood and interpreted. There were those who believed that they possessed the requisite discernment, and that it lay within their power to gain from the letter of the Law guidance for every possible emergency of life that could be imagined. Those who, by diligent and increasing study of the Law, had gained this proficiency were the *Sopherim* ("Scribes") and *Chachamim* ("Wise men"), called in the New Testament γραμματεῖς, in reference to their making copies of the Scriptures, and νομικοί or νομοδιδάσκαλοι ("Lawyers," or "Teachers of the Law"), in reference to the decisions from the Law which they gave. In course of time these decisions increased to a large mass of legal matter; this was handed down *by word of mouth*, for "that there should be two *written* Laws was as unthinkable as that there could be two Gods." [3] Thus arose the *Oral Law*. To the Pharisaic orthodox Jew at the time of Christ this Oral Law was equally binding with the Written Law. Indeed, it must have been at a relatively very early time that the Oral Law was declared to have been *coeval* with the Written Law, both being thus attributed to Moses himself; for the teaching of Rabbi Simeon ben Lakish (end of third century A.D.), preserved in the Baby-

---

[1] An Oral Law of some kind must, of course, have existed long before the time of Ezra, but not the Oral Law in the later Jewish technical sense.

[2] See *e.g.* Philo, in Eusebius, *Praep. Evangel.*, VIII. vi, (Migne).

[3] H. J. Holtzmann, *Lehrbuch der neutestamentlichen Theologie* (2nd ed.), i. 38.

Ionian Talmud (*Berakhoth*, 5a), on this subject, is as follows:—

"What is that which is written: *I will give thee tables of stone, and the Law, and the commandment which I have written, to teach them?*[1]

Tables: These are the Ten Words [*i.e.* the Ten Commandments];

Law: This is the Scripture;

And the Commandment: That is, the Mishnah;

Which I have written: These are the Prophets and the Writings [*i.e.* the Hagiographa];

To teach them: That is, the Gemara;

thus instructing us that all these were given to Moses from Sinai." Josephus refers to this when speaking of the policy of Alexandra, who became regent on the death of her husband, Alexander Jannæus (died 78 B.C.); he says, in reference to her two sons: "She made Hyrcanus High-priest, because he was the elder, but much more because he cared not to meddle with politics, and permitted the Pharisees to do everything; to whom also she ordered the multitude to be obedient. She also restored again those practices which the Pharisees had introduced, according to the traditions of their forefathers, and which her father-in-law, Hyrcanus, had abrogated."[2] The reference to the "traditions of their forefathers" is interesting; it is equivalent to the "tradition of the elders" (παράδοσις τῶν πρεσβυτέρων) spoken of in Mark vii. 3, 5 (*cf.* Matt. xv. 2; Gal. i. 14). That this "tradition" emanated originally from Moses was, of course, the merest fiction;[3] but it was, nevertheless,

---

[1] Exod. xxiv. 12.

[2] *Antiq.*, XIII. xvi. 2. *Cf.* also XIII. x. 6: "The Pharisees have delivered to the people a great many observances by succession from their fathers, which are not written in the laws of Moses."

[3] It is extraordinary to notice how this belief has continued among the Jews. Moses Maimonides (died 1204 A.D.), the greatest of all Jewish teachers since Biblical times ("From Moses to Moses there hath been none like unto Moses"), writes in his Preface to *Yad Ha-chazakah* ("The Strong Hand") as follows:— "All the commandments which were given to Moses on Sinai were given with their interpretation; for it is said, *And I will give thee the tables of stone, and the Torah* (Law), *and the Mitzvah* (Commandment). *Torah:* that is, the Written Law. *Mitzvah:* that is, its interpretation. He commanded us to observe the *Torah* in accordance with (עַל־פִּי, lit. 'according to the mouth of') the *Mitzvah*.

accepted as a fact by the bulk of the Jews in Judæa who were under the influence of the Pharisaic oligarchy; and therefore this "tradition" (Oral Law) was as binding upon them as the Written Law. This is an important fact, as it explains what appears at first sight to be the inconsistent attitude of Christ towards the Law; we shall deal with this in the next section. In speaking, therefore, of the Law it is this twofold element that is included; and this applies to New Testament times as well as to both earlier and later periods.

To the modern mind it is difficult to realise how a religion could be a religion of Law, such as Judaism was; but this difficulty is due to the fact that we do not, as a rule, quite understand what the term "Law" meant to the Jew. The term *Law* or *Nomos*, as Schechter has well pointed out, "is not a correct rendering of the Hebrew word *Torah*. The legalistic element, which might rightly be called the Law, represents only one side of the *Torah*. To the Jew the word *Torah* means a teaching or an instruction of any kind. It may be either a general principle or a specific injunction, whether it be found in the Pentateuch or in other parts of the Scriptures, or even outside of the Canon. The juxtaposition in which *Torah* and *Mitzvoth*, Teaching and Commandments, are to be found in the Rabbinic literature, implies already that the former means something more than merely the Law. . . . It is the Torah as the sum total of the contents of revelation, without special regard to any particular element in it, the Torah as a faith, that is so dear

And this *Mitzvah* is called the Oral Law. Moses, our teacher, wrote down the whole Law with his own hand before he died ; . . . the *Mitzvah*, that is, the interpretation of the Law, he did not write down, but he commanded it to the Elders and to Joshua and to the rest of Israel ; for it is written, *All the words which I have commanded you, these shall ye observe and do* (DEUT. xii. 28). And, therefore, this is called 'Oral Tradition' (תורה שבעל פה)." He states the same thing more concisely in the Preface to his Commentary on the Mishnah : "Know that with every commandment which the Holy One (Blessed be He) gave to Moses our Teacher (Peace be with him), He gave also the interpretation." And there follows then a minute account of how the Almighty communicated both the commands as well as their interpretations to Moses. This, while undoubtedly intended to be in the nature of *Haggadah*, does, nevertheless, witness to the belief that the Oral as well as the Written Law came directly from Moses, and were, therefore, both equally binding.

to the Rabbi." [1]   But it was not only the Rabbis of later ages
to whom the Law was dear; there is ample evidence to show
that in much earlier days, even in New Testament times,
and before, the observance of the Law was a joy to the pious
Jew; [2] when the Psalmist sings—

> " Oh, how I love thy law !
>   It is my meditation all the day long," [3]

and in many other passages gives vent to his religious feelings of affection and delight for the Law, it is difficult to
believe that there is much truth in the contention of some
modern Christian writers that the observance of the Law
was a burden, and wearisome to the Jews. [4]   How could that
be the case with a truly religious Jew who was convinced
that the Law expressed the Divine will?   He might have
been wrong in his conviction, but that it can have been
irksome to a pious Jew to keep even the minute precepts
of the Law, as far as this was in his power, cannot have
been the case if he believed (and he did believe) that the
Law was a Divine revelation. [5]   When, therefore, we speak
of Judaism as a religion of Law, it must be remembered
that by the Law is meant the great body of Divine precepts, the expression of the mind of Jahwe, the Wisdom
of God, the Knowledge of God, which had in loving condescension been accorded to His Chosen People.   One can
thus understand how the belief arose of the inseparability
between God and the Law, the idea that wheresoever the
Law was practised there the Divine presence was *ipso facto*
manifesting itself; the thought was expressed in later days

[1] *Some Aspects of Rabbinic Theology*, pp. 117, 127.

[2] See Schechter, *op. cit.*, chap. xi., "The Joy of the Law."

[3] PSALM cxix. 97.

[4] It should also be remembered that for the majority of the nation, *i.e.* for
those who were not rich and had no leisure, the observance of the Law in all its
minutiæ was an absolute impossibility ; the ruling classes despised the "people"
for this reason, *cf.* JOHN vii. 49.   See H. J. Holtzmann's interesting discussion
on this subject, *op. cit.*, i. pp. 184 ff.

[5] *Cf.* the words of Rabbi Nechonyiah ben ha-Qanah : " Whoso receives upon
him the yoke of *Torah*, they remove from him the yoke of royalty and the yoke
of worldly care ; but whoso breaks from him the yoke of *Torah*, they lay upon
him the yoke of royalty and the yoke of worldly care" (*Pirqe Aboth*, iii. 8).   See
further, *Christian Evidences for Jewish People*, § 163 (A. Lukyn Williams).

by Rabbi Chananiah ben Tradyon in the words: " Two that sit together, and are occupied with the words of *Torah,* have the *Shekhinah* among them." [1]   This belief in the inseparability between God and His Law, which explains better than anything else the reason why Judaism was a religion of Law, is very charmingly illustrated by a parable preserved in the Midrash *Shemoth Rabba,* sec. 33 : [2]

> " It is as though a king had an only daughter ; and one of the kings comes and marries her.   He then wants to return to his own country and to take his wife back with him.   Then the king says to him, ' She whom I have given to thee is my only daughter ; I cannot bear to be separated from her ; yet I cannot say to thee, Take her not, for she is thy wife.   But show me this kindness ; wherever thou goest prepare me a chamber that I may dwell with you, for I cannot bear to be separated from my daughter.'   Thus spake the Holy One to Israel : ' I gave you the Torah ; I cannot separate Myself from it ; yet I cannot say to you, Take it not. But whithersoever ye journey make Me a house wherein I may dwell.'   For it is said : *And let them make me a sanctuary that I may dwell among them* (Exod. xxv. 8)."

It was this conception of the Law standing for God that, generally speaking, made Judaism a religion which was truly spiritual.   But there were three dangers which inevitably arose here, and which, among many, counteracted the spirituality which was essentially a characteristic of Judaism.   The first has already been referred to, viz. the growth of the Oral Law ; we have seen that this was a positive necessity ; and had its real character always been made clear no harm would necessarily have followed.   But when precepts, which were originally only put forth because of passing exigencies, were declared to be of Divine origin, and therefore binding for all time, and upon all men, then a real

---

[1] *Pirqe Aboth,* iii. 3.   *Cf.* MATT. xviii. 20 : " Where two or three are gathered together in My name, there am I in the midst of them."

[2] At the beginning of the *Seder Teruma;* it is quoted by Weber in his *Jüdische Theologie,* p. 17.

danger arose; these both could, and did become, instruments of tyranny in the hands of the unscrupulous. Things which did not belong to the Law were declared to be part of the Law; and the bulk of the people accepted the *dicta* of their rulers.[1] A second danger was *Legalism,* by which we mean the idea that the external observance of legal precepts is in itself sufficient irrespective of the state of the heart. "The human mind is so constituted that, provided an outward show of duty is maintained, men are content to slur over the inner life, the thoughts and intents of the heart, which are invisible to their fellows, and which they cannot be summoned before a human tribunal to account for. It is the history of all religious organisations, only more patent and developed in the Jews of this (the New Testament) time."[2] That many fell victims to this danger was natural; but the extent to which this was the case has been much exaggerated by some Christian writers. And thirdly, closely connected with the foregoing, there was the danger of regarding the observance of legal precepts as meritorious *per se.*[3] This, again, is a danger common to all men, but it was intensified among the Jews because the doctrine of Divine grace played a relatively unimportant part in Judaism.

These evils must be fully taken into consideration when contemplating Judaism as a religion of Law; only we must be on our guard lest we overstate their prevalence and effect among the Jews during the New Testament period. It cannot be too strongly insisted upon that if the Jews were the people of the Law, they were also the people of Jahwe; and the Jewish doctrine of God is so exalted that it would have been impossible, at any rate among the bulk of the people, for a mere external legalism to have quenched the love and trust which the individual Jew felt for and in his God.

---

[1] It may be worth while, in passing, to utter a protest against the still prevalent view among Christian writers that these rulers (*i.e.* the Scribes and Pharisees) were *all* unscrupulous, or hypocritical. It can be proved, by a careful study of the Gospels, that our Lord did not include *all* the Pharisees in His denunciation of them. The subject is dealt with in some detail in Oesterley and Box, *The Religion and Worship of the Synagogue,* 2nd ed., pp. 120–131.

[2] Toy, *Judaism and Christianity,* p. 243.

[3] *Cf. e.g.* Matt. xxiii. 4 ff.; Luke xviii. 9 ff.

III.—CHRIST AND THE LAW

We must restrict ourselves here to a few examples illustrative of Christ's general attitude to the Law as an institution, without considering a number of subsidiary, but not unimportant, matters more or less closely connected with the subject.

(*a*) That Christ accepted the Law as such, and acknowledged its binding character, is evident from a number of indications in the Gospels; His protestation that He came not to destroy but to fulfil (see Matt. v. 17–19) is in itself sufficiently striking; the excellence of the Law as a whole is pointedly emphasised in Mark xii. 29–31; Matt. xxii. 34–40; Luke x. 25–28, where its entire content is declared to consist in love to God and one's neighbour (*cf.* also Matt. vii. 12; Mark x. 17–20; Luke xviii. 18–21). But in addition to this there are various details of the Law, the observance of which are evidently approved by Christ: "The scribes and the Pharisees sit in Moses' seat; all things, therefore, whatsoever they bid you, these do and observe" (Matt. xxiii. 2, 3); the cleansed leper is bidden to go and show himself to the priest, and to offer for his cleansing "the things which Moses commanded" (Matt. viii. 4; Mark i. 44): so, too, in the case of the ten lepers who were cleansed; they likewise are told to go and show themselves to the priests (Luke xvii. 14).[1] In Matt. vi. 2–4, 5 ff., 16 ff. the laws concerning almsgiving, prayer, and fasting are regarded as binding; it is only the method of observance with which Christ finds fault. Christ pays the Temple-tax[2] in accordance with the command given in Exod. xxx. 13, 14 (Matt. xvii. 24), where it is said that every Jew "from twenty years old and upward" is to make this offering to the Lord. Mention may also be made of Christ's observance of the feast of the Passover (Mark xiv. 12 ff.; Matt. xxvi. 17 ff.; Luke xxii. 7 ff.; *cf.* Luke ii. 41, 42).[3] These examples are sufficient to show

---

[1] For the law concerning a cleansed leper, see LEV. xiii. 2–14, xiv. 2–32.

[2] On this see Schürer, *H.J.P.*, II. i. pp. 249 ff. (English edition).

[3] On the other hand, there is no indication of the observance of the law given in DEUT. xvi. 16, according to which three times a year all males were required to "appear before the Lord." But silence on the subject does not mean that the Law was ignored.

that the general principle of observing the commandments of the Law had Christ's approval.

(*b*) But there are also a large number of passages in the Gospels which describe Christ's attitude towards the Law as critical, and in some cases as directly antagonistic. It is impossible to deal exhaustively with these now; but it can be shown that in the passages in question Christ is either spiritualising the letter of the Law, or supplying what was inadequate, or else abrogating what was wrong. In some cases, moreover, it is clear that what Christ finds fault with is not the Written, but the Oral Law. It is fully realised that to deal with only a few passages on this subject is inadequate; but more thorough treatment is out of the question here.

Christ's attitude towards the Law, to be properly understood and appreciated, must be considered in the light of His teaching as a whole; only so can it be seen in its true perspective. Mr. Montefiore expresses himself very excellently in reference to our Lord (though writing in a different connexion) when he says: "A great personality is more than the record of its teaching, and the teaching is more than the bits of it taken one by one. It must be viewed as a whole. It must be judged as a whole—so far, at least, as this is possible. It has a spirit, an aroma, which evaporates when its elements or fragments are looked at separately. . . . Righteousness is more and other than a number of excellent positive commands and excellent negative ones." [1] Nevertheless, some insight, it is to be hoped, may be gained by a brief consideration of a few appropriate passages.

Instances of the spiritualising, or "deepening the letter" [2] of the Law are the following:—

Matt. v. 27–28 : "Ye have heard that it was said, Thou shalt not commit adultery (Exod. xx. 13 ; Deut. v. 17): but I say unto you, that every one that looketh on a woman to lust after her hath committed adultery with her already in his heart." In spite of what Mr. Montefiore says (*op. cit.*, ii. 506) on this passage, the Law nowhere condemns adultery of the

---

[1] *The Synoptic Gospels*, i. p. civ.
[2] The expression is Mr. Montefiore's, *op. cit.*, ii. p. 506.

thoughts; he strangely misunderstands the point in saying:
" . . . what Jesus says is not the whole truth,

> "'Tis one thing to be tempted, Escalus,
>   Another thing to fall;'"

for there is no question of temptation here; what is referred
to is the deliberate harbouring of adulterous thoughts, tem-
porising with impure desires.

Matt. **v.** 21 ff. deals with the teaching of the law on
murder, which Christ "fulfils" in the same way as in the
case of adultery. Whatever interpretations may be given to
the words of Christ in verses 22 ff., it is certain that He teaches
that "not only will the external act receive due punishment
at human tribunals, but the inner feeling that prompts it is
liable to the verdict of condemnation which will be pronounced by God." [1]   (See for other examples Matt. v. 33 ff.,
38 ff.; xxiii. 16 ff., &c.)   In Matt. v. 43 ff., which offers
another example, we have a case of what is probably a pre-
cept of the Oral Law side by side with one from the Written
Law: "Thou shalt love thy neighbour," these words are
from the Written Law (Lev. xix. 18), but "Hate thine enemy"
nowhere occurs in the Written Law; the clause may be, as
Archdeacon Allen suggests, "an inference from the distinction drawn in the Old Testament between conduct
towards Israelites and conduct towards Gentiles," but that
inference had been made long before the time of Christ; the
words are clearly a quotation, with which Christ's hearers
were familiar; it is, therefore, in the highest degree probable
that they had been embodied in the Oral Law; and it is this
which Christ is combating.[2]   But Christ's attitude to the
Law is more pointedly illustrated by considering some matters
which touched the every-day practical life of the Jews more
closely.   In Mark vii. 2–5, Matt. xv. 2, 3 (*cf.* Matt. xxiii. 25,
26; Luke xi. 38, 39), we have references to the washing of

---

[1] Allen, *St. Matthew*, p. 48. For another example of this principle see
Mark vii. 9 ff. (= Matt. xv. 3 ff.).

[2] Or, if not a formal statement in the Oral Law, at any rate one which had
become stereotyped in the popular religion of the ordinary man, and which the
Teachers of the Law did not try to correct.

hands and the cleansing of utensils.[1] In the Written Law there are numerous precepts regarding questions of cleanness and uncleanness (*cf.* Lev. xi.–xv. ; Num. v. 1–4, xix.), but they are as nothing when compared with the abundance of enactments which had gradually increased by means of the Oral Law, and which were ultimately stored up in the Mishnah ; [2] " no less than twelve treatises deal with the matters appertaining to this subject." [3] The Scribes and Pharisees, in the passages referred to, speak of these washings as the "tradition of the elders," *i.e.* the Oral Law, the transgression of which they regarded as just as reprehensible as the transgression of the Written Law ; [4] Christ's reply, on being asked why His disciples transgress this "tradition," reveals an attitude of direct opposition. "It would seem," says Mr. Montefiore, "that Jesus did really take up a position of definite antagonism to the ominously increasing Oral Law." [5]

In Mark vii. 14, 15 (= Matt. xv. 10, 11) a principle of supreme importance is laid down by Christ ; but in this case His opposition was not only to Rabbinical Law, but also to Pentateuchal Law ; Christ's words amounted to nothing less than an abrogation of the *Dietary Laws*. Regarding this subject we may be permitted to quote some remarks of Mr. Montefiore, which are the more striking as coming from one who is a Jew by race and religion : [6] " According to the principle laid down by Jesus, no *thing* can make you unclean. You can only make yourself unclean by sin. The principle seems profoundly true. It destroys with a prophet's blow the terrible incubus from which all ancient religions suffered,

[1] On these subjects, *cf.* Büchler, *Der galiläische 'Am-ha'Areṣ des zweiten Jahrhunderts*, pp. 41 ff., 96 ff.

[2] Mr. Montefiore truly says that " the 'Oral Law,' codified later on in the Mishnah, was then [*i.e.* at the time of Christ] in its formative period " (*op. cit.*, I. 162).

[3] Schürer, *op. cit.*, II. ii. 106.

[4] *Cf.* Josephus (*Antiq.*, XIII. x. 6), where, in writing of the antagonism between the Sadducees and Pharisees, the former say as against the Pharisees : "We are to esteem those observances to be obligatory which are in the written word, but are not to observe what are derived from the tradition of our forefathers."

[5] *Op. cit.*, i. 163.

[6] Mr. Montefiore belongs, however, to the Reform Jews, whose views differ in many important respects from those of the Orthodox Jews.

that certain objects or physical states are in themselves taboo or religiously unclean. Doubtless our modern conceptions of clean and dirty may have had a religious origin; doubtless, too, there is a certain moral duty in physical cleanliness, a certain inter-connexion between the material and the spiritual. But this is a totally different thing from the theory of *religious* uncleanness. That rested upon very ancient superstitions, which, again, themselves depended upon polytheistic or 'animistic' conceptions of still greater antiquity. Ritual religion (which made up a considerable part of priestly religion) was largely concerned with practices which turned upon, or were developed out of, these superstitious conceptions. . . . The outward conception of religious uncleanness as caused by things, and not only by immoral acts, is still present in the Pentateuchal Laws; it was maintained and sadly elaborated by the Rabbis. . . . The world is profoundly indebted to Jesus for His liberating and clarifying words. They are spoken in the true spirit of Amos and Hosea. The true province of religion needed to be defined. It was made the greater and the purer by being limited to the realms of spirit and personality." [1]

Another subject of importance in the present connexion is that of *Sabbath observance;* this is dealt with in Matt. xii. 1–14; Mark ii. 23–iii. 6; Luke vi. 1–11; here we have another pointed instance of Christ's repudiation of the Oral Law. It was no transgression of the Pentateuchal Law to pluck ears of corn on the Sabbath (*cf.* Deut. xxiii. 25), but, according to the tradition of the elders, it was regarded as work, and therefore forbidden on the Sabbath. Christ's protest is, however, not only against the minute observance of Rabbinical Law here; He again lays down a far-reaching principle, viz. that if the Law (the Written Law) is such that it makes the Sabbath a burden to man, then the Law defeats its own ends, and may rightly be ignored; "the Sabbath was made for man, and not man for the Sabbath" (Mark ii. 27).

Finally, there is the law of *Divorce* (Mark x. 2–12 [=Matt. xix. 3–12]; Matt. v. 31, 32; Luke xvi. 18; *cf.* 1 Cor. vii. 10, 11). This is, perhaps, the most striking in-

[1] *Op. cit.,* i. pp. 170 ff.

stance recorded in the Gospels of Christ's opposition to both
the Written and the Oral Law; the former is repudiated by
His saying that Moses permitted divorce "for the hardness
of your heart," but that "from the beginning of the creation,
male and female made he them . . . so that they are no
more twain, but one flesh; what therefore God hath joined
together, let no man put asunder" (Mark x. 5–9). The latter
is repudiated by the words: "Whosoever shall put away his
wife, and marry another, committeth adultery against her;
and if she herself shall put away her husband, and marry
another, she committeth adultery" (Mark x. 11, 12). The
Written Law is contained in Deut. xxiv.; the Rabbinical
Law was based in the first instance upon Deut. xxiv. 1, 2:
"When a man taketh a wife, and marrieth her, then it shall
be, if she find no favour in his eyes, because he hath found
some unseemly thing in her, that he shall write her a bill of
divorcement, and give it in her hand, and send her out of
his house. And when she is departed out of his house, she
may go and be another man's wife." Rabbinical Law was
concerned mainly with what was implied by an "unseemly
thing"; Hillel and his followers explained it in reference to
a large variety of things;[1] Shammai and his school maintained that it referred to adultery; the former, therefore,
taught that divorce was permitted for almost any reason,
the latter allowed it only for adultery. Christ, as one would
expect, taught a higher ideal than either, and would not
sanction divorce for any reason whatsoever.[2]

These few examples (and there are others, but the most
important have been selected) will suffice to illustrate
Christ's attitude towards the Law. He accepted it in
principle, but modified and expanded it where necessary;
in other respects He abrogated it altogether because He
taught a higher morality and a more spiritual religion.

[1] The later Rabbis followed Hillel, whose view has prevailed up to the
present time.

[2] The words containing the exception mentioned in MATT. v. 32, xix. 9, are
later insertions. *Cf.* the later insertion of "without cause" in MATT. v. 22.

14789

IV.—JUDAISM AS A RELIGION OF HOPE

If it be asked in what respect Judaism can be spoken of as a religion of hope, the reply must take the form of referring the questioner first of all to the prophetical literature of the Old Testament. It is impossible to read the books of the prophets without realising that hope for the nation underlies the bulk of their teaching;[1] their belief in the omnipotence and righteousness of God impelled them to prophesy concerning a time to come when God would reign supreme on earth through His Anointed Instrument, and that the centre of His rule would be the nation of Israel, purified and made perfect in righteousness, whereby they would be made the means of drawing all the nations of the world within the sphere of the Kingdom of God, where peace and justice would reign supreme: "And it shall come to pass in the latter days, that the mountain of the Lord's house shall be established in the top of the mountains, and shall be exalted above all hills; and all nations shall flow into it. And many peoples shall go and say, Come ye, and let us go up to the mountain of the Lord, to the house of the God of Jacob; and he will teach us of his ways, and we will walk in his paths; for out of Zion shall go forth the law, and the word of the Lord from Jerusalem. And he shall judge between the nations, and shall reprove many peoples; and they shall bend their swords into ploughshares, and their spears into pruning hooks; nation shall not lift up sword against nation, neither shall they learn war any more."[2] "For unto us a child is born, unto us a son is given; and the government shall be upon His shoulder; and His name shall be called Wonderful Counsellor, Mighty God, Everlasting Father, Prince of Peace. Of the increase of His government and of peace there shall be no end, upon the throne of David, and upon His Kingdom, to establish it, and

[1] Even denunciations and prophecies of judgement are intended as a means, not an end in themselves; they are intended to be the means of rooting out wrong-doing and of purifying the nation in order thereby to bring about the fulfilment of the national hopes.

[2] Is. ii. 2-4; MICAH iv. 1-3.

to uphold it with judgement and with righteousness from henceforth even for ever. The zeal of the Lord of hosts shall perform this."[1] These words express most fully the hope that is implied in all the teaching of the prophets; it is a hope which is primarily a state of confidence in God, "the expectation of the Sovereignty or Reign of God, which can only be set up by a prophet, and necessarily results in public and private peace."[2] But as time went on this expectation seemed again and again to be disappointed, and that in spite of loyalty to the Law of Jahwe, which was the condition of its fulfilment; there seemed to be an abiding contradiction between the prophetic ideals and the actual conditions; in spite of the Divine promises the state of the nation was grievous; oppression and persecution was their lot; and their task-masters were heathen, the enemies of Jahwe. Well might Israel cry, with one of their psalmists, "Hath God forgotten to be gracious?"[3] But hope was ingrained in the nation, for its religion was a religion of hope —"Though He slay me, yet will I wait for Him."[4] It was not the righteousness of God which was at fault, but the impatience and blindness of men; what was wanted was clearer vision into the ways of God, deeper insight regarding Divine purposes. And men pondered and looked; then they saw, and wrote down their visions in order that Israel's hope might grow ever stronger. This hope was centred chiefly upon the nature and characteristics of the kingdom of God; the revelations concerning this kingdom and its establishment on earth formed the main theme of the earliest and noblest contributors to what has come to be known as the *Apocalyptic Literature*. According to these, the kingdom which was revealed to their inner vision was a kingdom not of this world; for this world was seen to be steeped in iniquity; the children of the kingdom "hated and despised this world of unrighteousness," they "hated

---

[1] Is. ix. 6, 7.

[2] Hart, *The Hope of Catholick Judaism*, p. 31 ; see further, pp. 32 ff. of this interesting book.

[3] Ps. lxxvii. 9.

[4] Job xiii. 15 ; so the R.V., but the Hebrew is susceptible of a different rendering.

all its works and ways."[1] In the same way the Messiah, upon whom these Apocalyptists set their hope, was a King not of flesh and blood, but one "whose countenance had the appearance of a man, and His face was full of graciousness, like one of the holy angels"; "the Son of Man who hath righteousness, with whom dwelleth righteousness, and who revealeth all the treasures of that which is hidden, because the Lord of Spirits hath chosen Him; and His lot before the Lord of Spirits hath surpassed everything in uprightness for ever";[2] "the Elect One who sitteth upon the throne of His glory,"[3] whose "glory is for ever and ever, and His might unto all generations."[4] The Kingdom and its Righteous Ruler; the thoughts and teaching concerning these constitute the essence of the Apocalyptic Literature.[5]

Further, this literature, as Professor Charles has pointed out, "strove to show that, in respect alike of the nation and of the individual, the righteousness of God would be fully vindicated; and, in order to justify its contention, it sketched in outline the history of the world and of mankind, the origin of evil and its course, and the final consummation of all things."[6]

By the time of the New Testament period the great body of eschatological ideas was fully developed; these ideas, though in their germ (as we have already pointed out) reaching back to prophetical times,[7] matured and became more or less crystallised during the two eventful centuries which immediately preceded the rise of Christianity. It was these centuries which saw the unfolding and

---

[1] Enoch xlviii. 7.   [2] Enoch xlvi. 3.

[3] Enoch xlv. 3; *cf.* xl. 5; lv. 4; lxii. 3, 5; lxix. 27, 29.

[4] Enoch xlix. 2. See also *Sib. Oracl.*, iii. 46–50, 652–730 (belonging to the middle of the second century B.C.); *Test. xii. Patr.*; Lev. xviii. 2–13 (belonging to the end of the second century B.C.).

[5] That there should be diversity of view in this literature is natural enough when it is remembered that the various books which belong to it were written at different periods, and that the apocalyptic outlook was almost always conditioned by the political circumstances of the time. In judging of this literature as a whole the fairest and most generous procedure is to look at it at its best.

[6] *Encycl. Bibl.*, i. 214.

[7] It is, of course, realised that the Jewish Apocalyptists were also to a considerable extent indebted to Persian influence in their conceptions; *cf.* Krüger, *Hellenismus und Judentum im neutestamentlichen Zeitalter*, pp. 22 ff.

rich growth of the apocalyptic movement with its vast eschatological developments.[1] It is important to remember that the Apocalyptic Literature, as a whole, is a *popular* literature; that is to say, it reflects the thoughts of religious circles which were outside the Rabbinical schools; and it embodies religious ideas which in many points sharply conflicted with the strict scholastic orthodoxy of the Pharisees.

"The great mass of the people, the Ochloi ('*Am-ha'areṣ*) continued both before and after the Maccabæan struggle to be dominated by the Hellenistic spirit; and as in the case of the ruling classes, so also had these their teachers and their pious ones. These were the creators of the apocalyptic literature. It is true, the Apocalyptists acknowledged the same spiritual forbears as the Pharisees, namely, the pious ones of the Psalms and of the Daniel-Apocalypse; but while the Pharisees were the literal descendants of these, the Apocalyptists were their spiritual offspring."[2] It would, however, be a mistake to suppose that the Apocalyptists and their followers were unmindful of the authority and claims of the Law, but, unlike the Pharisaic Scribes, whose energies were centred on the building-up of the "Oral Law," they saw in the Law of Moses a code of morality which was inclusive enough to gather all the nations of the world within the circle of its admirers, and a means of drawing all men to acknowledge and worship the One God, the God of Israel. Their gaze was fixed not so much upon the earth, as upon Heaven and the world to come, where racial distinctions would of necessity be obliterated. The exalted religious scheme which dominates the Apocalyptic Literature tended, therefore, to overcome national and particularistic limitations.

---

[1] See, further, Oesterley and Box, *op. cit.*, pp. 35, 237 ff., and the present writer's *The Doctrine of the Last Things: Jewish and Christian* (2nd ed.), pp. 65 ff.

[2] M. Friedländer, *Die religiösen Bewegungen innerhalb des Judenthums im Zeitalter Jesu*, pp. 22 f.

V.—THE ESCHATOLOGY OF THE GOSPELS GENERALLY

That Christ accepted the eschatological teaching of the Jewish Apocalyptists, whatever more exalted direction and explanation it may have received at His hands, does not admit of doubt; but as this Jewish teaching lay at the base of the Eschatology of the Gospels, it will not be inappropriate to illustrate the truth, in the briefest possible way, by a few quotations from the Apocalyptic Literature. In doing this it will suffice to show the parallelism that exists as regards the more outstanding points in the eschatological drama, without touching upon a number of subsidiary matters, which, though of interest, are not of great importance. The question of "sources" need not, for the present, trouble us here,[1] for while the possibility of Christ's eschatological teaching having been subsequently elaborated is not denied, the very nature of Jewish Eschatology demands that it should be accepted as a whole; its constituent elements depend one upon the other; if the Gospels adopted any part of its fundamentals they must of necessity have adopted other parts as well; the general scheme of Jewish Eschatology does not lend itself to piecemeal acceptance. Schweitzer and others are undoubtedly right when they maintain (on whatever various grounds) that it is a logical necessity to supplement the eschatological teaching given in St. Mark's Gospel by that given in St. Matthew's Gospel.[2] There is also the fact that the apocalyptic literature, being a popular one, the people were familiar with its content as a whole; so that we should not naturally look for any differentiation

---

[1] Though, as will be seen below, discrimination has been used in the choice of the passages quoted.

[2] *Cf. e.g.* the following: ". . . Hieraus erkennt man zugleich, warum die Markushypothese in der Konstruktion des 'Lebens Jesu' sich auf die Hilfe der modernen Psychologie angewiesen sah und damit nothwendig immer unhistorischer wurde. Die Tatsache, welche das Verständniss allein ermöglicht, fehlt in diesem Evangelium (MARK). Ohne MATT. x. und xi. bleibt alles rätselhaft. Darum sind Bruno Bauer und Wrede die in ihrer Art einzig konsequenten kritisch-historischen Vertreter der Markushypothese, wenn sie zum Resultat kommen, dass der Markusbericht in sich unsinnig ist. Keim mit seinem realistischen geschichtlichen Empfinden fühlte richtig, wenn er den Aufriss des Lebens Jesu nicht einzig nach Markus entworfen haben wollte" (*Von Reimarus zu Wrede*, pp. 356 f.; *cf.* also pp. 330 f., 336).

as between one part and another of the apocalyptic content, as regards their relative importance, in the Gospels.

(a) *The signs which are to precede the end* consist of physical phenomena, described *e.g.* in *Enoch* cii. 1, 2 : "And in those days when He brings a grievous fire upon you, whither will ye flee, and where will ye find deliverance . . . ? And all the luminaries will quake with direst fear, and all the earth will be affrighted, and tremble, and be alarmed"; and in one of the fragments of the *Apocalypse of Noah*, preserved in this book (lxxx. 4–8), it is said : "And the moon will alter her order, and not appear at her (appointed) time . . . and many chiefs of the superior stars will err, and these will alter their orbits and tasks, and will not appear at the seasons prescribed to them . . ." (*cf. Sib. Oracl.*, iii. 71 ff., 83–85, 796–806; *Test. xii. Patr.*, Lev. iv. 1, &c.). The thoughts contained in these passages are reflected, *e.g.* in Mark xiii. 24, 25. Another of the signs is war among nations, together with domestic strife; see *Enoch* c. 1, 2 : " . . . For a man will not withhold his hand from slaying his sons and his sons' sons, and the smiter will not withhold his hand from his honoured brother; from dawn till sunset they will slay one another"; *Test. xii. Patr.*, Judah xxii. 1, 2 : "And the Lord will bring upon them divisions one against another. And there shall be continued wars in Israel . . ."; see for these thoughts Matt. x. 21, 34–36; xxiv. 6, 7; Luke xii. 51–53. The conceptions of the *Kingdom* in the Gospels are full and manifold (we shall refer to them again later), but in some particulars the thoughts of the Apocalyptic writers are reflected in the Gospels. *Enoch* civ. 1–6 contains some ideas which are not absent from Matthew and Mark: " . . . Your names are written before the glory of the Great One. Be hopeful; for aforetime ye were put to shame through ills and affliction; but soon ye will shine as the stars of heaven, ye will shine and ye will be seen, and the portals of heaven will be opened to you. . . . Be hopeful, and cast not away your hope, for ye will have great joy as the angels of heaven . . . for ye will become companions of the hosts of heaven;" with this, *cf.* Matt. v. 12; xiii. 43; xxii. 30; Mark xii. 25; Luke x. 20. Further, reference is made several times in the

Apocalyptic Literature to the Messianic Banquet which is to take place when the Kingdom is established; this is evidently referred to in *Enoch* lxii. 14: "And the Lord of Spirits will abide over them, and with that Son of Man will they eat, and lie down, and rise up for ever and ever." More detailed is the account given in the Syriac *Apocalypse of Baruch*[1] xxix. 3–8, where it says: ". . . Then will the Messiah begin to manifest himself. And Behemoth will begin to manifest himself from his land, and Leviathan will ascend from the sea; and these two mighty sea-monsters, whom I created on the fifth day of the work of Creation, and have reserved for that time (*i.e.* the Messianic era), shall then be for food for all those who are left" (*cf. Enoch* lx. 7, 8; *Sib. Oracl.*, Procœm. 87, iii. 746; 4 Esdras vi. 49–52); in connection with this see Matt. viii. 11; xxvi. 29; Mark xiv. 25; Luke xiii. 29; xiv. 15 ff. In the Gospels the references to this banquet are, of course, to be taken in a purely metaphorical sense; it is a popular way of describing prosperity and happiness.

As regards the *Messiah* in Apocalyptic Literature, Professor Charles points out[2] that the title "Christ," or "Anointed One," is applied for the first time to the ideal Messianic King that is to come in the "Book of Similitudes" (= *Enoch* xxxvii.–lxx.); in xlviii. 10 reference is made to the tyrants who "have denied the Lord of Spirits and His Anointed" (*cf.* Luke xii. 9; see also Acts iii. 14); He is also mentioned in lii. 4. Another title of the Messiah, which likewise occurs for the first time in this book, is the "Elect One" (*cf.* Luke ix. 35; xxiii. 35). But most important is, of course, the title "The Son of Man"; the most significant facts in connexion with "the Son of Man" in the "Similitudes" are, first and foremost, that He is not conceived as being of human descent;[3] He sits upon the throne of God (li. 3); possesses universal dominion (lxii. 6); and all judgement is committed unto Him (xli. 9; xlix. 27).[4] The references in

---

[1] Though not written until the second half of the first century A.D., it reflects earlier beliefs and conceptions.

[2] *The Book of Enoch*, p. 51.

[3] This is, however, the case in ENOCH xc. 37.

[4] Charles, *op. cit.*, p. 315.

the Gospels to the "Son of Man" are so well known that there is no need to indicate them further. In the *Psalms of Solomon* [1] the Messiah is to be of the house and lineage of David [2] (xvii. 23–25); He will be "a religious King, and taught of God" (xvii. 35), who will gather together the dispersed of Israel (xvii. 28), and make them a holy people (xvii. 29, 30, 36); He will overcome sinners "by the might of His word" (xvii. 41); judgement is committed unto Him (xvii. 31); but, unlike the Messiah of the "Similitudes," He is mortal (xvii. 42). Here, again, it is unnecessary to give references to the Gospels; we would only emphasise the fact of the judgeship of the Messiah; the subject will come before us again.

The *Advent* of the Messiah is spoken of in the "Similitudes" (xxxviii. 2) thus: "And when the Righteous One shall appear before the eyes of the elect righteous, whose works are wrought in dependence on the Lord of Spirits ..."; and in the portion of *Enoch* called "The Book of Celestial Physics," [3] the Advent is referred to in the words: "And the Lord of Spirits seated Him (*i.e.* the Messiah) on the throne of His glory, and the spirit of righteousness was poured out upon Him . . ." (lxxii. 2 ff.); important, too, is the passage lxix. 27 ff. : "And He sat on the throne of His glory, and the sum of judgement was committed unto Him, the Son of Man . . . " (see further *Sib. Oracl.*, iii. 55–61, 625–658; *Test. xii. Patr.*, Zebulon viii. 8; Levi xviii. 2–14). With the above, *cf.* Matt. xix. 28; xxv. 31 ff.; Mark xiv. 61, 62. These points (without referring to others specially, such as the appearance of false Messiahs, the gathering of the elect, the punishment of the wicked, the reward of the righteous, the Resurrection, &c.), are amply sufficient to show that Christ utilised the eschatological teaching of the Apocalyptists. It has been necessary to lay stress on this fact; firstly, because it was an inevitable first step in the

---

[1] Belonging to 70–40 B.C.

[2] Contrast with this what is said in the "Similitudes" just quoted; such contradictions are frequent in the Apocalyptic Literature; but this is not to be wondered at when one takes into consideration the varying conditions, historical and other, under which the books were written.

[3] Chaps. lxxii.–lxxxii., belonging, according to Charles, to 166–161 B.C.

eschatological teaching of Christ; secondly, because it is well to realise that without it the ear of the people would not have been gained; and, thirdly, because it has to be set in relief against some other elements in the eschatological teaching of Christ, to which attention will be called presently. When speaking of the eschatological teaching of Christ as contained in the Gospels we would guard ourselves from being misunderstood, especially as the references given above have been, in some extent, chosen indiscriminately. No one would, it may be hoped, dissent from the position taken up by von Dobschütz, for example, when he says: "There is not only some vague possibility of alterations brought into the Gospel in the course of its transmission, but there is plenty of evidence that sayings of Jesus were coloured afterwards, and this at first by eschatological additions and changes;"[1] later on, however, he says as truly: "But if one were to conclude that all eschatological material found actually in the Gospel was but later addition or transformation, one would be wide of the mark . . . plenty of eschatological sayings remain, which must come from original tradition."[2] It may be permissible to go even further than this, and to say that a great deal of Christ's teaching on this subject has not been recorded at all;[3] for the study of the Apocalyptic Literature suggests that in such an immense complex as is presented in the eschatological drama, knit together in their essence as the various elements are, it would be hazardous to say that such and such parts were accepted, while others were rejected; it is maintained that Christ accepted the scheme as a whole,[4] that Schweitzer is perfectly right when he says, for example, using one of his many apt similes: "Just as a water-plant blooms in beauty as long as it remains in its native element, but fades and becomes unrecognisable as soon as it is torn

---

[1] *The Eschatology of the Gospels*, pp. 79 ff.; and see the examples given on the pages which follow.   [2] Pp. 90 f.   [3] *Cf.* John xxi. 25.

[4] "Looking at the contents of the Gospels broadly, we are struck by the fact that so many of the leading terms employed in them should be either directly apocalyptic or closely associated with apocalyptism," Sanday, *Hibbert Journal*, October 1911; this article did not appear until after the present essay had been written.

from its home, so it is with the historical Jesus, whom some detach from the soil of Eschatology, and then seek to comprehend historically as a stupendous Personality unaffected by time (*als zeitlose Grösse*)." [1]   Jewish Eschatology was accepted by Christ in its fulness as a basis for what He had to teach; but that offers only one side of His eschatological teaching.   There are some other points in His teaching on this subject which are of greater importance.   The consideration of these must be our next task.   All is, of course, centred upon the conceptions of the Kingdom, and the *rôle* that Christ assigns Himself in relation to it.

(*b*) First of all, there are some conceptions regarding the *Kingdom* which are as different as possible from anything taught in Jewish Eschatology on this subject.

In Matt. xii. 28, Luke xi. 20 occur the words: "If I by the Spirit of God [Luke, 'by the finger of God'] cast out devils, then is the Kingdom of God come upon you (ἔφθασε)." [2]   However we may explain the casting out of devils here will not affect the sense of the word ἔφθασε; [3] it is evidently used of set purpose in preference to "is at hand" (ἤγγικεν) in Mark i. 15 and elsewhere, and can only mean that the action of our Lord proved that the Kingdom had already come.   The same truth seems to be implied in Mark ix. 12, 13: [4] "And he said unto them, Elijah indeed cometh first, and restoreth all things. . . . But I say unto you that Elijah is come . . ."; as the Transfiguration took place some time after the announcement of the near approach of the Kingdom, the implication seems to be that Christ must have regarded the Kingdom as already in existence.   In Mark viii. 11–13, in reply to the Pharisees who ask a sign, Christ says: ". . . There shall no sign be given unto this generation."   It was the uncertainty regarding Christ that prompted this desire for a sign; if He was truly the Messiah who had come to inaugurate the Kingdom, according to Jewish apocalyptic ideas, some sign ought to

---

[1] *Op. cit.*, p. 399.   [2] The passage does not occur in Mark.

[3] It does not occur elsewhere in the Synoptic Gospels; the perfect rather than the aorist would have been expected.

[4] The passage occurs in an explanatory form in Matt. xvii. 11–13; it is omitted in Luke.

have been forthcoming. The request was not unreasonable from the Pharisaic point of view; but the Kingdom which Christ brought in came not "with observation"; there was no "sign" connected with it. The additions about "the sign of Jonah" found in Matt. xii. 38, 39 ; Luke xi. 29 read very much like later exegetical notes incorporated in the text; they mar the point of the words as found in Mark. We shall have to return to this passage later on in a different connexion.

Once more, the words of Mark x. 14, 15: ". . . Suffer the little children to come unto me; forbid them not, for of such is the Kingdom of God " (Matt. xix. 13 ; Luke xviii. 16), likewise speak of the Kingdom as something actually present ; the words which follow in Mark and Luke (*cf.* Matt. xviii. 3), ("Whosoever shall not receive the Kingdom of God as a little child, he shall in no wise enter therein "), describe the attitude of mind required in those who would enter into the Kingdom. Again, when Christ says to the scribe: "Thou art not far from the Kingdom of Heaven" (Mark xii. 34 only), the distance is evidently not one of time, but refers to the state of the heart which is not yet quite what is required for entrance into the Kingdom. Perhaps the most striking passage of all in the present connexion is Luke xvii. 20, 21 : " And being asked by the Pharisees when the Kingdom of God cometh, he answered them and said: " The Kingdom of God cometh not with observation ; neither shall they say, Lo, here! or there! for lo, the Kingdom of God is within you." The expression " within you " (ἐντὸς ὑμῶν) can scarcely have been used if it were not intended to emphasise the actual presence of the Kingdom, *i.e.* its influence and power, within the hearts of men ;[1] as von Dobschütz says, it can only have been chosen "with the aim of giving to '*in*' the peculiar colouring of inwardness." [2] The words must, there-fore, point to the Kingdom as something actually present ;[3]

[1] The Old Syriac has "among you," and the Peshitta "in the midst of you"; but the Diatesseron reads "within your heart" (Burkitt, *Evangelion da-Mepharreshe*, ii. 198).

[2] *Op. cit.*, p. 131.

[3] *Cf.* Rom. xiv. 17 : "For the Kingdom of God is not eating and drinking, but righteousness and peace and joy in the Holy Ghost."

and they receive their illustration in such a passage, for example, as Matt. xxv. 34 ff.: ". . . for I was an hungred, and ye gave me meat; I was thirsty, and ye gave me drink; I was a stranger, and ye took me in; naked, and ye clothed me; I was sick, and ye visited me; I was in prison, and ye came unto me. . . . Verily I say unto you, inasmuch as ye did it unto one of these my brethren, even these least, ye did it unto me."

Pointing to the same truth of the Kingdom of Heaven being the power of God working unhindered in the hearts of men, are the words, "Thy Kingdom come" in the Lord's Prayer; when one considers that this petition is followed by those which have as their context the asking for the physical and spiritual wants of every day, it is difficult to believe that it refers primarily to a future Kingdom, though that thought may conceivably enough be included in it.

In Matt. xi. 11 the words spoken in reference to John the Baptist: ". . . yet he that is but little in the Kingdom of Heaven is greater than he," likewise point to the Kingdom as being something present. Finally, we have the difficult words in the verse which follows: "And from the days of John the Baptist until now the Kingdom of Heaven suffereth violence, and men of violence take it by force"; in Luke xvi. 16 somewhat differently: ". . . from that time the Gospel of the Kingdom of God is preached, and every man entereth violently into it"; whatever these words may mean, and they are certainly susceptible of more interpretations than one, there is this concerning them which is abundantly clear: "The time of Jesus is set in opposition to the time until John, the present to the past, and it is to this present that the Kingdom of God belongs, not to a third form, the future. And because it is present, it is to be taken as something inward, some experience of happiness which men try to get so eagerly that they jostle one another in the effort to reach it."[1]

The passages cited do not profess to be exhaustive (*cf.* *e.g.* Matt. xxi. 31, &c.), but they present thoughts and ideas about the Kingdom which are as far removed as possible

[1] von Dobschütz, *op. cit.*, p. 134.

rom the conception of the Messianic Kingdom pictured in he Eschatological Drama of the Jews. Everything has now become spiritualised; the Kingdom means the rule of God in the heart. This will be seen to be further illustrated in the next section.

(*c*) In the next place, a brief consideration of some of the parables of the Kingdom will show some further elements in Christ's teaching on the subject.

The parable of the *Seed growing in secret* occurs only in Mark iv. 26–29; this parable is, in effect, an illustration and amplification of the words: "The Kingdom of God cometh not with observation" (Luke xvii. 20); the Kingdom, like a seed, springs up and grows, a man "knoweth not how." The parable seems to teach, further, that the growth of the Kingdom of God in the heart of man is a process of development—"first the blade, then the ear, then the full corn in the ear." In this case the Kingdom is taught to be something that is present; but it is more; in its completeness it is still to be looked for, and, therefore, something that lies in the future. In the words, "But when the fruit is ripe, straightway he putteth forth the sickle, because the harvest is come," it is perhaps not fanciful to discern a reference to a catastrophic consummation. But the main point of the parable is to emphasise the gradual growth of the Kingdom, so that these words would not be required were they not intended to teach something further; and the apparent sudden end of all things as far as the seed and its growth are concerned, at the harvest, points to the termination of one æon, or state, preparatory to a new one, just as in the case of the parable of the wheat and tares: "Let both grow together until the harvest: and in the time of the harvest I will say to the reapers: . . . but gather the wheat into my barn" (Matt. xiii. 30).

The parable of the *Grain of Mustard Seed* (Mark iv. 30–32; *cf.* Matt. xiii. 31, 32; Luke xiii. 18, 19) points again to the Kingdom as something already present and in process of growth; but the picture implies rapid growth, and the Kingdom is here thought of as extensive, while in the preceding parable its intensive character is rather presented.

H

The parable of the *Leaven* (Matt. xiii. 33, Luke xiii. 21)
emphasises the permeating character of the Kingdom;
normally all the world should be embraced within the
Kingdom. The repentance which is the condition of entry
is demanded of all, *i.e.* all men are at first unfit, the good as
well as the bad; all fall short (*cf.* Rom. iii. 23); but all
could belong to the Kingdom if they would, so is the will of
God (*cf.* 1 Tim. ii. 4); the Kingdom is for all. This is, again,
in striking contrast to the usual teaching of Jewish Apocalyptic Literature.

The parable of the *Wheat and Tares* (Matt. xiii. 24–30)
describes the actual state of things as distinct from what is
ideally intended; good and bad live side by side in the
Kingdom, which is again clearly seen to be something
already in existence (*cf.* ver. 41). On the other hand, the
Kingdom, as at present constituted, is represented as preparatory; it endures for a limited time; in the not very
distant future it is to come to an abrupt end; thereupon, at
any rate for the righteous, a new era breaks in (" Gather the
wheat into my barn "). The same lesson is taught in the
parable of the *Draw-net* (Matt. xiii. 47–50). The two
parables of the *Hid Treasure* and the *Merchant seeking
goodly pearls* (Matt. xiii. 44, 45) are probably meant to
teach nothing more than what is upon the surface, namely,
the overwhelming importance of the Kingdom, which is
worth more than every other possession. In each case the
Kingdom is represented as something present.

In connexion with Christ's teaching of the actual existence of the Kingdom while He was on earth, the words which
conclude this whole series of parables in Matthew are worth
remembering: "Therefore every scribe who hath been
made a disciple to the kingdom of heaven is like unto a man
that is a householder, which bringeth forth out of his treasure
things new and old."

(*d*) We turn now to the consideration of some sayings
regarding the Kingdom which seem to stand in a different
category from all that has been noticed hitherto.

In the passage (Mark viii. 11–13), already considered in
another connexion, the Pharisees seek a sign from Christ

the emphasis in Christ's reply is laid upon *this generation*, twice repeated (ver. 12), the implication being that it is not the request for a sign that is deprecated, but that those of "this generation" should have asked for it; the sign will be forthcoming, but not before the proper time. One is justified in reading in connexion with this passage Mark xiv. 61, 62: "Again the high priest asked him, Art thou the Christ, the Son of the Blessed? And Jesus said, I am; and ye shall see the Son of Man sitting at the right hand of power, and coming with the clouds of heaven." It is true, these words are addressed to those of "this generation," but this objection cannot be pushed, as the reference is to a different age or æon. Mark viii. 11–13 at any rate, especially when read in conjunction with other passages, seems, by implication, to point to the inauguration of a new age. But from other passages it is to be gathered that this new age, though in the future, is not in the distant future, from the point of view of the time at which Christ lived; for example, Mark ix. 1: "Verily I say unto you, there be some here that stand by, which shall in no wise taste of death till they see the kingdom of God come with power" (= Matt. xvi. 28: ". . . till they see the Son of Man coming in His kingdom; = Luke ix. 27: ". . . till they see the kingdom of God "). At first sight it seems difficult to reconcile such a passage as this with the teaching that the Kingdom is already present; but, as is well pointed out by Wellhausen, the expression ἐν δυνάμει used in connection with the Kingdom gains its real significance when it is realised that in this way it is differentiated, or placed in contradistinction to, an existing, invisible Kingdom, working in the hearts of men.[1] But, in any case, it points to a visible coming of the Kingdom in the future. Again, pointing to the Kingdom as something future, is the request of the sons of Zebedee, together with Christ's reply: "To

---

[1] *Das Evangelium Marci*, p. 74: "Das Reich Gottes ἐν δυνάμει empfängt seinen Sinn erst durch den Gegensatz eines anderen, schon gegenwärtigen, und innerlichen Reiches Gottes. Aristotelisch wäre dies letztere ἐν δυνάμει und das andere ἐν ἐνεργείᾳ zu nennen gewesen." *Cf.* H. J. Holtzmann (*Lehrbuch der N.T. Theologie*, II. i. 294 f.), who also says that the Kingdom of God coming with power, "ohne Zweifel im Gegensatze zu einem früheren, latenten Zustande des Reiches Gottes zu verstehen ist."

sit on My right hand or on My left hand is not Mine to give;
but it is for them for whom it hath been prepared" (Mark
x. 40 = Matt. xx. 23; omitted in Luke); so, too, Mark viii. 38:
". . . The Son of Man also shall be ashamed of him, when
He cometh in the glory of His Father with the holy angels"
(*cf.* Matt. x. 33, xvi. 27; Luke ix. 26, xii. 9); and Mark
xiv. 25: "Verily I say unto you, I will no more drink of the
fruit of the vine, until that day when I drink it new in the
kingdom of God" (= Matt. xxvi. 29: ". . . in My Father's
kingdom"; omitted in Luke). All these passages, and there
are some others to the same effect, tell of the Kingdom which
is still future, but not far distant (*cf.* Mark xii. 1–9, xiii. 10).

(*e*) Closely connected with what has just been said is the
teaching of Christ concerning the suddenness and unex-
pectedness of His *Parousia*. It is noteworthy that this
element is, with one exception, not found in Mark; the
exception is xiii. 35, 36: "Watch therefore; for ye know
not when the lord of the house cometh . . . lest coming
suddenly he find you sleeping." But in view of some undoubtedly genuine passages found in both Matthew and Luke,
it is certain that this element was an integral part of Christ's
eschatological teaching. For example, in Matt. xxiv. 27
(= Luke xvii. 24, though the form of the words is somewhat
different) it is said: "For as the lightning cometh forth from
the east, and is seen even unto the west, so shall be the
coming (ἡ παρουσία) of the Son of Man."[1] The unexpected-
ness of the Coming is emphasised in the passage Matt. xxiv.
37 (*cf.* Luke xvii. 26), 40–44, ending with the words: "For
in an hour that ye think not the Son of Man cometh"
(= Luke xii. 40; see also ver. 50), and this is also part of the
teaching of the parable of the Ten Virgins (Matt. xxiv. 1–13);
in Luke xvii. 30 the technical term ἀποκαλύπτεσθαι occurs;
cf. also Luke xix. 11: ". . . and because they supposed that the
kingdom of God would immediately appear (ἀναφαίνεσθαι)."
Fully in accordance with the teaching about the sudden and
unexpected coming of the Kingdom is the fact that the time
of its coming is altogether unknown—Mark xiii. 32: "But of

---

[1] The words which follow, "Wheresoever the carcase is, there will the eagles
[properly 'vultures'] be gathered together," are apparently an echo of ENOCH xc. 2.

that day or that hour knoweth no one, not even the angels in heaven, neither the Son, but the Father" (= Matt. xxiv. 36).

The teaching of Christ concerning the Kingdom (which is the central core of all Eschatology), its nature and characteristics, the time of its coming, and His relationship to it, seems, therefore, to have been variable, inconsistent, and sometimes directly contradictory; how is this to be accounted for? Some attempt to explain this difficulty must be made.

VI.—CHRIST AND ESCHATOLOGY

When all the phenomena are taken into consideration one thing seems to stand out clearly, and that is that if an explanation is to be sought of the problem presented in the Gospels concerning Christ and His eschatological teaching, it will not be along any *one* line of argument. There are at least four elements, so it seems to the present writer, which come into consideration, and which contribute their *quota* to the solution of the difficulty.

(*a*) From the nature of the case it seems probable that those who were originally responsible for the Oral Gospel, *i.e.* the disciples (not necessarily restricting these to the Twelve, or even to the Seventy) of Christ, misunderstood in some cases the tenor of His teaching. This would have been natural for three reasons; they were unlearned, simple-minded men, for the most part; the traditional Eschatology with which they were familiar was the point of view from which they would regard and understand all Christ's teaching on the subject; and, thirdly, they were not in a position to realise the fuller and deeper meaning of so much that Christ taught; for the Palestinian Jews were brought up in a school of literalism. The Gospels themselves have not left us without some indications regarding the inability of the disciples to understand and appreciate the essence of much that Christ taught; indeed, it is surprising to notice how many indications of this kind there are. The perplexity felt with regard to the Person of Christ is an important factor in this connexion, see *e.g.* Mark iv. 41: " And they feared exceedingly, and said one to another, Who then is this, that

even the wind and the sea obey Him?" (= Matt. viii. 27;
Luke viii. 25). The same perplexity, but owing to a different
cause, is evinced in the Baptist's question: "Art thou He
that cometh, or look we for another?" (Matt. xi. 3; not
mentioned in Mark or Luke). A misapprehension of Christ's
Personality is to be discerned in the episode of the healing
of the woman with an issue of blood, when in reply to Christ's
question: "Who touched My garments?" the disciples say:
"Thou seest the multitude thronging thee, and sayest thou,
Who touched me?" (Mark v. 30–32 = Luke viii. 45; in Matt.
ix. 20–22 these words do not occur); see also Mark vi. 2.
But instances of the inability of the disciples to understand
Christ's teaching are more frequent; in Mark iv. 10 we are
told that "they that were about Him with the twelve asked
Him of the parables"; Christ, in His reply, says: "Know ye
not this parable? and how shall ye know all the parables?"
He then proceeds to explain the parable of the sower; it is
evident that without such explanation the disciples found a
difficulty in understanding what Christ taught (*cf.* Mark iv.
33, 34): "And with many such parables spake He the word
unto them, as they were able to hear it; and without a
parable spake He not unto them; but privately to His own
disciples He expounded all things (see also Matt. xiii. 34–36;
Mark x. 10; Luke xxii. 38). On several occasions Christ
uses words which amply show the dulness of the disciples,
e.g. Mark vii. 18: "Are ye so without understanding also?"
(= Matt. xv. 16); Mark viii. 17: "Do ye not yet perceive,
neither understand? have ye your heart hardened? Having
eyes, see ye not? and having ears, hear ye not? and do ye
not remember?" (= Matt. xvi. 5–11 approximately); see
further, Mark vi. 52, ix. 39, x. 14 (= Matt. xix. 14); Matt.
xvii. 20; Luke xxiv. 25; *cf.* John xx. 29. It is also worth
noting how mystified the disciples appear to be when Christ
refers to His resurrection; see *e.g.* Mark ix. 10: "And they
kept the saying, questioning among themselves what the
rising again of the dead should mean." In the parallel
passage in Matt. xvii. 9 the disciples make no remark on this
part of Christ's words (*cf.* Matt. xx. 18, 19); the same is the
case in Matt. xvii. 23, where, after Christ has spoken of His

death and rising again the third day, it merely says that
they were "exceeding sorry"; so, too, in Mark viii. 31 ff.;
here St. Peter rebukes Christ for speaking of His death and
Resurrection; clearly the latter had no meaning for St. Peter.
Evidently the meaning of this is to be sought in the words
of Mark ix. 32, where again Christ speaks of His Passion,
and Resurrection after three days, but the disciples "understood not the saying, and were afraid to ask." Even after
the Resurrection; according to Matt. xxviii. 17, "some
doubted" (*cf.* John xx. 25). A very interesting instance
of a misunderstanding of Christ's words, and of the arising
of a mistaken tradition in consequence, is furnished by
John xxi. 21–24: "Peter therefore seeing him saith to
Jesus, Lord, and what shall this man do? Jesus saith
unto him, If I will that he tarry till I come, what is that
to thee? follow thou Me. This saying therefore went forth
among the brethren, that that disciple should not die; yet
Jesus said not unto him, that he should not die; but, If I
will that he tarry till I come, what is that to thee?" The
writer of the Fourth Gospel clearly believes in a visible
Second Coming of Christ; but he does not expect that this
will necessarily take place before his death, which the
brethren erroneously believed would be the case. But
most significant in the present connexion are the mis-
apprehensions of the disciples concerning the Kingdom;
this comes out clearly, *e.g.* in the request made to our Lord
by the sons of Zebedee (Mark x. 35 ff. = Matt. xx. 20 ff.); the
words of Christ in Mark x. 43–45 seem to show that the
rest of the Twelve had ideas about the Kingdom quite as
erroneous as the sons of Zebedee: ". . . Whosoever would
be great among you shall be your minister, and whosoever
would be first among you, shall be servant of all"; the
context shows that Christ is speaking of conditions in the
Kingdom (*cf.* Mark ix. 33–37; Luke ix. 48); see also Matt.
viii. 1 ff. These few passages are sufficient to show the
probability of the fact that the first disciples of our Lord,
those who "from the beginning were eye-witnesses" (Luke
i. 2), gave a colouring to their reports of some of Christ's
sayings, which was due to a natural inability to understand

the full significance of these; this would likely enough be especially the case with Christ's eschatological teaching, both on account of their own preconceived ideas, as well as on account of a new and spiritual element in Christ's teaching with which they were unfamiliar.

(*b*) But the record of the shortcoming of the disciples in this respect suggests that, embodied in our Gospels, there are the reports of some who realised the inability of certain of their colleagues to appreciate to the full the essence of Christ's teaching; though they themselves took His teaching in a fuller, more spiritual sense. When in the Lucan Preface reference is made to the many who had drawn up narratives, and when the Evangelist himself says that, "having traced the course of all things accurately," he also is going to write an account, we may, not unreasonably, infer that in St. Luke's idea the other accounts were not as accurate as he would wish; otherwise what was the object of his writing for the benefit of Theophilus? It is generally acknowledged that St. Luke's Gospel has less of catastrophic apocalypse than either of the two other Synoptists, and the fact is indubitable; what is the reason of this? The question opens up the whole subject of the development of the Gospel records; this is not the place to deal at any length with the Synoptic Problem; but a brief reference to one or two points is indispensable for the purpose in hand. Very recently two prominent scholars have reached diametrically opposed conclusions regarding the steps of development in the Gospel records, as far as the eschatological problem is concerned; the fact that these two opposing conclusions have been reached by scholars whose opinions rightly carry great weight, is in itself an exceedingly interesting phenomenon. Mr. Streeter holds that "in the series Q, Mark, Matthew, there is a steady development in the direction of emphasising, making more definite, and even creating sayings of our Lord of the catastrophic apocalyptic type, and of thrusting more and more into the background the sayings of a contrary tenor."[1] Archdeacon Allen, on the other hand, holds that the exact reverse is more probable: " Q, Mark, Matthew, Luke, John, represent a steady develop-

---

[1] Mr. B. H. Streeter in *Studies in the Synoptic Problem*, p. 433.

ment in the direction of emphasising, making more definite the non-catastrophic apocalyptic teaching of Christ, and of dropping out sayings of the opposite kind." [1] In seeking to decide which of these positions is the more correct, there is one thing which strikes one on reading the arguments on either side, and that is that to treat "Q" as a single written document, and one of which the characteristics are known, cannot yield really satisfactory results.[2] It seems far more probable that "Q" represents no one source, but a conglomerate, fragments from various sources, written pieces and oral reports, gathered from various people.[3] So that when it is said, on the one hand, that in "Q" there is a less developed Eschatology than in Mark, and on the other, that the eschatological element in it is more strongly in evidence than in Mark, &c., it is possible that both statements are correct, if only it be allowed that "Q" embodies material representing more than one point of view.[4] What is here tentatively maintained is that, among the followers of Christ, two tendencies soon began to manifest themselves, so far as eschatological conceptions were concerned; just as there were, as

---

[1] *The Interpreter*, July 1911, p. 359 (vol. vii. No. 4).

[2] *Cf. e.g.* the results of the conclusions come to by Wellhausen, Harnack, Streeter, and Allen, in their reconstructions.

[3] Archdeacon Allen does believe in this composite character of "Q"; in attempting a reconstruction of one of the sources of the First Gospel, he says: "It will be seen that the source reconstructed above is a source for the First Gospel not for the Third. On the same kind of principle, *i.e.* of putting together passages homogeneous in character, and characterised by a special phraseology, it might be possible to reconstruct for the Third Gospel one or more sources in addition to Mark. But these sources would not be the same source that we have constructed for the First Gospel, though one or more of them might contain matter parallel to that found in the source of the First Gospel" (*Studies in the Synoptic Problem*, pp. 281 f.).

[4] Mr. Streeter's arguments in favour of "Q" being a "single written source" are, as one would expect, extremely ably put, and require a good deal of answering (see *op. cit.*, pp. 141 ff., 166 ff.); this, however, is not the place to attempt to enter into the details of the question. The present writer, while realising the cogency of Mr. Streeter's words, cannot but feel that the theory of "Q" being a single written document raises more difficulties than that of its representing a variety of sources. It is a question of the balance of probabilities. Mr. Streeter holds (very rightly, as we venture to think) that Mark utilised "Q"; he says, for example (*op. cit.*, p. 177): "It is highly improbable that the authors of Mark, Matthew, Luke, writing at different dates, and evidently for Churches widely separated in their theological leanings, and probably also in their geographical

has already been pointed out, particularists and universalists, legalists and apocalyptists, literalists and spiritualists among the Jews prior to the coming of Christ, so (it is suggested) similar divergent mental tendencies manifested themselves among the followers of Christ, and the records, both oral and written, were coloured by these tendencies. It is frankly admitted that direct proof of this is not forthcoming; but on the other hand, it may be confidently asserted that it lies in the nature of things that this should have been so.[1] The bent of mind of many men is towards literalism, of many others towards a more spiritual perception of things; among the Jews especially, in those days, their early training was calculated to lead them in the direction of a somewhat narrow legalism. Upon many the spirit and teaching of Christ must have exercised a modifying influence, while in the case of many others the power of early training still asserted its sway. What is more natural than that in handing down the tradition, whether orally or in written form, the bent of either should have manifested itself? There is also the high probability that the diverging tendencies of Hellenistic Judaism and Orthodox, or Pharisaic, Judaism played a part among Christ's disciples. Then there is another consideration: assuming that "Q" is made up of various elements, one of which contained catastrophic apocalyptic material, then "Qapoc" is the earliest Christian source which we have containing such material; the next would be Matthew, together with Mark xiii.; the influence of the same type of apocalypse is seen, further, in 1 Pet. (*cf.* iv. 7, 13, 17; v. 1, 4), 2 Pet. iii. 9–14 (*cf.* on the other hand iii. 8), and the Book of the *Apocalypse*; finally, as witnessing still to the influence of the same type of apocalypse in the early Church, we have

situation, would yet all three have drawn so extensively from a single source if that common matter had been either a cycle of floating traditions or due to the overlapping of a number of separate written documents." But does this not seem to imply that all our three Gospels were substantially taken from one written document? If so, it would mean that there was an earlier, and more complete *written* account of the life and teaching of Christ than that contained in any of our present Gospels. This is difficult to believe.

[1] It is perhaps not fanciful to see the echo of something of this kind in the passage John vii. 40–43; see especially the last verse: "So there arose a division in the multitude because of Him." *Cf.* x. 19.

the *Slavonic Enoch*,[1] the *Apocalypse of Baruch*,[2] and 4 *Ezra*.[3] On the other hand, assuming again that "Q" is made up of various elements, then we have the series "Q[non-apoc]," Mark, Luke, John, representing a continuous development in the opposite direction, viz. of emphasising the non-catastrophic apocalyptic teaching of Christ. St. Paul, in his Epistles, illustrates the latter process; the Church generally, at any rate implicitly, the former. These two opposing tendencies are certainly striking; and it is difficult to account for their continued existence excepting on the supposition that they manifested themselves from the earliest times; on the other hand, the fact that they did exist in later times goes to support the contention that two similar mental attitudes were at work long before; we may believe even during Christ's lifetime on earth. If this was so, it is not without significance as regards the particular point with which we started; for not only were many of the disciples unable to apprehend the true essence of what Christ taught

---

[1] 1–50 A.D. : "The book was much read in many circles in the first three centuries of the Church, and has left more traces of its influence than many a well-known book of the same literature" (*cf.* Morfill and Charles, *The Book of the Secrets of Enoch*, p. vii., see pp. xvii.–xxiv.).

[2] Latter half of first century A.D. : "Written by Pharisaic Jews as an apology for Judaism, and in part an implicit polemic against Christianity, it gained nevertheless a larger circulation amongst Christians than amongst Jews, and owed its very preservation to the scholarly cares of the Church it assailed" (Charles, *The Apocalypse of Baruch*, p. viii.).

[3] *Circa* 90 A.D. Though undoubtedly the most important element in this book, namely the so-called "Salathiel Apocalypse," belongs to the type of thought mentioned above—its Eschatology is of the most radical kind, it gives up the present world as hopeless, it has no hope of any political future for Israel, nor any restoration of the earthly Jerusalem; the seer simply awaits impatiently the catastrophe which is to bring the present world-order to an end—it is yet a remarkable fact that the Apocalyptist seems to be aware that the future remaining to the present world-order may, after all, be indefinitely prolonged, though he fervently hopes that this will not be the case; the passage in question is 4 Ezra v. 36, where the Angel says to the seer : "Number me the days that are not yet come" (so the true text). As the context shows, the point of this remark lies in the seer's inability to do what is suggested; the Angel poses him with a number of difficulties, which he is unable to solve, and then tells him that just as he is unable to do these things so he cannot comprehend the judgements of the Most High. When the Angel then says : "Number me the days that are not yet come," he implies that the seer cannot do so—he cannot know them; the days that are yet to come may be few or many (see further G. H. Box, *The Ezra-Apocalypse*, in loc.).

regarding Eschatology, but there were among the disciples two tendencies in the *mode of interpreting* what Christ taught on this subject. Both factors must have played their part in the colouring of the reports drawn up of the life and teaching of Christ.

(*c*) And then there is this further consideration ; it is quite clear from the Gospel records that Christ's self-revelation to His disciples was gradual. Whatever may have been the reason, it was His will that the disciples' conception of Him should develop slowly. "It is remarkable," says Professor Sanday, "that from the first those possessed with demons publicly confessed Him for what He was; but it is no less remarkable that He checked these confessions: 'He suffered not the demons to speak, because they knew Him' (Mark i. 34, iii. 12; Matt. xii. 16). He imposed a like injunction of silence on one healed of leprosy (Mark i. 44). The farthest point to which Jesus went in the way of self-revelation at this early period was by taking to Himself the special title 'Son of Man.' There was probably some precedent for the identification of this title with the Messiah, but it was at least not in common use, and therefore served well to cover a claim which was made but in no way obtruded. . . . This marked reticence of Jesus in regard to His person is clearly part of a deliberate plan. One of its motives was to prevent the rash and reckless violence which one who appealed to the Messianic expectation was sure to excite (John vi. 15). But it was in full keeping with the whole of His demeanour, and with the special character which He gave to His mission. . . . The hour for the Leader to come forward was the hour when teaching was to give place to action. Hence it was well that at first, and for some time to come, the King should remain, as it were, in the background, until the preparation for His assuming the Kingship was complete." [1] It seems certain, at all events it is in the nature of things, that if the disciples were thus largely in the dark as to the real Person of Christ the effect of His teaching upon them would be modified accordingly. Had they apprehended His divine nature from an early period His teaching would have been bound to

[1] *Hastings' D. B.*, ii. 616 f.

have had a different effect upon them than it did when it
came to them from One whom they regarded only as a
human Messiah; this would be more especially the case
where Eschatology was concerned.   Since they saw in Him
only the Messiah of Jewish Apocalypse, the reports they
gave of Him (*e.g.* during the mission recorded in Mark vi.
7 ff.) would be in accordance with this.   Christ's gradual
self-revelation would have had this effect.

(*d*) And, lastly, there is the fact that what Christ taught
was a "transmuted eschatology."   The expression is von
Dobschütz's, and by it he means "eschatology transmuted in
the sense that what was spoken of in Jewish eschatology as to
come in the last days is taken here as already at hand in the
lifetime of Jesus; transmuted, at the same time, in the other
sense that what was expected as an external change is taken
inwardly; not all people seeing it, but Jesus' disciples
becoming aware of it." [1]

It will not be questioned that there is an immense deal of
truth in what is said here regarding "transmuted eschatology"; such transmutation was an absolute necessity if
there was to be any sympathy between traditional teaching
and increase of spiritual perception; and the two can never
be really divorced, for *some* aspects of truth are contained
in all teaching.   However great the increase of spiritual
perception may be, it will not fail to see elements of truth
in past teaching; and just because Christ was the Son of
God He would the more readily perceive the truths contained in the traditional eschatological doctrine which He
adopted.   But if the entire content of pre-Christian Jewish
Eschatology had to be "transmuted," in the sense that what
was spoken of in Jewish Eschatology as to come in the last
days is taken as already at hand in the lifetime of Christ, if
everything it taught had to have a transformed meaning
put upon it in order to make it fit to be utilised by Christ,
if it contained nothing that was in its essence true, then we
might be justified in wondering why Christ made any use of
it at all.   It will, of course, be retorted that in teaching the
people of His own generation it was obviously necessary

[1] *Op. cit.*, pp. 150 f.

that Christ should base His teaching upon that with which His hearers were familiar. And with this every one will be agreed. But the fact, from which it is difficult to get away, is that Christ Himself believed, at any rate, in a catastrophic consummation of all things as far as this world is concerned, and in His actual return upon this earth as Judge; this much must be conceded, unless it be maintained that the series Q^{apoc}, Matt., Mark xiii., &c., merely reflects the colouring of later thought as far as its Eschatology is concerned. There are probably few who will be inclined to go as far as this. Mr. Streeter truly says: ". . . The argument, however, must not be pushed to the length of entirely eliminating the Apocalyptic element from the authentic teaching of our Lord. The beliefs of the early Church may have modified, and did modify, the records of His utterances, but it is too great a paradox to maintain that what was so central in the belief of the primitive Church was not present, at least in germ, in what the Master taught." [1] But if the apocalyptic element cannot be entirely eliminated from Christ's teaching, if the germ was contained therein, of what did these consist? Is it possible to reduce them to less than this: The Second Advent of Christ, as Judge, which is the central core of all? [2] If it be asked, as it necessarily must be, how one is to represent to one's own mind, on the basis of Christ's teaching, such a Second Coming—is it to be understood as a literal, visible Coming, an actual appearance upon earth? Is it to be only to the infinitesimal fraction of mankind which is all that can possibly be on earth at any given time whatsoever? Does the Second Coming mean anything for the countless millions of those who are in the world of spirit? In a word, does the idea of a Second Coming represent something real, something that will actually take place eventually? The reply, we feel convinced, must be in the affirmative, otherwise the entire apocalyptic teaching of the Gospels means nothing; a Second Advent of Christ, as the Judge of the quick and

---

[1] *Op. cit.*, p. 433.
[2] *Cf.* the summing-up of eschatological teaching contained in the *Te Deum:* "We believe that Thou shalt come to be our Judge"; and see LUKE xii. 41-48.

the dead, is the core of that apocalyptic teaching. While in the Gospels the question of the time of this Second Advent is variable, in Jewish apocalyptic literature it is designedly left to the "last times." That the Second Advent should have been expressed as a visible appearing of Christ upon the "clouds of heaven" was, as we can fully understand, a necessity; it was the only way whereby the men of those days could have been made capable of apprehending the truth; but if the method of presentation was necessarily pictorial, that does not mean that the central truth embodied was not to be taken literally. To each individual soul, whether in the flesh or in the spirit, Christ will again appear; if the evidence of the records forces us to the conviction that this is the truth, it is a matter of small moment if we find ourselves unable to realise the way in which it will happen. That at His Second Coming Christ should appear as *Judge* will commend itself as belonging to the nature of things to all whose moral sense is possessed of any vitality; it is not only that "the general notion of a divine decision respecting human conduct, with appropriate rewards and punishments, belongs to the essence of the conception of the deity," [1] but it is also what the human conscience demands as necessary.

. . . .

Gospel Eschatology has a real and vital lesson for us in these modern days; the tendency to see in Christianity nothing more than an excellent system of Ethics, the tendency to eliminate all that is mystical and supernatural, the tendency to regard all that is not within the ken of human understanding as mere remnants of primitive superstitions, the tendency to cast contempt upon tradition —these tendencies denote a narrowness which is not less narrow than the attitude of those who would ignore the immense and beneficial results of modern criticism. Gospel Eschatology should be helpful in contributing to counteract the tendencies referred to, and in directing attention more to the other-worldliness of Christianity, which is, after all, its most important and greatest element. It is the great

[1] Toy, *Judaism and Christianity*, p. 395.

merit of Schweitzer's book, unbalanced and one-sided as it
is, that it lays such stress on Christ's teaching concerning
that which is to come; to serious minds the thought of the
Hereafter is, when all is said and done, of greater, infinitely
greater, importance than the petty affairs of everyday life,
essential, necessary, and absorbing as these are.   The eschatological teaching of Christ directs men's minds to things
higher and more abiding than those of the world.

"I doubt if we have realised how far the centre of gravity
of our Lord's teaching lay beyond the grave. . . . I doubt if
we have realised to what an extent He speaks of the Kingdom
of Heaven as essentially future and essentially supernatural.
. . . I doubt if we have appreciated the preliminary and preparatory character of His mission." [1]

VII.—Conclusion

It has been our endeavour to try and show how the two
essential and fundamental elements in the Jewish religion,
viz. Right living (Law) and Hope (Eschatology), were recognised by Christ as constituting the elementary bases of
man's religious requirements here on earth.   The Jewish
presentation of these great truths, and all that they stood
for, was inadequate; and therefore Christ "fulfilled" the
one and spiritualised the other.   He comes before us as
a Teacher and a Prophet; His ethical teaching is always
coloured by something higher; it is not enough to do the
Law, one must hope for God; right conduct in this life is
taught with the gaze fixed on the life which is to come.
There have been tendencies on the part of some scholars to
lay overmuch stress on the ethical side of Christ's teaching,
just as there have been tendencies on the part of others to
over-emphasise His eschatological teaching.   "The ethical
note is the purest and most unmistakable element in the
teaching of Jesus, and the essential core of Christianity." [2]

---

[1] Sanday, *The Life of Christ in Recent Research*, p. 121.

[2] Baur, *Christenthum der ersten drei Jahrhunderte*, p. 35, quoted by Peabody
in the *Transactions of the Third International Congress for the History of
Religions*, ii. p. 308.

"The ethical ideas of Jesus are incontestably the essential element in the spiritual experience of the modern world." [1] On the other hand, Schweitzer, who may be regarded as the most thorough-going among those of the modern "Eschatological School," takes up an equally one-sided attitude in the other direction; we agree wholly with him (though for reasons differing from his) in his contention that Christ's public activity contained within it something which was altogether incomprehensible to men; [2] we sympathise with his complaint that the "Eschatological School" in the past, while recognising Christ as an eschatological teacher, saw nothing corresponding to this in His life; [3] but we feel that he approaches the subject from a wrong standpoint when he says: "Is it not *a priori* the only thing thinkable, that He Who was shortly expecting His Messianic *Parousia* should in His words and acts be influenced not by the natural course of events, but solely by that expectation?" (Ist es nicht schon *a priori* das einzig Denkbare, dass der, welcher seine messianische *Parousia* in Bälde erwartet, in seinem Handeln nicht mehr von dem natürlichen Gang der Ereignisse, sondern nur von jener Erwartung bestimmt wird?) [4] What we contend for is a more rational balance in seeking to estimate the relative spheres and importance of these two elements in the teaching of Christ. In these days there is, generally speaking, little danger of not according to Christ's ethical teaching its proper place; [5] the modern spirit takes kindly to everything that it understands, or thinks it understands; and Christ's ethical teaching can be clearly and easily understood, in spite of its transcendent beauty. But with Eschatology it is different; here there are elements which are mysterious, and which cannot be treated in a cut-and-dried fashion; here we have to do with that which is

[1] Hermann, *Die sittlichen Weisungen Jesu*, p. 29, quoted by Peabody, *ibid.*
[2] *Cf. op. cit.*, p. 348.
[3] " Die Lehre Jesu und die Geschichte Jesu waren in verschiedenen Tonarten gesetzt " (*op. cit.*, p. 348).
[4] *Op. cit.*, p. 348.
[5] It is the exception when Schweitzer, for example, propounds his theory of " Interimsethik," *i.e.* a system of ethics only intended to serve during the interim between Christ's first and second Coming.

I

unknown, unknowable—"But of that day or that hour knoweth no one, not even the angels in heaven, neither the Son, but the Father" (Mark xiii. 32, Matt. xxiv. 36)[1]—and to many moderns this is intolerable; hence arises what is conceived to be the necessity of eliminating from Christian Eschatology everything that savours of the supernatural. We are far from denying, as the preceding pages will have shown, that traditional conceptions regarding this subject demand modification; but when every deduction has been made from the eschatological content of the Gospels on grounds which are manifestly reasonable, there still remains, firstly, the Personality of Christ, and secondly, the fact of His eschatological teaching, viz. that He proclaimed Himself to be the Divine Messiah, and that He would come again and judge all men. The Personality of Christ was a mystery to the men of His own day; but to those who accept His teaching concerning Himself that Personality is at least as great a mystery to the men of to-day;[2] and the same is true as to the essence of His eschatological teaching. All schools of thought accept as genuine Christ's ethical teaching; but if the truth of this teaching appeals to us because we can understand it, is it reasonable to seek to explain away His eschatological teaching because in some particulars it transcends our understanding? In his *Christianity at the Cross-Roads*, Tyrrell concludes his chapter on "The Christ of Eschatology" with the following words: ". . . It is not, then, wonderful that, even in the Churches, while the once central interest of the coming judgement has dropped into the background, if not altogether into oblivion, the incidental moralism of the Gospel should stand out as its principal value, and the central apocalypticism be overlooked as a troublesome incident. And this tendency, in an age that repudiates the miraculous and distrusts the transcendent, can only be accentuated by those whose aim is to secure the sanction of Christianity for the best ideals of the

---

[1] *Cf.* Acts i. 7: "It is not for you to know times and seasons, which th Father hath set within His own authority."

[2] To put down everything that is supernatural about the Person of Christ t "Gemeindetheologie" (*i.e.* the popular theology) of later times is unscientific with the records that we have before us.

time; to alleviate the friction between religion and reason as much as possible; to transform what was at most an ethical religion into a religious ethic" (p. 61). These words undoubtedly express a lamentable truth, lamentable because "to alleviate the friction between religion and reason" is only too likely to result in a loss of spirituality, though this should not necessarily be so. But what right has any age, if it professes a belief in Christianity, to repudiate the miraculous and to distrust the transcendent, when it is a question of relationship to God? If there was any truth in Christ's words, "I and the Father are one" (John x. 30), then His apocalyptic teaching must be regarded as *divinely* spoken; the inner truths, if not the verbal form, must be recognised as having God's sanction. "The great point about Apocalyptic, and the great value of its recognition to us at the present day, is that it postulates throughout a real manifestation of God upon earth, and not merely a teacher more eminent than the rest. If it did this under the form of figure and symbol, that was only a common feature of biblical religion."[1] Reason has its right place in religion, but it becomes mere arrogance when it displaces faith; there is a point at which reason, human reason, must give way to faith; in the domain of Eschatology that point is reached when, instead of seeking the why, and wherefore, and when, we must say:

"I believe . . . He shall come again with glory to judge both the quick and the dead; whose Kingdom shall have no end."

[1] Sanday, in the article in the *Hibbert Journal* referred to above.

ESSAY V

SOME CHARACTERISTICS OF THE SYNOPTIC WRITERS

BY

H. G. WOOD, M.A.

Formerly Fellow and Lecturer of the College

ANALYSIS

The purpose of the essay is to throw into relief the special characteristics of each of the synoptists.

The Gospels are admittedly written by believers to promote belief. It is argued that this does not render them useless as historical authorities, as M. Reinach supposes, but that it does make a knowledge of the standpoint of each writer important for the interpretation of his work.

The difficulty in discovering the special interests of each writer is greatest in the case of Mark. A clue may be found in his references to the teaching of Jesus. Following this and other indications, the radical Paulinism attributed to Mark by Loisy, Bacon, and others is largely discounted, but at the same time Mark's conception of the Gospel is framed to appeal to the Gentile world.

The leading characteristics of Matthew and Luke are then considered, emphasis being laid on the contrast between the pessimistic Judaism of the former and the sanguine universalism of the latter.

SOME CHARACTERISTICS OF THE SYNOPTIC WRITERS

THE nature of the Synoptic narratives is not an open question. They are not, and they do not pretend to be, lives of Jesus. They are Gospels—good news about Him. They are not the work of impartial observers or scientific historians, though Luke has some of the historian's outlook and purpose. They were written by believers to create and instruct faith. The Synoptics agree with the fourth Gospel at least in aim. "These things have been written, that ye may believe that Jesus is the Christ, the Son of God: and that believing ye may have life in His name." [1]

The recognition of this somewhat obvious fact is sometimes supposed to deprive the Gospels of all historical authority. Thus M. Reinach declares that "apart from the authority of the Church the Gospels are useless documents for the history of the true life of Jesus. They can and should be used only to teach us what the primitive Churches believed about Him." Elsewhere he says that but for the evidence of Paul's epistles, "it would be no paradox to call in question the historicity of Jesus." But to make an initial divorce between the beliefs of the primitive Churches and historical fact is in itself to assume the improbable. In no other inquiry would the scientific historian despair of getting at historical truth because all the witnesses were biased. Indeed, if the witness of believers is to be ruled out of court, there is no prospect of establishing any facts in the history of religious teachers at all. It may be the case, as Wellhausen suggests, that we have no criteria at our disposal to enable us to go behind the traditional picture of Jesus. It is perhaps

[1] JOHN xx. 31.　　　　[2] *Orpheus*, pp. 328, 339.

impossible to distinguish the actual historic person from the idealised portrait of faith. If so, there may be reason for suspecting that the ideal and the actual are not far enough apart to admit of distinction. At least, it is not reasonable to conclude that there is no historic figure behind the ideal. The fact that the Gospels are written by believers to promote belief is no valid ground for dismissing their claims as historical narratives. The unfavourable verdict is, as a rule, a *petitio principii*. It proceeds on the assumption that the faith did not originate in some historical happenings. This assumption, psychologically improbable, requires to be proved. If we may assume that an actual Person called forth the Faith, then the relation of the actual history would be an effective evangelistic power. The scientific historian could not trust as reliable an account of Jesus which did not show how men came to believe in Him.

In the realm of memory and tradition, the bias of belief will, in the first instance, act as a selecting and exaggerating influence rather than as a purely independent creative force. Memory guided by faith will naturally dwell on the things that are significant for faith. Only those actions and sayings will be recalled which serve to set forth the nature and justification of the disciples' interpretation of their Master. Given its starting-point in fact, faith may indeed embroider its history with legend and even draw on myth for the purpose. In cases where faith is deliberately and even fraudulently creating its credentials it still requires its *point d'appui* in the actual. But so far as early Christianity is concerned, even where a dogmatic purpose is obvious, the growth of legend is rather the unconscious extension of history than a conscious fraud. In the Synoptics, the influence of creed must be traced rather in the selection of incidents and in the modifying and recasting of historical narratives than in additions prompted by pious fancy, though such additions may exist. It is the incomplete, not the legendary, character of the Synoptic records which betrays the bias of the writers. The trivial is almost entirely lost to us, save in so far as it could be charged with larger meanings. It is not unlikely that some recorded sayings and deeds of Jesus have been robbed of their original simplicity through the prepossessions of the evangelists. The historian's quarrel with the Gospels is not that they do not give him history, but that they do not give him enough. The Gospels do not satisfy the historian's curiosity. But they were never intended to do that. They were meant to meet a religious need.

This common characteristic of the Synoptic writers is nothing less than the general atmosphere of the Church. The material at their disposal had been submitted to this influence of belief on tradition before it assumed the differing forms which they have given it. The Synoptics set forth a common Gospel. But they do not regard the Gospel in the same way. They are not all interested in the same aspects of their common message. It is well to remember that the term Synoptic means "that can be viewed together" rather than "taking the same view together." The contrast between the fourth Gospel and the Synoptics tends to obscure, for the average reader at least, the individuality of the first three evangelists. The aim of the present essay is to study the points of view peculiar to each synoptist. How did they in succession conceive the Gospel? In what were they individually most interested? Which side of the good news does each particularly illuminate? Each Gospel is presumably adapted to the needs of particular Churches in a special social environment. Is it possible to determine how these conditions have shaped the narratives?

It is in relation to Mark that the inquiry is most difficult. We cannot arrive at a satisfactory answer by confining attention to the small amount of material peculiar to the Gospel. The omissions of Marcan details by Luke or Matthew throw light on the mind of the omitters rather than on idiosyncrasies of Mark. And, on the other hand, where Luke and Matthew coincide with Mark, such material is not necessarily neutral. That the first and third Gospels are largely coloured by the second is hardly open to dispute. At the same time, some sentences and expressions in Mark are clearly editorial, as, for example, the notice of Jewish washings at the beginning of chapter vii. Furthermore, it can scarcely be wrong to argue from the general distribution of space in the Gospel.

Thus, the space allotted to Passion-week suggests the centrality of the Cross in this writer's conception of his message. And though the Gospel may be intended for readers who had a separate record of Christ's teaching, yet the small amount of attention devoted to the sayings of Jesus indicates a mind or an audience interested rather in action than in speech. What is recorded of the teachings of Jesus may give valuable insight into the writer's standpoint. For it seems probable that he was familiar with Q—that problematic record of the sayings of Jesus—and that he made some slight use of it. Since he did not intend to give any full account of this side of the ministry of Jesus, his coincidences with Q may be taken to betray his interests. If he goes out of his way to insert fragments of Q it may be presumed that he had special reasons for so doing.

Selected details, the general character of his material and distribution of his space, his handling of such sayings as he is interested in, will afford the best clues to the mind of the author and of those for whom he writes.

It is not without significance that Mark uses the term "Gospel" in an absolute sense, which is not paralleled in the other two evangelists. Matthew has "this Gospel" in xxvi. 13, a passage dependent on Mark. Elsewhere Matthew has the phrase "the gospel of the Kingdom," which must mean the "good news that the Kingdom of God is at hand." Luke does not use the term. But in Mark there are phrases like that in i. 15, "repent and believe the gospel," and more significant still, he associates the term with Jesus rather than the Kingdom. The superscription to his book is "the beginning of the Gospel of Jesus Christ, the Son of God," and he twice speaks of the double motive, "for my sake and the gospel's" (viii. 35, x. 29). Perhaps the phrase does not stand for a double motive, but is simply tautological. Be that as it may, the actual coming of Jesus already constitutes a gospel to Mark. It is not the whole of it; the Gospel is still the Gospel of the Kingdom (i. 16), and the Kingdom is still future. But the phrase "the beginning of the gospel of Jesus" may mean more than "Here I begin to tell you the good news about Jesus." It may mean "This, the earthly life of Jesus, is the beginning of the good news about Jesus." It is not the whole Gospel, but it is the essential start.

The good news relates, in the first instance, to something that has happened and is happening, to benefits that Jesus conferred and confers. Nor does Mark leave us in any doubt as to the direction in which the salvation wrought by Jesus may be most easily recognised. The first great truth about Jesus which gripped the popular mind was that "with authority He commands the unclean spirits, and they obey Him." Mark glories in the fact that Jesus is stronger than the strong, and that no demonic power can stand before Him. The ministry of Jesus may be summed up in the words "preaching and casting out demons."[1] To the same ministry the disciples are called. "He appointed twelve . . . that He might send them to preach and to have power to drive out demons."[2] The other evangelists in parallel passages add or substitute references to healing.[3] Mark hardly admits the ministry of healing as a distinct activity. In a truly popular manner he subsumes the healing of sickness under the work of driving out demons. It is interesting to notice how his successors tend to moderate the popular diagnosis. Thus it may not be accidental that in the story of the Syro-Phœnician woman, the woman's assumption that her daughter is vexed with a devil is accepted by Mark (vii. 25) as correct, and endorsed by the saying attributed to our Lord, "the devil is gone out of thy daughter." In Matthew xv. 22 it is only in the mouth of the woman that we find a reference to the devil. Similarly, in narrating the healing of the Gadarene demoniac (chap. v.) and the demoniac boy (chap. ix.), Mark enlarges on the symptoms, and describes them in popular terms. Luke curtails these descriptions, and Matthew simply omits all that Mark says of the Gadarene demoniac, while in the second case he describes the boy as an epileptic, and makes no reference to an unclean spirit at all. In his handling of disease, Mark represents the standpoint of humble folk. Thus, in the Ephphatha story (vii. 35), the phrase "the

[1] MARK i. 39. [2] MARK iii. 15, vi. 7. [3] Matt. iv. 23, x. 1.

bond of his tongue was loosed" implies demonic influence; as Deissmann has clearly shown,[1] the bond is similar to that by which Satan bound a daughter of Israel eighteen years.[2] Not only is the theory of disease adopted in Mark, the popular one of demonic influence, but also the methods of healing, by touching and spitting,[3] betray the same social outlook.[4] It is, I think, beside the point to suggest that these stories of gradual cure, as they are sometimes called, stories peculiar to Mark, are related with some secondary didactic purpose. Professor B. W. Bacon seems to me to be clearly wrong in regarding as symbolical the interest of the writer in the gradual emergence of the man of Bethsaida from blindness. "Two stages are expected in Israel's conversion—first the elect remnant, afterwards all Israel."[5] This story, like its companion, is too naïve and simple for this kind of exegesis, and probably Matthew and Luke fought shy of these two miracles because they savoured too much of folk-lore and magic. At the same time, it is not very easy to regard such stories as exaggerations due to the evangelist's love of thaumaturgy. It is useless to try and minimise an element in the Gospel which offends modern taste, by throwing love of thaumaturgy in the face of St. Mark. The fact is, the tradition he hands on was formed by men who shared this weakness, if it be a weakness. There is no particular evidence to show that Mark is going beyond his brief in reporting cures and exorcisms, or that he is misrepresenting the impression Jesus actually made on the minds of Galilean peasants. This delight in wonderful works is not a personal idiosyncrasy: it is a popular characteristic.

[1] *New Light on the New Testament*, p. 84.

[2] LUKE xiii. 6.

[3] MARK vii. 33, viii. 23.

[4] The parallel with the cures wrought by Vespasian in Egypt is curiously close. "E plebe quidam luminibus orbatus, item alius debili crure pro tribunali pariter adierunt, orantes opem valitudini demonstratum a Serapide per quietem : *Restiturum oculos, si inspuisset :* conformaturum crus, si dignaretur calce contingere" (*Suet. Vesp.*, ch. vii.). For the parallels from secular literature, which show how clearly the Gospel stories of exorcisms reflect the popular feeling of the age, see Wendland, *Die Hellinistisch-Römische Kultur*, p. 124.

[5] Bacon, *Earliest Gospel-story*, p. 99.

Mark must, however, have been interested in this aspect of Christ's work. Not only is the bulk of the first half of the Gospel devoted to this subject, but his first considerable coincidence with Q is the discussion between Jesus and the scribes as to the significance of the driving out of demons. This section of the recorded utterances of Jesus is obviously of special importance for him. It may be merely the accident of ignorance or lapse of memory which caused him to omit the reference to the exorcisms wrought by the sons of Pharisees. If such omission is intentional, the reason must lie in his unwillingness to risk minimising the peculiar power of Jesus by comparing Him with Jewish exorcists. But the whole passage is significant, because it defends the character of Christ's cures. For later on, Celsus echoes the verdict of the scribes;[1] and where belief in demons prevails, it is often supposed that demon will drive out demon. That Gentile Christians had to meet such a charge of relying on demons to work exorcisms is not improbable. But the passage not only rebuts a charge, it triumphantly announces the binding of the strong man. The power of Jesus over demons is evidence of the nearness of the Kingdom, and in itself it constitutes a Gospel. The driving out of demons was evidence of the truth of Christianity to the Gentiles for whom Mark wrote. It was also a large part of the message of salvation, for which they longed. Indeed, the Gospel stories themselves brought relief and healing. For Origen tells us: "It is not by incantation that Christians seem to prevail over evil spirits but by the name of Jesus, accompanied by the announcement of the narratives which relate to Him : for the repetition of these has frequently been the means of driving demons out of men, especially when those who repeated them did so in a sound and believing spirit."[2] For this kind of service man might well turn to the Gospel, which represents Jesus as first and foremost the destroyer of demons.

The aspect of Mark's Gospel so far discussed is not the only evidence that the Gospel was destined for the Gentile world. Taken by itself it would not be conclusive evidence

---

[1] Origen, *contra Cels.*, Book I. chap. vi.   [2] *Ibid.*, Book I. chap. vi.

on that head.   But if one thing is more certain than another
about the earliest Gospel, it is its Gentile destination.   The
lengthy, and it would seem inaccurate, note on the Jewish
customs of washing is obviously intended for readers who
knew little of Jewish ways and habits.   Omissions and some
characteristic additions alike bear out this deduction.   Thus,
attention is rightly drawn to the comparative silence of Mark
about John the Baptist.   He does indeed relate John's end
in detail, because he cannot resist a good popular story.
But of the ministry of John he says very little, and the
discourse of Jesus about His forerunner is omitted.   To
Jews, John's ministry had an interest of its own.   To
Gentiles, the work of John was only of importance in relation to Jesus.   Perhaps one reason for his reduced account
of the teaching of Jesus may be found in the want of the
Jewish background that would make it intelligible to his
readers.   It is curious that he does not relate the healing of
the Centurion's servant, and the saying of Jesus " I have not
found such great faith, no not in Israel."   The collection of
sayings with which he was familiar must have lacked that
incident, and in all probability Mark did not know exactly
the record of the teaching common to Matthew and Luke.
This circumstance renders rather dubious arguments based
on Mark's omissions from Q.   And, on the other hand, Mark
retains the story of the Syro-Phœnician woman, which is not
calculated to flatter Gentile readers.   It is true that he has
to some extent modified the story, and his modifications are
suggested by his interest in Gentile Christians.   The woman
is described not as a Canaanitish woman, as in Matthew,
but as a Greek ('Ελληνίς).   She is a Syro-Phœnician, but she
stands for the Gentile world.   Mark, by inserting the clause
"let the children *first* be filled," further suggests that Jesus
anticipated and intended the mission to the Gentiles.   And,
as Professor Bacon points out, the whole incident has the
advantage for Mark of bringing Jesus on to foreign soil to
confer the grace of healing there.   For all this, that Mark
has retained this story at all, is a witness to the faithfulness
with which he sticks to his sources.   Though Mark writes
for Gentiles, there is no such universalising of the Gospel as

appears in Luke. The slight references to the Gentiles in the closing chapter of the Gospel may therefore be the more confidently relied on. They are too slight to be conscious adaptations. Chapter xiii. presupposes a general evangelisation of the world, apart from the special phrase in ver. 10, "and the gospel must first be preached to all the nations." This chapter may be of doubtful value as a source for the teaching of Jesus, but there is no reason to regard this characteristic as a peculiarity of Mark. Similarly, with the reference to the preaching of the Gospel throughout the whole world, in the story of the woman who anointed the Lord's feet with ointment, such an allusion is too trivial to be a carefully designed introduction of the Gentiles. More important is Mark's version of the cleansing of the Temple in chapter xi. Here he alone in quoting from Isaiah includes the words "for all nations." "My house shall be called a house of prayer for all nations." Has the evangelist deliberately created a fresh allusion to the Gentiles? or has he simply completed the quotation unconsciously? or does his version really give the earliest tradition and the true point of the incident? Professor Gwatkin has suggested that the latter interpretation is correct. The temple-market would be held in the Court of the Gentiles, whose religious privileges in the temple were of small account to the Jews. The theft in question is spiritual rather than mercantile. This interpretation has not yet received the attention it deserves; but whether the deliberate act of defiance to the Jerusalem authorities was also a championing of the Gentiles or no, the impression which Mark gives, that towards the close of the ministry Jesus was conscious of the world-wide significance of His coming, is apparently derived from the earliest tradition, and not imported into it. "The others," to whom the vineyard is to be given, in the parable of the wicked husbandmen, are not necessarily the Gentiles. But Jesus perished largely because He refused the part of national Messiah, and interpreted Messiahship, not only in a more transcendental but also, I think, in a more œcumenical sense than suited popular sentiment.

These slight references to Gentiles are not in themselves

very important, though the impression they convey may well be designed. The main evidence for the characteristic of Mark's Gospel now under consideration is usually sought in the attitude of the writer towards Judaism and his alleged Paulinism.

It is sometimes asserted that Mark is rather hostile and contemptuous towards the Jews as a nation. The phrase in chap. vii. 3, which refers slightingly to the washings of "the Pharisees and all the Jews," does bear this interpretation. Other texts cited by Professor Bacon (*op. cit.*, p. 23) are less convincing. Thus the quotation from Isaiah in chap. vii. "This people honoureth me with their lips," is applied to Pharisees and scribes, and not, as Professor Bacon claims, to the Jewish people as a whole. Beyond this, the most damaging incrimination of the Jews as taking upon themselves the responsibility for the death of Christ—"His blood be on us"—is not recorded by Mark. But while there is little trace of any great hostility towards the Jewish people, it is true that Mark's main conception of the teaching of Jesus is that it breaks down the limitations of Judaism, and subjects the parent-faith to a searching moral and religious criticism. Consequently he represents the Pharisees as hostile almost from the start—a representation which perhaps does not put the facts of Christianity in their true perspective. Mark does not tell us the content of the first sermon of Jesus to which he alludes, but he does emphasise the impression the sermon made on the popular mind. Men were captivated by the freshness and originality, the sense of a direct message from God, which surprised them in what Jesus said. "He taught them as one having authority and not as the scribes." Here was new wine, destined inevitably to burst the old wine-skins of Judaism. Whatever may have been the first application of the saying about the wine and the wine-skins, its meaning to Mark is not in doubt. To him the Gospel of Jesus was a new life that must make its own forms, unfettered by the past. From this point of view even the most definitely Mosaic laws must be tested anew. Mark alone records the saying, "The Sabbath was made for man and not man for the Sabbath," the most searching criticism of the law, and indeed of all ecclesiasticisms, ever attributed to Jesus. In the case of the Sabbath Jesus condemns a strict observance of the law which defeats its original humanitarian purpose; in the case of divorce, He denies religious validity to a lax concession which defeats God's original ideal of human marriage. Jesus looses where Moses binds, and binds where Moses left men free. The Jesus of Mark's Gospel overrides the Mosaic law. In chap. vii. the writer forces upon the reader the significance of Jesus' teaching about the things that defile a man, by noting expressly, "(This he said), making all meats clean" (vii. 19), a phrase which must, I think, be referred to Jesus, awkward though the construction is. The point for Mark is that Jesus, implicitly at least, decided for the freedom of the Gentile against the scrupulousness of the Jew in regard to meats. In all these instances I do not see much reason to suppose that Mark has seriously heightened the antagonism of Jesus to Judaism, though there may be some editing and expansion of an originally simpler incident in chap. vii. But that Mark is "radically anti-legalist" and, in that sense, anti-Judaistic, is undeniable, and this has certainly affected his selection of teaching to illustrate the Galilean ministry, and also his conception of the early hostility of the religious teachers of Palestine towards the new prophet.

That Mark should have been influenced by Paul is *a priori* probable. Their traditional association may very well be historical, and in any case the writer of a Gospel for the Gentiles is not unlikely to have fallen under the spell of the Great Apostle. It is natural enough that attempts should be made to interpret the Gospel as a manifesto of the Pauline school. The radical anti-legalism discussed in the previous paragraph is nothing but an extreme development of the essential attitude of St. Paul. The explanation of the failure of the Jews to understand and accept Jesus by the quotation from Isaiah [1] is quite in line with the apologetic position taken up by Paul in Romans, chap. xi. Throughout the Gospel the relatives and

[1] See MARK iv. 11.

K

first disciples of Jesus are spoken of with scant courtesy. This might be expected from a strong partisan of St. Paul. But it is unnecessary to underline particular points of contact. "The Paulinism of St. Mark is supremely manifest in this evangelist's whole conception of what constitutes the apostolic message."[1] The Gospel, as Mark conceives it, is Paul's Gospel of Christ crucified. The ethic of Jesus is simply the doctrine of the Cross as unfolded in chapters ix. and x., where, again, "the principle so dear to Paul of rank through service" is clearly emphasised. The ethic of the Cross takes the place of the Sermon on the Mount! In this we may find the explanation of the remarkable characteristic—common to Mark and Paul—namely, both know some record of the teaching of Jesus which they very sparingly use. It is hardly necessary to add that the reference to Jesus' death as a ransom for many[2] may be an echo of Paul's doctrine of Atonement, and Paul's view of the Eucharist may have coloured Mark's narrative of the Last Supper (xiv. 24). In some such form as this Professor Bacon presents the case for the Paulinism of Mark.

The real difficulty here lies in appreciating the distinctive elements of Paulinism. It is possible that Paul himself would fail to recognise as distinctive many of the elements which are so regarded by some of his modern interpreters. We have not yet overcome the tendency to treat Paul's Gospel as a complete refashioning of primitive Christianity. Perhaps this tendency is nowhere more misleading than where it results in supposing that Paul was the discoverer of the Cross. Whatever else is distinctive in Paul, his proclaiming a crucified Messiah is no private monopoly. It is sometimes forgotten that St. Paul stumbled at the Cross preached by others before he became the soldier of the Cross himself. The Cross must have been near the centre of the Gospel at the outset. Even if the initial message was one of hope and warning—the announcement of the coming of the risen Christ to judgement—yet the first missionaries cannot have escaped the question, Why did Messiah die? And if we may trust the opening of

---

[1] Bacon, p. 28.   [2] MARK x. 45.

Acts, they did not wish to escape it. The paradox of the Crucified Messiah was the common theme of early Christian preaching. Nor were the earliest preachers content with simply acknowledging the fact. They sought to interpret it, and Paul can hardly have been the first to give the death of Christ an atoning significance. When we read in 1 Cor. xv. 3 that "Christ died for our sins according to the Scriptures," we are surely dealing not with distinctive Paulinism but with the earliest Christian reflection on the subject. Is Luke simply misled by Paulinism when he describes the evangelist Philip as preaching Jesus from Isaiah liii.? or must not the first disciples have been compelled to ponder on this and other Old Testament passages in connection with the death of Christ, even before Paul submitted to the scandal of the Cross? Again, the deduction of the ethic of the Christian life from the Cross is not a peculiarity of St. Paul. It is pre-supposed in the martyrdom of Stephen, and became indeed a factor in Paul's conversion. There is no reason to suppose that the centring of interest on the Cross, the conviction of the atoning purpose of the Cross, or the development of the ethic of the Cross, must have come to Mark through Paul. Is not Mark's Gospel much more an independent witness to the extent to which Paul's Gospel coincided with the earliest preaching than a mere echo or reflection of distinctive Paulinism?

This probability is strengthened by the close coincidence between Mark's Gospel and the earliest preaching as it is recorded in Acts. Not only is there correspondence in range—from the Baptism of John to the Ascension is the range of the Apostolic testimony, Acts i. 22, and significantly enough Mark begins with John, and presumably ended with the Ascension — but also the main topics assigned by Luke to the sermons of Peter are parallel to the main interests of the Gospel. Peter spoke of Jesus, "A man approved of God among you by signs and wonders which God wrought through Him in the midst of you." [1] Clearly if Peter developed this head of his discourse *he treated the Galilean ministry very much as Mark treats it.* Beyond

[1] Acts ii. 22.

this, Peter touches in some detail on the crime of the crucifixion, claiming, however, that it was divinely planned.[1] Again, if this is summary, Peter must have dwelt on the fact of the Cross, and he may well have shown how Jesus Himself was prepared for it and accepted it as God's will. Here, too, Mark may be simply a faithful reporter. The same is true of the place assigned to the Resurrection, and to the call to repentance, in expectation of the Lord's return. These two topics must have been all-important in the primitive Christian testimony. This, indeed, is clear from Acts. Though the end of Mark is lost, it is safe to say they were of fundamental importance in his Gospel also.

The eschatological chapter—chapter xiii.—is in any case a striking feature of the second Gospel. It is doubtless coloured by the experience of the Church, and it may in part be motived by the desire to repress agitation aroused by the fall of Jerusalem. But even in its caution the eschatological discourse may be in line with the earliest form of the Christian hope. There is little evidence for the view that the expectation of the Parousia began at fever-heat and gradually cooled. Some of the most guarded utterances may be among the earliest, and feverish enthusiasm was a spasmodic phenomenon. In any case, the conclusion of Mark's chapters, verses 28–37, agrees in temper with the summary of Peter's preaching in Acts iii. 20–21. Thus there is some positive evidence for supposing that the second Gospel reproduces the main lines of early Christian preaching. It may be worth while to ask whether there is not a similar agreement in omissions. In addition to, and perhaps in place of, the reasons already assigned for Mark's neglect of the teaching of Jesus, possibly the fundamental reason is that the teaching of Jesus never can have played a prominent part in the work of evangelisation. The Sermon of the Mount never was the centre of the Gospel. The first disciples never tried to gain converts primarily by repeating what Jesus said. Chronologically as a document Q may be earlier than Mark. In essential character and in the spiritual life and activity of

[1] Acts ii. 23 ; iii. 13, 14.

he Early Church, Mark is more fundamental, more primitive than Q. Mark is the instrument of conversion, Q of instruction. The second Gospel need not be designed to supplement Q. The author may have omitted any detailed account of the teaching of Jesus because he was not conscious that the teaching had any particular place in a Gospel—a record of the missionary message with which the Church was entrusted.

On the whole, the argument for the distinctive Paulinism of Mark, which is based on his whole conception of the Gospel, seems inconclusive, because it neglects to consider what must have been the nature of the earliest Christian preaching which, it is traditionally claimed, Mark reproduces. One or two of Professor Bacon's other arguments[1] call for examination. The explanation of Jewish blindness by citing Isaiah may be due to Pauline influence, but it does not necessarily reveal the attitude of Mark himself. It does not fit in with verse 13 or verse 33 of chapter iv., which have at least as much claim to represent the author's mind as verses 11, 12. I am inclined to hazard the suggestion that Mark retained verses 11, 12 out of loyalty to his source, but that they puzzled him, and he seizes the opportunity to quote sayings which emphasise the openness of the Gospel, in verses 21, 22. He does not appreciate the suggestion of concealment. An instance of the same kind is to be found in chapter xi., where the author tells the story of the cursing of the fig-tree. The narrative is compressed. It suggests in itself that the writer was puzzled by what he had to record. At the close of the section he adds the apparently irrelevant logion, "And when ye stand praying, forgive if ye have anything against any, that your father in heaven may forgive you your trespasses" (xi. 25). Is this conclusion intended to remind readers that, in spite of the difficult and curious story just related, Jesus was not the patron of cursing, that faith would not remove mountains apart from a forgiving spirit? If this impression is correct, the explanation given in Mark of the disbelief of the Jews may be distinctively Pauline and yet not distinctively Marcan!

[1] See *supra*, pp. 145, 146.

Even less convincing, it seems to me, is the argument based on the references to the Apostles in the second Gospel. It is certainly the case that these references are suggestive of limitation and even of blameworthy failure and mistake on the part of the disciples. There is a *prima facie* ground for suspecting that the writer intends to disparage the Twelve. Any adequate discussion requires a brief review of these references, and they are of interest in themselves. Mark represents the disciples as constantly amazed and perplexed by Jesus, and often afraid and ashamed in His presence. Jesus, on the other hand, is said not infrequently to have rebuked them. This impression is not altogether lost, but it is considerably modified by the other evangelists. Thus Mark introduces the explanation of the parable of the sower with the somewhat scathing question of Jesus to the disciples, "Know ye not this parable? Then how will you understand all the parables?" [1] In the parallels [2] the question is transformed into a colourless phrase. At the close of the same chapter Mark relates the stilling of the tempest. In his version of it the cry with which the disciples awake the Master is more blunt, and the question with which He rebukes their want of faith is more cutting than the corresponding utterances in Matthew and Luke.[3] Only in Mark does the form of the question suggest that the disciples have no faith at all! In the feeding of the five thousand Mark alone preserves the ironical question of the disciples, "Shall we go and buy two hundred penny worth of bread? [4]—a question which shows how greatly Jesus took the disciples by surprise on this occasion. Indeed, He was always doing and saying the unexpected. The story that immediately follows the miracle of the multiplied loaves affords a remarkable study in contrasts. Mark finishes his account of Jesus coming to the twelve on the sea by saying, "And they were exceedingly astonished in themselves for they did not understand about (or at the time of) the loaves, but their heart was unresponsive." [5] Matthew, on the contrary, records that "They

---

[1] MARK iv. 13. [2] MATT. xiii. 18 ; LUKE viii. 11.
[3] *Cf.* MARK iv. 38, 40 with MATT. viii. 25, 26, and LUKE viii. 24, 25.
[4] MARK vi. 37. [5] MARK vi. 52.

in the boat worshipped Him, saying, Truly thou art God's son." [1]   This contrast is repeated in other instances, where Mark gives the impression that the disciples were left in a state of fear, astonishment, and dull misunderstanding, while Matthew removes or tones down any such impression. A further example may be seen in the discussion arising out of the two miracles where, in Mark, we end with the unanswered question of Jesus, "Do ye not yet understand?" While Matthew adds, "Then understood they that He spake not of taking heed from the leaven of bread, but from the teaching of the Pharisees and Sadducees." [2]   Similarly, in relating the second announcement of the Passion, Mark says "The disciples understood not the saying, and were afraid to ask Him." Matthew tells us, "They were exceeding sorry," implicitly correcting Mark. Luke follows Mark more closely, but he inserts a clause to obviate the suggestion that the disciples' failure to understand was due to natural obtuseness—"And it was concealed from them that they should not perceive it." [3] It is not surprising to learn that Mark alone claims that when Jesus referred to the Son of Man rising from the dead, the disciples had laid hold of the saying and puzzled over it, wondering what the resurrection from the dead may mean. [4] It is in keeping with this that Mark does not tell us, though Matthew does, that when Jesus spake of Elias as already come, the disciples understood His saying to refer to John the Baptist.[5]   And when Jesus set His face towards Jerusalem, and led His disciples to the final crisis, Mark alone records the mingled astonishment and fear that pervaded the disciple-band—"And they were amazed, and those who followed were afraid." [6]   In the same way Mark brings out the element of rebuke in the dealings of Jesus with the Twelve. He uses the word ἐπιτιμᾷν [7] of the answer of Jesus to Peter's expostulation, though the terms of the answer itself are as strong in Matthew as in Mark. It is Mark too who says that Jesus was vexed with the disciples for sending

---

[1] MATT. xiv. 33.
[2] *Cf.* MARK viii. 21 with MATT. xvi. 12.
[3] MARK ix. 32 ; MATT. xvii. 23 ; LUKE ix. 45.
[4] MARK ix. 10.
[5] MATT. xvii. 13, no parallel in MARK.
[6] MARK x. 32.
[7] MARK viii. 33.

away the children (x. 14). This is one of the few recorded occasions on which we learn from Mark that Jesus was angry. The scene described in ix. 33 and following is particularly illuminating. According to Mark, Jesus questioned the disciples as to the rather discreditable subject of their road-side discussion. They held their peace, and the Lord then taught the lesson of humility without waiting for an open confession. In Matthew the disciples initiate the discussion by asking the question, " Who then is greatest in the kingdom of heaven ? " [1] In Luke Jesus divines the thoughts of the disciples, but does not shame them with a direct question.[2]

A further instance may be found in the reply to Peter's " What shall we have therefore ? " If we follow Mark, there is a shade of rebuke in the answer of Jesus, which ends with the saying, " Many that are first shall be last, and the last first." The suggestion that the disciples may not rank highest in the Kingdom after all is expressly avoided in Matthew by inserting the clause, " Ye shall sit on twelve thrones judging the twelve tribes of Israel "; while the passage from Mark which follows is made to apply to every one else, not to the Twelve. Luke has a simpler way out of the difficulty. He omits the clause about the first and the last.[3] In Mark the sons of Zebedee put their selfish, ambitious request themselves; in Matthew it is their mother who is the petitioner, and on whose shoulder the responsibility rests; from Luke the story is absent. I have only observed two instances in which this general relation between the Gospels is reversed. Matthew says expressly that the disciples objected to the anointing at Bethany, whereas Mark speaks vaguely of " them that sat at meat," and Luke alone suggests that the question of precedence in the Kingdom was actually discussed at the Last Supper. Reviewing the evidence as a whole, Mark's references to the disciples are almost uniformly disparaging, and their bluntness is almost uniformly discounted by the later evangelists. The case of the relatives of Jesus is on a similar footing. Mark alone says that they thought Jesus was beside Him-

---

[1] MATT. xviii. 1. [2] LUKE ix. 46, 47.
[3] MARK x. 28, 31 ; MATT. xix. 27, 30 ; LUKE xviii. 28, 30.

self, and wished to put Him under restraint (iii. 20, 21), and the phrase "among His own kin" appears as a peculiarity in Mark's rendering of the saying, "A prophet is not without honour save in his own country" (vi. 4). How is this characteristic of the second Gospel to be interpreted? Are we reading the work of a rampant partisan of Paul, who is anxious to undermine the prestige alike of the Twelve and of the relatives of Jesus, who were doubtless honoured in the Jerusalem Church? It is not unnatural to urge that the application of the detached saying about the first and the last to the twelve is Mark's own, and is intended to suggest that Paul stands higher than the Twelve. In one or two other instances (perhaps Mark vii. 18), which is reproduced in Matthew, the upbraiding of the disciples may seem artificial and out of place, very much as the command for silence after miracles of healing seems sometimes to be added as a matter of course by Mark, whether the occasion is really suitable or not. But, on the whole, it is difficult to sustain a charge of wilful disparagement against Mark. The points on which the disciples are represented as failing to understand are not points of doctrine in which Paul could claim superior insight. They are rather the historical developments which must have actually perplexed those nearest Jesus. Some of Mark's references justify themselves. Thus, the account of the relatives of Jesus wishing to put Him under restraint, omitted by Matthew and Luke, is required if we are to understand the subsequent answer of Jesus to His relatives, which the later evangelists retain. The bulk of these Marcean references read like history. They are too straightforward and simple to be the expression of a Pauline polemic. They epitomise the self-confession of the earliest disciples. They are signs of the excellence of Mark's traditions rather than of the bias of his associations.

So far the proof of distinctive Paulinism is inconclusive. It rests on features of the Gospel which seem to be either elements of the earliest Christian preaching to Jews as well as Gentiles, or else characteristics that may be expected in a genuine apostolic tradition about Jesus. The general probability of Pauline influence remains, though it is unlikely that Mark's Gospel is a tendency-document at all. If, then, Mark is content with a narrower definition of the Gospel than was adopted by Matthew and Luke, if to him the teaching of Jesus is still something outside the essentials of the good news, if he centres attention on the Cross, there is no reason to doubt that he was confirmed in this attitude by what he knew of Paul's work. That Paul should quicken his appreciation of the Cross lies in the nature of things. His experience in the Gentile world would favour the same concentration. Here was a world haunted with the myth of the dying God, a world seeking redemption through the sacrifice of a Divine victim. Is it conceivable that Mark did not know how the story of the Cross met this hunger of the Roman world? He would learn through Paul the wonderful effect of "placarding" Christ crucified before men's eyes. And it is noteworthy that in the Gospel the great confession of the Divinity of Jesus is drawn from the Roman centurion by the sight of the Cross. This act of confession Mark would fain persuade the Gentile world to share.

In thus drawing the picture of Jesus as the dying God, Mark can hardly have been ignorant of the part this conception played in the religious thought of the time. For all that, there is no reason for regarding the crucifixion as a variant on the myth of the dying God, and there is no evidence that the stories of Dionysos and other Divine victims has influenced the Gospel narratives. The advantages which the preaching of the crucified Messiah had over the mysteries of dying gods were primarily two. Firstly, the Christian message enshrined history, not myth. It was not the idea but the fact of the suffering Christ that created the Christian movement. Secondly, the Christian moral standard, as well as its moral power, was essentially bound up with, and expressed in, the Cross. The significance of this may be illustrated from the restraint of Mark's narrative. The central act of the tragedy is described in the bare phrase, "And they crucified Him." There is no description of the horrible process, no picture of the shed ding of blood inseparable from this kind of punishment. The wounds of Jesus, on which Christian piety has sometimes dwelt with almost morbid fancy, find scant recognition in the earliest Gospel. On the other hand, in the mysteries part of the sombre attraction, part of the emotional shock, part of the guarantee of spiritual benefit, would seem to lie in the crude horror of the myths on which they were founded. The would-be initiate pondered in meditation, saw in dramatic spectacle, or faintly repeated in physical wounds the tearing of Osiris limb from limb, the hacking of Dionysos to pieces, the mutilation of Attis. Mithraists went to the extreme of realism in their blood-bath. But there is no pandering to the blood-lust in Mark's story, no emphasis of the horror of it all. It is throughout the moral tragedy, the spiritual pathos which he forces upon the reader. The indifference of the soldiers who mocked and divided their victim's raiment at the foot of the Cross; the revilings of those who passed by and unconsciously summed up the moral meaning of the Cross when they said, " He saved others, Himself He cannot save "; the awful gloom and the one strange cry which convinced the very centurion of the majesty of the crucified King—these are the things Mark would persuade men to ponder. Here he found and sought to display the power that should transform the moral practice of mankind. " Among the Gentiles, men lord it over one another; but it shall not be so among you. For even the Son of Man came not to be ministered unto, but to minister and give His life a ransom for many." Here, then, Mark found the heart of the Gospel, the power of God unto salvation.

If it is permissible to sum up his message in phrases, Mark proclaimed Jesus the conqueror of demons; Jesus the giver of a new religious life in which the Gentile might know the true God, apart from the fetters of Jewish Law; Jesus, the God who died and rose again in actual fact, to transform the moral character of men; Jesus the coming Judge and Lord of all. That is the good news of Jesus Christ. It is not original with Mark. It is not distinctively Paul's. It is in the main the testimony of the Early Church to its first missionary period. Mark's distinction is that he was among the first to write down this common message, and in giving it literary shape he determined for ever the outlines of the Gospel story.

In relation to the other two synoptists the task of determining individual interests is easier than in the case of Mark. Good evidence is afforded by the treatment Matthew and Luke mete out to the material they derive from Mark (or relate in common with him). Further, in these instances, peculiar material—the sections peculiar to each Gospel—may more confidently be relied on to reveal the direction in which the minds of the two evangelists severally worked.

The atmosphere of the first Gospel is unmistakably Jewish. The temper of the writer's mind is revealed in his verbal preferences. Thus, he alone of the synoptists uses the term "lawlessness." He thinks naturally of ἀνομία where Luke writes ἀδικία. The adjective δίκαιος is found frequently in Matthew, and the noun δικαιοσύνη occurs six times in Matthew and only once in Luke. When Luke speaks of prophets and kings desiring to see the revelation of Christ, Matthew substitutes "just men"[1] for kings, and it is to Matthew that almsgiving is pre-eminently righteousness.[2] Another minor indication of his interest in Judaism may be found in his citations from the Old Testament. He has a larger number of direct quotations from the Old Testament than the other two evangelists taken together, and half of his quotations are found only in his Gospel. But his whole presentment of the teaching of Jesus is conditioned by his Jewish sympathies. He conceives the teaching of Jesus as a new law. It is a law of perfectness—its aim is to make men perfect as their Father in heaven, and if thou wilt be perfect, thou must, over and above the law of Moses, take upon thee the law of Christ. Matthew alone uses the term "perfect" in this kind of connection.[3] The follower of Christ pursues a righteousness which exceeds that of Scribes and Pharisees, and which fulfils the law in a deeper sense than merely carrying it out. The law of Christ is also the law of liberty.

[1] MATT. xiii. 17.   [2] MATT. vi. 1.   [3] See v. 48 and xix. 21.

The incident of the coin in the fish's mouth [1] would seem to indicate that the children—Jesus and those who follow Him —are in fact free from the minor obligations of the old law, though, to avoid offence, they naturally fulfil them. But the main point here is that the whole teaching of Jesus comes under the category of law. Matthew is emphatically under law to Christ. Christ is for him the prophet of whom Moses spoke. The Sermon on the Mount fulfils and eclipses the law of Sinai. Matthew clearly belongs to Jewish Christianity, and it is for a Jewish Christian Church, presumably the Jerusalem Church, that he is writing.

It is natural that in systematising the teaching of Jesus he runs it into Jewish moulds. It is also natural that he groups and perhaps develops the material to meet the needs of the Church-life with which he was familiar. Thus, in reference to the first point, not only is the new righteousness defined by contrast with the old, but the main duties of religion are alms, prayers, and fasting (in chap. vi.); and in setting in order what Jesus said on these topics, Matthew is writing for persons whose religious life follows the ordinary Jewish model. As to the second point, there is no doubt that Matthew's collocations of different sayings are artificial and determined by the convenience of later believers. Thus chapter x. is a discourse on the occasion of sending out the twelve to evangelise, which is clearly made up of sayings uttered on widely differing occasions. The bulk of the material there collected cannot in the nature of things have been spoken at the time to which they are supposed to refer. Incidentally, it is extremely hazardous, not to say unscientific, to reconstruct the life of Jesus as Schweitzer does, on the assumption that a saying like "Ye shall not have gone over the cities of Israel till the Son of Man be come," [2] must have been spoken at an early period in the ministry. Matthew brings together a number of sayings on the conditions of evangelisation in his own day; he has no intention of giving a strictly accurate report of what Jesus said when the twelve first went out to preach. His aim is to make the general teaching of Jesus on evangelisa-

---

[1] MATT. xvii. 26, 27.   [2] MATT. x. 23.

tion available for a later generation. It is not improbable
that he elaborates or embroiders his text with an eye to
existing practices or needs. Thus the developments of the
main teachings of Jesus against anger and against swear-
ing [1] have a touch of artificiality, not to say casuistry, about
them.[2]   The assignment of varying penalties to varying
forms of anger, and the parallel assignment of special
reasons for rejecting particular oaths, suggest a distinct
flavour of Rabbinism.   But even if these illustrations come
from Jesus, the collecting of them together and the legislative appearance put upon them may confidently be assigned
to the evangelist.   Similarly in chapter xviii. there is a development of Church-law on the subject of offenders, which
may indeed go back to a principle laid down by Jesus, but
which clearly indicates a settled Church order, and in its
present form ("Let him be unto thee as a Gentile and a
publican") can scarcely be attributed to Him who was condemned for eating with publicans and sinners.   It looks
much more like a corollary from the teaching of Jesus than
an actual part of it.   It is an addition made by the power of
binding and loosing entrusted to the disciples.   Matthew
almost hints as much by connecting a reference to this
legislative or judicial power (which even two or three met
with Christ in the midst might exercise) with the practice
enjoined on believers in the preceding verses.[3]   It is not
without significance that the word "Church" is found in
sayings of Jesus in Matthew only, and that in the first reference the Church is founded on Peter, to whom is expressly
given the legislative power (of the keys) already mentioned.[4]
In picturing Jesus as the Divine legislator, Matthew assumes
that He regulated His community beforehand and provided
for a continuance of a judicial authority to guide and
control it.

If the Gospel reflects in this way the life of the Jewish
Christian Church it is by no means a Judaising document.
A polemic against Paul has indeed been suspected.   Is the
teacher who authorises the breaking of one of the least

---

[1] Matt. v. 21–23, 34–37.   [2] See Montefiori *in loc.*
[3] See Matt. xviii. 15–20.   [4] Matt. xvi. 19.

commandments, and who is in consequence least in the kingdom of heaven, Paul, or some ardent follower of Paul? Should this be the case, it is still noteworthy that the Christianity of Paul or his follower is only depreciated, not denied. The author may have viewed with suspicion some sides of Gentile Christianity, but he approves and endorses the admission of Gentiles into the Church, and it is not clear that he intended some of his more strictly Jewish affirmations to apply to Gentile converts. Chapter x. takes for granted the evangelisation of the Gentiles, and the general missionary text "Go ye into all the world" is the climax of this distinctively Jewish Gospel. The writer is keenly alive to the significance of the mission to the Gentiles, and there is not much evidence that he wished to interfere with it. He is not a Judaiser. But while friendly towards the Gentiles, his primary concern is to commend the Gospel to the Jews, or at least to defend the Gospel to the Jews, for if the two may be distinguished Matthew is often an apologist rather than an evangelist. It is in accordance with this leading motive that he develops the argument from prophecy. This interest is at its strongest in narratives peculiar to his gospel, *e.g.* the birth narrative, when each development of the story is expressly connected with the fulfilment of a prophecy. He strains prophecies to fit events, as may be seen in his endeavour to discover an Old Testament anticipation of the connection of Jesus with Nazareth. He modifies his narrative to fit into prophecy, *e.g.* when he pictures Jesus as riding into Jerusalem on two asses, in order to indicate a closer fulfilment of the passage from Zechariah which the evangelist misunderstands, or when Mark's myrrhed wine becomes wine mingled with gall, under the influence of Psalm lix. 21. It is a tenable view that some traditions such as that concerning Judas[1] have simply grown out of reflection on prophecy. But be that as it may, Matthew is very anxious to show that he can prove Jesus to be the Christ from the Scriptures. At the points where Jesus most irretrievably offended Pharisaic sentiment, in eating with the

---

[1] Matt. xxvii. 3-10.

publicans, and in lax observance of the Sabbath, Matthew
hastens to justify his Master from Hosea, "I will have mercy
and not sacrifice." [1] That Jesus appealed to this passage is
probable enough, but that Matthew alone records it and
repeats it is due to the necessity he felt of Old Testament
support at critical points in the ministry of Jesus. Only
thus could Jewish opinion be conciliated.

He does not merely justify from the Old Testament deeds
and sayings of Jesus that gave offence. To the Jews Jesus
must be presented as fulfilling all righteousness. The conservative attitude of Jesus towards the law is very carefully
defined. Jesus is come to fulfil, not to destroy, and not one
jot or tittle shall pass from the law till all be fulfilled. The
scribes sit in Moses' seat, and their decisions must not be
neglected. The Christian will attend more earnestly to the
weightier matters of the law; at the same time he will not
leave the other undone. Jesus pays the Temple tax, and
Matthew's interest in the cleansing of the leper lies in the
fact that Jesus enjoined the strict observance of the law of
Moses. His treatment of the story is worth studying. In
Mark the connection of the story is of importance. It helps
to explain why Jesus could not escape crowds. This conclusion which unites the story with what follows in Mark
is omitted by Matthew. He detaches the story from its
original setting, appends it to the Sermon on the Mount
(perhaps to discourage revolutionary anti-legalist conclusions that might be drawn from the Sermon), and he concludes the story with Jesus' injunction of obedience to
Moses. That injunction now becomes the central point of
the story, and it is not an isolated example of Matthew's
method of showing that Jesus was a good Jew. It is part
of the same appeal that leads him to emphasise the strictly
national character of Jesus' own ministry.[2]

While the first evangelist is endeavouring to present as
strong a case for the Gospel of the Jews as he can, it must
be admitted that his tone is far from hopeful, and the wooing
note of the preacher is apt to pass over into denunciation.
The Gospel of Matthew is perhaps the most sombre of the

[1] MATT. ix. 13; xii. 5–7.   [2] See MATT. x. 6, 23; xv. 24.

four Gospels. There is a vein of pessimism running through it, and it is haunted by the thought of judgement. This tinge of sadness is apparent in the contrast of emphasis exhibited by Matthew and Luke in parallel passages. Both refer to the saying of Jesus about the light of the body being the eye. Matthew ends in darkness—"If the light that is in thee be darkness, the darkness—how great!" Luke, on the other hand, ends in light—"If thy whole body be light."[1] Similarly both record the saying "Judge not, that ye be not judged"—a solemn warning, unrelieved in Matthew, but in Luke connected with the thought that if judgement brings judgement, charity wins charity! "Give, and it shall be given you." It is a troubled soul that remembers, as Matthew does, the words of the Lord Jesus, how He said, "Give not that which is holy unto the dogs," or "Sufficient unto the day is the evil thereof." Does the evangelist write as one whose message has been rejected before, and who expects little better from the future? It is characteristic of Matthew that he records the saying, "He that is not with Me is against Me," but omits the companion saying, "He that is not against Me is with Me." This sadness becomes bitterness in the denunciation against the Pharisees and Sadducees, and against the Jewish people. Matthew couples Pharisees and Sadducees throughout his Gospel. In Mark the Sadducees have very little to do with Jesus until the end. In Matthew they are equally in opposition with the Pharisees. The Pharisees and Sadducees ask for a sign, and it is of the leaven of the Pharisees and Sadducees that Jesus bids His disciples take heed.[2] This may reflect the experience of the Church, which found the chief persecutors in Sadducees, and was inclined therefore to regard them as enemies of Jesus from the beginning. The polemic against the religious leaders of Judaism is unsparing. According to Matthew, Jesus on two occasions borrowed from John the Baptist the phrase, "generation of vipers" to describe them.[3] The absence of the phrase from Luke suggests that it is Matthew's own choice. The term "hypocrites" is re-

[1] MATT. vi. 23 ; LUKE xi. 35, 36.
[2] MATT. xvi. 1, 11. In MARK, Pharisees and Herodius; in LUKE, Pharisees only.
[3] MATT. iii. 7, xii. 34, xxiii. 33.

peated in Matthew.   It is applied to Pharisees and Sadducees
about three times as often as in Luke.   The evangelist
himself must have underlined a criticism which he felt to
be obviously true.   The Pharisees are plants which the
heavenly Father hath not planted.   They are to be rooted
out (xv. 13).   Nor is the case of the Jewish nation more
hopeful.   The experience of the man who lost one devil
only to receive seven worse in exchange, will be fulfilled
in Jewish history.   "Even so," Matthew tells us, "shall it
be to this generation." [1]

The condemnation on the spiritual blindness of those who
do not understand parables is expanded in Matthew (chap.
xiii. 10–15).   Even that which they have shall be taken
from them.   The moral of the parable of the vineyard
is explicitly drawn—"Therefore I say unto you that the
Kingdom of God shall be taken from you, and given to a
nation bringing forth the fruits thereof" (xxi. 43).   And
above all, it is Matthew who relates the tremendous self-
imprecation of the Jews when they cried, "His blood be on
us and on our children" (xxvii. 25).   But the foreboding
of judgement, the sense of the awful responsibility of rejecting Christ, dominates the first Gospel.   This thought is
reflected in most of the parables peculiar to Matthew.   We
have but to recall the parables of the tares and the drag-net,
and those which make up chapter xxv.   Matthew records
the teaching of Jesus on the conditioning of the Divine
forgiveness by human forgiveness, but he dwells on the
negative side of it.   If we do not forgive we shall not be
forgiven.   His teaching on the subject is embodied in the
parable of the unmerciful servant.   Matthew and Luke
both record parables of the king's marriage feast.   Luke
dwells on the fact that the host compelled all sorts of
persons to come in.   Matthew concentrates attention on the
fate of the man who forced his way in without a wedding
garment.   It is indicative of the same pre-occupation with
judgement that the phrase "There shall be wailing and
gnashing of teeth" occurs six times in Matthew and only
once elsewhere.   It is natural that Matthew adds to the

[1] MATT. xii. 45 ; contrast LUKE x   26.

phrase about the coming of the Son of Man, "Then shall He render to each man according to his works" (xvi. 27). The picture of the Son of Man on His judgement throne is characteristic of the temper of the whole Gospel. With this emphasis on judgement is bound up the strengthening of the apocalyptic element in the first Gospel. The judgement is essentially eschatological. The evidence for this has been ably handled by Streeter in the appendix to *Oxford Studies in the Synoptic Problem*, and it is unnecessary to repeat his analysis here. But it may be conjectured that the thought of judgement not only lends power to the hope of the Parousia, but also affects the portrait of the Judge. Whether this be the only or the main cause, it is certain that in Matthew an increasing majesty is attached to the person of Jesus, or rather the essential impression of majesty already given in Mark is more and more set in relief and disentangled from any obscuring element. Thus, all Mark's casual references to the human emotions of Jesus are carefully obliterated. An exception is made for "pity," on which indeed Matthew dwells. Otherwise he gives us a passionless Christ.

In the first Gospel Jesus seldom asks questions. Mark's graphic stories are retold and curtailed apparently in part to avoid the suggestion that Jesus needed information. Thus Jesus, in Matthew's Gospel, does not ask the Gadarene demoniac his name. He may be presumed to know it. Again, Jesus turns and sees the woman who touched the hem of His garment. He does not, as in Mark, ask the disciples "Who touched Me?" Jesus does not question the father of the epileptic boy about the symptoms of the disease. Such details are known or needless. From the first miracle of feeding the multitude the inquiry, "How many loaves have ye?" is absent. Instances might be multiplied. The process of editing out questions is not consistently carried through, but it is so pronounced a tendency in Matthew that the omission of the phrase "neither the Son" from chapter xxiv. 36 becomes probable. Matthew has nearly reached the position of John, that Jesus needed not that any man should tell Him anything.

It is perhaps due to the same tendency that in Matthew

Jesus is not informed of the fever of Peter's wife's mother. He reads her condition at a glance, and heals her of His own accord—the miracle thus ranking with the raising of the widow's son, as one of the few spontaneous works of mercy attributed to Jesus.

The wish to safeguard the majesty of Jesus is probably responsible for the omission of stories like the Ephphatha story. Matthew is inclined to avoid the mention of practices which savour of magic. They are unworthy of his subject. Is it possible that the thought of Jesus as Judge has influenced Matthew's account of the Transfiguration? In the vision of the exalted Jesus in Revelation (i. 16), "His face was as the sun appearing in its might." Matthew alone tells us that at the Transfiguration the Lord's face did shine as the sun. Was it the dread Judge of all that the three disciples saw in the glory on the mountain-side? This may be speculation, but Matthew conveys the impression that normally the presence of Jesus prompted worship. No fewer than ten times does Matthew speak of men rendering worship or paying homage to Jesus (προσκυνεῖν). Mark has the term twice—once of the Gadarene domoniac, and once of the mockery of the soldiers. In both cases Matthew avoids the term, reserving it for genuine human devotion. Luke uses the word once of the disciples at the Ascension (xxiv. 52), and probably the verse does not belong to the original text. The significant thing is that Matthew regards as normal during the earthly life of Jesus the attitude of worship or homage which all must adopt at the judgement— "At the name of Jesus every knee shall bow." The mediæval conception of Jesus as ever on the judgement-seat, in so far as it rests on the Gospel tradition, goes back to Matthew. Prominent though this feature of the Gospel undoubtedly is, it must not be suggested that the peril of rejecting Jesus is its only lesson. At least this persistent undertone is itself reinforced by a more positive conception of the wonder of the Gospel. It is Matthew who recalls the parables of the pearl of great price and the hid treasure. The kingdom of heaven is a treasure of surpassing worth, which sometimes comes to the patient seeker and sometimes meets a man at unawares, but in any case demands and more than repays the completest sacrifice. In Matthew we find the saying, "Come unto Me all ye that are weary." If the evangelist warns men to prepare to meet their judge, if he underlines the awful responsibility of neglect or rejection, it is because he knows that Christ's yoke is easy, and that in Him there is rest for men's souls.

Matthew then conceives Christianity as the fulfilment of Judaism. It is a moral law at once higher and easier than that of Moses. The Divine Lawgiver who has thus fully revealed the word of God is the Jesus whom the Jews rejected and crucified. He cometh quickly to judgement. Prepare ye then to meet Him.

If we may regard as conclusive the very strong argument for attributing the third Gospel to St. Luke, we may safely claim to know more of the third evangelist than of either Matthew or Mark. From external evidence we know that Luke was a Gentile, a Greek of some culture, a physician, and a friend of St. Paul. On the whole, the internal evidence of the Gospel confirms this characterisation.

It is neither necessary nor possible to summarise here the case for supposing that the author of the third Gospel had some acquaintance with medicine. Perhaps his toning down of the rather severe stricture passed on physicians in Mark's story of the woman who had suffered many things at their hands will suffice for illustration.[1] That Luke is a Greek, well educated, and with a wider outlook than is natural to Mark or Matthew, is apparent from a number of details. The rather elaborate sentence which forms the introduction is in itself adequate evidence on this head, and when it reveals a definitely historical purpose, and also shows Luke dedicating his work to one in good society, possibly a government official, there can be no doubt that we are dealing with a man of education. His wider experience and outlook explain a number of minor peculiarities in the Gospel. The substitution of the term "Lake of Galilee" for the local phrase, "Sea of Galilee" is natural in one who had travelled the Mediterranean. Luke's representation of the man sick of the

---

[1] MARK v. 26, 27 ; LUKE viii. 43.

palsy being let down through the tiles, suggests, as Sir W. Ramsay has pointed out, the impluvium of the Roman house, and certainly shows no familiarity with the wattled roofs of Capernaum.   As we should expect in a Greek, Luke is not always as clear about local conditions as the other evangelists.   Thus he vaguely substitutes crowds for the more definite groups, *e.g.* Pharisees, which figure in the parallel narratives.[1] This may be due to that contempt for the crowd, which is obvious in his account of events at Ephesus in Acts xix.   But it may also be due to the other cause already indicated.   It belongs to his wider outlook that Luke not only endeavours to commend the Gospel story to educated readers by stylistic improvements— many of Mark's slang terms, κράββατος, ἐσχάτως ἔχειν, &c., are avoided—but he also endeavours to conciliate official opinion.   Much of the peculiar material in his account of the trial is directed towards showing the favourable view which Pilate took of Jesus.   He brings out Pilate's *desire* to release Jesus, and he makes emphatic Pilate's repeated declaration of the innocence of Jesus.   The apologetic purpose is obvious here.   It is superfluous to labour this point, but it is worth while to remember that the Hellenistic culture of Luke is evidenced by numerous details in his writings, as well as by his universal humanitarian conception of the Gospel message.

The internal evidence that the third evangelist was a companion of St. Paul is less conclusive but very suggestive. No one could say that the characteristics of the Gospel which we are now to consider must of necessity be due to association with St. Paul.   Nevertheless, they are the characteristics such an association would naturally strengthen.

It would be a mistake to lay much stress on the fact that Luke is the only evangelist to use the term "grace," though the description of the preaching of Jesus as "words of grace" may be a small indication of the writer's familiarity with Paul's central conception of the Gospel.   Technical Pauline theology is not to be traced in Luke's writings, though he uses the verb "to justify" or "to be justified" more nearly

---

[1] See LUKE xi. 14–15, 29, and parallels.

in the Pauline sense than any other evangelist. The parable of the Pharisee and the Publican, with the comment "This man went down justified rather than the other," comes nearer to Paul's point of view on justification than anything else in the Gospel. The condemnation of the Pharisees in Luke xvi. 15—"Ye are they that justify yourselves in the sight of men: but God knoweth your hearts, for that which is exalted among men is an abomination in the sight of God"—might almost be an echo of Paul's judgement on his first faith. But two broader characteristics may be adduced which, while not necessarily Pauline, would be natural and inevitable in one to whom Paul was a hero. The first is, roughly, Luke's asceticism. As Burkitt has shown by comparing Luke xx. 34, 35 and Mark xii. 25, Luke is inclined to exalt celibacy. Those who are counted worthy to attain the resurrection life do not marry here or now— so Luke implies. If he does not share Paul's estimate of women, he does take Paul's view of marriage. Luke's ideal Christian, like St. Paul, is unmarried. Luke prefers the harsher form of the saying which puts the closest humanships second to love to Christ. "Whosoever *hateth* not father and mother and wife . . . is not worthy of Me." Had his friendship with one who had given up all things for Christ made him realise that the stronger word was not too strong? Again, Luke transforms the saying about taking up the Cross by adding to it the word "daily"—"If any man will come after Me let him take up the cross daily." [1] Does this show that he had been with Paul who would say, "I die daily?" Luke alone hands on the teaching of Jesus as to counting the cost (xiv. 33). One aspect of Luke's asceticism—his attitude towards wealth—is less certainly to be traced to St. Paul. That he learnt from Paul to be content with little and to reverence poor and humble folk is quite conceivable. But St. Luke is the Francis of Assisi among the evangelists, and he has something of the indignant defender of the proletariat about him, in spite of his contempt for crowds. According to him, Jesus condemned the rich as rich, and blessed the poor simply because they were poor. It is possible that Luke

[1] LUKE ix. 23.

approached the mind of Jesus from the wrong angle, and did not succeed in conveying an exact impression, but in any case he gives us more material for the teaching of Jesus about wealth than either of the other synoptists. It is Luke who records the woes on the rich, and who gives us the parables of the rich fool, and Dives and Lazarus. It is only in Luke that the Pharisees are accused of the love of money. His denunciation of the rich is matched by the value he sets on giving. He exalts the virtue of charity, and perhaps reads the lesson of indiscriminate giving into the parable of the unjust steward. With all his culture Luke is patron of the cult of poverty, voluntary poverty. He is clear that Christianity means the surrender of wealth. He may well have companied with the Apostle who interpreted the Incarnation in these terms.

The second and perhaps even more significant characteristic is Luke's insistence on prayer. He tells us more of the prayers of Jesus than Mark or Matthew does. At the baptism, as Jesus came up out of the water, and, adds Luke, as He was praying, the heavens opened (iii. 21). Luke mentions prayer as habitual with Jesus. "He was in desert places and praying" (v. 16). Before choosing the twelve, Jesus spent the night in prayer, and it was as He prayed, the fashion of His countenance was altered, and He was transfigured before them. Luke may have no direct historical authority for his insertions, but his spiritual insight is correct. It is to Luke that we owe the fuller record of the teaching of Jesus about prayer. The parables of the unjust judge and importunate friend are among Luke's treasures. Is it extravagant to suggest that he learnt from St. Paul to see in prayer the secret of the Christ-life? The same influence may be detected in some of Luke's references to the Holy Spirit. We may note in this connection his use of the phrase "full of the Holy Spirit" (iv. 1), and his substitution of the "Holy Spirit" for Matthew's "good things" in the sentence, "How much more shall your heavenly Father give the Holy Spirit to them that ask Him!"

Both Gentile sympathies and experience with St. Paul would force on Luke his presentation of the Gospel. For him the message of Jesus was from the first addressed to mankind. The distinctly national element in the ministry of Jesus disappears. The story of the Syro-Phœnician woman is omitted, together with passages like Matthew x. 23 and x. 5-6. On the other hand, the ministry opens in Nazareth with a passage from Isaiah, which makes the coming of Jesus an act of mercy as wide as human need. At the very outset, according to Luke's interpretation, the men of Nazareth rejected Jesus, and Jesus reminded them of the widow of Sarepta and Naaman the Syrian, in token that the Gentiles would welcome the Saviour whom the Jews denied. The mission of the twelve to Israel is supplemented in Luke by the mission of the seventy, symbolising the appeal of Christianity to the traditional seventy peoples of the world. Luke alone narrates the healing of the ten lepers, only one of whom turned back to give thanks, and he was a Samaritan. It is Luke who recovers for us the parable of the Good Samaritan, which once and for all brings out the inherent universalism of the great commandments. There are no national limitations to the appeal or the significance of Jesus. But there is little or no anti-Jewish feeling in the Gospel. The keynote is struck in the Nunc Dimittis—" For mine eyes have seen the salvation which thou hast prepared *in the sight of all the nations, a light to lighten the Gentiles* and the glory of thy people Israel."

There is, indeed, an element of election in Luke's view of the Gospel, though it does not run on national lines. The mission of Jesus is to the weak, the needy, and the sinful. Luke's Gospel presents Jesus pre-eminently as seeking and saving that which is lost. It contains the parables of the lost things, particularly the story of the Prodigal Son, in which so many have found the purest expression of the spirit of the Gospel. The phrase in Q, " Friend of publicans and sinners," is perhaps the most exact and most undoubtedly contemporary description of Jesus which we possess. The material for realising it is drawn almost entirely from Luke's Gospel. The calling of sinners to repentance is his constant theme. The very word " sinner " occurs as often in Luke as in the other three evangelists taken together. It is the corollary to all this, that Luke impresses on his readers, as no other writer does, the graciousness, the infinite tenderness of Jesus. Thus his Gospel is distinctly the women's Gospel. No one has touched more beautifully on the friendship of Jesus with women. But more generally, Luke relates the stories which show the immense influence of personal contact with Jesus. Peter falling at the feet of Jesus and saying, " Depart from me, for I am a sinful man, O Lord "; the woman that was a sinner drawn in penitence and hope to a Pharisee's house by the presence of Jesus ; Mary, unable to tear herself away from converse with the Master; Zacchæus, the publican, stung into generosity by the willingness of Jesus to lodge with him a man that was a sinner; the callous thief broken into repentance and faith by the sight of the sufferer on the central Cross—all these pictures come from St. Luke. He forces his readers to recognise this essential love of Jesus in the Passion. For he leaves out the mysterious, despairing cry recorded in Matthew and Mark, and instead he relates the words addressed by Jesus to the women : " Daughters of Jerusalem, weep not for me, weep for yourselves," and the prayer, " Father forgive them, for they know not what they do." The dying Jesus spends His last moments in an act of pardon to the thief, and in an act of trust in His Father.

If, then, Matthew is the Gospel of judgement, Luke is the Gospel of mercy. If there is something of pessimism in Matthew, Luke is full of hope. If both present a seeking Shepherd, Luke's Shepherd seeks the lost sheep *until He find it*. The third evangelist knows a Saviour who works moral miracles among poor men. He is aware of the fact that not many rich, not many mighty are called, and he rejoices in it. " He hath filled the hungry with good things, and the rich He hath sent empty away." Of the three synoptists, Luke has detached the permanent evangelical impulse from all temporal and national limitations, and consequently Luke makes the directest appeal to the modern world. From no other writer does the reader derive such a sense of the joy of the Gospel as from St. Luke.

The study of the individual characteristics of the evangelists attempted in this essay certainly impels an element of caution in trying to reach Jesus even through His earliest interpreters. But, in conclusion, it may be observed that these very prepossessions or tendencies of the evangelists are in the nature of equipment for their task. Some aspects of the work of Jesus would never have been adequately represented if the evangelists had not been men of varying outlook. The passing of the tradition through minds of differing but definite colour, while it raises some difficult problems, is on the whole a source of strength rather than weakness. For the process throws into relief the dominant features of the influence of Jesus, and at the same time compels attention to those elements which the distinctive temperaments of the evangelists led them to emphasise.

ESSAY VI

ST. PETER AND THE TWELVE

BY

W. K. LOWTHER CLARKE, M.A.

*Rector of Cavendish, Suffolk, and late Fellow of
Jesus College, Cambridge*

ANALYSIS

INTRODUCTION. Purpose of Essay.

I. THE EDUCATION OF THE TWELVE.

(a) In their native Galilee.

(b) By the national awakening under the influence of John.

(c) In the School of Jesus.

II. THE CHURCH UNDER THEIR RULE.

(a) The development of Acts i.–xv.

(b) Substantial accuracy of the account.

(c) The personality of St. Peter.

III. THE DISAPPEARANCE OF THE TWELVE.

(a) Later accounts of their activity.

(b) Are they ideal figures?

IV. LATER WORK OF ST. PETER.

(a) Activity at Rome.   The First Epistle.

(b) Petrine Christianity.   Its relations to Pauline.

V. SUBSEQUENT INFLUENCE OF PETRINE CHRISTIANITY.

ST. PETER AND THE TWELVE

Introduction

THE New Testament contains "all things necessary to salvation," in so far as it can afford complete satisfaction to the spiritual cravings of the soul. The case is different when a historical critic comes to the New Testament in search of accurate information about the early Christian community. To such a one it is in many ways a perplexing book, remaining silent on many subjects about which he desires information, since it reveals just enough to raise endless questions in his mind. The shelves of our libraries bear witness to the divergent answers given to these questions, and the innumerable theories propounded during the last hundred years as to the meaning of the life and sayings of our Lord and His disciples. These studies have been concerned not only with the facts of the Gospel, but also with the contributions to Christian thought made by the interpreters of the mind of Jesus Christ, among whom St. James,[1] St. Paul, and St. John stand out with most distinctness. Their teaching represents three great streams of thought welling forth from the one Source. The Epistle of St. James is mainly a manual of ethics, St. Paul is by far the greatest theologian of the Church, while in St. John mysticism finds its supreme exponent. As these three conceptions of Christianity, in which emphasis is laid on the ethical, the theological, and the mystical side respectively, are still to be found in the Church, a study of the New Testament writings in which they are represented is of direct practical value for the

---

[1] According to Hegesippus (Eus., *H. E.*, ii. 23), James was a typical Jewish righteous man, and exercised great influence over his fellow-countrymen.

needs of to-day. But the New Testament is largely th work of exceptional men; and it is about the average ma that we should like to know more. What was the Chri tianity of those interesting figures in the Acts that ai little more than names to us, such as John Mark, Philip th Evangelist, Agabus the Prophet, or of the first generatio of believers in Antioch, Pontus, Asia, Bithynia, and else where? The question is an important one. For it is cle that the sub-apostolic Church failed to appreciate the hig level of thought found in St. Paul and St. John, and owe its characteristics mainly to other influences. This failur was only relative. The actual standard to which the sub apostolic Church attained was no unworthy afterglow t the glories of the apostolic age. There is no exaggeratio in speaking thus of glories. The Church, of whose life th New Testament was a product, must have been even greate than its greatest names. St. Paul and St. John have exei cised such an influence over the world by their writing that we are tempted to forget that they were but the highei of a chain of mountain peaks. The very fact that th author of so brilliant an exposition of Christianity as i found in the Epistle to the Hebrews could so soon be fo: gotten is clear proof, if proof were needed, of the high leve of spiritual and intellectual attainment in the Apostoli Church. "The hearing ear is always found close to th speaking tongue, and no genius can long or often utte anything which is not invited and gladly entertained b men around him"[1] Those who listened to the voices an read the letters of the great masters were capable of passin on to the next generation many a lesson worth learning Are we not apt to underrate the importance of this mai stream of Church life, which can only partially be recon structed from the New Testament? To complete our pictur we must argue back from the Church life of the second cen tury, which owed much of its development to influences othe than those of St. James, St. Paul, and St. John. It is a: attractive hypothesis that the chief element in its develo ment was the central party, represented by St. Peter an

[1] Emerson, *English Traits*, chap. iv.

the non-literary apostles, whose views find scant expression in the New Testament. If this be so, then the First Epistle of St. Peter may be selected as most clearly reflecting the doctrinal standards acceptable to the majority of first century Christians. It will be the object of the following pages to trace the development of St. Peter, and, in a lesser degree, of the rest of the twelve, to estimate their position as leaders and rulers of the Church, and to show, if possible, that the world-Church of the second century was, as a historical fact, founded on St. Peter.[1]

I.—THE EDUCATION OF THE TWELVE

The disciples of Jesus seem to have been chosen from the same class as that to which their Master[2] belonged, so that much of what we say about the education of Jesus applies also to His disciples. In thus drawing a parallel between the education of our Lord and that of His disciples, we are surely justified in following the evangelist who tells us that the Child Jesus increased in wisdom, as well as in stature,[3] and so may fitly speak of His "education." Jesus was far from being brought up as an ignorant peasant. As the Child of a pious Jewish home, He had a thorough knowledge of the Old Testament and of the past history of His race. To know such a collection of books as the Hebrew Scriptures thoroughly was an education in itself. The Jews were literally at that time "the most highly educated people in the world."[4] He knew Hebrew, and could read the Scriptures, translating them at sight into the vernacular Aramaic.[5] Again, Galilee was definitely a bi-lingual country.[6] Even in Jerusalem every Jew with pretensions to

[1] I am indebted to the Rev. H. W. Fulford, Fellow of Clare College, for some references and a number of valuable suggestions.

[2] Thus James and John, the sons of Zebedee, were apparently cousins of Jesus ; *cf.* JOHN xix. 25 with MARK xv. 40.

[3] LUKE ii. 52.

[4] Ramsay, *Education of Christ*, p. 67 ; see whole of chap. iii.

[5] The *prima facie* meaning of LUKE iv. 16. The textual problems of MARK xv. 34 are best explained by assuming that Jesus quoted PSALM xxii. in Hebrew.

[6] Buhl in *Hastings' D. B.*, v. ˙47, 48 ; *cf.* Is. ix. 1, "Galilee of the Gentiles."

M

higher culture spoke Greek; it was essential as a medium
of communication between Jew and Roman.   Jesus was
able to speak with Pilate apparently without an interpreter
Paul addressed the listening crowd at Jerusalem in Aramaic,
but the narrative assumes that they could have understood
him had he spoken in Greek.   Still more in Galilee was
Greek in common use.   There were many enclaves of
purely Hellenic communities, and Greek must have been
indispensable for trading purposes.[2]   Philip of course could
speak Greek,[3] and, besides him, Andrew and Peter bore
Greek names.   It is not necessary to point out the value
of living in a bi-lingual country.   "With each newly-learnt
language one wins a new soul."   If the Epistle of James, with
its "wide culture," "acquaintance with classical as well as
Jewish writings," and "rhetorical and idiomatic Greek style,"[4]
could be rightly attributed to the brother of the Lord, no
further testimony to the education of Galileans would be
necessary.

The social conditions in Galilee in the early part of the
first century A.D. were calculated to stimulate the minds
and enlarge the horizon of receptive young men.   The
Synoptic Gospels afford a picture of a rich and varied life,
full of colour and movement.   Galilee was a half-way house
between the Judaism of Jerusalem, stern and uncompromising as its own grey hills, and that of the Dispersion, where
Jewish rigour was perforce profoundly modified by the
necessity of earning a livelihood amid the conditions of
Gentile life.[5]   Even in Old Testament times there had been
a difference in tone between the North and the South.
Galilee had always been more inclined to welcome alien
culture than Jerusalem, which was ever imbued with the

---

[1] ACTS xxii. 2 ; *cf.* J. H. Moulton, *Grammar of New Testament Greek*, i.[2]
7, 8.   Zahn, *Introd.*, i. 34 ff. ; but see Jos., *B. J.*, vi. 2, 5, where Titus uses
Josephus as an interpreter to speak to the people of Jerusalem.

[2] The knowledge in some cases was slight.   Peter could not express himself
freely in Greek, but needed an interpreter (Pap. ap. Eus., *H. E.*, iii. 39).

[3] JOHN xii. 21.

[4] Moffatt, *Introduction to New Testament*, p. 469.

[5] A striking instance of this is found in the theatre at Miletus, where an
inscription shows us that a special block of seats was reserved for the Jews.
See Deissmann, *Light from the Ancient East*, p. 446.

fanaticism of the desert which crept up to its gates.[1] When Galilee was repeopled from the South after the Maccabæan wars the same tendency asserted itself. The Galileans were distinctly more receptive than the Judæans.

In keeping with this we should expect to find the Galileans more open-minded with regard to the Law. There are indications that such was the case. Dr. Büchler has assured us that scholars are under a serious misapprehension as to the extent to which the rules of Levitical purity were observed in Galilee by lay Jews.[2] We know that Jesus adopted an independent attitude towards the Law. He attended the feasts as a loyal Jew, but He prophesied the destruction of the Temple,[3] and the worship of the sanctuary found no place in His teaching.[4] His position is reflected in the behaviour of His disciples. There is no sign that they were shocked by their Master's attitude towards the Law. In fact the opposition came mainly from the scribes from Judæa.[5] Peter tells us with reference to the Law as interpreted in his day that neither their fathers nor they had been able to bear it.[6] Then there was a large class that went further than the disciples, and was clearly indifferent to Levitical purity. These are the "sinners" of the Gospels, not necessarily immoral, but affected by Gentile influences. They may have respected the Pharisees, but did not attempt to follow their example. Jesus definitely chose these as His associates.[7] In estimating the influences that played on the disciples in these early days, we must not forget the apocalyptic element. The literature containing it, so Dr. Sanday reminds us,[8] is mainly provincial;

---

[1] See G. A. Smith, *Jerusalem*, i. 12 ff., 454.

[2] *Expos. Times*, October 1909 ; *cf.* Abrahams in *Camb. Bibl. Essays*, p. 167.

[3] John ii. 19 ; *cf.* Mark xiv. 58.

[4] G. A. Smith, *Jerusalem*, ii. 542 ff. ; *cf.* Denney in *Hastings' D. B.*, iii. 73 ff. Hort, *Judaistic Christianity*, p. 13 ff.

[5] Mark iii. 22.   [6] Acts xv. 10.

[7] In some cases ἀμαρτωλοὶ = Gentiles, especially in Luke (*cf.* vi. 32 ff., xxiv. ; Gal. ii. 15). But these cannot have been Gentiles. The earthly mission of Jesus was confined to the lost sheep of the house of Israel (Matt. xv. 24). They were as sheep not having a shepherd (Mark vi. 34). But their self-appointed guides were many. We conclude that they repudiated the guidance of the scribes.

[8] *Hastings' D. B.*, ii. 608a.

there are indications, too, that the teaching of the early prophets, with its high ethical demands, was still a powerful influence. The apocalyptic element is important enough to deserve more than a mere allusion such as the foregoing, but my purpose here is to guard against the attaching of undue importance to the legal element of Judaism by pointing out that it was but one aspect of contemporary Judaism. Generally speaking, in Galilee the more repellent features of Judaism were toned down. In coming to this conclusion we are taking the Synoptic Gospels as our main authorities. The Rabbinic testimony [1] is of little service here, because Galilee, after the fall of Jerusalem and the setting up of the Jewish headquarters in Tiberias, was a place very different from what it had been at an earlier date.[2]

Jesus and His disciples apparently belonged to the middle class; they were certainly not *fellahin*. In the early days of the ministry they could support themselves when on their travels without the offerings of the faithful women. Peter could leave his wife presumably provided for. The fisher-disciples were master-men,[3] and there is a great difference in the mental horizon of master-men and labourers. There was money enough for the simple needs of the disciples. Their renunciation was in a measure voluntary; their privations were the more real, because they could at any time return to their old life of comparative comfort.[4]

Jesus, at any rate, must have ranked high in popular estimation in virtue of His Davidic descent, which was

---

[1] Till recently scholars have assigned the Rabbinic literature to the second century. There is now a tendency on the part of Jewish scholars to put back both the Mishnah and the Midrash to a date before the fall of Jerusalem. See discussion by Abrahams in *Camb. Bibl. Essays*, p. 184.

[2] See Sanday in *Hastings' D. B.*, ii. 608b.; *cf. Recent Research*, p. 50. "The Judaism of the time of Christ had a wider and more open horizon than that of 100 years later."

[3] Mark i. 20.

[4] As they do in John xxi. 3. *Cf.* Matt. xvii. 24; Mark iii. 9, vi. 37 xi. 2, xiv. 14; John ii. 2, 12, xiii. 29, all of which presuppose a certain amount of financial independence. On the subject see *Hastings' D. B.*, v. 49; *D. C. G.* ii. 385; Zahn, *Int.*, iii. 187, 190; G. A. Smith, *H. G. H. L.*, p. 463.

generally acknowledged in His lifetime. In the East pre-eminence is willingly accorded to the man, however poor, who can trace his ancestry to an honoured name.

We have tried to show the sort of men whom our Lord chose. The disciples were ordinary Galilean Jews of the best type, but such Jews were at that time extraordinary men. Steeped in a noble national literature, brought up amid the free and wholesome surroundings of Galilee, in close contact with Gentile life and thought—where could better instruments have been found for the work on which they subsequently engaged? There is no need to exaggerate the miracle of Pentecost. A well-known theologian describes the disciples as "stupid, slow-minded persons."[1] By what standard does he judge them? The Founder of Christianity brought into the world a wealth of new ideas respecting the relations of God and man, and the values of life, which even now we find great difficulty in assimilating. Do the disciples deserve the reproach of stupidity because they were slow to take in these new ideas? Besides, their slowness and hardness of heart may well be overstated in the Gospels. A converted man is wont to see his life before conversion in the worst possible light. May not the disciples have been unduly severe on themselves in looking back on their early intercourse with Jesus? The Master who knew what was in man did not choose stupid men to be shepherds of His flock. John the son of Zebedee at least, if either the Gospel or Apocalypse can be rightly attributed to him, is proved by his writings to be a genius. Peter, and probably others of the twelve, had administrative powers of a high order. It is true the twelve incurred the supercilious contempt of the aristocracy of Jerusalem,[2] but such criticism is entirely relative to the point of view of the priests. The prejudice, such as it was, did not prevent Peter from exercising an acknowledged primacy in the Church at Jerusalem, which included "a great company of the priests."[3]

---

[1] A. B. Bruce, *Training of the Twelve*, p. 482.
[2] ACTS iv. 13; *cf.* JOHN vii. 49; MATT. xxvi. 73.
[3] ACTS vi. 7.

Such were the men that were going about their daily work in Galilean towns and villages when news came that a prophet had arisen. For some time there had been a feeling of expectancy in the air. The political situation was strained, and patriotic Jews believed that the coming of the Messianic Kingdom could not be long delayed.[1] This vague expectation was focussed in John the Baptist, who began to proclaim the immediate advent of the Kingdom, and to demand an inward purification of heart as a necessary preliminary to its coming. As an outward symbol[2] of this purification he insisted on baptism. This rite had been demanded for some time past as the condition of admittance into the ranks of the covenant people.[3] But for John to demand such an initiation of Jews was a startling innovation. He was putting them in the position of outsiders, and practically saying, "Ye must be born again, before ye can enter the Kingdom." Mere physical descent from Abraham did not avail to make them members of this spiritual Israel.[4] Perhaps only a few of those who accepted baptism appreciated the logical consequences of what they were doing, but that so many were induced to undergo the rite is a clear proof of the potency of the Baptist's teaching.

To understand the excitement we must remember that prophecy was generally acknowledged to have ceased for centuries.[5] "All men counted John, that he was a prophet indeed,"[6] and his appearance marked an epoch in the spiritual history of the nation. He preached the Kingdom, otherwise he would hardly have got a hearing. His message was on the surface apocalyptic, but its emphasis lay rather on the necessity of inner purification, and, having

---

[1] Schürer, *The Jewish People*, Div. II., vol. ii. p. 126 ff.

[2] I use the word in its primitive sense ; *cf.* Harnack, *History of Dogma*, i. 211. "There was as yet no reflection on the distinction between symbol and vehicle ; the symbol was rather regarded as the vehicle and *vice versâ*."

[3] "No reasonable scholar doubts that baptism of proselytes was earlier than John the Baptist, but it is not easy to demonstrate this indisputably from actual dated references." Abrahams in *Camb. Bibl. Essays*, p. 187. *Cf.* Oesterley and Box, *The Religion and Worship of the Synagogue*, p. 255. Edersheim, *Life and Times*, vol. ii., App. xii.

[4] MATT. iii. 9.

[5] *Cf.* 1 MACC. iv. 46, ix. 27, xiv. 41.   [6] MARK xi. 32.

gained the people's attention, he used it to inculcate the ethical standards of the old prophets.   He was not opposed to the Law, but simply passed it by.   If the account in the fourth Gospel is correct, the Pharisees followed his course with interest and curiosity, without, however, identifying themselves with the movement.   According to the first Gospel, the Pharisees and Sadducees came from Jerusalem to be baptized, but were greeted with scornful invective.[1]   The narrator leaves it an open question whether or not they actually fulfilled their purpose.   In any case John's work was sufficiently on the old lines to make them on a later occasion contrast him favourably with Jesus.[2]   He succeeded in stirring the nation to its depths, and the crowds came from all parts of the land.[3]   Even a year or two after the death of the prophet,[4] to have spoken against him might have provoked a riot.[5]   It was essentially a revival, with the weakness and strength of all revivals, not a new religion making a slow progress in the face of prejudice.   The movement died down, and in a year or two there was little to show for it;[6] but as in all movements of the spirit, there

---

[1] John i. 19 ; Matt. iii. 7.   In Luke iii. 7 the words "O generation of vipers," &c., are addressed to the multitude.   Luke has a tendency to omit anti-Pharisaic polemic.

[2] Mark ii. 18.

[3] According to Matt. iii. 5, it was the dwellers in Judæa and round Jordan who went to John.   But in Matt. xi. 7 the Galilæan multitudes are said to have gone also.   So Judæa in iii. 7 possibly means the whole country, as in Luke iv. 44 (אּ BCL).   *Cf.* Luke vii. 29.

[4] John was essentially a prophet.   He foretold the coming of One greater than himself, *i.e.* Elijah (John i. 21).   Jesus was thought to be Elijah (Mark viii. 28).   He discloses to His disciples the secret that John was really Elijah (Mark ix. 13 ; Matt. xi. 14, 15).   See Schweitzer, *Quest of the Historical Jesus*, p. 371.

[5] Mark xi. 32.

[6] Though perhaps more than appears on the surface of the New Testament. The preaching of John may have prepared the way for the conversions of Acts. The reference to the Baptist in Paul's speech at Antioch (Acts xiii. 24, 25) shows that the Baptist's propaganda was well known in a synagogue of Asia Minor ; or, if we do not accept it as a genuine record of the apostle's speech, that the subject was still of interest at the time of the composition of Acts. There is perhaps an anti-Baptist polemic in the fourth Gospel ; *cf.* John i. 20-33, iii. 28-30, and the omission of any reference to the Baptism of Jesus by John.   See Inge in *Camb. Bibl. Essays*, pp. 255, 266 ; *cf.* Acts xviii. 25, ix. 3.

were permanent results in the lives of some, who must in the coming years have looked back to those early days and said, " It was good for us to have been there." Some, perhaps all,[1] of the future disciples of Jesus were swept into the current and went out to hear John in the wilderness, where they underwent baptism at his hands. Whatever leaning they may have had towards the apocalyptic and prophetic sides of Judaism, or comparative indifference to the traditional requirements of Levitical purity—and we have seen that both of these are probably to be postulated— would be strengthened by the influence of John's teaching.

No violent breach of continuity was experienced by the disciples in forsaking the Baptist and attaching themselves to Jesus. Our Lord Himself takes up the message of the Baptist, and opens His ministry by calling on the Galileans to repent, for the Kingdom of God is at hand.[2] "The Kingdom" has played an important part in recent theology, and there is little doubt that it is the dominant factor in the Gospel history. There is, however, a danger of construing the phrase in too abstract a sense. Its primary meaning may well be "The Theocracy" or "The Sovereignty of God,"[3] but an abstract idea must receive a concrete embodiment, if it is to be of importance on the stage of human history. Nor should we be prepared to find an exception to this rule in the Jews, who, as a nation, certainly leaned towards the concrete.[4] During the ministry of our Lord the disciples obviously held materialistic views about the Kingdom,[5] while after the Ascension the return of Christ was conceived of in a concrete way for many years to come.

---

[1] From JOHN i. 35–45 we conclude that Andrew, Peter, James, and John, also probably Philip and Nathanael, were disciples of the Baptist. As the publicans are said to have received John's baptism (LUKE vii. 29), probably Matthew is to be added to the list.

[2] MARK i. 15.

[3] See Dalman, *Words of Jesus*, p. 91 ff.

[4] An interesting example of this is found in the word δικαιοσύνη, *righteousness*, which came to be used, as in MATT. vi. 1 (א BD), in the specialised sense of *almsgiving*; cf. DAN. iv. 27 (24), LXX. The Jews were of course *theologically* minded, but a *philosophical* conception of the Kingdom as an abstract Sovereignty of God on earth is not quite congruous with what we know of Palestinian Judaism.

[5] MARK x. 35–45 ; cf. ACTS i. 6.

There is much to show that the idea of a community [1] was present from the very beginning of the ministry of Jesus, the primary purpose of which was to draw out from the mass those who had the requisite qualifications for membership of the Kingdom.

Baptism was the outward sign of such membership, both before the Crucifixion and after Pentecost. As practised by the disciples [2] during our Lord's Ministry, their baptism was essentially one with that of John; and the Baptism of Acts grows naturally out of the baptism of the Gospels. [3] All who received baptism now were potentially members of the Kingdom, and, when the Kingdom was manifested, might expect to receive a pledge of their membership in a baptism of the Spirit such as was foretold by the prophet Joel. [4]

It is possible to see in the Gospels traces of this community as it would appear to the minds of the twelve. It may perhaps be described under the figure of three concentric circles—

(a) The twelve themselves, who were *with* the Master, and preached the advent of the Kingdom. [5] They, and especially Peter, James, and John, were destined to be the rulers of the community.

(b) There is a wider circle of "followers" of Jesus, who rank after the twelve, and yet are in a closer personal relationship to Him than the crowds who also

---

[1] So Allen with reference to the use of ἐκκλησία in MATTHEW. "That Christ should have spoken of His disciples as forming a community . . . marked off from their Jewish fellow-countrymen by their belief in Him as the Son of Man, is intelligible and natural" (*Studies in the Synoptic Problem*, p. 280).

[2] JOHN iv. 1. A passage such as this may be used in evidence without prejudging the question of the historicity of the fourth Gospel. There seems no motive for its invention.

[3] Note that repentance and baptism are inculcated both by John (MATT. iii. 2, 6) and Peter (ACTS ii. 38). The 120 of ACTS i. 15 are swollen by 3000 converts in ii. 41. If baptism was necessary for the latter, the former must also have been baptized. By whom? Probably John. Apollos is baptized by John, and is not, so far as we know, re-baptized (ACTS xviii. 25); but *cf.* xix. 5. See *Studies in the Synoptic Problem*, p. 213.

[4] JOEL ii. 28. The above follows Schweitzer's attractive exegesis of MARK i. 8. See *The Quest of the Historical Jesus*, p. 376.

[5] MARK iii. 14.

"followed" Him. It is to this body that the in-quirers seek admission in Luke ix. 57, 61. In verse 49 John resents the action of one who was outside the community and did not "follow with" them in cast-ing out devils. In Mark x. 21 Jesus invites the rich young man to leave all, as the twelve had done (verse 28), and follow Him. This means more than a following in the ethical sense, which is urged upon the crowd in Mark viii. 34. This body of adherents was a shifting one. We read of the defection of some of the disciples in John vi. 66. In the journey to Cæsarea Philippi and back to Capernaum [1] only the twelve seem to have been present; on the last journey to Jerusalem they were reinforced by a number of women. Many of the 120 must at some time or other have thus "followed" Jesus.[2]

(c) While it is easy to say of certain people that they are inside the community, it is harder to determine who is outside it. There was, however, a wider circle of holy and humble men of heart, in sympathy with the new doctrines, to whom the Kingdom belongs.[3] In practice these would tend to be identified with the recipients of John's baptism.

Our present concern is, however, with the inmost circle formed by the twelve. If we are correct in assuming that there were outer circles the position of the twelve was from the first one of authority. Our Lord needed officers for His community, and, as was most natural, chose twelve to re-present the ideal spiritual unity of Israel, and to be con-sciously trained by Him for their future responsibilities. The invitation to become fishers of men, the part played by them in feeding the multitudes, the exhortations of Matt. x. and the parables, some of which were addressed to the special needs of the twelve, all imply this position of responsibility. They certainly realised the privileges and

---

[1] MARK ix. 35.

[2] ACTS i. 15. We should include the seventy in this class.

[3] See the Beatitudes (MATT. v. 3 ff. ; *cf.* MARK x. 14).

duties which lay in front of them.[1] If the Pharisees could devise a world-wide propaganda,[2] the disciples may well have had similar visions. If they anticipated a heaven-descended theocracy, in which they were to hold office, there would still remain the task of bringing in the Gentiles. It is not too much to say that the training of the twelve for a future position of influence and power is represented in the Gospels as the main task of the Ministry of Jesus.[3]

Let us now inquire what impression the apostolic brotherhood would make on a thoughtful contemporary observer. It would have appeared to him in the light of a peripatetic religious community, based on principles of an eclectic Judaism, and the resemblances it bore, at least on the surface, to the Essenes, might well have led him to confound the new brotherhood with the latter sect. The existence at this time of eclectic Jewish sects cannot be ignored; the resemblances between them and the disciples of Jesus may be only superficial in our eyes, but they must have appeared significant to contemporaries. It is sufficient here to refer to the abundant literature on the subject of the Essenes and Therapeutæ.[4] There is a growing tendency to see in them the influence of Greek ideas on Judaism. If this is so, and especially if the connection was recognised in Palestine in our Lord's day, the point is of some importance. We do not wish to suggest that our Lord was anything but supremely original; but, as far as the disciples are concerned, it explains much in the subsequent development and Hellenisation[5] of the Church.

We have tried to describe the men to whom was entrusted the task of guiding the destinies of the Church

---

[1] MATT. xix. 27 f. ; MARK x. 41.　　　[2] MATT. xxiii. 15.

[3] See Bruce, *The Training of the Twelve;* Latham, *Pastor Pastorum ;* Hort, *The Christian Ecclesia,* p. 22 ff.

[4] Essenes were found in villages, even in Jerusalem, where there was a gate of the Essenes. They observed celibacy, had a common purse, used no oaths. See *Hastings' D. B.,* i. 767 ff.; *D. C. G.,* i. 273. Schürer, II. ii. 188 ff. Friedländer (*Zur Entstehungsgeschichte des Christentums*) says they were a Greek sect of Jews. They had a Pythagorean régime. Philo clearly connects them with the Therapeutæ, and leaves the purely Jewish schools of Palestine unnoticed. For the Therapeutæ, see F. C. Conybeare's *Philo de vita Cont.*

[5] *Cf.* Harnack, *History of Dogma,* passim.

in its earliest days. They possessed considerable natural powers, which had developed by a stimulating and wholesome education in their native Galilee. Their spiritual interests had been awakened by the revival of the Baptist, and they had enjoyed, possibly, three years of intercourse with Jesus, during which He who knew what was in man had trained them designedly for their future work. We do not wish to minimise the outpouring of Divine grace at Pentecost, but nothing is gained by decrying the preparation of the twelve for it. We may well ask, Were there any men of that age so fitted for the task that was to be laid upon them? Also, in the Gentile surroundings of Galilee, and in the resemblance that the disciples bore to the eclectic sect of the Essenes, we have seen some ground for supposing that the religion of the first followers of Jesus was never entirely and nakedly Judaic; that the primitive Church in absorbing much of the spirit of Hellenism was not cutting itself completely adrift from its early moorings.

II.—The Church under the Rule of the Twelve

We will now proceed to trace the expansion of the Church in its early years under the guidance of the twelve. According to the traditional view, some four years [1] elapsed before the conversion of St. Paul, at which time we find Christians at Damascus,[2] and Churches firmly established throughout Judæa, Samaria, and Galilee.[3] This expansion must have been very rapid, all the more so, perhaps, because the twelve made Jerusalem their headquarters, in order to build up a strong centre, and to let intensive work precede extensive. Jerusalem was the natural centre for any propaganda among the Jews. From it the seed could be sown broadcast. The stream of pilgrims which flowed thither from all parts must have come into contact with the new teaching, and have carried back news of it to their homes in distant lands.

---

[1] See Turner in *Hastings' D. B.*, i. 424b, for a statement of the different views. The time varies from one year (Harnack) to six years (Turner).

[2] Acts ix. 19.   [3] Acts ix. 31.

Besides this work at Jerusalem, the twelve may well have carried on evangelistic work in Galilee. It is most unlikely that they made an abrupt break with their old home. The Galilean churches are mentioned quite incidentally in Acts ix. 31, as if their origin was well known in the Church. Whom are we to postulate as their founders with such probability as the Galilean disciples, who had already undertaken missionary journeys in their native land under the direction of Jesus?

All this activity is, however, confined to Jews. The Church as a whole has not yet risen to the conception of a mission to the Gentiles. Even in chapter xi. Peter feels it necessary to justify the baptism of Gentiles at some length. Can such a state of mind be reconciled with the universalist ideas to be found in the Synoptic Gospels, and especially in the third Gospel, or with the genuineness of the great Commission in Matthew xxviii. 19? It is an old difficulty. Some solve it by assuming the passages in question to be later additions to the primitive report of our Lord's words, though nothing is more probable than that One, who was, at the very least, the greatest religious genius the world has known, should have looked forward to the widest possible diffusion of His teaching. It may be said that the apostles were practical men, who did the work nearest to their hand, without reflecting much on the principles involved, so that when the logic of events taught them the necessity of admitting the Gentiles, the lesson came as a surprise. Even so, however, there remains the difficulty, Why did no one appeal to the words of Jesus, if they were known?

It is possible that they were known, but were not interpreted in what was subsequently seen to be their true sense. The primitive Church might well have imagined that our Lord had proclaimed a universal Judaism. In fact it would be surprising, in view of their Jewish upbringing, if the first Christians of Jerusalem had entertained any other conception of His meaning; in which case the baptism of the uncircumcised Cornelius could not but seem a startling innovation.

The following may be advanced as a possible suggestion. Does not the primitive eschatology of the early chapters of Acts throw some light on the matter? The apostles may well have looked forward to the incorporation of the Gentiles into the community, but have imagined that it would take place after the Parousia. Their duty during the interim was to prepare themselves and as many Jews as possible for the coming of the heavenly Kingdom. As Jews, they would naturally imagine that Gentiles, if admitted at all, would enter through the usual door of proselytism. After the Parousia Jew and Gentile would alike share in the blessings of the Kingdom, a theocracy would be established with its centre at Jerusalem, and the twelve would rule under Christ over His world-wide Kingdom. Such a hope had animated Hebrew prophets of old,[1] and seems consistent with the state of mind of the apostles as revealed in the Gospels. What they failed to realise was that the spirit of the Gospel demanded the immediate admission of the Gentiles on equal terms, and as Gentile believers, not as proselytes to Judaism.

Their primitive eschatological hope was rapidly modified by the teaching of events. The growth of the Church was a patent fact and tended to fill the foreground of their thoughts, and the future heavenly Kingdom to fall into the background. They began to see that their present duty was to gather in disciples from all quarters. When Samaritans could be admitted, the Gentiles' turn could not be long delayed. It seems probable that the march of events would in any case have taught the disciples the lesson before long; that they learned it so soon as they did was due to the clear and logical vision of Paul.

The narrative of Acts i.-xv. is carefully written, and the author traces the stages of the Church's expansion with precision and distinctness. There is an early period of rapid growth, during which the authorities refrained from

---

[1] MICAH iv. 1 ff., v. 7; ZECH. viii. 22 f.; *cf.* Is. xviii. 7, xix. 24 f. In ZECHARIAH the position of the Gentiles is clearly intended to be subordinate. Even Paul said "the Jew first" (ROM. i. 16), and described the Jew and Gentile under the figure of the good and wild olive tree (ROM. xi.). *Cf.* Harnack, *Neue Untersuchungen zur Apostelgeschichte*, p. 28 ff.

active persecution, and the attitude of the people in Jerusalem towards the new movement was favourable. The increase in numbers was so great that it soon became necessary to inaugurate a new order of officers, in order to relieve the apostles of business details.

A second period began with the preaching of Stephen, which instantly provoked a persecution. Many of the disciples left the city, and carried the Gospel to other parts of Palestine, including Samaria. The mission of Philip to Samaria and the conversion of Cornelius are both described at some length. They are test cases, and indicate the relaxation of Judaic prejudices. Converts were presently made as far afield as Cyprus and Antioch,[1] and Barnabas was sent to aid the development of the Church in the latter city. Then came the first missionary journey of Paul with its wholesale appeal to the Gentiles, followed by a conservative reaction in the Church of Jerusalem. Intense feeling was aroused, nor could it be allayed except by a Council in Jerusalem, at which the status of the Gentiles was settled. This concludes the second period. The rest of the Acts is devoted to the fortunes of Paul. When the narrator returned to Jerusalem in xxi. 18, James, the Lord's brother, was in charge of the Church, and none of the original apostles, apparently, were left in the city.

Despite some inconsistencies the narrative is on the whole straightforward. How far can it be accepted as an accurate record of facts? The answer is not easy. The tendency of recent criticism has been to vindicate the Lukan authorship of the third Gospel and Acts, and to form a high estimate of Luke's work as an historian.[2] Where he is an eye-witness of the events described, he is generally acknowledged now to be eminently trustworthy. But he is not an eye-witness for these early days; and his work must be examined and criticised on its merits. It is idle to deny the difficulty of certain passages. How many, for instance,

---

[1] If we read ''Ελληνας with א ᶜAD * in Acts xi. 20, we have here the first large accession of Gentiles to the Church.

[2] It must be sufficient here to refer to the well-known works of Ramsay and Harnack on the subject.

can accept the Ananias and Sapphira incident as a literal record of facts?[1] Or, again, the Story of Pentecost is beset with difficulties. There have been many explanations of it,[2] but, while the story is evidently given in all good faith, we cannot resist the impression that an eye-witness might have described the occurrences differently. The moral miracle of Pentecost is so great that it does not need the symbolical additions of Luke's narrative.

When, however, all has been said, these chapters remain a remarkable record, and we may claim their substantial accuracy. Luke had access to excellent sources of information. On his visit to Palestine he met Philip the Evangelist,[3] who was in touch with the events of the first years. Through him Luke may even have learnt some of John's reminiscences.[4] He is in close connection with Mark, who is the link binding Paul, Barnabas, and Peter together in the later apostolic age; as the companion of Paul, when he wrote the Epistles of the Captivity, Mark was in touch with Luke, who has incorporated the greater part of the Marcan Gospel into his own.[5] Mark's exceptional opportunities of knowing about the early days of the Church were at the disposal of the writer of the Acts, who is even able to tell us the name of his mother's maidservant.[6] In one way or another, then, nearly all the leading figures of these chapters come within the sphere of Luke's personal knowledge.

The question of miracles need not detain us. Every great religious movement—down to the Welsh Revival of 1905 —is accompanied by events believed to be miraculous. Paul for one believed that he had the power of working

---

[1] A writer so conservative—in his attitude towards Acts—as Ramsay, says (*St. Paul the Traveller*, p. 370): "The episode of Ananias and Sapphira excites reasonable suspicion. That Ananias should be carried forth and buried un known to his family, unmourned by his kindred and friends, is not merely contrary to right conduct, but violates the deepest feelings of Oriental life. . . A moral apologue has found here an entrance alongside of real history."

[2] Chase, *Credibility of Acts*, p. 34 ff. Wright, *New Testament Problems*, p. 277 ff.

[3] Acts xxi. 8.

[4] Certain affinities of the third and fourth Gospel have been frequently pointed out. See Bartlet in *Studies of the Synoptic Problem*, p. 352 f.

[5] Col. iv. 10, 14 ; 1 Peter v. 13.

[6] Acts xii. 13. See Harnack, *Luke the Physician*, p. 19.

miracles, in common with the other apostles.[1] We should rather be tempted to suspect something if there were no mention of miracles. As Professor Deissmann says, "The whole ancient world is full of miracles; definite types of miracle become fixed by the tradition of thousands of years, and occur again and again in all sorts of places. Viewed amid the surroundings of its own age and social stratum, the New Testament is seen to be shy, rather than otherwise, of narrating miracles."[2]

The fidelity of Acts i.–xii. to early conditions is a strong argument in its favour. Although the book is written perhaps forty years after the events, there is no attempt to read existing features of Church life into those early days. It may be noted[3] that the Sadducees are the first persecutors, that both Christology and eschatology are of a markedly primitive type, that Jesus is the Jewish Messiah, and that the doctrines of the Atonement and of the pre-existence of Christ, all-important in Pauline circles, are conspicuously absent. The speeches are of course not short-hand reports, but they may well reflect the apologetic of the primitive Jewish-Christian Church.

Throughout these chapters there looms the imposing figure of Peter. He is indubitably the shepherd and ruler of his brethren. Now that he is converted, he strengthens them to good purpose. He is also a great popular figure, besieged by crowds when he goes out in the streets of Jerusalem. His greatness is that of character and personality rather than of subtle or powerful intellect. Conceivably Paul might have vanquished Simon Magus in argument, Peter cuts him short with a majestic rebuke. Generally speaking, his position is so assured that it does not need to be asserted. The contrast between this characteristic of Peter and the self-assertion of the Pauline Epistles is striking. We need not of course attribute this attitude on the part of Paul to any lack of humility; for he, unlike Peter, was subjected to a continual succession of personal attacks involving, as he deemed, the honour of his

[1] 2 Cor. xii. 12.   [2] *Light from the Ancient East*, p. 393.
[3] See Headlam in *Hastings' D. B.*, i. 32 ff.

N

Master as well as his own. The apostolic council sh
us the position occupied by Peter. He was not presid
for his evangelistic journeys had already begun;[1] but
voice was enough to quiet the strife of tongues. T
was "much disputing,"[2] but after some words from
"all the multitude kept silence" and listened to
Paul and Barnabas had to say.

III.—THE DISAPPEARANCE OF THE TWELVE

After the Council the original apostles disappear
the pages of the New Testament. Peter emerges in
First Epistle, and John in the writings attributed to
Otherwise, there is no first-hand account of their
activities. The traditions of the later Church are
and varied, but of singularly unequal value. Thus
traditions connecting Peter with Rome and John
Ephesus[3] are too strong and intrinsically probable t
ignored; whereas any one attempting to trace the tra
of certain obscurer members of the band is soon los
a maze of inconsistent traditions. The apocryphal
are really the historical novels of the Early Church, an
no single instance do their authors seem to have had
definite facts unknown to us to go upon.

The starting-point of our inquiry is the fact that Ja
the Lord's brother, was apparently the only apostle in J
salem at the time of Paul's last visit,[4] and the agreer
recorded in Gal. ii. 9, by which Paul was to preach to
Gentiles, Peter, James and John to the Circumcision. J
stayed in Jerusalem; the arrangement, which was at

---

[1] GAL. ii. 8. [2] ACTS xv. 7, 12.

[3] Room must be left for the possibility of the early death of John th
of Zebedee, and of the Ephesian traditions referring to another John
Moffatt, *Introduction to New Testament*, pp. 596–619, and Sanday, *Critic
the Fourth Gospel*, for summaries of the evidence respectively favourabl
unfavourable to this hypothesis.

[4] Though not one of the original twelve, he ranked as an apostle, an
apparently filled the place of his namesake the son of Zebedee. *Cf.* Ra
St. Paul the Traveller, p. 378 : "The want of any reference to Peter in x
must, in our view, be taken as a proof that he was not in Jerusale
the time."

only a rough working agreement—for Paul continued to
appeal to the Jews when an opportunity offered—would,
whilst leaving them perfect freedom of choice, direct the
steps of Peter and John primarily to the great Jewish
dispersions of Rome, Syria, Alexandria and Chaldæa.[1]

The earlier movements of John are unknown, but his
chief work was done from Ephesus as a centre, where he
became the "great light" of the province of Asia. His
activities need not be discussed here, as they form the subject
of another chapter in this book. Peter, so far as we know,
never went to Chaldæa or Alexandria, but there are strong
traditions connecting him with Antioch, which was of great
importance as a centre both of the Jewish dispersion[2] and
of the earliest Christian propaganda. In Galatians we find
Peter at Antioch; if he continued his work there the
complete withdrawal of Paul from a place of such importance, which was also the scene of his early ministry,
becomes intelligible. If Antioch were Peter's centre[3] he
would naturally extend his work to Cilicia, which ranked
geographically with Syria. Once more, the absence of any
reference to Cilicia in the Pauline Epistles is significant.[4]
It is an attractive suggestion that Peter laboured in Asia
Minor. Certainly the Church of these provinces owed much
to teachers other than Paul, and the work of Paul as founder
left very few traces in the next generation.[5] It is even
possible that the reason why Paul was forbidden to preach

[1] See Gwatkin, *Church History*, i. 60.
[2] For the importance of the Jews in Antioch in Chrysostom's time, see
Stephens, *St. Chrysostom*, p. 132 ff.
[3] Chase in *Hastings' D. B.*, iii. 768 : "The simple tradition which associates
St. Peter with the early period of the Church at Antioch seems to go back
to the second century, and is intrinsically probable." On p. 779 he assigns
the period 44–61 to "work in Syrian towns with Antioch as its centre." *Cf.*
Chrys., *Hom. in Ign. Mart.* (Migne, *P. G.*, l. 591). Work in Syrian towns,
along the sea-coast from Cæsarea to Antioch, is assumed in the Ebionite Acts
of Peter, embedded in the Clementine Recognitions (*Clem. Rec.*, iv. 1, vii. 1,
5, x. 68).
[4] Except the retrospective reference of GAL. i. 21. Antioch, Syria, and
Cilicia are assigned to Peter by the Syriac *Doctrina Apostolorum* (Cureton,
Ancient Syriac Documents, p. 33).
[5] 2 TIM. i. 15 shows a defection ; *cf.* APOC. i.–iii., addressed to the Pauline
churches.

in Bithynia [1] was that other teachers, perhaps Peter, were at
work there.   If we can put any trust in the statements of
the Apocryphal Acts, there is ground for supposing that
Peter had laboured " in the land of the barbarians," probably
the country to the south-east of the Euxine.[2] There is
no obvious tendency at work here to make us discount the
statement, as there is in the visit to Corinth recorded by
Dionysius.[3] In the latter case the Jewish-Christian desire
to disparage Paul, and to introduce Peter's influence into
the chief Pauline spheres may well have been operative.

Andrew [4] is an interesting figure in the Gospels, ranking
after the three, but before the other eight apostles.   In
Acts he is only a name, but later accounts bring him to
Scythia ; that is, European Scythia on the Euxine, which fits in
with the fairly constant tradition connecting his preaching
with Sinope.[5] His martyrdom was assigned to Patræ in
Achaia.[6] The Muratorian Fragment [7] records his connection
with John at Ephesus, which is not unlikely when we
remember the position occupied by Andrew in the fourth
Gospel, where he is mentioned four times.

Bartholomew is said to have preached to the tribes of
Lycaonia, also in the kingdom of Polemon.   Polemon II.
became for a time a convert to the Jewish faith,[8] and the
presence of Jews in these regions makes an apostolic visit

---

[1] ACTS xvi. 6, 7.   There is, however, no trace of Petrine work in later
times.   Marcion, from Pontus, is Pauline to an extreme.

[2] *Acta Petri et Andr.* (Tischendorf), p. 162.

[3] Eus., *H. E.*, ii. 25 ; *cf.* 1 COR. iii. 22, ix. 5.

[4] See lists of apostles, also MARK xiii. 3 ; JOHN xii. 22 ; *cf.* Orig. ap. Eus.,
H. E., iii. 1.   M. R. James in *Hastings' D. B.*, i. 92.

[5] Where Andrew's white stone chair was long pointed out (*Epiph. Monachus*,
ed. Dressel, p. 47 ff.).   Hort reminds us (*Comm. on I. Peter*), that Christianity
was very strong in Pontus—*cf.* Pliny's letter to Trajan—but that it probably
came by sea from Asian coasts, or Rome, not from the south.

[6] *Acta Andreæ* (Tischendorf), p. 105.

[7] " Eadem nocte revelatum andreæ ex apostolis ut recogniscentibus cunctis
johannis suo nomine cuncta discriberet " (Gwatkin, *Selections from Early
Christian Writers*, p. 84).

[8] Jos., *Ant.*, xx. 7, 3.   In these speculations we must remember that the
Pontic sea-board was full of Christians at an early date, while Neo-Cæsarea
had seventeen Christians only in the time of Gregory Thaumaturgus (Greg.
Nyss., *Vita Thaum*, Migne, *P. G.*, xlvi. 954).

quite probable. The reference in Eusebius,[1] according to which he was a missionary to the *Indians*, is probably to be explained by a confusion with the Sindians, a tribe to the north-east of the Euxine, over which the kings of the house of Polemon held sway. If Bartholomew is to be identified with Nathanael, the prominent position of the latter in the fourth Gospel might lead us to surmise that Bartholomew, like Andrew, was associated with the province of Asia in his later years.

Philip, in spite of a possible confusion with his namesake Philip the Evangelist, may be located with fair certainty in the province of Asia. Polycrates, Bishop of Ephesus, *c.* 180 A.D., categorically asserts this. Two aged virgin daughters long survived him in Hierapolis.[2]

Thomas is the apostle of Parthia,[3] also of India.[4] India here seems to mean Aria, Drangiana, and Arachosia, over which the Gundaphorus of the Gnostic Acts of Thomas reigned in the first half of the first century A.D. There is every likelihood of the Christian propaganda having reached Parthia at an early period, for Edessa was under Parthian suzerainty,[5] and there were "innumerable Jews"[6] in the regions round that city. Professor Burkitt, however, cannot find any evidence for Christianity in Edessa before the first half of the second century.[7] The legendary labours of the other apostles may be omitted from this survey, as there is nothing certain to be said about them. The above, however, is enough to show an imposing array of evangelistic work, dwarfed perhaps by the superhuman activities of Paul, but in itself a great and permanent contribution to the expansion of the Church.

It is frequently asserted that the idea of an apostolic

---

[1] Eus., *H. E.*, v. 10.

[2] Eus., *H. E.*, iii. 31, 39, v. 17, 24 ; Clem. Al., *Strom.*, iii. 6. See Lightfoot, *Colossians*, p. 45, and M'Giffert on the passages of Eusebius.

[3] Orig. ap. Eus., *H. E.*, iii. 1 ; *Clem. Recog.*, ix. 29.

[4] *Acta Thomæ* (Tischendorf), p. 190 ff. ; *cf.* Rendel Harris, *The Dioscuri*, p. 20.

[5] Burkitt, *Early Eastern Christianity*, p. 8.

[6] Jos., *Ant.*, xi. 5, 2 ; *cf.* ACTS ii. 9, "Parthians, Medes, Elamites."

[7] Burkitt, *op. cit.*, p. 34 ; *cf.* The Doctrine of Addai (in Cureton, *op. cit.*, p. 6 ff.).

college entrusted with rule over the Church is a purely dogmatic invention of the early Christian writers. Thus Dr. M'Giffert, in his *History of Christianity in the Apostolic Age*, says: "They held no official position in the Church at Jerusalem, and were not regarded as in any way entrusted with its government or empowered to exercise authority within it . . . the notion is evidently purely dogmatic."[1] Now it is clear that the apostolate was wider than the twelve,[2] also that the logic of events caused the idea of the college to be given up. With the death of individual members the vacancies were not filled up.[3]

But to deny the primacy of the twelve in these early days at Jerusalem is to go behind the documents to an extent quite unwarranted. Acts vi. 2 ; viii. 1, 14 ; xi. 1 are clear proofs that the twelve occupied a unique position. As we have seen above, Luke exhibits a wonderful fidelity to early conditions and modes of thought in the opening chapters of Acts, and he had access to excellent sources of information. What ground is there for supposing that in this instance he departs from his usual custom? The words attributed to our Lord in Matt. xix. 28 are evidence from an early date of the importance attached to the number twelve, as typifying the ideal unity of Israel—"Ye shall sit on twelve thrones, judging the twelve tribes of Israel." It is true that a modern man, in starting a new sect, would be unlikely to form a college of twelve as the first custodians of its traditions, but would be more likely to invite the whole body of adherents to elect a committee ; this, however, is no argument as applied to the first century.

The twelve were chosen not primarily because of their eloquence or brilliant gifts, but to fulfil the special function of witnesses. It was necessary to have been a witness of the events from the time of the Baptist onwards, and especially to be able to testify of the Resurrection from personal experience.[4] Even the brilliant achievements of Paul could

---

[1] P. 45, 47 ; *cf.* Harnack, *History of Dogma*, i. 161.

[2] Paul and Barnabas, *e.g*, were apostles, and even apparently Andronicus and Junias (Rom. xvi. 7). *Cf.* the apostles in the *Didache*.

[3] After the one instance of Matthias.   [4] Acts i. 21 f.

not rob the obscurest member of the twelve of the peculiar
glory of his position. The Church was founded in the last
resort on the impression made by Jesus on the minds of
His immediate followers, and primarily on those of the
twelve. To deny all this, to claim that the earliest Church
was a pure democracy without any official leaders, is at least
as much due to dogmatic prepossessions as is the old Church
tradition, according to which the twelve composed the
Apostles' Creed by each contributing a clause.

It is important, however, not to overstate the case. The
Church grew so rapidly in all directions that new conditions
arose within a very few years, and in the nature of things
the position of the twelve became relatively, if not absolutely, less important. The great mission to the Gentiles
overshadowed all else, and the apostolate of Paul, the validity
of which had been doubted at first, was generally recognised.
The vigorous young Church of Antioch was led by the Spirit
to ordain Barnabas and Paul for their missionary journey,
and these two apostles proceeded to ordain elders in every
Church.[1] Laying-on of hands, then, was no longer confined to the twelve, as it seems to have been at first.
The very fact that Luke gives us no clear or consistent
account of the important rite of ordination, and that the
advocates of so many different theories of the Christian
Ministry have appealed to his words, is good evidence that
he is not over-estimating the status of the twelve in the
earliest stage at Jerusalem.

IV.—LATER WORK OF ST. PETER

Let us now return to Peter whom we left, in all probability, labouring at Antioch. We find him next at Rome.
For years he had been engaged in missionary labours and
journeys in company with his wife, who seems to have been
a heroine of the primitive Church.[2] The circumstances that
led him to the Metropolis of the Empire are unknown.

[1] ACTS xiii. 3, xiv. 23.
[2] Clem. Al., *Strom.*, iii. 6, vii. 11 ; Eus., *H. E.*, iii. 30. Why should she
not be referred to in 1 PETER v. 13 ; *cf.* 1 COR. ix. 5.

Perhaps he too, as well as Paul, had felt an overpowering longing that prompted him to say, "I must see Rome." If the Gospel of the circumcision had been entrusted to him, there could be no place more suitable for his activities than Rome, which was one of the largest centres of the Jewish dispersion.[1] Rome had never been, strictly speaking, a Pauline Church. It was a spontaneous growth, springing, so it seems, from the faith of Christians who had come from the East to the imperial city. Among them a not unimportant section would be formed by Jews who had come into contact with Christianity on their pilgrimages to Jerusalem. To such Peter would speak with an authority fully equal to that of Paul.

It is clear that Peter left his mark on the Roman Church, as the legend of the twenty-five years' episcopate would seem to indicate.[2] The patient labour of archæologists has collected a good deal of cumulative evidence[3] of late years, showing how early and wide-spread was the tradition of Peter's martyrdom at Rome. Another important piece of evidence is the close connection between Rome and Mark's Gospel,[4] which has generally been held to represent the witness of Peter. In fact, with the evidence we now possess nothing but the distorting influence of anti-Romanist polemic, conscious or sub-conscious, could lead a student to reject the sojourn of Peter at Rome and his influence upon the Roman Church. "Babylon" in 1 Pet. v. 13 is definitely seen to be Rome, and the other suggested interpretations are obsolete.[5]

The First Epistle of Peter must now claim our attention. The limitations of an essay, and the necessity of confining it to manageable proportions, limit us to this writing, though

---

[1] *Cf.* Acts ii. 10.

[2] See Clem., Rom. v., associating Peter and Paul in suffering, also Iren., iii. 1 ; Ign., Rom. iv. ; Dion. Cor. ap. Eus., *H. E.*, ii. 25 ; *cf.* Lightfoot, *Clem.* ii. 48 ff. Chase in *Hastings' D. B.*, iii. 769 ff., 777. Puller, *Primitive Saints and the See of Rome*. Fouard, *St. Peter*.

[3] Summarised by Chase in his invaluable article.

[4] Papias ap. Eus., *H. E.*, iii. 39 ; Iren., iii. 1 ; Canon Mur. ; Clem. ap. Eus., *H. E.*, vi. 14 ; Eus., ii. 15, vi. 25.

[5] There is no tradition of Peter's visit to the real Babylon, nor evidence of the existence of a church there in early times.

there is much that bears on the subject in the Second Epistle, and the pseudonymous Petrine literature. It must be sufficient to say in passing that the anxiety felt by later writers to use the name of the great apostle is indisputable proof of the supremacy of his authority in the sub-apostolic Church. The First Epistle is a very important document, if it really represents the apostle's work, which there is little reason to doubt, as there is strong evidence in favour of its authenticity. Dr. Chase sums up his exhaustive discussion of the problem as follows: "The only natural interpretation of the facts—the early and wide influence of the epistle on the one hand, on the other the consistent and unwavering attribution of it to St. Peter on the part of all writers from Irenæus' time onward—is that from the first it was regarded as the work of that apostle." [1] The exact part played by Silvanus [2] in its composition is a vexed question. Those who uphold the genuineness of the Second Epistle are compelled to attach great importance to his part in the production of the First; only thus can they reconcile the divergences in style between the two epistles, and claim the second as the work of the apostle. They would assert that the expression of the First Epistle is entirely the work of Silvanus though the ideas are Peter's. This is very likely true, but it will be remembered that the case against the authenticity of 2 Peter rests on many more grounds than its dissimilarity in style to 1 Peter. It may be thought, however, that the external testimony is insufficient to substantiate the authenticity of 1 Peter, in view of the strong internal improbability of its apostolic authorship. For instance, the allusions to persecutions have been held by many to demand a date within the reigns of Vespasian or Domitian. Professor Ramsay argues strongly for this later date, and is even ready to postpone the death of the apostle to the same period. [3] His arguments have not won general acceptance, and the results of recent research would seem to show that the references of this epistle are not inconsistent with the little that is really known on the subject of the

[1] *Hastings' D. B.*, i. 781b.   [2] διὰ Σιλουανοῦ ἔγραψα.   1 PETER v. 12.
[3] *Church in R. E.*, (5) pp. 279–295.

Neronic persecution.[1] A weightier objection is the *a priori* impression felt by many scholars, that a Galilean fisherman is unlikely to have composed such a pastoral.

We have tried to meet this difficulty by laying stress on the training that Peter must have received for his life-work, and drawing attention to Silvanus' share in the epistle. May not also the thought of *inspiration* be introduced in this connection without incurring the reproach of "uncritical conservatism"? There are times in the world's history when men are swept along by the current of a great movement, and are able to achieve far more than their natural abilities would lead us to expect. The apostolic age was one of these great creative epochs, and we must be prepared to find the actors in it at the very top of their powers, or even at times, surpassing their own best achievements. The phenomenon may be described as an uprush of the subliminal consciousness, on which forces hitherto unsuspected have been working, or, in traditional language, as an inspiration of the Holy Ghost. In either case it is a fact to be reckoned with.

It is often said[2] that the First Epistle is thoroughly Pauline, and that the writer was saturated with Pauline phraseology and doctrine, and especially that he borrows freely from Romans and Ephesians. In reply to this it may be urged[3] that the resemblances are superficial and can easily be accounted for by the part played by Silvanus, a follower of Paul. The draughtsman of the epistle had often heard Paul preach, and in compiling the practical exhortations he fell naturally into the groove traced for him by his former companion. Besides, must not something be allowed for the common "pulpit formulæ" of the time? Original as Paul was, he did not originate everything. When he was converted he became a member of a Church which already throbbed with abounding life. Original men are generally receptive as well as original.

[1] See Moffatt, *Intr.*, pp. 323–327, and literature cited therein.

[2] See Jülicher, *Introduction to New Testament*. Harnack, *Chronol.* p. 451 ff.

[3] As by Bigg in his Commentary on 1 PETER, to which the following paragraphs are largely indebted.

They learn what other men have to teach, and, after reflection on what they have learned, they see the short-
comings of current doctrine and strike out a line of their
own. During the seven or more years of quiet preparation at Tarsus and elsewhere Paul must have absorbed
much. So that the close resemblances of certain sections
of 1 Peter to Romans and Ephesians [1] does not necessitate
the conclusion that Peter consciously borrowed from Paul,
though it will seem to many the most probable explanation.

In matters of deeper importance Peter is singularly independent. Nowhere does he refer to the great Pauline
antitheses of Law and Gospel, Spirit and Flesh, Faith and
Works. He has no doctrine of inherited sin, or imputed
merits; for him ἁμαρτία is concrete.[2] In the characteristic
Pauline theology the world is essentially dualistic and dis-
continuous. Is it fanciful to see in this a reflection of
Paul's experience—a persecutor of the Church turned into
a saint by the Finger of God? Even though his conversion
involved no passing from indifference or immorality, yet
the revulsion was tremendous, and involved an entire re-
versal of his former attitude. Paul repeatedly insists on
the difference between the two periods of his life; and
though he says in Acts xxiii. 6, "I am a Pharisee," he may
in this case only be referring to the particular doctrine of
the Resurrection.[3]

Peter's experience, on the other hand, was essentially
continuous. Unlike Paul, who had been brought up in the
atmosphere of cities and schools, Peter as a fisherman had
been in contact from boyhood with the influences of Nature.
The countryman's mind develops more slowly than that
of the townsman, but truths once grasped are held more
tenaciously. In company with other Galileans he had looked
for the coming of the Kingdom, and had eagerly welcomed
the preaching of the Baptist. He became a disciple of John,
from whose side he had passed to become a pupil in the

---

[1] 1 PETER ii. 13 ff. = ROM. xiii. 1–7 is one of the most striking.

[2] Except perhaps in iv. 1.

[3] *Cf.* Harnack, *Neue Untersuchungen*, p. 61 : "Sofern der Apostel an die
Auferstehung der Toten glaubte, war er noch immer ein Pharisäer ja er und
seine jüdischen Glaubesgenossen waren allein die rechten Pharisäer '

School of Jesus. Day by day during these years new visions
of God unfolded themselves. Left in charge of the Christian
Community at Jerusalem, his mind grew with the growth
of the Church. First came the greater consideration due
to Greek-speaking Jews, then the admission of Samaritans,
then of Gentiles—step by step he was led to understand the
possibilities of the Gospel. After such a training his mental
outlook was bound to differ considerably from Paul's. And
surely his experience was nearer to that of the normal
Christian, of which the parable of the seed growing secretly
is the best picture.[1]

Dr. Bigg calls him essentially a Disciplinarian, as opposed
to Paul the Mystic. As a Disciplinarian his leading ideas
are Grace considered as an external gift,[2] Law,[3] and Godly
Fear.[4] He dwells on God as an external object of worship
and trust, rather than as a Spirit within him, to be apprehended by faith. Paul had never known Christ in the
flesh, but Peter looked back to wonderful times spent in
His company on earth; he had not the mystic temperament
of John, and, like a plain man, looked forward to a renewal
of the old companionship when Christ returned once more.
So in his thoughts the future outweighs the present.[5]

Again, Peter, though a devout son of the law, had never
expected it to do so much for him as had Paul, so that
when he came to comprehend the meaning of the Gospel,
the reaction from legalism was not so acute. For him, as
for James, Christianity is a New Law,[6] transfigured and
brought to fulfilment, but still essentially a law. In har-
mony with this he does not assume spiritual maturity in

---

[1] *Cf.* Inge, *Truth and Falsehood in Religion*, p. 81: "I do not think the
'instantaneous' experience is the most wholesome or normal."

[2] 1 Peter i. 10, 13; iii. 7; iv. 10; v. 5.

[3] 1 Peter ii. 12–17; iv. 15.

[4] 1 Peter i. 13, 17; ii. 18; iii. 2, 15.

[5] *Cf.* especially i. 7, 9, 13; v. 4. There are many such passages in the
Pauline epistles, but the point is the *absence* in Peter of the characteristic
Pauline doctrine of the mystic indwelling of Christ.

[6] The word νόμος does not occur in 1 Peter, but the affinities with the
epistle of James, especially in 1 Peter i. 6 ff., 23; ii. 1, 11; v. 6, 9; and
generally the emphasis laid on fear, probation, and subordination to authority
justify this statement.

his readers. They are still *babes* to be fed with milk, while for Paul babes are formalists, to be blamed for their stagnation.[1] Christians for him are in constant need of direction, so Christ is the Shepherd and Overseer of souls, titles never applied to Him by Paul. Again, the advice to married couples given in 1 Pet. iii. 1–7 is entirely based on practical grounds, whereas, according to Eph. v. 22–33, the highest Pauline teaching on the subject, the duties of husbands and wives, spring ultimately from the mystical relation of Christ to the Church.

In conclusion, the entire absence of Christian prophecy from the pages of 1 Peter is most significant. Paul is essentially a prophet, Peter as essentially a pastor. It would be idle to ask which is the better type. Wisdom is justified of all her children. But we may at least inquire which would have appeared more valuable to the average contemporary Christian. Can we doubt that Peter during his lifetime would have occupied a position of unassailable pre-eminence? There is no sign of rebellion against his authority, whereas Paul's position, we gather from his epistles, was being continually challenged. His opponents have left no record of their case, and they must not be judged entirely by what Paul wrote in the heat of the struggle; in some instances no doubt they acted with perfect conscientiousness and good faith.[2]

Or, again, the two preached the same Gospel, but with a difference of emphasis. Which presentment would seem at the time more correct and better representative of the teaching of Jesus? Would not the apostle who had been one of the chosen three be considered a more trustworthy guide? Besides, written accounts of the words of Jesus were already circulating in the Church.[3] If the messages of the two great apostles were compared with them, it would be noticed that, wherever Peter diverges from Paul, he follows

---

[1] 1 PETER ii. 2 ; 1 COR. iii. 2 ; *cf.* HEB. v. 12.

[2] *E.g.* in PHIL. i. 16 we can hardly accept the justice of the apostle's verdict.

[3] LUKE i. 1. Recent criticism puts Q very early, considerably earlier than MARK. See Streeter in *Studies in the Synoptic Problem*, p. 210 ff., and Harnack's recent works.

Christ as represented in the Synoptic Gospels. According to the synoptists the teaching of Jesus is that Christianity supplements the Law, fulfilling and enriching it,[1] and this is the teaching of 1 Peter. Whereas Paul could see the good side of the Law,[2] but he was a man who as a rule saw only one side at a time, and his dominant thought is certainly that legalism is opposed to grace. It would seem then that he overstates the antithesis between Judaism and Christianity. There is an antithesis, as evident in the words of Christ as elsewhere, yet in Paul the discontinuity is unduly marked ; the new does not grow out of the old in any normal and harmonious way.

Once more, the teaching of Peter that Christians are waiting for the coming of the Chief Shepherd differs in emphasis from Paul's mystical conception of Christ dwelling in the believer. But in the parables of Jesus we constantly have the thought of an absent Lord away on a journey, to whose return his servants must look forward. Once more Peter is nearer the Synoptic Gospels. It is true Paul has the other thought,[3] but the mystical conception is more characteristic. He would probably have approved of all the Petrine teaching, but the difference in tone between the two might be sufficient to cause misconception. Our point, it should be noted, is not that Paul misrepresented Christ, but that Peter's main ideas were nearer to the side of His teaching that is represented in the Synoptic Gospels. It has been argued with ingenuity that "the Gospel" is to be looked for primarily in the Pauline epistles, rather than in the Gospels, for Christ came not to preach the Gospel, but that there might be a Gospel to preach. This is hardly convincing. We want to get back to the sources of Christianity, and Peter, with his fidelity to his memories of Christ,[4] and his lack

[1] MATT. v. 17, 18 ; xv. 6 ; xxiii. 23 ; LUKE xvi. 17 ; xxiv. 44. The conception is most marked in MATTHEW. Streeter and Bartlet, *op. cit.*, pp. 222, 362, would object that MATTHEW is in this respect a "secondary and rabbinising" version.

[2] ROM. vii. 12, 14 ; GAL. iii. 21, 24. See Ramsay, *Pauline Studies*, p. 34.

[3] ROM. xiii. 11, 12 ; 1 COR. xi. 26 ; COL. iii. 4 ; PHIL. i. 10 ; ii. 16 ; 1 THESS. iv. 15 ff. ; 1 TIM. vi. 14 ; 2 TIM. i. 12 ; TIT. ii. 13.

[4] Peter is the rock, James and John the impulsive Sons of Thunder. If not loved so much as John, Peter is trusted more. LUKE xxii. 32.

of intellectual originality, may well be a more valuable *witness* than Paul with his creative genius. And so to-day the Petrine Gospel, Mark, has become to many perhaps the most precious book of the New Testament.[1]

We may sum up by saying that, in the mind of the average member of the Church, for instance, in the province of Asia, Peter would have occupied a more prominent position than Paul, and those who received 1 Peter would consider it more authoritative than Ephesians. It may be remarked incidentally that they would understand it better.[2]

V.—SUBSEQUENT INFLUENCE OF PETRINE CHRISTIANITY

Whereas Paulinism is all-important in the apostolic literature as it has come down to posterity, it played little part in the development of sub-apostolic Christianity. The pathetic remark of the author of 2 Peter[3] about the unintelligibility of Paul's letters gave expression to the thoughts of the average believer. The name of Paul was held in the utmost reverence. He was "The Apostle," his martyrdom had finally silenced all controversy,[4] but the Church was expanding on different lines. By the reign of Domitian[5] there was little trace of his influence in the province of Asia. At Rome, which witnessed the closing scenes of his life and his martyrdom, the Church grew on non-Pauline lines. Historians have often been attracted by the moral grandeur of the Roman Church in ante-Nicene times. Its catholic sympathies, its wise toleration, and its power of preserving the doctrinal balance gave it a unique position. It is far the best representative of the second and third century Catholic Church. But it is the spirit of Peter that survives,

---

[1] Streeter is very bold when he asks, "Who does not feel that St. Mark, the oldest of the Gospels we still have, is the one we could best spare?" *op. cit.*, p. 226).

[2] If the Pastoral epistles are genuine, they present an aspect of Paulinism considerably more akin to 1 PETER in many respects than the four great epistles.

[3] 2 PETER iii. 16.

[4] This is true of the Church as a whole, though in certain circles, as the Clementine literature testifies, a different spirit prevailed.

[5] We accept this date for the Apocalypse.

the note of a wise and moderate discipline. The First Epistle of Clement and the Shepherd of Hermas come from the pens of men who are evidently most worthy and pious Christians, but just a trifle dull. They have quite failed to catch the spirit of the Epistle to the Romans, which must, one would think, have been well known in their Church. Was the sub-apostolic Church making a grand mistake in thus following the lead of Peter rather than of Paul? Surely not. The course of development seems to have been inevitable. In the matter of government, for instance, we cannot deduce from the New Testament that Paul's methods were altogether successful. He gave too much liberty to the young communities, with the result that liberty degenerated into license, and personal visits were necessary to put things straight. Neither Paul's principle of the liberty of the Spirit, nor his short way with offenders, was adopted by the Roman Church. The keynote of sub-apostolic Christianity is the gradual suppression of prophecy, with a number of sporadic revolts against its disappearance. In view of our personal needs we may feel strongly prejudiced against such a development, but "Is the religion of the Spirit a working religion for mankind?"[1] Whether it is so now is another question, but Paulinism was certainly too strong meat for the average Christian of these early days. There was no conscious policy, yet unconsciously these early builders of the City of God were building wiser than they knew. They were building on Peter the rock, as Christ had ordered. The Architect of the City of God ordained this foundation with full insight into the needs of humanity. Mystics were in a minority, and always will be; besides, they can take care of themselves. The Church must consider the average Christian majority rather than the elect few.

The body of Pauline doctrine remained with the Church, and only needed a master-spirit to inspire it with life. With Augustine it became a living force once more. Yet perhaps even he was born out of due time; his influence has been

---

[1] The title of an article by Dom. C. Butler in the *Hibbert Journal*, April 1906; *cf.* Sabatier, *The Religions of Authority and the Religion of th Spirit.* There is of course no necessary antinomy of Law and Spirit.

mixed, and productive of many strange results in the
Western Church. Have not the Once-Born after all a
truer vision than the Twice-Born? The Twice-Born lean
instinctively to dualism, the Once-Born to unity, and unity
is the deeper truth.[1]

The foundations were duly laid, and what had been the
peculiar glory of the Catholic Church became its special
weakness. Discipline and order, in themselves indispensable
as a foundation, were exaggerated out of all proportion.
Discipline tamed the Northern Conquerors, but itself grew
rigid and corrupt. The outburst of liberty seen in Arnold
of Brescia, Francis of Assisi, and the German mystics was
a presage of the greater movement of the Reformation,
when the Northern nations broke their bands. In the
foregoing pages I have tried to appreciate the position
and influence of Peter in the Apostolic Church at its true
value. In thus trying to do justice to the subject of one's
essay, it is difficult to avoid the impression of holding a
brief for him. Few would doubt, however, that the liberty
of prophesying secured by the Reformation was as necessary
as it was inevitable. The nations had been kept in bands
so long, so long in fact that the idea of liberty was strange
to them and difficult of comprehension, and Protestantism
showed itself only too willing to return to the weak and
beggarly elements of a barren scholasticism. Much has
happened since the seventeenth century, and Protestant
scholasticism has ceased to be a living force. The claims
of individualism in the sphere of religion are fully recognised
nowadays, and Protestants at least may learn valuable lessons
from a study of Petrine Christianity.

In conclusion, Paul and John were the two great master-
builders of New Testament theology, but Peter was the
foundation upon which they built. Historically speaking,
their ideas could not come to fruition until this firm founda-

---

[1] In a preceding paragraph I have traced the essential unity of Peter's
spiritual experience, which I do not consider to have been impaired by his
denial in the palace of the high priest. Terms such as Once-Born or Twice-Born
would be incongruous if applied to Christ. It seems clear, however, that
there was in His spiritual experience nothing corresponding to the crisis in
Paul's life.

O

tion had been laid. Moreover, in a sense Peter was m
than Peter. He stands for the average Christian,
multitude of nameless men and women who laboured fa
fully in those early days when the foundations were be
laid. And if Peter was the Rock, so too in a sense t
Rock was Christ, for it was on Peter's testimony to Ch
his fidelity to his early memories of Christ, his witnes
Christ's life, words, death, and resurrection, not on P
himself, that the Church was built.

ESSAY VII

THE THEOLOGY OF ST. PAUL

BY

G. B. REDMAN, B.A.

*Formerly Scholar of the College and Naden
Divinity Student of St. John's*

ANALYSIS

1. Early years and training.

2. Conversion and what it meant.

3. His Christology—(a) As seen in 1 Thessalonians, (b) as developed later
   (i) The Epistles of the Second Missionary Journey ; Christ and the Spirit
   —(ii) The Epistles of the Captivity.
   The whole based on St. Paul's own experience of Christ.

4. Soteriology—The work of Christ. Faith, justification, liberty. The place
   of the Law and St. Paul's relation to Judaism. Sin, deliverance, and
   reconciliation.
   All based on the death of Christ.

5. The Christian Life—The new life following on death with Christ to sin—
   in Christ—Flesh and Spirit. The spiritual life essentially ethical.

6. The Church—Growth of the idea in the primitive community. St. Paul's
   teaching—the building, the body, and the bride—(a) As seen in the
   Epistles of the Third Missionary Journey, " The churches "—(b) In the
   Epistles of the Captivity, " The Church."

7. Eschatology—Change of emphasis and perhaps of expression between
   1 Thessalonians and Ephesians. Permanence of essential idea.

THE THEOLOGY OF ST. PAUL

No man putteth new wine into old wine-skins : else the ine will burst the skins, and the wine perisheth, and the :ins : but they put new wine into fresh wine-skins." [1]

So the Lord had clearly defined the relation of His aching to the old religion. But the apostles were slow understand their Master's mind. They seemed for some me to imagine that the Christian Society was a special :otherhood within the Jewish Church, united in their elief in Him Whom God had glorified and proved to be the essiah,[2] and by their hope of His return; but they did not em capable of realising that Christianity could exist apart om Judaism. Thus for the world-wide expansion of the reaching of the new faith a special instrument was needed, id St. Paul was raised up for the great work of freeing hristianity from the fetters of the Law without breaking s continuity with God's earlier revelation. He was, more-ver, the great constructive thinker by whom the meaning id content of the new revelation were first clearly grasped id expounded. In character and training he was admir-ɔly fitted for his task, being by birth a Jew of Tarsus, of ιe Dispersion, yet strictly brought up in his religion, and ιerefore probably not allowed to mingle much in the life id activity of that great intellectual and commercial centre, ιough it cannot have failed to exercise an attraction over is mind.[3] He was, further, a free-born Roman citizen,

[1] ST. MARK ii. 22. The quotations throughout are taken from the Revised ersion.

[2] ACTS ii. 36.

[3] Mr. H. S. Chamberlain in *The Foundations of the Nineteenth Century*, .ap. vii. (Eng. trans., vol. ii. p. 57 f.), sees so much of the Hellene in St. .ul that he is compelled to infer that his mother was a Greek proselyte.

enjoying privileges which he did not shrink from claimin on occasions, though it is noteworthy that he never allud to this in his epistles.   To it, however, is no doubt large due the apostle's great vision of a Church coterminous wit the Empire.

He was educated as a Rabbi in the centre of Judais under the most famous teacher of his time.   All his mor earnestness and fiery ardour were given up to the servi of his national religion, all his keen mental faculties devote to the study of the Scriptures.   He was a Pharisee—his ze for God unmixed with Sadducean worldly ambition, his fait not weakened by Sadducean scepticism.   A Pharisee—ther fore he looked for the salvation of Israel in the Messia Recent research has somewhat changed our views on Jewis Messianic hopes.[1]   The warrior king who was to deliver h people from the Romans was not the universal, perhaps n even the general ideal.   St. Paul, we may be sure, with a the best Pharisees of his time, was looking for a Messia to set wrong things right.   This was his fundamental cor ception—to vindicate God's righteousness, which seeme liable to be called in question, to set up a judgement fro which some would pass to death, some—and they the r deemed—receive life, a life under new conditions, a life i the glory of God, free from wars and from the tyranny oppressors, in which all the inequalities of the present worl would be redressed.

With these ideals he came across a sect preaching crucified Messiah.[2]   Such a thought was impossible; it w treachery not only to the nation but to God.   He thre himself into the struggle against such teaching, and, to h angry astonishment, was unable to refute it.   Moreover, h opponents asserted that their Messiah had risen again, an quoted the Scriptures to support their statement.   Unable t overthrow them in argument, he took his share in the attemp to silence them by force.   He became the prime mover in

[1] *Cf.* J. H. A. Hart, *The Hope of Catholic Judaism*, especially chap. ii.
[2] It is perhaps only fair to say that this paragraph was written before I ha seen Professor Percy Gardner's new book on *The Religious Experience of St. Pau* otherwise it might seem merely a summary of his chapter on the subject.

violent persecution. Yet while he opposed he was attracted; he fought the attraction and persecuted yet more fiercely till —the vision. He saw the Lord.

It meant for him first of all that his whole life hitherto had been on a false basis; his opponents were right and he was wrong; and recognising this he surrendered himself wholly to his new Master. With that surrender came a new life, first realised and thought out perhaps in Arabia. Messiah had come, Messiah claimed him, and, to his life-long amazement, required his service.[1]

That meant that he must think out his position from this new standpoint—a long process, but no doubt it began somewhat in this way.[2] The life, redemption, blessings of the Messianic Kingdom, which he had been trying to win by strict obedience to the Law, had been won for him by the Messiah. That to which he had been looking forward as an aspiration in the future he now realised might be his immediate possession; and the epistles show how he grew into the practical experience of this truth.[3]

How soon[4] he grasped it all we cannot say. We read of his early activity at Damascus and Jerusalem,[5] showing that re-interpretation of Scripture was with him, as with the other apostles, one of the first and most important steps. There followed a further period of comparative leisure at Tarsus, then pastoral work at Antioch, and missionary journeys to the unevangelised world.

For our knowledge of his thought and teaching we are dependent on two main sources—his evangelistic sermons,[6] as reported in the Acts, and his own epistles. In both the

---

[1] EPH. iii. 8.

[2] For this thought, as for much else in the essay, I am indebted to the Rev. C. A. Anderson Scott.

[3] The blessings of the Messianic Kingdom may be summed up as—(1) No condemnation at the judgement; (2) the destiny resulting, life; and (3) the conditions of life, peace with God. *Cf.* ROM. viii. 1; GAL. ii. 20, ROM. vi. 11; ROM. v. 1, GAL. v. 22, &c., and the constant salutation.

[4] The difficulty is that after fifteen years of Christian life, apparently without much originality of thought, a rapid development seems to take place during ten years of his later life.   [5] ACTS ix. 20, 22, 28.

[6] For the general trustworthiness of the sermons in the Acts see Harnack, *Acts of the Apostles* (Eng. trans.), p. 130. For a rather less favourable view, Professor Gardner in the *Cam. Bibl. Essays*, p. 380 f.

supreme subject is Jesus Christ. In his sermons to non-Christians, whether through Scripture when addressed to Jews, or through Natural Religion when addressed to Gentiles, all leads up to Christ; so much so that the general description of his sermons is " he preached Jesus." In his epistles the fact of Christ dominates the whole of life; Christ is the final revelation, at once the standard and the power. And this is not set down in the dispassionate phraseology of theological definition, but in the burning words of one who speaks out of a full heart of that which he has found Christ to be to him, summed up in the marvellous phrase, " To me to live is Christ." [1]

In the middle of strenuous and successful work come his first letters, not written as formal treatises, but the more valuable on that account as giving the thoughts that came naturally to his mind.

Probably the earliest Christian document extant is 1 Thessalonians; its Christology therefore has a unique interest and may well be made the starting-point for a consideration of St. Paul's system.

The following points may be noticed : [2]—

(1) The constant reference to " Christ Jesus," " the Lord Jesus," " the Lord Jesus Christ." The Master Himself is the subject of this as of all St. Paul's epistles.

(2) It is the historic Jesus of whom St. Paul speaks, Who lived a life that is the pattern for His servants (i. 6), and died a violent death at the hands of the Jews (ii. 15). Hence definite instruction about the life and death of our Lord must have formed a part of St. Paul's early addresses to his converts. [3]

(3) With the insistence on the human life goes the

---

[1] PHIL. i. 21.

[2] They are mainly borrowed from a little volume of brief studies on 1 THESSALONIANS by the Bishop of Durham, entitled *Light from the First Days*.

[3] Harnack, *Date of Acts and the Synoptic Gospels*, p. 116, well says that if we were dependent on the Acts alone for St. Luke's knowledge of the Gospel history, we should conclude that he had never heard of it, or at least thought it wholly unimportant. Is there any reason to consider St. Paul's interest or knowledge on this subject less than that of St. Luke ? Compare the minute description of the Lord's Supper, given incidentally, as a reminder, 1 COR. xi. 17 f.

extraordinary position given to this Person. Not only is He the Messiah, not only has He so completely fulfilled all Messianic hopes that "Messiah" has become His personal name, He is Κύριος, The LORD, as the regular natural thing; for He is more than man. If He died He rose again (i. 10), and His death and resurrection affect man's future state (v. 10). He is the Son of God (i. 10), who is linked with God the Father in salutation and prayer and as Lord of Providence (iii. 11). Not that Jesus in any sense takes the place of God; the Apostle's teaching on the Father is essentially that of His Master; but in dignity, nature, and function the crucified and risen Jesus is put on an equality with God.

(4) The characteristic Pauline phrase "in Christ" appears as a general description of the Christian life both of the individual (iv. 1, 16) and of the Church (ii. 14), and is used as the equivalent of "in our God" (ii. 2).

(5) His future coming is the object of Christian expectation; it will complete the Christian's salvation (i. 10, ii. 13, &c.).

Thus in Christ provision has been made for the past, the present, and the future; while the essential features of the doctrine of His humanity and His divinity are clearly expressed.

But St. Paul's was a receptive mind ever ready to assimilate new methods of expressing more clearly the truths which he was commissioned to preach. Thus in the second group of his epistles—those of the Third Missionary Journey—new terms are adopted. Possibly his stay in Ephesus, bringing him more into contact with the philosophical conceptions of the day, made him reconsider his Christology; not that he abandoned his former ideas, but recognised their need of enlargement and precision. Perhaps his intercourse with Apollos [1] brought him into touch with the Græco-Judæan speculation of Alexandria.[2] At any rate, in the two letters written during

---

[1] 1 COR. xvi. 12.

[2] For the connection of Apollos with the "wisdom" so highly prized in the Corinthian Church and its consequent derivation from Philo and Alexandria, see J. H. A. Hart, art. "Apollos" in *Journal of Theological Studies*, vol. vii. p. 22 f.

or immediately after the sojourn at Ephesus, we meet with phrases which bear close resemblance to Philo's language.[1]

Thus in 2 Cor. iv. 4 our Lord is called the "image of God," ἐικὼν θεοῦ, a term which Philo applies to the Logos. The thought is repeated two verses lower, but it is not till the Colossian Epistle that it finds full exposition. Philo's language would be familiar in Ephesus at the time, owing to the constant communication between that city and Alexandria, and St. Paul may well have adapted the current phrase for his own use, charging it with a richer significance; but in 1 Cor. xi. 7 he uses the identical expression applied to man in general, with a clear reference to Gen. i. 26–7,[2] so it may be really the Old Testament phrase that is in his mind here; the only man who was really in God's image was the Man Christ Jesus.

More striking, because unique in St. Paul, are the phrases in 1 Cor. xv., ὁ ἔσχατος ῎Αδαμ (ver. 45), ὁ δευτέρος ἄνθρωπος, ὁ ἐπουράνιος (verses 47–48), "the last Adam, . . . the second, the heavenly man." This is naturally explained as referring to the new[3] creation in Christ. Its immediate context is the doctrine of the Resurrection. St. Paul has been asked, "With what body are the dead raised?" The reply is, with a body which is a new creation. As all men were made according to the type of Adam, so the spiritual body of the risen Lord is the pattern which the new creation will follow. It is a "heavenly" body, for Christ is "in the heavens,"[4] and the new life is one in which death and corruption have no place. Christ is the "first-fruits of them that are asleep," just as in the Colossians He is "the first-born from among the dead," for His Resurrection is the pattern and pledge of that of all believers.

So once again it is the creation story to which St. Paul is referring, to the Old Testament that he turns for proof or

---

[1] For the resemblances and differences see Lightfoot's notes on COL. i. 15 in his commentary on that epistle.

[2] Philo used this text of the Logos as the "image" after which man was created.

[3] Obviously distinct from the new creation of the spiritual life which has taken place already in each believer, 2 COR. v. 17.

[4] EPH. vi. 9.

illustration, though it may well have been the current use of the phrases which turned his thoughts in that direction.[1]

In 1 Corinthians again there is much emphasis on the Person of Christ. Were there factions? A right conception of the Person of their Lord would allay them. Were there misunderstandings of the position and authority of their teachers? Consideration of the personal allegiance owed to the Christ would correct them. Were there problems of conduct? A true grasp of their relation to Him would solve all. And, again, as to the Thessalonians the life of Christ is held up as the supreme example.

This causes the position of Christ to the Church to be discussed—an important side of St. Paul's thought, but one that need only be mentioned here. In these epistles the Pre-existence of Christ is definitely stated; He is the Mediator in creation, the Revelation of the Father.[2] Thus the great doctrines elaborated in the later epistles are already clearly taught; the emphasis, however, lying not so much on the Divine Nature of Christ as on His work for and in the believer. In the latter it is noticeably difficult to draw a distinction between the work of Christ and that of the Holy Spirit, particularly when such a phrase as " dwelleth in " is employed; while there appears to be something like actual identification in the words, " Ye are . . . in the spirit, if so be that the *Spirit of God* dwelleth in you. But if any man hath not the *Spirit of Christ*, he is none of His. And if *Christ* is in you," &c.[3] Not that the two ideas are really identical, for St. Paul's conception of Christ was twofold: The Messiah, sitting at the right hand of power, ruling in heaven, directing the way of His servants; and Christ, as He is experienced, dwelling in the heart of the believer; and it is in this latter aspect that St. Paul speaks of Him as in function equivalent to the Spirit.[4]

---

[1] In one instance St. Paul seems to be specifically correcting Philo. Philo said first the heavenly man came, then the earthly; *cf.* 1 COR. xv. 46. Several cases of parallel thought or expression are quoted by Robertson and Plummer (*Intern. Crit. Comm.* 1 *Cor.*), none of any great importance.

[2] 1 COR. x. 4, GAL. iv. 4, 2 COR. viii. 9; 1 COR. viii. 6, 2 COR. iv. 6, &c.

[3] ROM. viii. 9–10.

[4] See Swete, *The Holy Spirit in the New Testament*, p. 300 f.

In his teaching on the Holy Spirit St. Paul is more
explicit than the early apostles, as may be seen in the opening
chapters of the Acts, where the Spirit is mainly an influence,
a supernatural force proceeding from God as in the Old
Testament. Closely, however, as St. Paul and St. John are
allied in emphasising this personality they represent Christ
as doing the work on earth which He accomplishes in the
believer. Thus both He and the Spirit are Paracletes, and
the presence of the Spirit is the Presence of Christ.[1]
"Another Paraclete . , . he abideth with you, and shall be
in you." [2]   But there, too, the presence of the Spirit means
the Presence of Christ—"I come unto you." But St. John
also gives the Spirit a work to the outside world not mentioned by St. Paul, and he seems to distinguish the Persons
still more explicitly—"*I* will send *Him*." [3] Not that this
distinction is wanting in St. Paul, as may be seen from
2 Cor. xiii. 14.[4]

The later epistles show development as expressing in
terms of the whole Church what St. Paul had before said
with reference to the individual (whether Church or person),
though points merely noticed before are now emphasised and
more clearly stated. But even here St. Paul does not set
himself to expound the doctrine of the Person of Christ, but
only dwells on one side or another incidentally to enforce his
message. The most explicit, dogmatic statement is to be
found in Philip. ii.[5] Here the points which deserve attention
are :—

(1) The fundamental conception—$\dot{\epsilon}\nu\ \mu o\rho\phi\hat{\eta}\ \theta\epsilon o\hat{v}\ \dot{v}\pi\acute{a}\rho\chi\omega\nu$
—the essential Deity of our Lord, which underlies all that
follows, before the Incarnation.

---

[1] In the other epistles this aspect is less clearly treated ; in Hebrews the
Spirit is not necessarily personal, save possibly in chap. x. 29, and in passages of
Scripture introduced by the formula "the Holy Ghost saith," nor in St. Jude ;
St. James has nothing to say on the subject (but *contra Swete, op. cit.,* p. 356) ;
St. Peter is thought to have been influenced by St. Paul, but even with him the
Spirit seems more often a Force than a Person.

[2] There appears to have been some confusion in the Early Church ; *e.g.* in
Hermas the "Son of God" seems to mean the Holy Spirit. See Duchesne, *Early
History of the Church,* pp. 170–71.   [3] St. John xiv. 17, 18 ; xvi. 7, 8.

[4] *Cf.* also 1 Cor. ii. 10, 11, where the Spirit of man is defined as "the spirit
of man which dwelleth in him," not so the Spirit of God.

[5] *Cf.* Lightfoot *ad loc.*

(2) His Incarnation was (*a*) In His mind the thinking little of His position of equality in circumstances with God (ἴσα εἶναι, not ἴσος εἶναι), and (*b*) In execution the assumption of the actual status of a slave (δοῦλος, a word not of nature but of relation).[1]

(3) Then after dwelling on the utter abasement of His human life, St. Paul describes His exaltation; that He has become the supreme object of man's adoration, "the Name which is above every name."

The position of this passage is instructive. The apostle is appealing for humility, and enforces it by the example of the Master.[2] It is just an indication of the place Christ held in his thought, how truly Christ was everything in his preaching. The same is brought out still more strongly in Colossians. Christ Himself is the solution of every problem of conduct, the answer to all questions of doctrine. The apostle hears of false teaching and false standards of life at Colossæ. Against superstitious angelolatry he sets the Person of Christ as the true object of worship; against mistaken and pernicious standards he sets the meaning of His work.

This refutation of the Colossian heresy leads to one of the sublimest passages in the New Testament on the glory of the pre-existent Son of God, written that St. Paul may let the Colossians see Whom they have disregarded by allowing the angels to take the place that is His alone.

Here, again, occurs the interesting question how far St. Paul was influenced by the Logos doctrine of Philo.[3] We have already indicated that his use of apparently Philonic language may possibly be derived from the Old Testament. We cannot examine the subject in detail; it may perhaps be enough to say that if St. Paul borrowed current phraseology to express his own conceptions, his doctrine rested on the Scriptures and on his personal experience of his Lord.

---

[1] *Cf.* "under law," GAL. iv. 4.

[2] It is noticeable that all specific references to the example of Christ are references to His condescension, *e.g.* 2 COR. viii. 9; ROM. xv. 3.

[3] Besides εἰκὼν θεοῦ again, πρωτότοκος has a close parallel in Philo's πρωτόγονος and πρεσβύτερος υἱός of the Logos as the archetypal idea of creation. See Lightfoot *ad loc.*

What Christ was to St. Paul above all was Saviour. On the road to Damascus he realised that Jesus was the Messiah and therefore the Deliverer—"Jesus who delivereth us from the wrath to come." This great truth seems to have been grasped by him with special clearness, and his exposition of it is his pre-eminent contribution to Christian thought. Not that his teaching differs from that of the other apostles. "Christ died for our sins" was part of the "tradition" which he had received; St. Peter and St. John use almost identical language on the subject. Yet their treatment is less full than his; moreover, there are thought to be traces that St. Peter was largely influenced by him, while St. John's real emphasis lies elsewhere. To St. Paul "Christ died for our sins" is the basis of his theology, "the Son of God loved me and gave Himself up for me" the foundation of his personal religion.

Nor are there any signs of altered views of this doctrine. It is clearly stated in 1 Thessalonians, dwelt on in Colossians, found in the Pastoral epistles.[1] But its fullest exposition is to be found in the four letters of the Third Missionary Journey. There are constant references to it in 1 and 2 Corinthians. St. Paul's own preaching, he reminded them, was of "Christ and Him Crucified," a fellow-Christian is "a brother for whose sake Christ died," his own sufferings for the Gospel he describes as "bearing about in the body the dying of Jesus." The question of the way of salvation had been forced into prominence through the activity of the Judaising Christians, who were insisting on the observance of the Jewish Law. These appear to have met with their greatest success in the cities of Galatia; it was to the Galatian Church that St. Paul sent his most vigorous reply. Hence it may be convenient for our purpose to begin with this letter, for though not a systematic treatise, it contains the main points in St. Paul's teaching on the subject, and just because of its spontaneity it reveals the thoughts that lay uppermost in his mind.

The general subject of the letter is Salvation through

---

[1] If the Pauline authorship of the Pastoral Epistles be rejected the argument still holds good ; St. Paul maintains this doctrine to the end.

Christ, a theme treated more systematically and at greater length in the Epistle to the Romans.[1] In the epistle before us the order is dictated by its polemic purpose; we may therefore rearrange the apostle's thoughts somewhat as follows:—

1. Salvation is the work of Christ for us (i. 4); that is the great outstanding fact. By that work He delivered us from this evil world (i. 4), He redeemed us from the curse brought by the Law (iii. 13), and freed us from bondage to the Law to make us sons of God (iv. 1–8). This He did by His death (i. 4), and that the death of the Cross (iii. 13). Moreover He died "for our sins" (i. 4), taking the curse of the Law upon Himself by His death on the Cross.

2. Wrought by Christ it is received by faith alone, defined as "faith in Jesus Christ"[2] (ii. 16). Works are valueless to obtain it; it is God's free gift (ii. 21). The meaning of faith is illustrated by the case of Abraham; not a mere intellectual assent, but taking God at His Word.[3] It is the faith of Abraham which is the type and model of the Christian's faith (iii. 7, 9).

3. This faith brings justification, which enables a man to stand as righteous in the sight of God. This the Law had failed to give; it offered it but on the impossible terms of keeping all its precepts (iii. 10–12); it was failure to keep the precepts that brought the "curse" from which Christ freed mankind. That is, the state to which St. Paul had hoped to attain in the Messianic age and after sufferings, was now a present reality, already obtained for him in this life by the sufferings of Christ—or, to put it in other words, he had already entered into the New Age.[4] The Jews had

---

[1] It is noticeable that neither σωτηρία nor the specially Pauline word ἀπολύτρωσις occurs in Galatians. Yet the idea is present all through the epistle, only looked at from a slightly different standpoint.

[2] Not put as a substitute for faith in God, but set side by side with it. See Rev. C. Anderson Scott in *Camb. Biblical Essays*, p. 356 f.

[3] It is striking that repentance is never mentioned in St. Paul's epistles in connexion with the way of salvation. It is only mentioned in practical cases, with the exception of ROM. ii. 4. Yet the speech to the Milesian elders (on which see *Camb. Biblical Essays*, pp. 401, 418) shows it was part of his teaching. The reason doubtless is to avoid giving the impression that repentance *brings* salvation.

[4] *Cf.* 2 COR. v. 17.

tried to obtain righteousness through the Law, but ha
failed, and some of them had come to see that faith i
Christ was their one hope, had turned to Him and obtaine
justification (ii. 16, iii. 24). They now saw that God ha
from of old appointed faith as the means of justificatio
(iii. 6, 11), and once more this justification was only to ł
obtained through Christ's death (ii. 21).

4. But this doctrine had a new and startling significanc
so new and so startling that St. Paul could only regard it ɛ
a direct revelation to him from his Master (i. 11, *cf.* Eph. i
1–9). If the Law is really of no avail for justification, if fait
in Christ is all, it means that the old privileged position ɛ
the Jew has gone. Justification is equally available for tł
Gentile; Jew and Gentile are on the same footing; tł
Gentile is no longer a dog, he is a brother (iii. 26, 28). Th
too Scripture had foretold (iii. 8, 14). But it involves alɛ
new consequences for the Jew. Salvation implies not onł
release from the curse of the broken Law, it means freedoɪ
from its shackles (iv. 3–5, 25, 31). So the aspect of salvatio
most emphasised is " our liberty which we have in Christ
(ii. 4, v. 1), liberty for Jew from bondage to the Law, libert
also for Gentile from bondage to observances to which ł
had been trusting as the Jew had trusted to the Lɛ
(iv. 8, 9); in a word, sonship for slavery.

Hence circumcision, the rite representing the oł
covenant, is valueless as a means of obtaining salvatic
(v. 6), a thing in itself wholly indifferent,[1] but one which,
made the ground of acceptance with God, may be positivel
harmful. On this the apostle uses strong language; thei
can be no compromise, no half measures; either Christ c
the Law, not both combined (v. 2–4).

At this point both in Galatians and Romans an insistei
question meets us—What then is the use of the Law ? I
not this minimising its value and function ? Against suc
an idea St. Paul protests.[2] In the Epistle to the Galatiar
he assigns to it a twofold function—(*a*) To reveal sin an

---

[1] Further expounded in 1 Cor. vii., where the whole subject of outwa
circumstances and the Christian life is broadly treated.

[2] Rom. iii. 31.

so show the need of a Saviour, to hold up a standard that men might see how far they had fallen short (iii. 21, 22), to make men realise that their own efforts were insufficient; and (*b*), on the other hand, to repress sin, and so prepare us for liberty in Christ as sons of God. This seems to be the meaning of "the Law hath been our tutor" (iii. 24, so Lightfoot *ad loc.*), and still more clearly of the simile of the heir (iv. 1–7). Hence the function of the Law is neither slight nor unworthy. But in Romans a further task is added which at first seems less attractive—namely, to incite desire for unlawful things by forbidding them, and so to increase sin.[1] This, however, in St. Paul's view does not seem a *purpose* of the Law as (*a*) and (*b*) above—else how could he call it "holy and righteous and good"?—but rather its effect as he found it in his own life; and there modern psychology will support him.[2] Yet with all this apparent depreciation of the Law, St. Paul really held it in high esteem. Its possession was the permanent glory of the Jewish race. St. Paul himself was proud of his Israelitish origin. We read in the Acts that he set great store by its feasts, and shaved his head for a vow,[3] while his passionate affection for his people and his belief in a great future for them in God's purposes is evident in every verse of Romans ix.–xi. Nor does he urge his Jewish converts to drop their Judaism. Circumcision was a divinely appointed state for some men; it was their duty to abide in it. He himself in preaching always went first to the synagogue. In fact his enemies could even accuse him of "preaching circumcision." It was only when it came to a question of the way of salvation or position in the Christian body that his opposition was aroused; it was against those who would make observance of the Law a condition of entering into full Christian privileges that his invectives were directed.[4]

But to St. Paul sin was not merely failure to keep the

[1] ROM. vii. 5–13.

[2] *E.g.* school-teachers are warned not to give orders in a negative form lest the prohibition of an act should suggest it.

[3] ACTS xviii. 18.

[4] For a discussion of "St. Paul and Judaism," see Harnack, *Date of the Acts and the Synoptic Gospels*, p. 40 f.

P

Law, mere imperfection; it was a power which held man enthralled, and that by his own fault.[1] The Gentile world was held in the grip of loathsome and degrading vices, springing from their rejection of the light which had been vouchsafed to them. Similarly the Jews were no better off for all their Law; it had not kept them undefiled. Jew and Gentile alike were not only guilty but helpless.

Further, it was a power that made enmity between man and God. Two problems are thus presented.

The solution of both is once more the death of Christ, which brings the soul ἀπολύτρωσις, emancipation,[2] from the bondage of sin, and καταλλαγή, reconciliation with God. And the constant insistence on it is due to the fact that St. Paul had himself experienced both. Romans vii. graphically describes the impotent struggle of the soul in bondage —a picture which must have been taken from life—ere he found in Christ crucified his emancipation, so that to the despairing cry, " O wretched man that I am! Who shall deliver me . . . " ? he could answer triumphantly, " I thank God through Jesus Christ our Lord." [3]

Again, the frequent references to enmity surely have their origin in the experience on the Damascus road, where St. Paul found he had been fighting against God; one thing alone could bring reconciliation—the Cross of Christ.[4]

So the Cross is to St. Paul his burden and his boast, the subject of his preaching and the constraining power of his life, for it meant the sacrifice of Love.

But the death of Christ is not merely a fact in history for St. Paul, it has its counterpart in his own life, for " I have been crucified with Christ." [5] Nor is this the unique experience of a man of special saintliness; all who were baptized into Christ Jesus were baptized into His death;[6] indeed, it is only because their faith unites believers with Christ in His death that they are justified,[7] for in Him all were crucified.[8]

---

[1] Rom. vi. 12, 16, 19.

[2] Dr. Armitage Robinson on Ephesians i. 14.   For the thought *cf.* St. Mark iii. 27, St. Luke iv. 18.

[3] I assume that the experience described is that of St. Paul before conversion *cf.* Sanday and Headlam, *ad loc*.   [4] Rom. v. 10.   [5] Gal. ii. 20.

[6] Rom. vi. 3.   [7] Rom. vii. 4 f.   [8] Rom. vi. 6, 11.

Again, as the Crucifixion was followed by the Resurrection, so in the believer there is an awakening to a new life.[1] Here lies the answer to a twofold difficulty—(1) If the Law is abolished as the rule of conduct, what is to be put in its place? and (2) Though freed once from sin's bondage, what guarantee has the believer that he will not be again enslaved?

Over against the Law—the external imposition of rules—is set a new principle, nay rather a Person, for "Christ liveth in me," and "your body is a temple of the Holy Ghost which is in you"; hence the natural injunction, "Present yourselves unto God . . . and your members as instruments of righteousness unto God."

And sin's bondage is, or may be, over for ever, for "the Law of the Spirit of Life in Christ Jesus hath made me free from the law of sin and death," and "sin shall not have dominion over you."

So the Christian life is one of double freedom—freedom from the bondage of legal observances, and freedom from captivity to a foreign power. It is a life inspired from within by a Divine Person, and therefore described as "in Christ," who dwells in the believer by faith,[2] or "in the Spirit,"[3] whom God has sent into our hearts as the proof of our adoption and the pledge of future glory.

"His Spirit that dwelleth in you"—the phrase brings up one of the most famous of St. Paul's antitheses, that between "flesh" and "spirit." These are the two parts into which the apostle divides human nature.

At first sight it seems mere oriental dualism of matter and the immaterial, the former sinful and the latter pure. For instance, we find such phrases as "The mind of the flesh is death, but the mind of the spirit is life and peace : because the mind of the flesh is enmity against God";[4] "If ye live after the flesh, ye must die; but if by the spirit ye mortify the deeds of the body ye shall live."[5] Again, the list of sins in Gal. v. 20 is summed up in the term "the works of the flesh."

---

[1] ROM. vi. 4.   [2] EPH. iii. 17.   [3] 1 COR. xii. 3.
[4] ROM. viii. 6, 7.   [5] ROM. viii. 13.

But further examination shows that it is not quite so simple. On the one hand, the spirit, like the flesh, is capable of defilement;[1] the "works of the flesh" in Gal. v. 20 are not all fleshly sins. On the other hand, the body as such need not be sinful; "your body is a temple of the Holy Ghost," "present your body," "present your members"[2]—to God.

Then what do phrases "body of sin," "flesh of sin," &c. mean? Not that the body as such is inherently sinful, but that it is the sphere of sin's operation, *cf.* "the law of sin which is in my members"; it is peculiarly open to attack. Yet "flesh" does seem to be used not of mere material, in itself non-moral, but with a distinctly ethical connotation as in the texts quoted above.

The question is further complicated by the use of "spirit" for (1) man's spirit, and (2) the Holy Spirit, often obviously personal, but the distinction is not always easy to draw. In Rom. i. 9 or 2 Cor. ii. 13 there is not much doubt, but Rom. viii. is puzzling; one shades off into the other; it is almost impossible to keep them apart.

Then the words "mind" and "soul" are used, increasing the difficulty as seeming to introduce a third division, though in Rom. vii. 23 "mind" seems to be equivalent to "spirit."

Probably the distinctions are not accurately maintained. St. Paul is using the language of experience not of psychology. But some meaning must be assigned to them.

σάρξ does seem to have a definitely ethical sense distinct from merely physical or material, though arising from it. In practice the distinction is not difficult. It is the lower nature, the home of such sins as envy, pride, and selfishness, as well as grosser vices—it is not material, for, as seen above, the body, though by nature subject to sin, is not necessarily so, and may be cleansed,[3] but the lower nature must be put to death, the flesh crucified.

Then πνεῦμα is the higher nature—the side of man which is turned towards God, the capacity for understanding and communicating with the divine, the "inward man" which delights in the Law of God. In the unconverted man this

---

[1] 2 Cor. vii. 1.   [2] Rom. xii. 1, vi. 13.

[3] 2 Cor. vii. 1 ; 1 Cor. vi. 20 ; Rom. vi. 13, &c.

higher nature is controlled by the lower, unable to make headway against sin, even if it is not conceived of as absolutely dead.[1] It is only on the advent of the Spirit of God to quicken it to new life that it comes to its own. Before the flesh reigned supreme, now the Spirit of God lays hold of man's spirit and energises it ; man is enabled to live in the spirit, the flesh is subdued. So the new governing principle that has come in with Christ sets the believer free from the domination of the sin that was entrenched in the appetites and desires of the lower nature.

Such, then, is St. Paul's description of the normal Christian life—the flesh subdued to the spirit and the Spirit of God over all. This life is not automatic ; it comes only as the response to a definite act of will. Hence the constant appeals to "present your bodies," to enter on the life governed by the Spirit, to realise the potentialities of union with Christ. It involves a choice, because even after acceptance of Christ it is possible for the believer to remain a "babe" instead of becoming a full-grown man ; but the choice once made the results are certain ; the old life is a thing of the past ; sin is a beaten foe ; its place in the life is taken by Christian virtues, which come not as the laboured effects of self-effort, but as the inevitable product of the working of the Spirit ; sonship is a relation to God realised in actual life, and manifested by the formation of the character of Christ in the individual heart.[2] "If any man be in Christ, he is a new creature : the old things are passed away ; behold they are become new."

The character developed in every relation of practical life is the theme of the closing chapters of almost every epistle in the form of exhortation ; it runs all through 1 Corinthians in answers to questions raised or comments on information received, while in 2 Corinthians especially, in others in varying degrees, the effect on St. Paul's own life stands out vividly. Here two points only can be briefly mentioned in passing.

The spiritual life has many manifestations—some in the physical realm, some in the ethical. The former attracted

---

[1] Eph. ii. 1. [2] Gal. iv. 19.

the more attention; it is upon the latter that St. Paul lays the greater stress.

The supreme ethical demand, the one great Christian obligation, the law that has supplanted the Law of Moses, is the law of love.[1] Of his converts the apostle demanded that love should show itself in mutual consideration and forbearance, and in scrupulous regard for the feelings and conscience of "the brother"; in St. Paul himself it took the form of a passion which considered no sacrifice too great, which yearned for his absent friends with a longing which he could only describe as in the heart of Christ; "for now we live if ye stand fast in the Lord."[2]

Love springs from the love of God in Christ to us. "We love because He first loved us"[3] is an excellent summary of St. Paul's teaching on the subject. To "know the love of Christ which passeth knowledge" is his highest aspiration.

Then joy—"The Kingdom of God is . . . joy in the Holy Ghost." "The fruit of the spirit is . . . joy." "Rejoice in the Lord alway." With all his insistence on the mortification of the old self-life, his disparagement of position or all that savoured of "the flesh,"[4] St. Paul is constantly asserting the duty of Christian joy. Amid all his anxieties and sufferings the note of joy is rarely if ever absent. He can truly say of himself "as sorrowful, yet alway rejoicing."

But the Christian is not merely an individual. His vital union with his Lord unites him also with other members of Christ's body; because he belongs to Christ he is linked in a fellowship. The doctrine of the Christian life is incomplete without the doctrine of the Church.

It is possible to trace in the early chapters of the Acts the growth of the idea of the Christian body as a Church.[5] The word first appears in the account of the sin and punishment

---

[1] Rom. xiii. 8–10; Gal. v. 14.   [2] 1 Thess. iii. 8.

[3] 1 St. John iv. 19.

[4] In the sense in which it is used in Phil. iii. 4. Not the ethical meaning defined above, but life in all its relations apart from Christ.

[5] In the LXX. ἐκκλησία is the regular translation of the Hebrew קָהָל, assembly, the whole body of people assembled. So it was more suitable than the national word λαός for the new society, being inclusive rather than exclusive (*cf.* Hort, *The Christian Ecclesia*, chap. i.).

of Ananias and Sapphira, as a result of which "fear fell on the whole Church." If Professor Ramsay is right in his view of St. Luke as a historian and literary artist, the use of the word here for the first time is no accident; it is intended to indicate that this incident brought home to Christians and perhaps to Jews as well the fact that "the brethren" were linked to one another by a bond no less strong than that which bound together "my people Israel" under the old covenant. There was no room for such a society within the commonwealth of Israel.

This was followed by organisation—the appointment of officials with administrative duties—while persecution by the religious leaders of the nation consolidated the young community and emphasised its separation from official Judaism.

So far the Church is a single body, a group of people in one place having possessions in common, living a life of fellowship with a common sacrament of admission, a common sacrament of continuance, and a common worship.

Now there comes a change; we read of "the Church throughout the whole of Judæa and Galilee and Samaria,"[1] of a Gentile Christian community at Cæsarea,[2] and finally, of "the Church that was [at Antioch],"[3] which is clearly contrasted with "the Church which was in Jerusalem."[4] "The Church" has become "the Churches."

The number of Churches soon grew apace; on the return from their First Missionary Journey St. Paul and St. Barnabas "appointed elders in every church," and in further journeys new churches were founded.

With this multiplication of churches there was obviously a risk of the unity of the Church being forgotten. The apostles were alive to the danger; and they strove to avert it by frequent intercourse between the churches, and especially at the great Council of Jerusalem. This is the point at which St. Paul's letters begin. He himself took an active, and even a leading, share in the efforts to maintain unity; he paid frequent visits to Jerusalem (observing the Jewish feasts there when possible) to take counsel with the other apostles, and insisted on the duty of the Gentile churches to contribute towards the need

---

[1] ACTS ix. 31.   [2] ACTS x.   [3] ACTS xiii. 1.   [4] ACTS xi. 22, 26.

of the mother Church at Jerusalem. The same may be seen in his letters. At first he writes to "the churches" of Thessalonica, Galatia, and Corinth; but afterwards always to "the saints" at Rome or Philippi. And this is no mere precaution against the misunderstanding of others; his own thoughts on the subject were expanding, and perhaps it was partly his own efforts to connect his newly founded churches with Jerusalem which showed him how important it really was. At any rate, the efforts came first, the exposition followed.

Yet his teaching on the Church is not inspired by perception of the need for a united whole, nor by the imperialist vision of a spiritual empire analogous to that of Rome. It is not the thought of the Kingdom of God [1] that he thus expands, though we know that it formed part of his preaching; it is the Church's inner life, her relation to her Lord.

As with most of his teaching this, too, was first called forth by circumstances. There was rivalry in the Church at Corinth, threatening to split the body of believers into separate and semi-antagonistic camps. St. Paul protests in vigorous language. Against it he asserts the unity of all Christians in their Lord.

Here his characteristic metaphors first appear—the building, the body, and the bride. All three are found again in the epistles of the Captivity, and the change of treatment is interesting and instructive to notice. But throughout they are mere metaphors; he is never bound down to them, nor does he always use them in exactly the same way.

Let us first examine them as used in the letters to the Corinthians. The metaphor of the *building* is opposed to factions.[2] The believers are all one building, the temple of God; schism within the Church is met by the stern warning, "If any man destroyeth the temple of God, him shall God destroy." Schism is sacrilege; it is tearing asunder the walls of God's sanctuary, which is hallowed by His presence.

The metaphor of the *body* [3] is aimed rather at personal dissensions and jealousies regarding the gift of the Spirit. Christ is the whole of which each believer is a part through

---

[1] That idea is rather developed in his eschatology.
[2] 1 COR. iii. 16, 17.   [3] 1 COR. xii.

union with Him. Therefore, all are members of each other; each has his place in the body; none can do without the rest. They have all become members of the body by the same sacrament, were all drawn in by the same Spirit. So, too, in Rom. xii. the unity of each individual believer with Christ carries with it union with all His other members. The Church is one because Christ is one; believers are united with one another because they are united to Him. The conception bears a striking analogy to the figure of the vine in St. John xv.

The metaphor of the *bride* is only incidentally used in these epistles. Apparently St. Paul has not yet seen its possibilities; he does not dwell upon it. Speaking as Hosea or Jeremiah might have done, he tells the Corinthians that he has espoused them to Christ, and urges them not to be led away by false doctrine.[1]

In all these the single Church is alone in view. He is writing to " the Church " at Corinth, and his words relate, primarily at least, to it only. The Corinthian Church is *a* temple of God. The Corinthians are members of Christ's Body, a virgin espoused to Christ. There is no thought of others.

In the later epistles he takes a wider view. In Ephesians the whole is seen, and with it comes a new thought. The Church is not yet complete; it is becoming. The same metaphors are used, but there is a change; it is not a static conception but a development.

He had called the Corinthian Church *a temple;* now he has a vision of one mighty temple slowly growing as all building everywhere is included in it;[2] the Christians whom he is primarily addressing form but a part of the whole.

So too with the *body.* Before Christ was the whole Body complete; but when the idea of growth is grasped the Christ becomes the Head, and in Him the body is coming to its full stature; it is being built up by each joint, each member, as each brings its own contribution to the whole,[3] while the parallel passage in Colossians[4] shows that the Head is not only the source of its unity, but also supplies the power of growth. Nor is the figure used merely as an appeal for

---

[1] 2 Cor. xi. 2.   [2] Eph. ii. 20–22.   [3] Eph. iv. 11–16.   [4] Col. ii. 19.

unity; it enriches and ennobles every function of life, for each has his share in the building up the body of Christ.

Thirdly, the *bride*. Here again it is the whole Church, not a portion of it, not the church in any one town or district, that is in question. The metaphor goes closely with the preceding one. Again Christ is the Head, but here the Head defined as Saviour. Once more stress is laid on the unity of Christ and the Church. Her preparation is given as the reason of the sacrifice of Himself, and nothing less than her completion and perfection is His purpose. Here, too, we seem to be brought to the verge of a Johannine conception.[1] The seer on Patmos saw the New Jerusalem, the Lamb's wife coming down, complete at last, out of heaven from God. St. Paul shows us the preparation that leads up to that great event.

In the busy rush of work, amid the calls to strengthen the positions won and attack those yet unassailed, St. Paul had had but little leisure. He met with matchless insight, guided by the Spirit, each problem as it came; but we may well be thankful to the Providence of God which called him apart in later life to reveal to him truths which have enriched the Church's life and thought through all ages.

So much for the Church on earth. But whither is she tending? Whatever the exact answer may be, one thing is clear, the future is bright. "Christianity," says Dr. Inge, "is not a religion of faith and love; it is a religion of faith, *hope*, and love." In contrast the heathen are those without hope.[2]

But hope of what? The answer does not seem always the same. The future to which the Thessalonian letters, in the middle of St. Paul's ministry, look forward, is held to be quite different from that which the Epistle to the Ephesians, near its close, expects. The former describe a catastrophe, the sudden appearance of the Son of Man for judgement, the gathering together and overthrow of the forces of evil, the resurrection of the saints to eternal glory. Thought and language alike remind us of the Jewish Apocalypses current

---

[1] For the New Jerusalem *cf.* GAL. iv. 26.

[2] EPH. ii. 12. The word "hope" had a rather bad flavour to the Greeks implying rather "unreasoning expectation." This is developed in J. H. A. Hart, *The Hope of Catholic Judaism*, chap. i.

between 200 B.C. and 100 A.D.   But most striking of all the catastrophe is expected within St. Paul's own life.

In the Epistles of the Captivity there seems to be substituted the gradual growth and perfection of the Church in this present world.

Did St. Paul really abandon his earlier ideas and replace them by conceptions quite different?   Certainly a diminution of emphasis on "the last things" may be traced from the first group of epistles, through the second and third, though if the Pastoral Epistles may be accepted as genuine, at the close of his lifetime there is a natural recrudescence of his hopes of Christ's manifestation, though he no longer expected to live to see it.   As a Pharisee by training, moreover, apocalyptic imagery to describe the future state would be natural for him, and its gradual disuse under new conditions not surprising.   Admitting, however, change of emphasis, admitting variation in the language he uses, and in his views on the nearness of the end, the theory above outlined seems to state the position more strongly that the evidence warrants.

A brief survey in outline of the apostle's eschatological teaching will be necessary.

In 1–2 Thessalonians eschatology has a very important place; the nearness of the end, which St. Paul seems to expect in his own lifetime, the resurrection at the appearing of the Lord, and the signs which must precede His coming—told in language which bears a striking resemblance to our Lord's own predictions in the Gospels—are all subjects which he treats with explicit emphasis.

1 Corinthians has a clear and reasoned presentation of the doctrine of the Resurrection, based on the fact that Christ has risen.   Elsewhere in the epistle too it is clear that St. Paul's eyes are fixed on the end.   He speaks of "the fire" of judgement and "the day" till which the Corinthians are to suspend their judgements; the Lord's Supper is a memorial "till He come," and the letter closes with *Marana tha* (come, Lord!).[1]

---

[1] So Professor Burkitt would divide and translate, *cf.* Rev. xxii. 20.   Otherwise divide with R. V. Maran-atha, "The Lord has come," a reference to the fulfilment of the Messianic hopes in Jesus.   Some take it as present, "Our Lord cometh," which again emphasises the nearness of the end.   See *Encyl. Bibl.*, iii., art. "Maranatha."

St. Paul, it would seem, still expects to see the end: "We shall not all sleep" (xv. 51).

In 2 Corinthians there is less reference to the Parousia. The future is one of glory, but St. Paul is not sure of living to see it; he is prepared himself to go first to be "at home with the Lord." The judgement is spoken of, but here, as in 1 Corinthians iii., believers only are in view.

In Romans again "the day is at hand"; the eighth chapter looks forward to the revelation of the Sons of God which is to set creation free, while the saints too are waiting for their complete emancipation, of which the gift of the Spirit is but the first-fruits. The present life is one of suffering; it is to be followed by glory.

The epistles of the Captivity are usually appealed to in proof of the theory under discussion.

Of these Philippians, which is generally acknowledged to be genuine, clearly states that a coming of a Saviour from heaven is expected (iii. 20, iv. 5), and that soon, and states it in a way which shows it to be an integral part of the normal Christian creed. But St. Paul no longer expects it in his own lifetime. The alternatives before him are life and work, or death and the Presence of Christ, which "is very far better." In Colossians too, which, by its close connection with Philemon has gained a wide acceptance, there is a definite statement of the glory to come for the Christian, as manifested with his Master—a manifestation contrasted with the earthly life which is "*hid* with Christ in God." Ephesians, the authenticity of which is more often questioned, is rather less specific, but if we may accept its evidence St. Paul is still looking for a world to come and a day of redemption (i. 14, 21). As in Romans the gift of the Holy Spirit is not itself the new age, but is the earnest of the inheritance (iv. 30), the pledge of something greater to follow, greater even than "to sit in heavenly places" of ii. 6.[1]

The Pastoral Epistles are more widely doubted in critical circles, but there is a tendency to accept at least consider-

---

[1] If the epistle is not genuine, then the chief authority for St. Paul's view of the establishment of the Church and the indwelling Spirit as taking the place of the coming of Messiah disappears.

able portions of 2 Timothy. In one of its most personal passages the apostle speaks of the crown of glory laid up for him " at that day," which is clearly not the day of his death, for it is not only for him but for "all them who have loved His appearing" (iv. 8, *cf.* i. 12). It seems natural to connect the ἐπιφάνεια here mentioned with the φανέρω[σις] of Col. iii. 4.

If 1 Timothy and Titus be admitted, in them too the "Epiphany" of the Lord Jesus has a definite place in St. Paul's thoughts and hopes.

Thus it is noteworthy that the one Epistle (with the exception of the letter to Philemon, which is purely personal) containing no reference to the Parousia is that to the Galatians, written, on any view of its exact date, at a time when, on the hypothesis, the Parousia still occupied a prominent place in St. Paul's thought. The reason may seem obvious—that the whole point of the letter was to make the Galatians realise their present privileges in Christ; but this at least suggests that there may have been special circumstances in other places which similarly regulated the emphasis given. We know that 1 Cor. xv. is the answer to doubts raised at Corinth; may not the prominence given to eschatology in 1 and 2 Thessalonians be due to a like reason ? Professor Findlay [1] makes the interesting suggestion that St. Paul's contact in Asia Minor with Emperor worship, which he recognised as the great opponent of Christianity, may have helped to make his thoughts run in that direction at the time. The Acts is a witness to the permanent place of the Judgement in his preaching.[2]

Hence the theory of a gradual development of St. Paul's thought, involving the abandonment of the old idea of the coming of the Lord to inaugurate a new order of things, in favour of a conception of the gradual improvement of earthly conditions by the work of the Spirit, seems insufficiently supported by the evidence. The Advent Hope retains a permanent place in his scheme of Christianity.

---

[1] 1 and 2 Thessalonians in the Camb. Greek Testament for Schools, Introduction, chap. iii.

[2] Acts xxiv. 25.

With all his doctrine of a present salvation, of peace with God here and now through the death of Christ, of a risen life of constant victory over sin through the power of the "Spirit that dwelleth in you," with all his magnificent visions of God's purposes for mankind and the Church, St. Paul still looks forward all through his life to a consummation which will be the manifest triumph of his Master, to a new life of which the present is but a foretaste, the Kingdom established, sin and death destroyed, when God shall be all in all.

ESSAY VIII

THE JOHANNINE THEOLOGY

B. T. D. SMITH, M.A.

*Formerly Lady Kay Scholar of the College.   Vice-Principal
of the Cambridge Clergy Training School*

ANALYSIS

THE JOHANNINE THEOLOGY :—

    In the Parting of the Roads.
    In relation to the work of St. Paul.

HISTORICAL CONTEXT :—

    The Christian Church at the end of the first century and opening years
    of the second—its environment and problems—

        i. The Gentile world. Twofold danger of Christianity :—Stag-
            nation—Submersion. The State.
       ii. The Jewish world.
      iii. The Christian communities and Judaistic Christianity—
            Millenarianism—Gnosticism—Baptist sect—Organisation.

THE JOHANNINE LITERATURE.

JOHANNINE DOCTRINE OF THE PERSON OF CHRIST.

    1. Logos Christology :—
        The Diaspora and the Alexandrian philosophy of religion.
        Philo and the Logos doctrine.
        The Johannine Logos doctrine in relation to the Philonian.
        The Prologue and the Gospel.
        Significance.
    2. Messianic Claims :—
        Attitude towards Judaism.
        "Christ" and "Son of Man."
        Answer to Jewish opponents.
    3. Person of Christ and the Baptist sect.
    4. The Incarnation. Doceticism. The Virgin Birth.
    5. The fact of the Incarnation :—
        Danger of Christianity becoming a tradition.
        Danger of Christianity becoming divorced from history.
        Johannine Christology and the historical life.

JOHANNINE SOTERIOLOGY :—

    1. Dualism.
    2. The Work of Christ. Change of categories. Life. Truth. Light.
    3. The Judgement of Christ.
    4. The Death of Christ.
    5. The appropriation by the individual of the work of Christ. Belief
        Knowledge. Love.
    6. The Mission of the Spirit and the Return of Christ. The Church,
        Sacraments and Ministry.

THE JOHANNINE THEOLOGY

THE last general contribution to the New Testament is to be found in a literature with characteristics of its own, bearing the honoured name of St. John. Grave questions affecting the very centre of our faith face the student of these writings, for it is the Johannine system that has set its mark most deeply on the theology of the Church, and given to it its distinctive character. To the chronicler of the " Parting of the Roads " these documents are of paramount importance. Even Pauline Christianity is not irreconcilable with the earlier Judaism.[1] The Johannine doctrine of the Incarnate Logos broke the last fetter which bound together the Christian and the Jewish faiths; and we pass by a natural transition from these writings to the anti-Judaism of Ignatius.

It is not without significance that Ephesus or its neighbourhood should have been the place of origin of the Johannine writings. For Ephesus was the mart of Asia, the meeting-place of East and West, famous alike as a seat of Greek art and learning and as a centre of religious life. It would seem, moreover, that its strategic position was appreciated by St. Paul the ecclesiastical statesman very early in his missionary career, and that it was in pursuance of a long-matured policy[2] that he made that city his residence for the space of two years, " so that all they which dwelt in Asia heard the word of the Lord." Only then did he venture to push his plans still further, and to fix his eyes on Rome. At a later date it was to the churches of

---

[1] Harnack, *History of Dogma*, Eng. trans., vol. i. p. 89.
[2] *Cf.* Hort, *Proleg. to Rom. and Eph.*, p. 82 f.

Q.

that district that he despatched his two great Christological epistles, the product of his ripest thought. When, therefore, the Gospel of St. John was put forth from Ephesus as the weapon whereby Christianity should win her place as a world-religion, it came also to crown the labours of the great Apostle of the Gentiles.[1]

Any discussion of the Johannine theology would, indeed, be incomplete without some reference to the work of St. Paul. This has been treated of in the preceding essay, but it may be summarised briefly here. As Saul the persecutor he had unwittingly set on foot the movement whereby the Christian Church spread from the confines of the city of Jerusalem " throughout the regions of Judea and Samaria "; as Paul the Apostle he had conceived and largely carried out his scheme for the evangelisation of the Roman Empire. It was his careful hand on the helm that saved the Church from shipwreck in the troubled waters of the controversy on the admission of the Gentiles, and as the first Christian theologian he had attempted to face the problems which inevitably confronted the convert from Judaism, and had done much towards developing and systematising the various elements which went to make up the primitive faith of the infant Church.

St. Paul had accomplished much: yet there still remained much to be done. If the Christian faith was ever to win the position that it claimed for itself in the world, another prophet must arise. The influence of St. Paul was circumscribed, not only by his limitations, but by his very greatness. By his limitations, for to the last he remained a Jew. His early training in the Jewish schools had formed his thought, and despite the use he made of Greek ideas, his theology was cast in Rabbinic moulds. And, again, the circle of his influence was narrowed by the singular greatness of the man, singular alike in his religious experiences and in the working of his mind. It may be doubted whether the system of St. Paul was ever really appreciated before Augustine except, perhaps, by the heretic Marcion, and he misunder-

[1] *Cf.* H. L. Jackson, *Fourth Gospel and some Recent German Criticism,* p. 225.

stood him.[1] Pauline Christianity alone could not hope to win the Græco-Roman world to Christ.

The period, then, of the Johannine writings was a critical one in the history of Christianity. Old problems remained to be solved, and new and urgent questions confronted the Church.

In the first place, the situation had changed with regard to the surrounding Gentile world since the days of St. Paul. The Church had now emerged from its first position as an obscure Jewish sect, and had joined the motley throng of systems that were clamouring for the empire of the religious world. It had escaped one danger when it first burst through the confines of Judaism ; a twofold danger now menaced it. On the one hand, it might fail to make good its new footing, and sink into the obscurity from whence it had emerged. Or it might, in the very process of adaptation, lose its uniqueness, sacrifice essential elements for the sake of accommodation, and become submerged under the pressure of alien forces. Nor was it suffered to fight its battles without interference from without. A new enemy had arisen, fearful enough to daunt a more experienced and more influential body than the early Church, in the person of the State. Against the Asian Christians there emerged from the sea a beast bearing upon his horns the imperial crowns, to lend his power and authority to that other beast of organised paganism which already pressed them hard.

Again, the sharp line of cleavage between Christianity and Judaism had become apparent. The Church and the Synagogue had by now discovered themselves to be rivals, and on the part of Judaism at least the hostility was very bitter. For the Jews, the Christians were intruders upon sacred ground, successful impostors who laid claim to their most cherished possessions. For the Christians, the Jews were the men who had crucified Christ. It was but a few years later that the Jews of Smyrna broke even a " great Sabbath " in their zeal to gather faggots for the pyre of Polycarp the aged Christian saint, and Tertullian could write, some half century after, *Synagogæ Judæorum fontes persecutionum.*[2]

---

[1] Harnack, *History of Dogma*, Eng. trans., vol. i. p. 89.   [2] *Scorp.* 10.

Nor were the Jews backward in entering the lists of religious controversy, for which they possessed special advantages. Both Justin and Eusebius tell us that the Jewish leaders organised a regular missionary propaganda to check the progress of the Christian faith.[1] Their controversialists pointed to the commonplace details of the Saviour's early life, to the obscure village which was His home, to the poverty of His kin, to the helplessness of His death, and to His betrayal at the hands of an intimate disciple. They did not hesitate to spread the vilest calumnies as to His birth,[2] and had their own version of the empty tomb.[3]

But the Church of this period had to deal with Jew and Gentile not only as outside and alien forces, but also as constituent elements, influencing her from within as well as from without; and some account of the difficulties which confronted the Christian communities in consequence of this fact must be given.

In the first days of Christianity the Gospel presented itself as an "apocalyptic message on the soil of the Old Testament."[4] Its early preachers proclaimed Jesus as the Messiah foretold by the prophets, whose condemnation by His own people had been reversed by God in that He had raised Him from the dead, and who would speedily return on the clouds of heaven to bring about the establishment of the Messianic kingdom. This is not the place to discuss the eschatology of primitive Christianity, or to determine whether its more catastrophic features formed an integral part of the teaching of our Lord. Nor can we here trace in any detail the later developments of the Christian hope. But the significance of the creed of early days, "Jesus is the Christ," to many, if not the majority, of Jewish Christians must be realised. They had accepted Jesus as the promised Messiah, and looked for His return as imminent. The interval of waiting, during which the Gospel was preached

---

[1] Just., *Dial.*, 17 ; Euseb. in *Jes.*, xviii. 1.   [2] *Cf.* JOHN viii. 41.

[3] For examples of Jewish controversy illustrating the general trend of their arguments, *cf.* Justin, *Dialogue with Trypho*, and Origen *against Celsus.* The Jew of Celsus, according to Harnack, is a more lifelike character than the more refined Trypho.

[4] Harnack, *History of Dogma*, Eng. trans., vol. i. p. 41.

to the Gentiles, was but the means chosen of God to provoke their Jewish brethren to jealousy, "and so all Israel" should "be saved."[1] But no trumpet had sounded; the heavens were still closed; the Messiah did not come. And now, after the destruction of Jerusalem and its accompanying horrors, the breach between the Jewish and Christian Churches was widening, so that there seemed little chance of its ever being spanned. Small wonder was it, then, that some of them began to cry "Where is the promise of His coming?" and to doubt the simple creed of their baptismal confession. In the days of Justin the small number of Jewish Christians had to be accounted for by appealing to prophecy.[2]

It is obvious that when the Church no longer restricted her attention to the Jews, but turned to the Gentiles, the form in which she preached her Gospel must be adapted to meet their needs. The circle of ideas connected with the Jewish hope would have been practically unintelligible to the Gentile world. They would, however, be able to appreciate the strict monotheism of the Christian message, and to share in the expectation of the Second Coming. The position of many Gentile Christians of those days might be summed up in St. Paul's description of those of Thessalonica—they had "turned unto God from idols, to serve a living and true God, and to wait for His Son from heaven."[3] Now one very real danger which threatened the Church at the period with which we are dealing was the exaggerated interest displayed in the promise of "the good time coming," despite the foresight of St. Paul. It is a mistake to suppose that this attitude was restricted to Jewish Christianity. It was shared by Gentile as well as by Jew, and the traditions of the elders handed on by Papias show the greedy appetite of early Christianity for information on the subject, however legendary in character, and however far removed from the Christian spirit.[4] Unless something was done to redress the balance here, Christianity, it would seem, was fated to pass away within a short period of time.

Over against this somewhat crude and unthinking

---

[1] Rom. xi. 11, 26. [2] Just., *Apol.*, i. 68.
[3] 1 Thess. i. 9. [4] *Cf.* Iren., *adv. hær.*, v. 33.

Apocalypticism, we have to set a tendency in the opposite direction, due to the introduction into Christianity of ideas which, at least in their origin, were Oriental in character. The speculative philosophy of the East transformed Christianity into Gnosticism, in the same way as it had previously affected Judaism and Hellenism.[1] The Church in the province of Asia where "cosmological speculation, mystic theosophy, and religious fanaticism all had their home,"[2] was from very early days exposed to these influences, and the heretical teaching attacked in the Epistle to the Colossians and in the Pastorals can only be ascribed to incipient Gnosticism. The developed Docetism, denounced in the Epistles of Ignatius, was already in existence in germ at the time of the publication of the Johannine writings.

A local problem which seems to have confronted the Asian communities at this time was the activity of a "Baptist sect." It will be remembered that it was at Ephesus that Apollos first arrived, who knew "only the baptism of John,"[3] and that it was at that city that St. Paul found certain who had been baptized only "into John's baptism."[4] The idea that the followers of the Baptist had become a separate sect is to a certain extent theoretical, but it is not an improbable one, receives some support from other sources,[5] and seems to be demanded by the references to the Forerunner in the fourth Gospel.[6] It has been suggested that "the Baptist controversy is bound up with the larger Jewish one."[7] The Jews themselves appear to have had no quarrel with John, and a reference in Justin would seem to show that his adherents ranked among the Jewish sects. Speaking to Trypho of some heretical Christians who "blaspheme the God of Abraham,

---

[1] *Cf.* Foakes Jackson, *History of the Christian Church*, p. 122.

[2] Lightfoot, *Colossians*, p. 95.

[3] ACTS xviii. 25 ; *cf.* J. H. A. Hart, *J. T. S.*, vol. vii. p. 16.

[4] ACTS xix. 3, 4.

[5] *Clem. Hom.*, ii. 22, 24 ; *Clem. Recog.*, i. 54 : "Some even of the disciples of John, who seemed to be great ones, have separated themselves from the people, and proclaimed their own master as the Christ." *Cf.* i. 60 ; ii. 7, 12.

[6] Lightfoot, *Colossians*, p. 401. "This Gospel indicates the spread of Hemero-baptist principles, if not the presence of a Hemero-baptist community, in proconsular Asia, when it was written."

[7] Scott, *Fourth Gospel*, p. 82.

Isaac, and Jacob," and deny the resurrection of the body, Justin says, "Do not imagine that they are Christians; even as one, if he would rightly consider it, would not admit that the Sadducees, or similar sects of . . . Hellenists, Pharisees, *Baptists* are Jews. . . ." [1]

The review of the environment and problems of the Christian Church at this period must not conclude without a reference to the development of the ecclesiastical organisation which was then taking place. The tradition [2] that the establishment of the monarchical episcopate in Asia was the work of "John" is most probably a true one, and the inevitable friction consequent upon the change was another difficulty that had to be dealt with.

Such were the conditions that saw the rise of, and in part gave rise to, the Johannine writings.

The Gospel, three epistles, and the Apocalypse which are covered by this title have been for many centuries ascribed to the apostle John, the son of Zebedee, and the disciple beloved of our Lord, who was first one of the pillars of the Church at Jerusalem, and then removed in later years to Ephesus, where he died at an advanced age in the reign of Trajan, after having suffered exile on Patmos " for the word of God and the testimony of Jesus."

In view, however, of the criticism to which these writings have been subjected in recent years, it is no longer possible to speak with the same confidence as formerly on the subject of their authorship. That they are the work of one school, and thus in some sense the product of a single type of mind, seems fairly certain. But few to-day find themselves able to ascribe both the Gospel and the Apocalypse to one and the same hand. Despite certain similarities, the profound differences which separate the two writings form a formidable barrier to unity of authorship.

On the same ground no use can be made of the Apocalypse in this essay, though it deals with one of the problems that have been outlined. The Christian prophet who gave it to the Asian communities was undoubtedly influenced by

---

[1] *Dialogue*, 80.
[2] *Cf.* Clem. Alex., *Quis Dives*, 42 ; Tert., *adv. Marc.*, iv. 5.

Johannine ideas, but the whole of his theology is of too distinct a type to serve to illustrate that of the fourth Gospel and the epistles save by way of contrast.[1]

The Gospel and the three epistles stand in much closer connection. It has, however, been suggested from quite early days in the history of criticism that the two smaller epistles should be ranged with the Apocalypse. But their size is too inconsiderable to afford much evidence either for or against this theory, and, for the same reason, the question is of little importance to our subject. It is difficult to separate the Gospel and the first epistle, and reasons will be given in the course of the following discussion for doubting the conclusion which many critics have drawn from certain contrasts in the two writings.

The further question as to whether any of these compositions can be ascribed to John the Apostle is in many ways the most difficult and most important of the problems which circle round the Johannine literature. Space, however, will not permit the discussion of this subject. Its omission does not imply a lack of appreciation of the issues involved.

Finally, mention must be made of recent attempts to trace the work of different hands in the composition of the fourth Gospel.[2] In so far as these proceed on the assumption that it is possible to find different theological ideas within the body of the Gospel, the subject has some interest for us. But nothing very convincing has yet been put forward in support of this theory. The differences which have hitherto been pointed out can be amply accounted for by supposing, as must indeed have been the case, that the

---

[1] Swete, *Apoc.*, cliv. : It is "not only in the region of eschatology that the book takes its own course ; its views of the Person of Christ, of the Holy Spirit, of Redemption, and of the Church are its own ; even its doctrine of God has no exact parallel in the rest of the New Testament." Réville's dictum is harsh, but in a sense is true : "Tous deux assurément ont eu une vision du Christ, mais où l'un voit avec les yeux du visionnaire ce qui est de la chair, l'autre voit avec les yeux de l'esprit ce qui est de l'esprit" (*Le Quatrième Évangile*, p. 36). Harnack is able to ascribe both Apocalypse and Gospel to the same author, by subscribing to Vischer's theory that Apocalypse represents the Christianising of a purely Jewish original.

[2] These can be conveniently referred to in Moffatt, *Int. Lit. N.T.*, p. 550 f.

Gospel was not written at one sitting. A writer of the genius of the author of the fourth Gospel will not be bound by the rigid rules of consistency which some critics have laid down for him.

The Johannine theology cannot well be studied apart from its historical context.[1] An attempt will accordingly be made in the following pages to discuss its several parts in relation to the situation, already briefly sketched, at the close of the first century and in the first decades of the second.

I. This discussion must inevitably start from the doctrine of the Person of Christ in the Johannine writings.

(1) The opening words of the Gospel, "In the beginning was the Logos," at once challenge attention. The time had come when the Church, if she would escape destruction, must in some way bridge over the gulf that separated the two worlds of Jewish and Hellenic ideas; this short sentence has already spanned them. With one hand it reaches back to the opening words of the record of the old dispensation, with the other it stretches forward and appropriates one of the most popular and productive ideas of Greek philosophy.

Yet if these words were to be fruitful in the future history of the Christian Church, it must not be forgotten that they themselves had not sprung full-grown into being, but were in part the fruit of former ages. Before the author of this Gospel could write his Prologue, a long period in the Præparatio Evangelica had first to be passed through, during which the Jew came into contact with and was profoundly influenced by Greek thought.

The situation recorded in the words of Zechariah, "Thy sons, O Zion, against thy sons, O Greece,"[2] soon ceased to be true of the Judaism of the Dispersion. The infinite number of Jews scattered throughout the empire adopted the language, imitated the civilisation, and interested themselves in the intellectual problems of the Gentiles, without abandoning the faith of their fathers. Thus it came about that while Palestinean Judaism cradled the infant Church,

---

[1] Wrede (*Charakter und Tendenz des Johannes Evangeliums*, p. 40) describes the Gospel as "eine aus dem Kampfe geborene und für den Kampf geschriebene Schrift." [2] ZECH. ix. 13.

Hellenistic Judaism levelled the path whereby she could pass
out into a wider world.

The Jews of the Dispersion, if they breathed a freer
atmosphere than their brethren of Judæa, found themselves
faced with new difficulties. How could they reconcile those
truths of philosophy and science which they had taken over
from their neighbours, with the revelation embodied in the
Old Testament Scriptures? This problem must have confronted the intelligent Hellenist throughout the empire; the
solution was worked out with the greatest thoroughness in
the flourishing school of Alexandria. On the one hand the
use of the allegorical method in the interpretation of Scripture, coupled with the aid of the Greek version of the Jewish
Bible, enabled the inquiring Jew to discover Greek philosophy in Moses, as well as the Mosaic teaching in the Greek
philosophers.[1] On the other hand, he was able to link on
his Platonic idealism to Old Testament conceptions, and at
the same time to answer a difficulty which was also troubling
his Palestinean brethren, though not so acutely—that of reconciling the transcendent character of the Deity with belief
in His Providence.[2]

The influence of this Jewish-Alexandrian philosophy of
religion can be clearly traced in the Apocrypha. Though it
is usually connected in our minds with the system of Philo,
that is only because his was the most thoroughgoing and the
best known. A short review of it is necessary here, although
in doing so we must traverse a well-beaten path.

Philo starts from a dualistic conception of the universe.
As a strict Jew he was bound to admit that "in the beginning
God created the heaven and the earth." But this he explained as meaning that God caused the undifferentiated
pre-existent matter, which in itself is neither good nor evil,
to be impressed with rational forms. The difficulty of bringing the transcendent God into touch with a universe thus
created is answered by Philo in these words: "Though He is
far off, yet is He very near, keeping touch by means of His
creative and regulative Powers, which are close to all, though

[1] *Cf.* Bigg, *Christian Platonists of Alexandria*, p. 6.
[2] Réville, *Le Quatrième Évangile*, p. 81 f.   [3] Born *c.* B.C. 20.

He has banished the things that have birth far away from His essential nature." [1] It is not hard to recognise in these Powers the Ideas of Plato, the Logoi of the Stoics, and the Angels of the Jewish schools.

The manifold phenomena of the universe, however, form a cosmos, and the varied Powers are summed up in the Divine "Logos." The term we are thus introduced to has had a long history. One can only transliterate it, not translate it, for no English word is exactly its equivalent. It denotes both the thinking mind, and the thought given outward expression in word or design. Its use in philosophy begins with Heraclitus in the sixth century B.C., who employed it to describe the rational principle underlying the phenomena of the world, "the seed of all that happens, and the measure of all order." The system of Plato, although he scarcely made use of the term, affected its later history. This philosopher conceived of a world of supra-sensible realities or Ideas, overshadowing this visible universe. Individual things come into being in accordance with the Ideas, and, indeed, only exist by participation in them, the ὄντως ὄντα. But all these Ideas are themselves subordinate to the Idea of Ideas—the Good. The next important step was taken by the Stoics. They were chiefly interested in ethics, and abandoned the Idealism of Plato. The Logos conception was once more taken up and developed, and to them is due the distinction between the λόγος ἐνδιάθετος and the λόγος προφορικός, the immanent reason, and reason projected and given outward expression. The Logos is both the governing principle of the universe, and (as the λόγος σπερματικός) the source of all separate realities. [2]

This term is now adopted and enriched by Philo. On the one hand he detaches it from the materialism of the Stoics and grafts it on to the Idealism of Plato, so that the Stoic world-spirit is practically identified with the Platonic Idea of the Good. On the other hand, he has to combine it with the revelation embodied in the Old Testament Scriptures, and here the way has already been paved for him. From early

[1] *De post. Caini*, 5 (i. 229).
[2] For this section *cf.* Scott, *Fourth Gospel*, p. 146 f.

times we find a tendency manifesting itself among Jewi
writers to avoid anthropomorphic conceptions of the De
by the use of such theologoumena as the Angel, Glory,
Name of Yahweh. In the later books of the Old Testame
and in the Apocrypha, partly under the pressure of Gre
ideas, an endeavour is made to safeguard the transcende
character of God by representing Him as mediating I
creative and revealing activities through His Word or I
Wisdom, and by endowing these with a kind of persor
existence. This is pushed still further in later Rabbini
speculation, and the Memra or Word of God is in the T;
gums practically hypostatised.[1] It is obvious that Ph
would have no difficulty in reconciling his Logos doctri
with his religion as a devout Jew.

The various functions ascribed by Philo to the Logos m
be summarised as follows:—In relation to the other Powe
and to the world He is the Idea of Ideas, which stamps t
thought of God on matter and is the bond of the univer
As the mind of God the Logos is Divine, Eternal, $\theta\epsilon\acute{o}\varsigma$-
though not $\acute{o}$ $\theta\epsilon\acute{o}\varsigma$, $\acute{o}$ $\delta\epsilon\acute{v}\tau\epsilon\rho o\varsigma$ $\theta\epsilon\acute{o}\varsigma$: as His Word, $\pi\rho\epsilon\sigma\beta\acute{v}\tau\alpha\tau$
or $\pi\rho\omega\tau\acute{o}\gamma o\nu o\varsigma$ $\upsilon\acute{\iota}\acute{o}\varsigma$, the Image and the Shechinah of G
In relation to man He is the Mediator, the Saviour, t
Physician, the High Priest, the Shepherd, and the Food
souls. For the Logos is not only the Image of God, but I
is also the archetypal man,[2] and it is by participation in t
Divine Logos that man becomes rational. Thus He is t
Door through which man passes to God. He it was wl
manifested Himself to the Patriarchs, and by whose i
spiration the Prophets spake. Man is saved by the Log(
inasmuch as he can enter into communion with Him, risi
above his lower physical nature, which seeks to imprison hi
as in a tomb.

When we turn back again to the Prologue of the four
Gospel, it is obvious that we are still moving within t
same circle of ideas, although from a vastly different stan
point. The Johannine Logos is Eternal and Divine, standi
in appositional relationship to God. He is the mediator

---

[1] *Cf.* Weber, *Jüdische Theologie* (2nd ed.), pp. 180–190.
[2] For Adam was made $\kappa\alpha\tau'$ $\epsilon\grave{\iota}\kappa\acute{o}\nu\alpha$ $\theta\epsilon o\hat{\upsilon}$.

creation and the source of its life, the organ of revelation, ever coming into the world. He it is who has declared the invisible God, for no man hath seen God at any time. His activities are opposed by the darkness which is in the world, but those who receive Him are thereby empowered to become children of God.

Yet despite the closeness of resemblance there are profound differences between the Philonian and the Johannine Logos doctrines, differences which in the main arise from the fact that the writer of the fourth Gospel takes a step which it is doubtful whether Philo could ever have taken. He asserts that the Logos became incarnate in the historical Person of Jesus Christ.

Many critics have accordingly denied any connection between the Christian writer and the Alexandrian philosopher. They have looked rather to the Old Testament and Rabbinical speculations for the source of the Johannine teaching. This solution, however, is too one-sided. Attention must be called to two points. First, that the term Logos is introduced abruptly into the Prologue, without any explanation being added. The readers, then, must have been quite familiar with the conception. Secondly, that while it would be possible to produce parallels from the writings of Philo to almost every clause of the Prologue, it is noteworthy that the Johannine writings are marked by the omission of many Philonian "catchwords."[1] These two points suggest the line along which the answer to the problem should be sought.

On the one hand, there is no need to assume that the Christian writer was acquainted directly with the works of Philo. Similar ideas must have been widely disseminated among the Jews of the Dispersion, and thus have found their way into the Christian communities.[2] And as a matter of fact we can trace their influence in Christian writings prior to the Johannine. Of the Epistles to the Colossians and Ephesians it has been said that Philo's "grand con-

---

[1] *Cf.* Sanday, *Criticism of the Fourth Gospel*, p. 191 f.

[2] *Cf.* Harnack, *Hist. of Dogma*, vol. i. p. 113. The "practical ground-thoughts (*i.e.* of Philo's philosophy of religion), though in different degrees, must have found admission very early into the Jewish circles of the Diaspora, and through them to Gentile Christian circles also."

ception of the Logos, though not expressly mentioned, is clearly indicated, and transferred to the person of Christ." [1] And in the Epistle to the Hebrews [2] the Alexandrian influences are plainly marked, both in the employment of the allegorical method, and in the use made of Logos phraseology. [3] Reference, too, might here be made to the recently discovered "Odes of Solomon," although the question of their date and provenance is still much in dispute. [4]

On the other hand, the interests of the Christian writer are religious and not philosophical. He is concerned, not with the problem of the cosmos, but with the Person of Christ. As a result, he takes up the "Philonian" conception of the Divine Logos, in whatever form it has reached him, and turns it to his own ends, transforming it and charging it with new significance in the process. "The very ideas which have most appearance of being derived (from Philo) have been brought under the transfiguring influence of an original and creative mind, and turned out stripped of their philosophical dress, and robed with a new spiritual beauty to captivate the world." [5] It is the religious interests of this writer which make him revert to the phraseology of the Old Testament when he wishes to describe the activities of the Word of God.

His purpose is to set forth, not the Doctrine of the Logos, but the Gospel of the Word-become-Flesh, and so he can afford but scanty space to trace the pre-incarnate life and operations of the Divine Word as he hastens on to record the momentous fact of the Incarnation. It is perhaps on

[1] Scott, *Fourth Gospel*, p. 54.

[2] *Cf.* Moffatt, *Introd. to Lit. of N. T.*, p. 27 f.

[3] It must not, of course, be forgotten that the idea of the Logos was as much in the air as that of evolution is to-day. Philo's Logos conception does not stand in isolation, but is only one adaptation of the popular Stoic doctrine. It must also be remembered that Heraclitus, who first speculated on the subject, taught at Ephesus, and seems to have been held in some veneration by the Christian communities of Asia at a later date ; *cf.* Just., *Apol.*, i. 46. But one would naturally conclude that the conception came to the author of the Gospel, in the first instance, through Jewish rather than through Gentile channels.

[4] Rendel Harris, *The Odes and Psalms of Solomon* (1909). Harnack, *Ein jüdisch-christliches Psalmbuch aus dem ersten Jahrhundert* (1910).

[5] Drummond, *Character and Authorship of Fourth Gospel*, p. 24; *cf.* also Loisy, *Le Quatrième Évangile*, p. 120.

count of this feature of the work that Harnack has committed himself to the strange statement "that the Logos
(of the fourth Gospel) has little more in common with that
of Philo than the name, and its mention at the beginning
of the book is a mystery, not the solution of one," [1] if his
judgement is not rather to be ascribed to his dislike of the
Logos doctrine.[2]

Dr. Sanday has compared the Prologue to a stately pylon
through which one approaches the sanctuary proper. But
we must see in this pylon an integral part of the whole
building, and not some bizarre structure which bears no
resemblance in style to the rest of the temple. To drop the
metaphor, the opening verses belong to the plan of the
Gospel, and are essential to the understanding of the body
of the work. The objections to this view lose their force
when it is realised that the Gospel is that of the Logos-
Christ, not of the Logos, and accordingly, quite apart from
the difficulty of inserting this term into the mouths of the
actors, the author naturally speaks throughout of the historical
Person. But as in the Prologue the eternal relations of the
Logos with God are insisted upon, so in the following chapters
the Son is said to have been pre-existent, sharing in the
Father's glory, and the object of His love, before the world
began.[3] As the Logos was the agent in creation, so the
Son mediates the activities of the Father.[4] As the Logos
imparts life and light, so the Son is the Light and Life of
the world.[5]

Further, not only are the ideas in the Prologue carried
on through the rest of the Gospel, but they seem to have
influenced its whole structure. The continuity between the
two parts of the work is first secured by extending to the
Person of Jesus the witness of the Baptist to the Advent and
the Incarnation of the Logos (i. 19–34). Then in what
follows it is almost possible to range in parallel columns the

---

[1] Harnack, *Hist. of Dogma*, vol. i. p. 97. *Ueber das Verhältniss des Prologs
des vierten Evangeliums zum ganzen Werk* (1892). *Cf.* also Zahn, *Introduction
to N. T.*, iii. 3, p. 327 f.

[2] Inge, *D. C. G.*, art. "John, Gospel of," ii. 2.

[3] vi. 62 ; viii. 58 ; xvii. 5, 24.   [4] xiv. 10.   [5] v. 21 ; viii. 12 ; ix. 5.

statements of the Prologue in regard to the Word and the corresponding sections in the Gospel.[1]

The Johannine theology, then, is dominated by the conception of the Logos-Christ. No longer need there be any fear lest the wine of the Gospel should be wasted by attempted enclosure in the old skins of Jewish Messianism. The new wine has been put into new wine-skins and thereby preserved, for "it is historically true that 'the Logos became flesh' is the formula which won Europe to Christianity."[2]

Yet the recognition of this is not unattended with difficulties for us of to-day. The old "Harmonies of the Gospel" have been discarded, and we realise acutely the gap between the Jewish doctrine of the Messiah and the Hellenic idea of the Divine Logos. At the same time we must not misapprehend the significance of the change of categories. The progress of Christian thought in regard to the doctrine of the Person of Christ is often coldly pictured as following a straight line from Judaism to Greek philosophy, passing through stations represented respectively by Paulinism, the doctrine of the

---

[1] Thus, the Logos is the Divine principle of creation (i. 3). The Logos-Christ is shown as the principle of the new creation in a series of manifestations to individuals or to groups of people, ranging from a few disciples on "the first day," to the Samaritans who confess Him to be indeed "the Saviour of the world" (i. 35–iv. 42).

The next statement in regard to the Logos is that "in Him was Life" (i. 4). So the Logos-Christ is shown as the Life of the World in three signs, which culminate in the miracle of the loaves and the discourse on the Bread of Life (iv. 43–vi. 71).

The Life of the Logos was the Light of men. It shineth in the darkness, but the darkness overcame it not (i. 4, 5). This description of the revealing activities of the Word is paralleled by the revelation of the Christ as the Light of the World in the highly controversial scenes at the Feast of Tabernacles and in the treasury—a revelation which is sealed by the miracle of the man born blind (vii. 1–ix. 41).

As the pre-incarnate Logos came into the world and the world knew Him not (i. 10), so the Incarnate Word manifests Himself to His own in the allegory of the Good Shepherd, and in the sign of the raising of Lazarus, and His own received Him not (x. 1–xii. 50).

But "as many as received Him, to them gave He power to become sons of God" (i. 12). The Christ pours forth His love in the intimate discourses of the supper room, and faith triumphs over unbelief in the closing confession of the doubting apostle, "My Lord and my God" (xiii. 1–xx. 29).*

[2] Inge, *Camb. Bibl. Essays*, p. 278.

---

* *Cf.* Réville, *Le Quatrième Évangile*, p. 116 f.

Epistle to the Hebrews, and the Johannine theology. These latter, no doubt, do represent points in its development, though the course taken was not so direct as seems at times to be suggested. The important question, however, is surely this—Did the potentiality of future development lie in the mystery of Christ's Person, or in the historical situation that saw the rise of Christianity? What was the motive force behind the advance? Was it impelled merely by the unaided working of the human intellect? Was it not also the outcome of the personal devotion of the disciple for his Master, which sprang from no less a root than actual experience of what Christ had done and was doing for him and in him, of the new light thrown by his faith upon the old problems of life, and the new power which was transforming the world, a devotion which led him under the guidance of the Spirit of Truth to find no title too high for Him, no dignity too great? The early Jewish-Christian did not indeed hail his Lord as Logos, but he gave to Him the title which was the highest at his command, and which represented the sum of his and his nation's hopes. He was the long-expected Messiah foretold by prophet and psalmist—the King of the royal line. The Hellenistic Jew had moved in a larger world, and his interests were not so circumscribed as those of his brother in Palestine. For him his Master was the Pre-existent Son of God, the archetypal Man, from whom and in whom and unto whom are all things. It only represents one step more in the same process when "John" recognises in Him the Divine Logos, the solution of the intellectual cravings of the Greeks and the religious aspirations of the .Hebrews, both the Wisdom and the Power of God.

(2) The relation of the Johannine portrait of Christ to the Jewish problem of the time must now be considered.

There can be no doubt both that the evangelist was a Jew and that he found in our Lord the Messiah foretold in the Law and the Prophets.[1] The titles of "Christ" and "Son of Man," that were bound up so intimately with the Jewish hope, are retained in the Johannine Gospel. Further, our Lord is not only represented as directly asserting His own

[1] i. 45.

identity with the Messiah,[1] but as giving His sanction to the most exclusive claim of the Jewish nation.[2]

Over against this, however, must be set the fact that throughout the Gospel "the Jews" stand in sharp contrast to Christ and His disciples. When not actively hostile, they are incredulous, and are always obstinately blind to the inner meaning of Christ's teaching.[3] This anti-Judaic tendency of the writer seems to reach its height when he represents Christ as severing Himself so completely from the Jewish people as to speak to them of "your Law."[4]

The evangelist's attitude must be explained in view of the fierce strife between the Church and the Synagogue at this period, which had embittered both parties, and not least in the province of Asia.[5]

Salvation indeed was of the Jews, but the old Dispensation of Law had now been superseded by that of Grace and Truth.[6] Here the writer is echoing St. Paul, and he seems to have followed him still further in his justification of the ways of God by drawing the same distinction between "the Jew" who was one outwardly and "the Israelite indeed" who recognised in Jesus "the King of Israel."[7] This will throw light upon his seemingly inconsistent standpoint.

At the same time it must be noticed that the Messianic conceptions of the evangelist are not those of the Jews nor yet those of the simple Jewish-Christians.[8] The very terms which he has taken over have suffered a subtle change. The title "Christ" in the mouth of the believer is charged with a new and fuller meaning. It is synonymous with the confession that He is "the Son of God" not merely in the loosely defined sense

---

[1] iv. 26.　　　　　　　　　　　　[2] iv. 22.

[3] This is an over-statement, but registers the impression left upon the mind of the reader. The Jews, who from time to time are mentioned as believing, do not seem to have persevered.

[4] viii. 17 ; x. 34, xv. 25.

[5] Rev. ii. 9 f.　　　　　　　　　[6] i. 17.

[7] i. 47 ; *cf.* Rom. ii. 28 f. and Rev. ii. 9.

[8] *Cf.* Wrede, *Charakter und Tendenz des Johannes Evangeliums:* "Der israelitische Horizont existiert nicht mehr. . . . Da drücken denn andere Begriffe wie der 'eingeborene Sohn Gottes,' der 'Heiland der Welt,' 'das Licht,' 'das Wort,' viel besser aus, was Christus auf dem Standpunkte des Evangeliums ist und bedeutet."

in which the title may have come from the lips of St. Peter,[1] but in that which the words bear in the Church's creeds.[2] Similarly, in the First Epistle the whole point of the heretical denial that "Jesus is the Christ" is completely missed if we substitute the term "Messiah."[3] The title "Son of Man," the self-designation of our Lord in the synoptists, is retained in the fourth Gospel, but with a special set of ideas attached to it. One would gather from the Synoptic Gospels that the term was chosen by Christ as referring to His Messianic office as the future Judge of the world,[4] without giving any sanction to the popular notions which had gathered round the title of Messiah. But He appears also to have selected it as expressing the peculiar relation in which He stood to the human race; on the one hand as sharing to the full their experiences,[5] on the other, as embodying in His own Person the prophetic description of the Servant, "the man of sorrows and acquainted with grief."[6] In the fourth Gospel one of these conceptions disappears entirely, the other is emphasised but viewed in a somewhat different light. No longer do we hear of the Son of Man of Daniel's vision who will come in His glory, but of the Son of Man who came down from heaven.[7] The thought throughout is that of the Incarnation, as the true Jacob's ladder uniting heaven and earth.[8] The title is brought into connection with the Passion, as in the synoptists; but the evangelist's doctrine of the Death of Christ (to which allusion must be made later) again alters to some degree the significance of the term, for the Cross is viewed, not from the hill of Calvary, but from the mount of the Ascension. The Christ now foretells, not that "the Son of Man must suffer many things," but that "the Son of Man will be glorified."[9]

The records in the fourth Gospel of the Jewish controversies with our Lord on the subject of His claims, although

---

[1] MATT. xvi. 16. The words are absent from MARK (viii. 29).
[2] xi. 27, xx. 31; *cf.* i. 49, iv. 42.
[3] 1 JOHN ii. 22, v. 1; *cf.* iv. 15.
[4] MARK viii. 38, xiii. 26, xiv. 62, &c.
[5] MATT. viii. 20; MARK ii. 10, 28, x. 45.
[6] MARK viii. 31, ix. 12, 31, x. 33, xiv. 41, &c.
[7] iii. 13, vi. 62. [8] i. 51; *cf.* vi. 53.
[9] *Cf.* iii. 14, v. 27, viii. 28, xii. 23, 34, xiii. 31.

they no doubt embody genuine reminiscences,[1] may be regarded in part as echoes of the "blasphemy of those that say they are Jews and are not" at the time of the composition of the work. The Jewish arguments closely resemble those that were brought forward at a later date in the controversy.[2]

The evangelist meets them in various ways. In the first place his presentation of the real nature of Christ's Messianic dignity causes many of their attacks to lose their force, and as a rule they are not so much answered as treated as irrelevant.[3] Then by reading back into the times of Christ the blind opposition of the Jews to the Gospel in his own day he is enabled to trace the Jewish rejection of our Lord to the same cause. They could not receive Christ because they had lost the capacity to see the things of God.[4] Intellectually arrogant, proud and self-centred, the character of Christ awakened no response in their hearts, for they had not "God's Word abiding in them."[5] It was doubtless to emphasise further the guilt of the Jewish nation that the evangelist represents Jerusalem as the centre of Christ's activities. Our Lord's Mission did not take place in some obscure corner but in the very centre of the chosen people.

And lastly, the evangelist drives his lessons home by pointed references to the present situation of the Jews. In such sayings as "When ye have lifted up the Son of Man then shall ye know that I am He,"[6] "I go away, and ye shall seek Me, and shall die in your sin,"[7] we seem to hear the unwilling recognition by the Jewish people of the compelling power of the Cross, as they watch the triumphal progress of Christianity, to see their fruitless searchings for a saviour as destruction grows imminent, and to mark the death of the nation in the ruins of Jerusalem.

(3) Something more than the necessities of the Jewish controversy would appear to be required satisfactorily to explain the references in the Gospel to St. John the Baptist, although the polemical element in them has been exaggerated.[8] The

---

[1] *Cf.* Brooke in *Camb. Bibl. Essays*, p. 318.
[2] *Cf. supra*, p. 244.   [3] v. 18 f., vii. 14 f.   [4] ix. 41.
[5] v. 38 f.   [6] viii. 28.   [7] viii. 21.
[8] *E.g.* by Baldensperger, *Der Prolog. des* 4 *Ev.* (1898).

Christians of Asia must have had to face either the activities of a Baptist sect, as has been already suggested, or at least distorted notions current in their midst as to the importance of the person of the Forerunner.

We need not suppose that the Baptist is dragged into the Prologue in the interests of controversy. His position as standing midway between the two Dispensations amply accounts for the introduction of his name. But this alone will not explain the emphasis laid upon the fact that "he was not the Light," and upon his subordinate character as a mere witness to the Christ. Indeed in one passage even the significance of his testimony is minimised.[1] He was the lamp, Christ is the Light; he was the friend, Christ the Bridegroom; he was of the earth, Christ from above.

(4) Even at so early a date as this questions were being raised as to the exact relation of the Divine and Human elements in the Person of Christ. St. Paul had not been directly confronted with this difficulty, although in his teaching on the Incarnation he had laid down the lines along which later ages might work out the problem. The Son who pre-existed in the "form"—the specific character and essential attributes[2]—of God had, by a voluntary act of self-beggary, "emptied Himself" and taken the form and fashion of a man.[3]

But by the time of the composition of the Johannine writings the problem had become more acute. Christianity had come into contact with a mode of thought to which the idea of a real Incarnation was intolerable, and the Christian teachers had acccordingly to accept or reject the solution proposed by Gnosticism in its many phases. This solution we may style broadly Doceticism, though it took various forms. The union between the man Jesus and the Æon Christ was but temporary. The Divine Being only seemed to have come in the flesh and to have undergone human experiences. The Christ left Jesus before the Passion. Simon of Cyrene, who carried the Cross, was crucified in His stead. His crucifixion was an illusion practised on His enemies.

---

[1] v. 36. [2] *Cf*. Lightfoot, *Philippians*, p. 127 f.
[3] PHIL. ii. 7 ; 2 COR. viii. 9 ; GAL. iv. 4.

Such ideas as these, however helpful they may have been to the Gnostic illuminati, robbed the mass of men of all that they valued most highly in the Christian religion, and met with a direct denial from the Church.

Although opposition to this form of heresy is most clearly marked in the First Epistle it is not absent from the Gospel in the emphasis laid upon the reality of the Incarnation. The Lord did not unite Himself for the purpose of His Ministry with a man, nor clothe Himself in some phantasmal body—He became flesh.

Ὁ λόγος σὰρξ ἐγένετο. No loophole is left for the introduction of Docetic ideas, and though the formula does not define the term "flesh," nor explicitly guard against the thought of an absorption of the Divine in the Human element, other references of the writer leave little doubt as to his meaning. What the Word "became" is placed in antithesis to what the Word "was" in His eternal Being.[1] There was no transference of personality at the Incarnation —it was the "Word-made-Flesh" who dwelt among us.[2] Yet the Humanity of the Incarnate Logos was complete and not confined to the bodily frame.[3] He it was who hung upon the Cross, and stress is laid on the effusion of blood and water from His pierced side, not only in view of its mystical significance, but as testifying to the reality of His human sufferings.[4] The idea of the substitution of Simon of Cyrene seems to be in mind when Christ is said to have gone forth "bearing His Cross for Himself."[5] Nor was the human nature of Christ laid aside as a worn-out cloak after His Resurrection. His Body still bears the prints of the nails and the scar of the spear wound when He appears to His disciples,[6] and the thought not only of the Passion but of the Ascension of the *Incarnate* Word is implicit in the frequent references to the "exaltation" of the "Son of Man."[7]

---

[1] *Cf.* the expressions in the Epp. "ἐν σαρκὶ ἐληλυθότα," 1 JOHN iv. 2, ἐρχόμενον ἐν σαρκὶ, 2 JOHN 7.

[2] *Cf.* xvii. 5.

[3] xvii. 2 shows that to "become flesh" is equivalent to becoming a member of the human race. *Cf.* also x. 11, 15, 17–18 with xiii. 37, 38, xv. 13.

[4] xix. 34 f.   [5] xix. 17.   [6] xx. 20 f.

[7] iii. 14, viii. 28, xii. 32, 34.

The evangelist has thus protected the doctrine of the Incarnation, the central point of his theology.

As to the Virgin Birth he says nothing directly,[1] although the narrative must have been known to him, and the Jewish calumnies on the subject may be alluded to.[2] The omission of any explicit reference to this is probably due to the fact that the account of the Birth, like the stories of the Infancy, did not fall within the scope of his Gospel. Perhaps also it is an early instance of the practice of " οἰκονομία " in view of the petty slanders of the Jews, which are sufficiently met by the doctrine of the Word-become-Flesh. Either of these suggestions appears more likely than the supposed difficulty felt by the evangelist in referring to the beginning in time of the human life of the Logos-Christ.[3]

It may not be out of place to notice here that just as the writer insists on the reality of our Lord's Humanity, to safeguard His unique position as the one mediator between God and Man, so for the same reason no mention is made throughout the Gospel of angelic intermediaries, nor yet of the cures of demoniacs, that are so often met with in the synoptic records. He is determined to afford no handle to Gnostic speculations.

But while the existence of these heretical views as to the Person of Christ can be clearly recognised as forming part of the historical background of the Gospel, in the First Epistle they come more to the front, and we can gain a better idea as to their nature.

This epistle seems to have been called forth by the activities of certain heretical teachers, and more immediately by the secession from the Church of a considerable body of their number [4] after some strife.[5] The writer views them

---

[1] Critics of such opposite schools as Zahn and Loisy agree in reading the singular in i. 13. This text is supported by b. Tert. Aug., and indirectly by Iren. lat. (3), Amb., Sulp., possibly by Just. Dial. lxiii. If it is accepted it is undoubtly a reference to the Virgin Birth. But one may well ask if this is not presupposed in the received text of this verse. "Why the elaboration of the theme, above all why the θελήματος ἀνδρὸς, unless he has in mind the supernatural birth of the Logos as a kind of pattern or model of the birth of the children of God." W. C. Allen, *Interpreter*, October 1905, p. 57 f.

[2] viii. 19, 41.   [3] *Cf.* Scott, *Fourth Gospel*, p. 187 f.
[4] ii. 19.   [5] iv. 4.

with so much apprehension that he regards their presence as a manifest sign that it is already the "Last Hour."[1]

The errors attacked by him in the epistle are of two kinds, practical and doctrinal, but while we may not separate these, and look for two classes of teachers, one distinguished by irregularity of life and the other by false doctrine, the references seem to show that he is not confining his attention to any one heresy, but warns his readers against many varieties of error, illustrating his point by elements in the heretical teaching which are most repugnant to him.[2]

It is often said that the writer is combating the Antinomianism found in some later Gnostic sects. But this is too sweeping a judgement. When we interpret the general references in the light of the more explicit statements we find that we can only accuse these heretical teachers on the practical side of a lack of the sense of sin and of a clear recognition of the moral obligations which are bound up with the Christian Faith. They would lower the standard set by Christ, and to this the writer attributes their popularity. More particularly they fail in the virtue of Christian love, the love which is ready to share the goods of this world with a brother in Christ, and if need be to die for him.[3]

Turning to the doctrinal references we recognise semi-Gnostic elements in the suggested claim to a superior knowledge of Christ or God,[4] and to a special spiritual enlightenment.[5] But the crucial test whereby the false teachers are to be tried is the confession of "Jesus Christ come in flesh." To deny this is to deny that Jesus is the Christ, or Son of God,

---

[1] ii. 18. [2] *Cf.* ii. 18 f. ; iv. 1 f.

[3] *Cf.* i. 8 f. ; ii. 3 f. ; ii. 15 f. ; iii. 10 f., 16 f. ; iv. 5 f. ; v. 3 f.

[4] ii. 4 ; iii. 6, *cf.* Tit. i. 16 ; Apoc. ii. 24. Perhaps this is hinted at in i. 5, ii. 23. In the latter reference the writer may have had his Jewish opponents in view as well, but it is impossible to follow Wurm and Belser in tracing all the doctrinal references to Judaizers. This particular verse can quite well cover even such teachers as Cerinthus, who taught that the Pre-existent Christ united to Jesus revealed "the unknown Father."

[5] ii. 9, 20, 27. Perhaps also the allusion to the Divine σπέρμα in iii. 9 may refer to such ideas as those of the Valentinians, who said that οὐ πρᾶξις εἰς πλήρωμα εἰσάγει, ἀλλὰ τὸ σπέρμα τὸ ἐκεῖθεν νήπιον ἐκπεμπόμενον, ἐνθὰ δε τελειούμενον (Iren., *adv. hær.*, i. 6, 4), or even to Jewish claims (*cf.* iii. 1.) ; see Moffatt, *Int. N. T.*, p. 587. But neither of these interpretations is necessary to explain the thought of the text.

and to confess not Jesus.[1] There can be little doubt that the error with which the writer is dealing, and which he regards with so much abhorrence, is that early form of Doceticism which drew a distinction between Jesus the Human Person and the Heavenly Being Christ. The heretics, as the early gloss on iv. 3 puts it, "dissolve" Jesus.[2]

But, the writer insists, not only had the Christ come in Flesh. He came also "through Water and Blood, not in the Water only, but in the Water and the Blood." That is to say, the Passion was an essential part of the saving Mission of Christ. The passage suggests that one or some of the false teachers recognised the Baptism alone, and taught that before the Passion the union between the Christ and Jesus was brought to an end. This may be illustrated by what is told us in Irenæus of the teaching of Cerinthus. It was alleged by him that after the Baptism there descended into the man Jesus, from that Principality which is above all things, the Christ in the figure of a dove, to announce the unknown Father and to perfect His powers, but that in the end the Christ flew back again from Him. Jesus suffered and rose again, while the Christ remained impassible existing as a Spirit.[3] The early tradition of the opposition of the Apostle John to Cerinthus may well be founded on fact.[4]

These doctrinal errors are met by the writer in two ways. In the first place he flatly controverts the claims of the False Teachers to any special knowledge or illumination in regard to spiritual things. Right knowledge, he tells them, is bound up with right action, and they prove the falsity of their claims by their own lives.

---

[1] ii. 22 f. ; iv. 2 f. ; v. 1, 5 f.

[2] For the variant reading here *cf*. Westcott, *Epp. John*, note p. 163. For the idea *cf*. Iren., *adv. hær.*, iii. 16 : "Some say that Jesus was a receptacle of the Christ, in whom the Christ descended from above as a dove." Contrast with the developed Doceticism of the Ignatian Epistles.

[3] Iren., *adv. hær.*, i. 26, 1.

[4] *Cf.* also the statement in Epiphanius (*adv. hær.*, ii. 1), possibly founded on the Syntagma of Hippolytus, to the effect that Cerinthus identified the Christ with the Spirit. This may throw light on the reference to the Spirit's function of "testifying" in v. 7 (*cf*. Ev. i. 7, &c.). For this and many of the points of the discussion on the False Teachers I am indebted to the Rev. A. E. Brooke's Prælection for the Lady Margaret Professorship, July 1911.

But his positive argument consists of an appeal to the historic facts on which the Church has based her message— to "that which we have heard, that which we have seen with our eyes, that which we beheld and our hands handled."

(5) This opens up the important but difficult problem of the relation of the Johannine presentation of Christ to history.

The subject of the historical character of the fourth Gospel has led to endless discussion, and the last word with regard to it has not yet been spoken. Here we can only touch on it in so far as it affects the question of the Johannine theology.

When it is recorded in the Apostles' Creed that Jesus Christ suffered "under Pontius Pilate," the intention is not to hold up the name of the Roman procurator to universal execration, but to register the fact that the Person who is the centre of the Christian revelation lived and died as man at a particular date in the world's history. In this fact lies much of the strength and attraction of the creed of Christendom, and yet it has its own peculiar danger, to which the Church of the second century was exposed in like manner, if not to the same extent, as it is to-day.

The early Christians, as we have seen, fixed their eyes on the future, and were concerned with the past or present only in so far as it was a preparation for that which was to come. But when the Parousia, though still eagerly looked for, was not regarded as so immediately impending as in the first days, and before the generation which had seen our Lord had passed away, it was but natural that increased interest should be aroused in the words and acts of the Saviour when on earth. The Synoptic Gospels, based on the oral traditions of the apostles, are the outcome of this demand for information concerning the earthly life of our Lord. They are not written without presuppositions—we have said this when we have styled them Gospels—yet, on the whole, the authors are content to let the facts narrated tell their own tale. And these facts have a value in themselves, both for writers and readers, as records of a never-to-be-repeated past. The Church indeed owes a deep debt to the Synoptic Gospels, yet in the very temper of mind which called them forth lies the danger to which allusion has been made, one that was stayed at the time by the enthusiasm of the Christian communities, but which would be threatening when this had passed away, as pass it must. When the vivid expectation of the Second Coming had gone, what would remain to nourish the life and devotion of the Church save the memory of a great fact of past history—unique and wonderful and winning enough— yet for all that, in the past.

At the time this peril was in part averted by the work of St. Paul. This apostle indeed did not say all that he is often represented as having said in the words, "Even though we have known Christ after the flesh, yet now we know Him so no more." [1] He had both some interest in and knowledge of the earthly life of Christ. But for him it was all over-shadowed by the Cross, viewed in the light of the vision of the Risen Master on the road to Damascus. The words just quoted, then, do to a certain extent represent his attitude towards the historical life. The incidents of the earthly mission were for him transcended in importance by Christ's heavenly activities. The original apostles, he insists, were placed in no position of advantage over him by the fact of their companionship with the Lord on earth. Was he not too an apostle ? Had he not seen the Christ ? Christianity was no mere tradition from the past, it was a life in Christ in the present.

But when once the weight of the emphasis was laid on the knowledge of the Exalted Lord Christianity was immediately exposed to a danger from the opposite direction, that it should be altogether divorced from history. Then Gnosticism would have represented not a side channel, but the main current of the development of Christian thought—and its grave.

Now, the abiding value of the fourth Gospel consists in the fact that it deliberately avoids both of these ex-tremes. On the one hand, the evangelist refuses to be cut loose from the past. The central figure of the Christian revelation was not some mythical abstraction, the subjective product of the religious consciousness, but the Jesus of Nazareth who had been seen, heard, gazed upon, and handled

[1] 2 COR. v. 16 ; *cf.* Inge, *Christian Mysticism*, 69 f.

when He lived on earth as Man. On the other hand, he equally refuses to be bound down to the past, as though the terms of the earthly life limited the activities of the living Christ, or as though the experiences of the first generation were the sum of the knowledge that could be gained of Him. Thus when he turns back to the life of Christ on earth it is to review it in the light of all that the Church had learned of her Master from the earliest days, and to exhibit it as a vast sacrament, which conveyed without concealing the inner permanent meaning of what was said and done. The whole significance of the historical life to him was not as a record of the past but as a symbol of the present. His Gospel consists, he tells us, of "signs" selected to produce belief that Jesus is the Christ, the Son of God. Let us grant, what is far from having been proved, that these signs are not historical in the strict sense, that his Gospel is of little use for a reconstruction of the life of Christ, that the narratives have been worked up from the synoptists or from tradition, yet we have not said all that needs to be said. If the writer of the fourth Gospel speaks of the healing of the blind, or of the raising of the dead, so do the synoptists. But he has recorded these works not so much as accounts of what Christ did as of what Christ does, because they are symbols of the present activities of Him who is the Light and the Life of the world, and because even then the eyes of the spiritually blind were being opened, and those who are dead in sin were coming forth from their tombs at the call of the Master. "We speak that we do know, and bear witness of that we have seen."

The evangelist has endeavoured to portray the permanent significance of the life of Christ. Whether he has succeeded or not it is scarcely the place of historical criticism to say. And the nature of the Gospel must be taken into account when the historical critic turns to subjects which more immediately concern him. The author has not attempted to draw a picture of the Christ which would register the exact impressions made by Him upon His contemporaries. He has deliberately chosen to take eternity and not time as his standpoint, and the history of Christ becomes, not a journal describing the rise of a Prophet among an obscure people and His tragic death at the hands of His countrymen, but a great drama staged between ⸢heaven and earth wherein eternal issues are wrought out. Much criticism is robbed of its force when it is realised that " it is not only his Christ who is not of this world. The believer also is not of this world, is not judged, doth not sin, is passed from death unto life." [1]

It is true that the Divine glory which radiates from the Johannine Christ as He moves among men sometimes dims the clear outline of the Human Figure,[2] yet it does not dehumanise it. And the Christ who claims to do and speak nothing of Himself, whose meat is to do the will of Him that sent Him, is not far removed from the Christ who spends lonely hours in the wilderness or upon the mountain top, and who strives in prayer among the olive trees. If the sevenfold " I am " takes the place of the Sermon on the Mount, yet the Beatitudes lingered in the ears of their disciples less for their beauty than for the weight of personal experience which lay behind them; and it was the authority wherewith the Christ lays down the Laws of the Kingdom that filled the people

---

[1] Inge, *Camb. Bibl. Essays*, p. 279.

[2] It is scarcely true to say that there is no κένωσις, *cf.* xvii. 5. Very unfair treatment is often meted out to the Johannine portrait of the Historical Christ. Thus Réville states that the Christ of the fourth Gospel does not pray, and instances in support of this the fact that, in speaking to the Father in the High Priestly Prayer, Christ uses the expressions ἐρωτῶ and θέλω (*Le Quatrième Évangile*, p. 223). Leaving on one side as too large a subject the general question of the prayers of Christ in this Gospel, and confining our attention to the linguistic point, we notice that if the Christ does not "pray " in this sense, neither does the Christian ! Like the Christ he *"asks."* Αἰτεῖν (αἰτεῖσθαι) is regularly used, but in xvi. 23 this verb alternates with and is practically equivalent to ἐρωτᾶν; *cf.* also xv. 7, ὃ ἐὰν θέλητε. (The distinction between αἰτεῖν and ἐρωτᾶν does not turn upon the relative dignity of the person asking and the person asked. *Cf.* Trench, *Notes on Translation of New Testament*, p. 101; Grimm and Thayer's *Lexicon*, p. 18a).

The human traits of the Johannine Christ are most clearly marked in the account of the raising of Lazarus, but here capital is made out of the strange expression ἐτάραξεν ἑαυτόν (xi. 33). This, *e.g.*, is singled out by Scott (*Fourth Gospel*, p. 170) as showing that " His very emotions do not come over Him involuntarily." But if any stress is to be laid upon the phrase at all, may it not be that the writer here again has in mind the Docetic denial that the Christ could suffer, and employs this expression to safeguard the unity of the Divine-Human Person against those who would "dissolve " Him. These violent emotions, he seems to say, were those of the Logos-Christ Himself. *Cf.* xi. 38, ἐμβριμώμενος ἐν ἑαυτῷ.

with astonishment. He who was not recognised by "the Jews" because He came not in His own name appears none other than "the meek and lowly of heart" of the synoptists; and it is to the "egotistical" and "arrogant" Christ of the fourth Gospel that the simple folk and the weary and heavy laden of this world turn for comfort.

II. We pass on to consider the Johannine soteriology.

The old controversy as to salvation by faith or by works, which in the days of St. Paul had threatened to split the Church asunder, has by now died down, and the faint echoes which reach us, while they bear witness to the widespread influence of the Pauline teaching on this subject, show, too, how far removed from the arena of practical interests the question has become. It is as a self-evident axiom which needs neither explanation nor justification that the author of the fourth Gospel lays down that "the Law was given by Moses. Grace and Truth came through Jesus Christ";[1] and the Pauline position is concisely summed up in the words, "This is the work of God, that ye should believe on Him whom He sent."[2]

But in their presentation of the saving work of Christ and subjects allied thereto the Church teachers of the time had other problems to face. The simple faith of the mass of Christians required to be enriched with new elements, a counterbalance was needed to the current "Millenarianism," and the question as to what was to be the attitude of the Church towards that mode of thought roughly styled "Gnosticism" had become pressing.

(1) At the outset of our inquiry into the Johannine teaching on this subject we are confronted by a strongly marked tendency of thought, which may be termed "Dualistic." The world—the sphere of darkness, death and falsehood—with its ruler and the men of this world, stand in sharpest contrast with God and Christ, and those who are of God, of the Truth, not of this world. In the Gospel we seem to hear no longer the call to repentance, nor the welcome extended to the publicans and sinners. Rather it would appear that mankind are by nature divided into two classes, separated by a

---

[1] i. 17. [2] vi. 29.

chasm which none can cross,[1] and that Christ's love and saving mission extended only to the one class.[2] That this is the thought of the evangelist has indeed been maintained by some critics, though in order to do so they have been obliged either to explain away other references which militate against this theory,[3] or to allow for inconsistencies in the mind of the writer. But the solution of the difficulty will not be found along this line. The Johannine dualism is not Manichee, for the world is represented as the direct object of God's love. Nor have we here to deal with the Gnostic division of mankind into pneumatic and psychic, for the Logos is the light of every man. Nor, again, must we see in the "Darkness" only the inert matter of the Philonian philosophy which offers its negative opposition to the action of the Logos; sin is here represented, not as a mere *privatio boni*, but as an active evil power which brings men into a state of slavery.[4] It is an ethical dualism which meets us in these writings. The writer's interests are throughout religious and not metaphysical; he is concerned with the fact of sin, and not with speculations as to its origin. Having assured his readers that "apart from the Logos nothing came into being," he is content to state the fact of the conflict between the Divine Light and the Darkness, and there to leave the matter. His presentation of the effect of the historic Mission of Christ is conditioned partly by temperamental reasons, partly also by apologetic. He intends to show that the rejection of Christ by the Jews was *morally inevitable*, and arose necessarily from the given facts. He paints his picture accordingly with a broad brush in black and white, and we may not quarrel with him if some of the fainter shades are blotted out.[5]

(2) The same change of categories that we met with in the Johannine doctrine of the Person of Christ we find again in the teaching as to His Work. Roughly speaking, the idea

---

[1] vi. 64; viii. 23, 44; x. 26, &c.   [2] xi. 52; xiii. 1.   [3] *Cf. e.g.* v. 24, 40.

[4] There is, therefore, no need to separate the Gospel from the First Epistle on this ground.

[5] *Cf.* Abbott, *Johannine Vocabulary*, p. 157: "Generally, we may say that John prefers to pass over local distinctions of sects, classes, and rulers, material distinctions of physical evil and moral distinctions of various sins, in order to concentrate the mind on the elements of the spiritual world, light and darkness, spiritual life and death, truth and falsehood."

of Life fills in the Johannine writings the place that the
Kingdom does in the synoptists, though it is not of course
absent from Christ's teaching there, and no doubt in both
places goes back to the same Old Testament fount. It is
the natural term in the language of religion to express
man's highest good and God's chief boon.

Only the Father and the Son by His gift can properly
be said to have life in themselves,[1] but it is the work of
the Logos to mediate life. All true life in every sphere
comes through Him. He is "the timeless Life of which
the temporal world is a manifestation," [2] and His Incarnate
Mission was to rescue men from death [3] and destruction [4]
that they may have life, and have it more abundantly.[5]
"Life" here then stands for "the fulfilment of the highest
idea of being" (Westcott); it is opposed, not to physical, but
to spiritual death. It is sometimes further defined by the
addition of *αἰώνιος*, but this marks it, not as laid up for
the future, but as belonging to another than the temporal
sphere. Indeed, the writer prefers to lay emphasis on it as
a present possession,[6] though at times it is referred to the
future and brought into connection with the Resurrection.[7]
But the idea that Christ's gift of life is limited to the
resurrection on the Judgement Day is expressly corrected.
"Martha saith unto Him, I know that he shall rise again
in the resurrection at the last day. Jesus said unto her,
I am the Resurrection and the Life." [8]

Another term to be noticed in this connection is that
of Truth. In the Johannine use of the term "the Truth"
(*ἡ ἀλήθεια*) is perhaps better translated "Reality," and the
conception goes back ultimately to Platonic idealism. It
signifies "all that really exists in every sphere," [9] and things
have "truth" in them in so far as they correspond to the
Thought and Will of God.

Inasmuch as the sinner is failing to realise the law of
his being, to live in sin is to lie and to do not the Truth.[10]

---

[1] v. 26, *cf.* v. 39.
[2] Inge, *Christian Mysticism*, p. 46 (on JOHN i. 4, W. H. text).   [3] v. 24.
[4] iii. 16.   [5] x. 10.   [6] iii. 36 ; v. 24, &c.   [7] v. 28 ; vi. 40, &c.
[8] xi. 24 f.   [9] Inge, *Dict. Christ and Gospels.*   [10] 1 JOHN i. 6.

Christ came to bear witness to the Truth,[1] and the Truth thus revealed frees men from the illusory life of sin.[2] In the last resort the Christ is Himself the Truth.[3]

"Light" is the third great leading idea that we meet with in the Johannine writings. Besides being the obvious symbol of illumination, joy, and purity, it contains also the thought of self-communication. God is Light.[4] Not only is His splendour undimmed by any moral imperfection, any limitation of knowledge, but it is His nature and property to reveal and to communicate Himself. The idea of Light thus fringes on that of Love. Light must impart as Love must give,[5] and the Prologue, which records the continued revelation to man through the Logos, culminates in the statement that the Word became Man, and by His Incarnate Presence completed and superseded all earlier manifestations.

But it is a characteristic of light to repel as well as to attract, and this the history of the earthly life is designed to show. First we watch the Light dawning upon the world as various witnesses and signs reveal His glory.[6] Then the inevitable sifting process begins, moral sympathy drawing men within the circle of His influence, moral antipathy driving them further back into the darkness.[7] As His day draws to its close the shadows lengthen.[8] There is one final manifestation of the Light to His own,[9] and then His foes gather against Him, as clouds around the setting sun. But the Light goes down upon the world only to rise again.[10]

(3) Thus, although the purpose of Christ's mission was to save men, it resulted in a κρίσις, whereby the true children of God were separated from among the mass of mankind. This will explain the contradictory statements on Christ's office as Judge that we meet with in the Gospel.[11] He Himself passes judgement on no man; men by their attitude towards His Revelation pass judgement on themselves. Here,

---

[1] xviii. 37.   [2] viii. 32.   [3] xiv. 6.   [4] 1 JOHN i. 5.
[5] *Cf.* iii. 16, "God so loved . . . that He gave."   [6] i. 19–iv. 54.
[7] v.–vi.   [8] vii.–xii.   [9] xiii.–xvii.   [10] xviii.–xx.
[11] *Cf.* iii. 17 ; v. 45 ; xii. 47, with v. 22, 27 ; ix. 39 ; xii. 31.

S

again, we find the Evangelist throwing emphasis upon the
present rather than upon the future. But to say that because
he does so he has no place in his system for the future judgement, and to explain all reference to this in the Gospel [1] as a
concession to orthodoxy or as an unassimilated fragment of
primitive Christianity, is to do less than justice to the
writer.[2]

(4) There has always been a tendency for Christian thought,
in contemplating the work of the Saviour, to concentrate its
attention upon one of these two salient points, either upon
the fact of the Incarnation, or upon the Cross. Pauline
theology centres in "Christ crucified," Johannine theology
in the "Word become Flesh." Yet in neither case does this
necessarily imply a lack of appreciation of the other clause of
the Christian creed. The Cross may be regarded as the
summary of the work of the Incarnation, and such it was
to St. Paul. The Incarnation, on the other hand, may be
held to imply and to include the Cross. What is the
Johannine doctrine of the death of Christ?

In the first place the Cross is viewed as the consummation of the Life, and the supreme manifestation of Divine
Love.[3] "Christ crucified" is for the evangelist "Christ
glorified." The life of the Son of Man reaches its sublimest
height of moral splendour, and the revelation of God attains
its most complete expression, on the hill of Calvary. The
apparent contrast between the ignominy of the Passion and
the glory of the Resurrection is found to be transcended in
a deeper unity, and the reproach of the Cross has lost its
sting.[4]

Stress is put upon the freedom with which the Good

---

[1] *Cf.* v. 28, 29 ; xii. 48.

[2] *Cf.* Inge, *Christian Mysticism*, p. 54. If such a critic "means that for
St. John judgement is now, *and therefore not in the future*, he is attributing to
the Evangelist and to the whole array of religious thinkers who have used
similar expressions a view which it is easy enough to understand, but which is
destitute of any value, for it entirely fails to satisfy the religious consciousness."

[3] x. 11 ; xii. 23 ; 1 JOHN iii. 16 ; iv. 7.

[4] *Cf.* Loisy, *Le Quatrième Évangile*, p. 116. "La pensée de l'évangéliste
s'est familiarisée avec elle (la mort du Christ) et l'a tournée de façon qu'elle n'a
plus rien d'effrayant ni d'inquiétant ; le Christ en parle et il la traverse avec une
telle sérénité que le lecteur n'en garde qu'une impression de vie."

Shepherd lays down His life.[1]   None can touch Him until His hour has come, and then He goes forth to meet His death with full knowledge of what was about to happen.[2] So self-determined is it all that He can already speak in the supper room of having completed His Father's work.[3]

Peculiar to the Johannine theology is the thought of the death as necessary for the universal extension of Christ's mission. His work on earth was confined within narrow borders, but by His death the limitations of His earthly life were removed, and thus He would gather into one the children of God who were scattered abroad.[4]   "Domini mors potentior erat quam vita" (pseudo-Cyprian).

Nor can we escape the conclusion that the death is also regarded in a sacrificial aspect.   In the Gospel John the Baptist bears witness to Christ as "the Lamb of God, which taketh away the sin of the world,"[5] and the Synoptic chronology is expressly corrected so as to make the Crucifixion coincide with the slaughter of the Paschal lambs.   Christ lays down His life for the sheep,[6] and as both Priest and Victim, consecrates Himself for death.[7]

Yet we are told that the death of Christ in the Johannine theology is of no value for salvation, and that it is not regarded as a sacrifice for sin.   This conclusion is surely an example of the evil results of starting with pre-suppositions. Because the death of the Logos could not well be reconciled with the Alexandrian philosophy it does not follow that it is of no importance in the eyes of the Evangelist.   To carry out this idea consistently it is usual to label many passages as concessions to tradition, and to separate the First Epistle from the Gospel.   As a matter of fact, however, there is little in the First Epistle that goes beyond what is suggested in the Gospel itself.   In the Epistle the blood of Christ is said to cleanse from all sin;[8] in the Gospel stress is laid upon the effusion of blood from the pierced side of the Crucified,[9] and to drink His blood is made a necessary condition for eternal life.[10]   Twice in the Epistle, Christ Himself, not His death

---

[1] x. 18.   [2] xviii. 4.   [3] xvii. 4.
[4] xi. 52; *cf.* iii. 14, 15; vii. 39; xii. 24; xvii. 1, 2.   [5] i. 29, 36.
[6] x. 11; *cf.* vi. 51; xi. 50 f.   [7] xvii. 19.
[8] 1 JOHN i. 7.   [9] xix. 34 f.   [10] vi. 53.

nor His blood, is said to be a Propitiation ($\dot{\iota}\lambda\alpha\sigma\mu\acute{o}s$) for our sins,[1] but this is scarcely more explicit than the sacrificial references in the Gospel. In both Gospel and Epistle Christ is looked upon as a sacrifice for sin; in neither is it clearly stated how that sacrifice avails for us.

(5) "Faith" is the necessary condition of the appropriation by the individual of the salvation wrought by Christ. The noun, $\pi\acute{\iota}\sigma\tau\iota s$, indeed, does not occur in the Gospel, and in the First Epistle only once (v. 4), where it is used in the restricted sense of the Christian creed. It is noticeable also that the noun $\gamma\nu\hat{\omega}\sigma\iota s$ is not to be found in any of the Johannine writings. In both cases the verbs, $\pi\iota\sigma\tau\epsilon\acute{u}\epsilon\iota\nu$, $\gamma\iota\nu\acute{\omega}\sigma\kappa\epsilon\iota\nu$, take their place. There can be little doubt that this avoidance of the nouns is due to their use as technical terms by the Gnostics. The Church teacher by employing the verb goes back to the simple root-idea of the words, and thereby strips them of their Gnostic connotation. "Salvation, he seems to say, is not dependent on $\gamma\nu\hat{\omega}\sigma\iota s$ and $\pi\acute{\iota}\sigma\tau\iota s$ in the Gnostic, esoteric sense, but on a real 'knowing' and 'believing.'"[2]

The Johannine doctrine of "Faith" falls in no way short of the Pauline. The favourite construction both in the Gospel and the First Epistle—it is rare elsewhere—is $\pi\iota\sigma\tau\epsilon\acute{u}\epsilon\iota\nu$ followed by $\epsilon\acute{\iota}s$.[3] For the writer, as for St. Paul, faith is self-surrender to a Person.

But he is concerned to show that it has many phases, and it is necessary to recognise that he employs the same construction to denote both the most rudimentary movement of belief and the most developed faith.[4] As he emphasises by the use of the verb, belief in Christ is a process,[5] which may take its rise from most imperfect beginnings, and which indeed may never reach maturity.

Faith which springs from "signs and wonders" is disparaged;[6] true faith, such as may be expected to develop,

---

[1] 1 John ii. 2; iv. 10; *cf.* Rom. iii. 25; Heb. ii. 17.

[2] Scott, *Fourth Gospel*, p. 94.

[3] $\pi\iota\sigma\tau\epsilon\acute{u}\epsilon\iota\nu$ $\epsilon\acute{\iota}s$ is not found in the LXX., occurs only in Matt. xviii. 6 of the synoptists, and is only rarely used by St. Paul. *Cf.* Swete, *Studies in Teaching of our Lord*, p. 152 f.

[4] *Cf.* vii. 31; viii. 30, with xi. 25, &c.

[5] *Cf. e.g.* xi. 15; xiii. 19; xiv. 29; xvi. 31, spoken to disciples, and xvii. 8.

[6] iv. 48; vi. 30.

is that which, penetrating beneath the mere outward marvel, seizes on the inner meaning of the σημεῖον.[1] Indeed the heinousness of the sin of unbelief consists in the fact that it is a confession of failure to recognise the Divine in the world,[2] a failure which arises from moral causes.[3] "Believe Me" (πιστεύετέ μοι), urges the Christ, "that I am in the Father and the Father in Me: or else for the very works' sake believe."[4]

The liberty of man to accept or reject the revelation of Christ is clearly recognised[5] — that "dualistic" tendency which appears to contradict this has been already noticed. But there still remain some passages which at first sight are difficult. "All that the Father giveth Me will come unto Me,"[6] says Christ; and again, "No man can come unto Me except the Father who sent Me draw him."[7] Such words, however, appear to stand for "the deepest religious truths, the prevenience of God and man's affinity to Him . . . Man's spirit, ever largely but potential, can respond actively to the historic Jesus, because already touched and made hungry by the all-actual spirit-God, who made that soul akin unto Himself."[8]

But if in the Johannine theology the importance of faith is fully emphasised, equal stress is laid upon the fact that it is not in itself the ultimate relation of the believer to Christ.[9] Faith leads to knowledge: the Christian life "begins with an experiment and ends with an experience."[10] "Believe," says Christ, "that ye may know and continue to know (γνῶτε καὶ γινώσκητε) that the Father is in Me and I in the Father."[11] Christianity is not a system of estoric "γνῶσις," but a life of progressive experience and illumination. Thus "eternal life"

---

[1] *Cf.* ii. 11 with ii. 23.

[2] iii. 18 f., 36 ; v. 35 f. ; ix. 41 ; xv. 21 f. ; 1 JOHN iii. 6.

[3] iii. 20 ; v. 44 ; vii. 7 ; xii. 43.   [4] xiv. 11 ; *cf.* x. 37.

[5] *Cf.* especially v. 40.   [6] vi. 37.   [7] vi. 44.

[8] Von Hugel, *Ency. Brit.*, vol. xv. p. 455b.

[9] *Cf.* Abbott, *Johannine Vocabulary*, p. 79 ff.

[10] Inge, *Christian Mysticism*, p. 52.

[11] x. 38 ; *cf.* vi. 69 ; vii. 17 ; viii. 32. Those few passages in which "knowledge" appears to be practically identified with "faith" (*cf.* i. 10 ; xvii. 8 ; 1 JOHN iv. 16) must be explained as referring to that "recognition" of God in Christ which synchronises with belief. Faith is not irrational.

can be spoken of as a process of acquiring knowledge of God and Christ.[1]

It may be that the Gnostics called forth this presentation of Christianity—heresy's great service to the Church has been in drawing attention to truths forgotten or overlooked—yet this is far removed from Gnosticism. To say that here "the purely religious view is overlaid and obscured by the conception of Christianity as a speculative system, which makes its primary appeal to the logical intelligence,"[2] is simply untrue. The knowledge of which the writer speaks is knowledge of a Person, and therefore not solely or even primarily a matter of the intellect—it is rather that of the heart than of the head. Only the union of love between the believer and Christ makes such knowledge possible; for "he that loveth knoweth."[3] Christ knows His own, and His own know Him; and as this mutual knowledge reflects in the sphere of the Incarnation that eternal relationship of love which exists within the bosom of the Godhead,[4] so the Highpriestly prayer which starts with the definition of eternal life as "knowledge" leads to the petition that "all may be one, even as Thou, Father, art in Me, and I in Thee . . . that they may be one . . . in Us."[5]

Here, then, we are presented with a conception of the Christian life that would prove not only an effective counterbalance to the current futuristic outlook, but one that the world has not yet exhausted, indeed cannot exhaust.

(6) It is, however, when we turn to the Johannine doctrine of the Holy Spirit that we find perhaps the greatest advance made, and one of the highest significance for the future history of the Church. The Return of Christ holds a place in the Johannine system as central as in the creed of the early Church—only it is not the Return at the Last Day but the Return under the dispensation of the Holy Ghost.

The Synoptic teaching on the Holy Spirit follows closely on Old Testament lines, but a development is discovered in the Pauline writings. St. Paul traces the action of the Spirit of God not only in the strange psychic phenomena, the occur-

---

[1] xvii. 3.   [2] Scott, *Fourth Gospel*, p. 98.   [3] 1 JOHN iv. 7.
[4] x. 14, 15.   [5] xvii. 21, 22; *cf.* 26.

rence of which in the Christian communities was regarded as a manifest token of Divine operation, but in all the graces and virtues of the Christian life. The Spirit is the sphere within which the Christian lives, the indwelling power which controls and transforms his life. Of great importance are those passages in which the activities of the Spirit are identified with those of the glorified Christ, as *e.g.* Rom. viii. 9 f., "If any man has not Christ's spirit, that man is not His. But if Christ be in you . . ."; 2 Cor. iii. 17, "The Lord is the Spirit, but where the Spirit of the Lord is, there is freedom. But we all . . . are being transformed . . . as by the Spirit of the Lord."

The ideas here seen to be latent in the writings of St. Paul find clear expression in the fourth Gospel, where the dispensation of the Holy Spirit is viewed as a real extension of the Incarnation.

The Spirit had descended and abode in full measure upon Christ at His baptism,[1] but, says the Evangelist, during the earthly life the Spirit was not yet given to men, for it could only be mediated to them through the glorified humanity of the Son of Man.[2]

The Coming of the Spirit, however, is a real Return of Christ to His own. For the Spirit is Christ's *alter ego.* If in one verse He[3] is differentiated from the Son, in the next they are identified. If Christ promises another Paraclete,[4] in the same breath He tells the disciples that they already know Him, even now He is abiding with them, hereafter He will be in them,[5] and this is immediately followed by the words, "I will not leave you bereaved. I come to you."[6] Throughout the Spirit in His temporal mission is regarded

[1] i. 32 ; iii. 34.　　　　　　　　　　　　[2] vii. 39.

[3] ἐκεῖνος is used of the Paraclete xiv. 26 ; xv. 26 ; xvi. 8, 13, 14.

[4] On the title *cf.* Swete, *Holy Spirit in N. T.*, p. 372. There can be no doubt that in its use here it should be translated "Advocate" and not "Comforter," despite its employment by Aquila and Theodotion in Job xvi. 2 in the latter sense. It is used by Philo of the Logos. It is a refinement of criticism to separate the First Epistle from the Gospel on the ground that in the Epistle the title is applied to the ascended Christ (ii. 1). This use is implied in the Gospel itself (xiv. 16).

[5] xiv. 17, reading ἔσται with א, A. B, D * read ἐστίν, and they are followed by W.H.　　　　　　　　　　　[6] xiv. 18.

as standing in the same relation to the Son as the Son to the Father. The Father sends the Son, and the Son the Spirit. As the Son does nothing of Himself, but reveals and glorifies the Father, so the Spirit does not speak of Himself, but reveals and glorifies the Son.[1]

It was indeed expedient that the Christ should go away, since only thus could the Spirit come to the Church.[2] His departure meant that for the presence under earthly conditions and earthly limitations there would be substituted a permanent indwelling;[3] for the temporary sight of Christ a perpetual vision and manifestation;[4] for the teaching clothed in "proverbs" (ἐν παροιμίαις), open speech, and the guidance of the Spirit of Truth.[5]

The mission and work of Christ then do not cease with the earthly life, but are extended through the work and mission of the Holy Ghost. Only when the Son of Man was lifted up would He draw all men unto Him.[6] The works that He had done, even greater works, would be wrought by the disciples, by reason of His Ascension to the Father.[7] And as He has been commissioned by the Father, so He sends His Church, in the power of the Holy Ghost, to forgive and to retain the sins of men.[8]

Christ returns in the mission of the Spirit. But it is untrue to say that there is no place for the Parousia in the Johannine system. It remains,[9] and it always must remain, as a permanent element of the Gospel, with the conviction that

> "There will at last appear
> The world, the order, which God meant should be."

The service that Johannine theology rendered to early Christianity was to set the Christian hope in its right perspective, and to restore the balance of the truth.

[1] xvi. 13 f. ; *cf.* v. 30 ; vi. 38, &c.   [2] xvi. 7.   [3] xiv. 16–20.
[4] xiv. 21 ; xvi. 16–23.   [5] xiv. 25 f. ; xv. 26 f. ; xvi. 12 f., 25.
[6] xii. 32.   [7] xiv. 12.   [8] xx. 21 f.

[9] v. 28 ; vi. 39, 40, 44, 54 ; xii. 48 ; 1 JOHN ii. 18, 28. It is said that the Epistle contains primitive eschatology which is absent from the "spiritual" Gospel. But there is a vast difference between the Antichrist of 1 JOHN and that of 2 THESS., and as Drummond has pointed out, the Parousia of the Epistle (the word does not occur in the Gospel) stands for the presence and manifestation of Christ, *i.e.* the conception is entirely "spiritual"—while the Gospel retains the Messianic function of raising the dead from their tombs !

The Water and the Blood, which in the First Epistle are described as bearing witness with the Spirit to the Christian creed, represent not only the two great facts of the Gospel history, the Baptism and the Passion, but, mystically, the two great sacraments of Christianity. "He that believeth on the Son," it is said, "hath the witness in himself." [1]

The Johannine doctrine of Baptism is to be found in the discourse with Nicodemus, where a birth from above of water and Spirit is declared to be necessary for spiritual life. Only the Spirit can generate the life of the Spirit—the flesh, which here appears to stand for human nature on its lower and animal side,[2] can only perpetuate itself.[3] It is noticeable that in the Johannine teaching the negative side of baptism as embodying death to sin is eclipsed by the positive idea of the imparting of Divine life. In the First Epistle as in the Gospel the Godward side of the Sacrament is emphasised. Believers are children of God, not only in name but in fact. "See what manner of love the Father hath bestowed upon us, that we should be called the children of God—and so we are." [4] Yet here, where the writer is confronted with a tendency to minimise the Christian obligations, he finds it necessary to lay stress upon the complementary truth, that Divine birth must be realised by human co-operation, that "he that doeth righteousness," [5] "he that loveth," [6] "he that believeth that Jesus is the Christ, hath been begotten of God." [7]

The sustenance of the life imparted by baptism is the dominant note of the great discourse at Capernaum, which enshrines the Johannine doctrine of the Eucharist. It is through this sacrament that Christ, the Bread of Life, dispenses Himself to the believer.[8] More particularly, the gift that He imparts is that of His humanity—the Flesh and Blood of the Son of Man.[9] It is, no doubt, to throw stress on this aspect of the sacrament that throughout the discourse the term "Flesh" takes the place of the "Body" of the words of institution. Further, the Eucharist gift is that of humanity which has ascended to God through sacrificial

---

[1] 1 JOHN v. 6 f. [2] *Cf.* Swete, *Holy Spirit in N.T.*, p. 349. [3] iii. 6 f.
[4] 1 JOHN iii. 1. [5] 1 JOHN ii. 29. [6] 1 JOHN iv. 7.
[7] 1 JOHN v. 1. [8] vi. 35. [9] vi. 53.

death.[1] The connection of the Eucharist with the death of Christ is not emphasised in the discourse, but is evident elsewhere.[2]

The Capernaum discourse is substituted for the record of the Institution, and where this should stand we find the account of the feet-washing. Some of the fathers saw in this incident a mystical allusion to the Eucharist, and the suggestion is not improbable. The thought then will be that the laver of baptism makes the disciple clean every whit, but that he yet has need to wash from his feet the travel stains of his journey through the world in the sacrament of God's love; and to this the further idea will be added of the Eucharist as the expression of the corporate life of love and service to which the disciples are bound by the example of the Master whose death they plead. Whether we can go further than this, and regard the last discourses as coloured throughout by the thought of the Eucharist and its liturgical ceremonial and prayers is more doubtful.[3]

The great commission of Christ to the disciples must always remain the inspiration of the ministry, and the allegory of the Good Shepherd furnish it with its ideal of the pastoral office. But only strained exegesis can find in this parable a direct allusion to the Christian ministry, and its immediate purpose in an attempt to raise the ideal of those who have been set over Christ's flock.[4] For a glimpse at the organisation of the Church at the time we must turn to the two minor Epistles. The monarchical episcopate appears to be just emerging, for Diotrephes " ὁ φιλωπρωτεύων " would seem to hold that office, and to resent the active interference and oversight of the Presbyter.[5]

---

[1] vi. 51, 62. It is perhaps not without significance that the "sign" is brought into connection with "the Passover, the feast of the Jews" (vi. 4).

[2] xix. 34 ; 1 John v. 6 f.

[3] *Cf.* Loisy, *Le Quatrième Évangile*, p. 760 : " La pensée de l'Eucharistie, mémorial de la mort salutaire, l'idée de l'agape-charité inspire toujours l'auteur : l'allégorie du la vigne est une allusion assez directe au cérémonial Eucharistique, et le chapitre xvii. est une prière d'actions de grâces, prototype des prières analogues qui se faisaient dans les communautés après le repas sacré. Jean imite le liturgie primitive."

[4] Scott, *Fourth Gospel*, p. 135 f.

[5] 3 John 9.

ESSAY IX

THE BREACH BETWEEN JUDAISM AND CHRISTIANITY

BY

EPHRAIM LEVINE, B.A.

Formerly Scholar of the College

ANALYSIS

1. IMPORTANCE OF JERUSALEM IN ISRAEL'S RELIGION, AND THE PHENOMENON OF JUDAISM SURVIVING 70 C.E.

The conditions at the origin of Christianity.

Sects—Pharisees, Sadducees, Essenes, Zealots, and the necessity for approaching their study without bias.

Jesus and His followers.

Paul—Weakening of the tie between Judaism and Christianity.

Fourth Gospel—Anti-Jewish.

Reign of Hadrian—Schism complete.

Points of difference between Judaism and Christianity.

2. REORGANISATION OF JUDAISM AFTER 70.

Jochanan ben Zakkai—Jamnia and its Schools.

Jewish methods of interpretation—Halacha—Agada—Midrash.

Gamaliel, and others—Prayers against Minim.

Akiba—His influence on Judaism—His methods of exegesis.

Aquila's version.

Babylon—Israel's home.

Permanent elements in Judaism.

THE BREACH BETWEEN JUDAISM AND CHRISTIANITY

IN this essay an attempt will be made to trace the narrative of religious progress to the point where Judaism and Christianity parted company; the greater portion of the essay will, however, deal with the reorganisation of Judaism after the destruction of the Temple, for this is the task that has been entrusted to me. It will be convenient to take the year 70 [1] as the centre of the investigations. For it was the destruction of the Temple and the sacking of Jerusalem that brought about the vital change in Israel's condition and emphasised the distinguishing mark between Jew and Christian. The religion of the Jew had centred round the Holy City; thither the pious Israelite wended his way three times a year, on Passover, on Pentecost, and on Tabernacles. Here lay the embodiment of all his hopes and ideals. The 122nd Psalm—" I was glad when they said unto me, Let us go to the House of the Lord "—is a description of the religious joy which the pilgrim could carry away from his visit to Jerusalem. One need only turn to the liturgy of the Synagogue to realise the intense longing for Zion which even now the Jew cannot throw off. [2] It is wonderful, then, that the plundering of the Temple did not annihilate Judaism. But there is a still more wonderful phenomenon to be considered. Side by side with Judaism there had been growing up a faith, almost identical, but differing in a few respects

[1] The year 70 does not mark the final breach. It is chosen as a convenient centre, because the destruction of the Temple gave an impetus to Christianity. The Bar-cochba war, 132 C.E., will more fittingly mark the dividing line.

[2] Especially in the Kinoth, or Prayers for the 9th of Ab. But the return to Zion is the theme of many a prayer even in the Daily Service. Modern Zionism is more of a national than a religious movement.

from the Mother whence she had sprung. It was a religion
that could exist apart from the Temple, apart from the Holy
City; it required no area to restrict it, no space to contain
it. It was to be an universal religion with the whole world
as its area and all mankind as its adherents. The question
then suggests itself—why did not Judaism become absorbed in
Christianity? We know that as a fact the course of religious
history went otherwise. Christianity developed gradually,
till it became a world-wide power with mighty influence.
Judaism continued and flourished, working silently, never
too anxious to gain new adherents, but preserving its old
traditions and maintaining its old hopes.[1] It is the nature
of this phenomenon that will come up for our consideration
in the following pages. It will be necessary first to go back
a few years.

The dawn of Christianity found the Jewish world in
a curious state. But the movements were on the whole
healthy. The noise of controversial strife is a better sign
than the quiet of indifference and apathy. The periods
when men think and argue and range themselves into
sects are always fruitful. Writers on the origin of Christianity are prone to regard the state of Judaism at this
time as ready for the establishment and development of a
new faith. It is a trite saying that the world was in a state
of expectancy when Christianity began, and that it came at
an opportune moment.[2] Jewish nationalism was growing
weaker and weaker. The rule of Rome was foreshadowing
the disaster that was to befall the Jews in 70. Political
independence was gradually slipping away; yet Judaism
was, if anything, stronger than it had been for many a day.
Hillel had done something to reorganise it and place it on
a surer footing.[3] There were many different sects, Pharisees,

---

[1] The proselytising spirit was not absent from Judaism. In fact, after 70
till perhaps 100 C.E., Judaism made many converts, especially in Rome. It
may be that the Epistle to the Hebrews refers to this tendency. *Cf.* Moffatt,
Literature of the New Testament, p. 450 ; *cf.* also Hort's *Judaistic Christianity*,
p. 156 ff. Later on, this tendency disappeared.

[2] See Gwatkin's *Church History*, vol. i., chap. ii., and elsewhere.

[3] Hillel and his work cannot be considered here. His influence on Judaism
is very great, and Hillel is an important figure in Talmudic pages. *Cf.* Graetz,
History of the Jews, vol. ii.

Sadducees, Zealots, Essenes, not to mention many others, whose views may be expressed in some of the apocalyptic literature which flourished at that time. These various sects must be briefly considered.

The Pharisees, whose purpose and aims have, I venture to think, been entirely misrepresented by many, were engaged in the further development of the faith of Israel. The Gospel statements and the evidence of the sources do not justify the condemnation of a body of God-fearing men for the misconceptions of individuals. Pharisee ought never to be used as synonymous with hypocrite.[1]

The Pharisees represented the best of the religious among the nation. Their name, derived from a word that means " separated," does not imply that their object was to separate themselves in superiority from the rest of the nation, but to keep themselves separated from sin and the taint of too much worldliness. This can best be accomplished by constant intercourse with God. Only a religion which abounds in ceremonial can aid one to this end. Judaism sanctified every hour of the Jew's life. When he rose in the morning, he thanked God for continued life; when he retired to rest, he thanked Him for the gift of sleep. Three times a day he prayed. When he ate or drank he offered up a blessing. Religion was never absent from his life. But ceremonial is apt to beget formalism and develop into routine. There must have been those amongst the Pharisees whose anxiety about the letter of the Law shut their eyes to its spiritual meaning. The Jew has not the monopoly of swallowing camels and straining at gnats. It is the failing of adherents to all systematised religions, and there may have been some Pharisees who answered the description of the synoptists. As a body, however, they were earnest, God-fearing men, imbued

---

[1] Recent works dealing with Pharisees have been more fair. *Cf.* J. A. H. Hart's articles in *Jewish Quarterly Review*, vols. xviii.-xx., and his more recent articles in *Encyclopædia Britannica*. *Cf.* also *Our Lord and the Pharisees*, by Canon Foakes Jackson (1909), &c. For Jewish works dealing with Pharisees and the sects, *cf.* Graetz, *History of the Jews*, Geiger's *Judaism and its History*, Eng. edit., 1911 ; Gerald Friedländer's *Jewish Sources of Sermon on the Mount ;* M. Friedländer's *Die Secten*. Also *Jewish Sectaries*, by Schechter, 1910. The 2nd edition of Oesterley and Box, *Religion and Worship of the Synagogue*, pp. 120–130, has a very fair account of the Pharisees and their standpoint.

with the real spirit of religion and actuated by a pious consciousness of the nearness of God to man, and His never-failing presence. They organised prayer as an institution, parallel with that of the Temple rites, and when the latter had ceased, as their substitute;[1] and they limited the power of the priesthood. They it was who established schools and synagogues. One notion they dispelled—the idea that the priest could make complete reconciliation for the people on the Day of Atonement. They insisted, on the other hand, upon sincere penitence and complete reparation as necessary preliminaries to a reconciliation with God.[2] This last idea is noteworthy in view of subsequent events. The Pharisees were a sound limb in the body of Judaism, and time proved how powerful they were. Combining, as they did, patriotism and religious zeal, they were yet moderate and tractable. The world might be bad and conditions might be hard, but man cannot be as the beasts that perish. In the life hereafter God would level things and the pious would come to their own.[3] Thus they lived with one eye to the future, the other fixed on the present, and they directed their energies towards the improvement of the conditions of their time. Such a body of men is bound to be often misunderstood. Even to-day one finds it difficult to understand another's point of view. In politics it is unpolitic to attempt to do so; in religion it is tantamount to heresy. But one point cannot be ignored—hostile as the Synoptic writers represent the attitude of the Pharisees to have been towards Jesus, they do not make them responsible for his death, and in the Acts[4] the Pharisees actually take the part of the Christians.

Aristocratic Judaism—if we may borrow the term—had its adherents in a sect called the Sadducees, composed for the

---

[1] *Cf.* Kohler in *Publications of Graetz College*, 1897, p. 193, where he argues that prayers went on alongside of sacrifices for a considerable period before 70 C.E.

[2] This idea is at the root of the Jewish conception of Repentance. *Cf.* Mishna Yoma : " Sins between man and man cannot be atoned for till the sinner has acknowledged his guilt and made reparation." For the question of Jewish conception of repentance, see a learned article in *J. Q. R.*, by C. G. Montefiore (1903).

[3] The belief in a future life was held very strongly by the Pharisees.

[4] Acts xv. 5.

most part of the priesthood and the rich Jews, whose leaning towards Hellenism on the one hand and devotion to the written letter of the Scripture on the other are predominant characteristics of the sect. To them the priesthood was rather a political than a religious office. This world was quite enough for them; anxiety about the future world did not concern them; the resurrection of the body they denied; indeed no future life was included in their religion. Their influence on Judaism in the period with which we are concerned was small and short-lived. A sect [1] with ideas such as these could not be expected to act in face of a calamity like the destruction of the Temple. Their Judaism lacked the very religious element—the consciousness of God's presence—which enabled the Pharisees to build up their New Judaism on the ruins of the Temple Service.

Then there was another sect—the Essenes—the remnant of the old Chassidim—the pious ones—whose share in the Maccabæan struggles averted a national calamity for the Jews in the time of Antiochus Epiphanes. [2] "The despised and rejected of men"—according to some—the suffering servants of God—this sect lived in the desert in seclusion away from the haunts of men, in strict communion with God. If the Pharisees represented religious Judaism, this sect may be called the type of mystical Judaism. They are the Jewish type of ascetics, and they strove even more than the Pharisees to preserve a standard of rigid purity. In the world this could not be achieved. They must needs live apart, like hermits in the wilderness, eschewing marriage, indulging in fastings, and embracing the idea of communism. In a sense they are akin to the early followers of Jesus, but

---

[1] Sadducean ideas often recur in Jewish History. *Cf.* the Karaites : but there is no continuous connection evident. The origin of the name Sadducee is obscure. The question is discussed in an article in the *Encyclopædia Biblica*, by A. E. Cowley.

[2] חסידים, the pious ones, were the people of the country who bore the brunt in the Maccabæan war. *Cf.* Kennett, *The Servant of the Lord* (1910), for the theory that the Servant Chapters in ISAIAH 40–66 refer to the Chassidim. Probably the Essenes were descended from those. Josephus, *Antiq.*, vol. ii., calls them צנועים, the modest ones (*cf.* MICAH vi. 8). *Cf.* Graetz ; M. Friedländer, *Die Secten;* Geiger. *Cf.* also Lightfoot's *Commentary on Colossians* for a long article on Essenes, &c.

T

theirs was not the type of Judaism that would be likely to make any lasting impression on the people as a whole. It has been supposed that John the Baptist belonged to this sect, and his call to repentance by washing would tally with their ideas of rigid purity. The Essenes did not influence the commonwealth; they won adherents and were respected because of their sincerity and their supposed gift of miracle working. In a sense they differed little from the Pharisees. The Sadducees they ignored and shunned. The Pharisees did not go far enough for them. They are said to have given up animal sacrifices. All this might increase their reputation and respect, but as healers, workers of miracles, prophets and saints, their influence upon the events of the history of the time did not count for much. We shall not be surprised, therefore, to find this sect dwindling away when the final catastrophe overtook Jerusalem.[1]

It is obvious, then, that no one of these three organisations could cope with the outside enemies of Israel. Even combined, they still lacked something that is essential to a people with an enemy knocking at its gates. Thus the way was open for another party—the Zealots[2]—a combination of burning patriotism and ardent faith—men ready to stand up for the rights and freedom of their nation so long as the smallest chance of defence was afforded them. "Forty years before the Temple was destroyed," say the Rabbis, "its gates were opened and could no more be closed." True or false, the legend is significant; there was a settled conviction in the minds of the Jews, years before the actual event occurred, that they were destined to experience a long final struggle and an almost overwhelming catastrophe.

When a nation is faced with a problem such as this it cannot stop to pick and choose its men. The enemy appears in the distance and nothing can stop its onslaught, therefore any and every means must be adopted; the chances of averting

---

[1] Foremost among those who maintain that there was an important ascetic influence on the subsequent development of the Synagogue and its ritual is Dr. K. Kohler, many of whose writings in the *J. E.* bear upon this topic. *Cf.* also *J. Q. R.*, early volumes.

[2] Hebrew קנאים. They were finally checked in 135, after the defeat of Bar-cochba.

the disaster may be hazy, but the worst that can happen is
to accelerate it; the end is bound to come either way. Such
conditions justified the sect of Zealots. For years they nur-
tured an implacable hate against the foreigners and their rule
of tyranny. Some say they even carried daggers[1] about on
their persons, ready at any time to take the law into their
own hands and rid themselves of an enemy. They were a
well-organised party too, and soon assumed such proportions
as to render themselves immune from the interference of
legal authorities. Revolts were frequent. They declared it
to be criminal to obey the Empire, or to yield to the rule
inspired by the foreigner. The Kingdom of Heaven was
the Kingdom to which they pinned their allegiance. To
touch a piece of money with the Emperor's head engraved
on it was a sin; to pay taxes was a crime; to sign contracts
dating them by the year of the Emperor was impious in the
highest degree. To such an extent did this sect grow that
even Josephus counts them as a power side by side with the
Pharisees and Sadducees.

The conviction, which now found such powerful expression
in Judea, rested on some spiritual foundation. As far back as
the days of the Maccabæans the idea that the "world is breaking up and the future world must soon come" made itself
felt among the Zealot Jews.[2] But if the world were passing
away there still remained the hope "That a Son of Man shall
arise hidden in the clouds of Heaven; that all Empires shall
bow to Him; and that many of them that sleep in the dust of
the earth shall awake, some to everlasting life, some to everlasting shame." Daniel's vision gives the promise of the
world to come. But the Maccabæans fell short of these
expectations. Warriors and soldiers, hard-headed Zealots
eager for victory, they never made nations obey them or
peoples give voluntary allegiance to them; the one thing
they did was to make Judæa independent for a time. And

[1] Hence their name Sikarioi. Judah of Gaulonitis and Theudas were two
Zealot leaders (*cf.* Josephus, *Ant.*, xx. 5). But Josephus should be read with
caution, for he is naturally biased in his description of the Zealots, whose
political views were opposed to his.

[2] The Book of Daniel most probably dates from the time of the Maccabees,
i.e. 165 B.C.

now, again, a crisis had come more serious even than before. Rome's iron heel was ready to stamp out Jewish independence and crush their spiritual lives at the same time. The Jew was to adore the Emperor as a god, to put up his image in the Temple, and to affix the eagles to the shrine at Jerusalem. The Jewish Zealots could not contemplate this. Now or never the time had come. The old world was passing and the lust thereof, but God rules in the kingdom of men. Only the Torah would rule and must rule; strict observance of the Law without swerving would cause even the political structure to fall. Righteousness exalteth a nation. Bear the yoke of the Law and the State will fall ultimately, but cast off the yoke of the Law and you will have to bear the yoke of the world.[1] What profit is there then? This world is full of evil and sin and misery, it is passing away; throw off its yoke then and cling to the Law. For even the Roman State will vanish like a puff of wind when the Lord God of Israel bloweth upon it, but the Word of God will stand for ever. Hopes such as these sustained the Zealots and gave them unbounded confidence. And though there was a strong and growing party who, like Jochanan ben Zakkai (whom we shall consider later), resolved to save the Law while remaining subservient to Rome, it was the Zealots who in the year 70 had gained the upper hand in the capital.[2]

Such, briefly, was the state of Judæa in the generation after Jesus had preached His Mission. There seems no adequate reason to doubt that conditions were essentially the same when His Mission began. In Galilee of the Nations things were different; here were people rude and uneducated, occupying a lower and simpler intellectual plane than those in Judæa. Here every violent and extreme movement found ready helpers. Here was the scene of much of the Ministration of Jesus.

---

[1] Cf. *Mishna Aboth*, iii. 8 : "Whoso receives upon himself the yoke of the Law, they remove from him the yoke of worldly care." *Cf.* Taylor's note. This is an utterance of later date, but it expresses the Zealot idea.

[2] The struggle for political independence and the demand for religious freedom sometimes merged, as at the outbreak of the Maccabæan revolt. But just as then the two ideas led to the formation of separate parties, so too at our period.

The early development of Christianity and the literature of the New Testament are not within the scope of the subject assigned to me. But writing as a Jew, and from a standpoint differing essentially from that of every other writer of this volume, I cannot omit mentioning a few facts which will help to indicate the distinguishing line between Judaism and Christianity. To the life of Jesus and His Ministry I need not refer, except to say that the Jew does not regard the Life-work of Jesus as a mission opposed to Judaism. Like many another inspired preacher and servant of God, He saw where faults lay and pointed them out. Formalism and routine He denounced only where spirituality was absent. For He came not to destroy, but to reassert the beauties of the religion to which He adhered during His own short pilgrimage on earth. His death on the Cross was a political step on the part of the Romans, deplored by Jews no less than by Christians. Jewish Law would not have sanctioned it. The fear that the " King of the Jews " would be a menace to the Roman State made the Mission of Jesus appear political, in the eyes of the Romans, and not religious.[1] The death of Jesus, however, made a profound impression on His disciples, and many of His words came back to them, and they recalled how He had spoken of His Kingdom which was not of this world, and soon the belief grew that their Master had risen from the tomb and was in the presence of the Father in Heaven. Nor did the work of Jesus stand still. The small band of His followers gradually increased in numbers, and worked silently by the side of Judaism, not in opposition to it. Here it is that our difficulties begin. We know that at first the Gospel was preached to the Jews exclusively. Churches were founded at Jerusalem and in other places of Judæa.

---

[1] There are many objections to any attribution of the death of Jesus to the Jews: (1) Crucifixion was not a Jewish, but a Roman mode of execution; (2) a threefold execution at one time is doubtful; (3) an execution on a Friday or on the day before Passover would be most unlikely. For an account of the objections see *Jewish Encyclopædia*, vol. iv. p. 374. There is an appendix to a book by Chwolson on *The Last Passover of Jesus* (1904), in which he maintains with great force the innocence of the Jewish Pharisaic party and the fact that Jesus had done nothing that could offend against their laws. His death was instigated by the Roman party. *Cf.* also C. G. Montefiore's *Synoptic Gospels* (Macmillan, 1909).

What the relation of these churches was to Judaism even Harnack does not clearly unravel.[1] Continual strife and persecutions seem to prove that the friendliest relations could not have existed. But, on the other hand, if we turn to the early literature, we fail to find any cleavage between Judaism and Christianity distinctly marked.

The work of St. Paul and his preaching began to separate Jew and Christian. St. Paul wished to enlarge Judaism and make it accessible to the whole world. But Judaism was a religion which it was no easy matter to observe. Circumcision was necessary for any convert; there were other ceremonial laws which made it difficult for intending proselytes. If circumcision must continue to be essential, then it would not be possible to establish an universal religion. The question perplexed St. Paul, as we see in the Epistle to the Galatians. It was not long before the ceremonial laws were abrogated, and thus Paul and his followers began the work of separation. It is unnecessary to give a complete summary of the lines of cleavage which made the parting between the two religions inevitable. The final rupture was gradually effected. With the sack of Jerusalem by Titus the severance began plainly to manifest itself; the fourth Gospel emphasised it still further. The revolt of Bar-cochba and his overthrow in 132 ended the matter. I shall here touch on the subject briefly.

At the death of Jesus there are no indications of a breach between Judaism and Christianity.

About the year 50 there is the Apostolic Conference, and obligation of the Jewish Law is not enforced upon the Gentile converts. This is a step towards separation. After this Paul is strenuously opposed by the Jewish people. Another step is the fall of the Temple in 70. Deprived of their home and scattered abroad, the Jews, unable to point to the Temple as their stronghold, and denied the opportunity of sacrifice, were weaker as a missionary or proselytising faith.[2] Yet, officially, there is no breach between Christian or follower

---

[1] See Harnack's *Expansion of Christianity*, vol. i. chap. v.

[2] Yet nevertheless there was a strong proselytising movement in Rome towards the end of the first century.

of Jesus and the Jew. The Synoptic Gospels give us no indication of it, and such a book as the Apocalypse [1] knows nothing of divisions in the camp. At the end of the century the fourth Gospel has a distinct anti-Jewish bias. It openly treats of the Jew as the enemy of the Gospel. This Gospel, written presumably by one who had known Jesus and had been a disciple, written too in old age, when the author had had time to reflect on the events that had happened since the death of his Master, marks an important epoch.

We have here an entirely new conception of the life of Jesus. "The fourth Gospel is a study or interpretation of His life, written in order to bring out His permanent significance as the Logos-Christ for faith." [2] The idea of the Logos as a man gave an altogether new colour to religious thought. The Jewish idea of a Messiah is a son of David, born like any other man, with a sublime mission for the benefit of mankind, but he is only a man. The Logos is different. Existing from the first ere the beginning of the world, He assumed human form and dwelt among men. "The word was flesh and dwelt among us." His death was a voluntary sacrifice— to give Himself as a ransom for many. The whole world had become corrupt, the process of emanation and effluence beginning with Adam reflected back to Adam. By Jesus assuming human form and taking upon Himself the sin of the world, the human race could be born again. "Marvel not that I say unto you, ye shall be born again." He chose to die as a man, but His Divinity remained to illumine the world and direct the path of mankind. Ideas such as these were woven out of the Jewish-Grecian philosophy; they produced radical changes in current Jewish thought concerning God and concerning man. To the Jew the question of original sin, the fall of man, and the innate evil of the world were never too perplexing. The Jew never held him-

---

[1] I know that many date the book of REVELATION much later than 70. But there seem to be good grounds for supporting the 70 date. *Cf.* Moffatt, *L. N. T.*

[2] Moffatt, *L. N. T.*, 525. The Jewish idea of the Logos, as seen in Philo, is essentially different from the conception in the fourth Gospel. For a clear account of this, see "Theology of the Fourth Gospel," by the present Dean of St. Paul's, in *Cambridge Biblical Essays*, 1909.

self responsible for the sins of others. Ezekiel made it clear that man dies for his own sins, and each one must bear the punishment for his misdeeds. God is a God of justice and mercy, and takes no delight in the death of the sinner. Each man can work out his own destiny uninfluenced by what has gone before. Already in the wilderness Moses had asked to be allowed to give himself as an atonement for his people, and he was answered by the declaration of God—"Whosoever sins against Me, him will I blot out from My book." To introduce such an idea into Judaism as vicarious atonement was to introduce something opposed to the spirit of Judaism.

Thus the close of the first century found Jew and Christian going further and further apart. When we come to the year 132—the Bar-cochba war—the final breach is emphasised. The Jews fought their enemy by themselves without the aid of Jewish Christians. It is more than possible that the Christians who opposed the Bar-cochba gained favour, and were not hindered when they set up a bishop in Aelia Capitolina, as Jerusalem was now named. The Jews, on the other hand, were not permitted to set foot there, and the Christians returned as Gentiles.[1] A few years later the Jews are openly pointed to as the instigators of the murder of Polycarp; and if such an accusation could be levelled against them, it seems clear that the separation must at this time have been complete.[2] The idea that Jesus was the Messiah and the Son of God who lived among men; the breach with tradition and abrogation of the ceremonial law; the impossibility for Jewish Christians to attempt to be Jews and Christians at the same time—all these causes led to the final rupture. Christianity was now a definite faith and not a phase of Judaism. There were even some who contended that Judaism was essentially bad and that the faith of Christ had never been an aspect of it.

[1] Gwatkin, *Church History*, vol. ii. p. 8.

[2] The statements in Harnack's *Expansion of Christianity Book*, pp. 65, 66, are not substantiated by any adequate testimony. The period during which Harnack supposes the Jews to have had the influence, to say nothing of the desire to instigate persecutions of Christians, was the very time when they themselves were barely able to maintain their own lives against Rome. The whole of this question stands in need of a thorough re-investigation, in which attention will have to be directed to other evidence than that of controversial writers against the Judaism of the Roman Empire.

Here we may leave Christianity, for now we must turn to the other side of the picture and examine the causes that enabled Judaism to maintain itself and keep itself alive. In spite of persecution, in spite of weapons, carnal or spiritual, fire and sword, in spite of expulsions and massacres, Judaism still flourishes alongside of Christianity to-day. It has endured persecution from Christian and Heathen alike. Its adherents have been tossed and buffeted from one country to another, from place to place, but dogged pertinacity has won the fight. To Judaism has been denied everything that is good—to Judaism has been attributed most that is bad. If the Old Testament contained any spiritual truth, it was merely a forerunner of the New, or it only marked a step towards ideas which were developed later, or which received their real application in the New Testament. But Judaism has not cared. Pure and undefiled, it has kept its tenets and doctrines, heedless of the dangers that threatened it continually. The Jew knows nothing of the Trinity—"Hear O Israel, the Lord our God is one" is still the axiom of the Hebrew's faith. Judaism knows nothing of all mankind suffering for the sin of Adam.[1] The Jew is governed by the Will of God, but he is a free agent. "Everything is in the hands of Heaven," say the Rabbis, "except the fear of Heaven." The Jew can conquer the evil inclination and the tendency to sin if he listens to the Word of God and lives in the fear of God. The Jew, too, knows nothing of a vicarious atonement. He cannot conceive of God requiring an individual sacrifice. But for God's mercy every man for his own sins shall die—the Jew still believes this, and regards himself accountable to God for his misdeeds. In the days of the Temple the sacrifice was considered useless unless the individual brought it himself and confessed his sin as he did so.[2] From this idea of individual responsibility the Jew has never turned. Judaism did not disappear as though it had served

---

[1] In 2 ESDRAS we get the idea of sin going back to Adam, but this idea meant to the Jew nothing more than the fact than sin came into the world with Adam.

[2] Talmud *passim*. Commentators on LEVITICUS i. 4, on the words "he shall lay his hand upon the head of the offering," where they lay emphasis on the words "his hand," not the hand of his servant, &c., but "his own hand."

its purpose and was destined to rank as a relic of antiquity in the religious history of the world. It was to assert itself, and justify its right to live and its power to regenerate man. How it strove to accomplish this remains now to be shown.

We left the Jewish people divided into sects at the time when Christianity arrived into the world. These sects were considered with their aims and potentialities. It was not expected that all could survive the destruction of the Temple. Nor did they. The Sadducees depended on the Temple; priests and aristocracy had no *raison d'être* now; the absence of sacrifice, the cessation of Temple service, the lack of any political office for which they might scramble, made existence seem a terrible catastrophe. They need concern us no more for the present. And the Zealots were almost as powerless in the face of the disaster. Anger and gloom could avail little against the power of the Roman Army and a Roman Empire. Revenge was their only hope, but it was a transient, delusive hope, and one that could not afford much comfort. Here and there they raised petty revolts, stirred up little insurrections; for a time they managed to annoy the Empire, but, about 132, they were finally suppressed in the War of Bar-cochba. Rome cared little for Judaism *quâ* Judaism.[1] But the people must be put down, and the disaster of Barcochba set the last stone on the grave of Jewish independence and called forth bitter persecution of Judaism itself. To observe the Jewish religion and to practise its ceremonies was now made a crime punishable by death, and even Akiba was one of the victims. So by 135 we see the Zealots disappear from the pages of Jewish history.

There are still the Pharisees, two divisions of them. The one, the followers of the strict school which inherited the tendency of Shammai, sought to preserve Judaism by asceticism, by forbidding the use of wine and meat because animal sacri-

---

[1] Rome regarded Jew and Christian alike as "atheists"—in their acceptation of the term.

For a description of the extent to which Jewish observances were prohibited by Hadrian, see Graetz, *History*, vol. ii. chap. xvi. *Cf.* also Midrash on LAMENTATIONS. The Christian persecutions in Lyonne about fifty years later, as described by Eusebius, Book V., seem almost the same events described again with the word Christian instead of Jew.

fices could no longer be offered in the Temple. This was not likely to preserve the religion; something quite different was required. But others of the Pharisees were men with the spirit of Hillel, imbued with the idea that conviction and belief were more necessary than ceremony and sacrifice. It was not the time to bewail the loss, but the time to reorganise the religion; the sacrifices had vanished, the Temple was gone, the outward aspect of the religion was no more, but Judaism had its inward aspect, and it was the duty of those who had seen the Temple destroyed to build up a Temple of faith, prayer, and charity. A more difficult problem than that which had faced Jeremiah after the destruction of the first Temple confronted them. They were to prove that even the fall of Jerusalem did not mean the end of Judaism.

Jochanan ben Zakkai [1] is the organiser of the religion of this period. His activity as a Jewish teacher began much earlier than 70, but it is after the destruction that he comes into prominence. Even while the war with Rome continued there were many among the Jews who advocated a policy of peace, and many a time they tended the advice to surrender and submit to the Romans. Among them was Jochanan ben Zakkai. It came to the ear of Vespasian that he advocated peace and surrender, and Jochanan, actuated either by fear of the Zealot party, or concern for the safety of the Torah which he taught in the schools of Jerusalem, resolved to betake himself to the Roman camp.

Tradition relates that in order to carry out his plan he had himself conveyed in a coffin to Vespasian; [2] thus he was able to trick the soldiers and reach the camp in safety. The Emperor asked him what request he desired to make, and Jochanan, so runs the story, asked that he might be permitted to establish a school at Jabne, a place situated between Joppa and Ashdod. Jabne lay in the private part of the Emperor's own property. Vespasian readily granted the request; it

---

[1] *Cf.* Graetz, *Hist.*, ii. 325 ff., Schlatter's *Jochanan ben Zakkai*, &c. For a condensed account of Jamnia and its school, *cf.* Abrahams' *Short History of Jewish Literature*, chap. i.

[2] *Talmud Gittin*, 56a; *Echa Rabb.*, i. 5, &c.

seemed to him an unimportant enough concession. But it was one fraught with important consequences, and could the Emperor have foreseen that he was giving a new lease of life to Judaism, perhaps he would not have acquiesced so readily. But God employs divers agents to perform His work. If the Assyrians of old were the rod of His anger to destroy, a Roman emperor could be His agent to build up. Thus it came about that Judaism was able to re-organise itself. Soon the news came that the Temple had fallen, and though Jochanan bewailed the disaster and was as concerned as any Jew for the welfare of his people who had been over-taken by such an awful catastrophe, he was far-sighted enough to see that it need not necessarily be the end. Like many of his contemporaries he could not regard the destruction as final; the near rebuilding was assured. But for the present—and this present still continues to our day—Judaism had to be placed on a non-sacerdotal basis. There is a time to weep, there is a time to pull down, but there is also a time to build up. In place of sacrifices and burnt-offerings, charity and love of mankind could continue the mission of Judaism.[1] If Jerusalem was no more the centre of the nation's worship the next best thing to do was to establish another centre.

Jochanan ben Zakkai is a typical representative of the Jewish teacher. Like so many others he followed a trade, besides engaging in the study of the Law.[2] Even before 70 he had been engaged in teaching, but now with the dis-appearance of the Temple a new centre had to be established in Palestine. Jabne or Jamnia became what Jerusalem had been. Here the college was set up, and the Sanhedrin estab-lished as it had been in Jerusalem. Jochanan was himself the President, the Ab-Beth Din, with supreme authority.

---

[1] The spiritual side of Judaism was certainly emphasised now. The pro-phetical books with their preference for charity, mercy, &c., over sacrifice have many parallels in the Talmud. "A day in Thy courts is better than a thousand" (Ps. 84) is taken to mean—God prefers one day's devotion and study of the Torah to a thousand burnt-offerings.

[2] Professional rabbis are not known at this early period. Many of the greatest rabbis gained their livelihood in a very humble way. Hillel's early poverty is proverbial, and Akiba's youth is said to have been one of great penury.

All the privileges that had been vested in the Sanhedrin at Jerusalem were transferred to Jabne. Such questions as the determination of the new moon were decided by the authority of the President. But the chief influence of Jochanan lay in the zeal for the Law which he imparted to his pupils. The Torah was not a crown wherewith man might aggrandise himself, or a spade with which to dig.[1] The study of the Torah was to be undertaken for its own sake, not for the sake of enabling one to gain a livelihood or to bring honour and praise to the student. This idea was always prominent in the teaching of Jochanan. "If thou hast acquired much knowledge of the Law, boast not of it, for to this end wast thou created."[2] Hence the admission to his school was guarded. Only earnest students were welcome, no triflers or traffickers in the Law. To consolidate Judaism which now had no Temple, to bring to it a unifying power, Jochanan had to investigate the Law and interpret it. In many ways he was a follower of Hillel, who had been the first to frame a sort of Jewish theology. The written Law, *i.e.* Pentateuch, and the Oral Law, *i.e.* precepts and customs which have been handed down from generation to generation, which were said to have been told by word of mouth to Moses on Sinai, were in the time of Hillel not considered as two distinct systems, but as complementary parts of one whole code. When the Rabbis studied the Pentateuch every verse received its careful attention. Here and there a word would suggest something, a parallel in one verse would be found with another verse; contradictions might appear, and from all these decisions had to be arrived at and deductions drawn. These laws (for such they became in time) were called Halachas. It required one gifted with a wonderful memory to know the Halacha on this or on that, for these Laws were not committed to writing, but were handed down orally from one to another; nor was there any connection of subject-matter or any attempt at classification; the name of the rabbi responsible for a de-

---

[1] *Aboth*, i. 14. A recorded saying of Hillel: "He who makes a worldly use of the crown of the Torah will perish" (see Taylor, who translates differently).
[2] *Aboth*, ii. 9.

cision was sometimes handed down, but that was all. Jochanan knew these Halachas better than anybody, and he now handed them on to his pupils and showed their connection with the Laws of the Pentateuch; here also we get the first fruits of Midrashic interpretation.[1]

Another method of exposition was called Agada. By this was meant the application of historical events to the present condition of Israel, or to their future hopes. The prophets or the historical books of the Bible would serve as the texts, so to speak, on which to base the discourses. Edom and Esau would be applied to Rome and its rule, and parallels would be drawn between the peoples' past history and their tyrannical oppressions, and their present subjugation to the Roman yoke. Agada brought out in clearer view the moral truths of Judaism and strengthened the hope of the Jewish people.[2]

With Jochanan there were working many other teachers in the vineyards of Jamnia.[3] Most of them are only known by name, but they helped in the work and kept the torch of Judaism burning. It is therefore not surprising that there should have been many able and ready to assume the head of the Sanhedrin when Jochanan had completed his work. There was also a desire to spread further and enlarge the area. Therefore, many other schools were established, those at Lydda and Bekiin being the most important of the new ones. But Jamnia still maintained its pre-eminence as a religious centre to which all others turned and from which all enactments went forth. The new head was Gamaliel II.,[4] the Nasi or Prince, a man after the heart of Jochanan, and imbued with the same ideas. Jochanan died in the arms of his disciples, his last words breathing complete confidence in the future of Judaism and the certain

---

[1] See article on "Halacha" in *Jewish Encyclopædia*.

[2] Halacha and Agada are not distinguished in the Talmud; both are found here and there; often the elucidation of a difficult Halachic passage will be helped by a sprinkling of Agadic explanation.

[3] Some of his disciples became famous—Eliezer ben Hyrcanus, Joshua ben Chananiah, Jose the Priest, Eleazar ben Arak.

[4] To be distinguished from an earlier one of that name. Under Gamaliel II. the question of excommunication was brought to the fore.

hope that the Messiah will yet come. But Gamaliel was faced with a different situation. The establishment of new schools and the spreading of the pupils, while it still left Jamnia the centre, yet prepared the way for differences of opinion and dissension. We constantly meet in the Talmud, when any question is under discussion, two opposing schools appealed to—Beth Hillel and Beth Shammai. Hillel and Shammai were the two teachers of Israel in the years preceding the commencement of the present era, about whose personality so much has been handed down. Both were great Jews, but whereas modesty and gentleness were the characteristics of Hillel's method of teaching, Shammai is represented as a harsh, overbearing man, impatient of disagreement and discussion. How many tales we read of the treatment intending converts received from Shammai and Hillel! The former would drive them away, the latter would argue quietly and seek to convince or discourage an intending proselyte.[1] Now the descendants (in a religious sense) or the followers of these two schools of thought were still divided into parties. Gamaliel and his school were the House of Hillel, and now the contest between the rival schools of thought broke out, and is said to have raged for three and a half years. The points on which they were at variance were not many, but no decision could be come to owing to the stubbornness of Beth Shammai. At last it was agreed (a voice from Heaven having been heard, according to legend) to decide the Law according to Hillel, though both Laws, they agreed, were the Word of God. Thus the dispute is said to have ended, and Gamaliel is credited with having united the two parties. Gamaliel also introduced fixed prayers into the synagogue service. Prayer took the place of sacrifice, and instead of each man offering a private prayer (which he might still do) public prayers were introduced. The eighteen Benedictions to be found in the Prayer Book to-day were fixed about this period.[2] On the whole, at this time, the Jews were a united and consolidated body con-

---

[1] *Cf.* especially Talmud Sabbath, 31*a*, where a great many stories typical of Hillel and Shammai are told.

[2] See Authorised Prayer Book, by S. Singer, pp. 44–54.

trasted with the new religion, which was already divided into sections and opposing factions. In one point, however, Judaism missed an opportunity. The schools were good for the lettered and educated classes; for them no danger was entertained as likely to come from Christianity. But the poorer peasant classes [1] were not so fortunate. The Law could not be grasped by them nor its contents understood so easily; hence the observance was restricted in their case to these things that appealed to their temperament. In Babylon in the following century the study of the Law was popularised by the institution of conventions held twice a year and attended by the masses as well as the experts. This institution had no place in Palestine. It is not necessary to press this difference too far. But it is not surprising that some of those to whom the Law had lost its appeal were easily absorbed by the growing power of Christianity; from their ranks the converts came, and Judaism was soon to realise that the Judæo-Christians were a foe more dangerous than the heathen enemies themselves. These Judæo-Christians or *Minim*,[2] as they were called, at first lived on friendly terms with their Jewish neighbours—perhaps till the end of the first century. But this state of affairs could not last long. When the Minim commenced to publish writings in opposition to Judaism, more dangerous to Judaism than plain attacks, the separation was not far off. "The writings of the Minim," says R. Tarfon, "deserve to be burnt, even though the Holy Name of God occurs therein, for heathenism is less dangerous than heresy: the former fails to recognise the truth of Judaism from want of knowledge, the latter denies what it fully knows." It soon became necessary to warn people against them, and a prayer written by Samuel the younger was introduced into the eighteen Benedictions testifying to the strong feeling that was entertained against the Minim. The wording of the prayer now does not contain

---

[1] Called Ami-haaretz. This term also embraces the laxer observances of the Levitical Law and customs. *Cf.* Büchler, *Der Gal. Am-haaretz.*

The view adopted in the text is pressed to its extreme, perhaps unjustified in the writings of Moritz Friedländer.

[2] Minim, derived from מין, "kind" or "sect," is applied in the Talmud to all sects and heretics—Gnostics, &c.

any reference to the Minim,[1] because the words of Samuel the younger underwent modification when Church Fathers accused the Jews of cursing the Gentile Christians in their services—a charge which they never succeeded in proving. Many other rules were passed against these Minim—all of which show that they must have been a menace to the Jewish body. They soon merged themselves into the Christian body, and broke with Judaism altogether. It has been supposed that the Epistle to the Hebrews is an appeal to the Minim to separate themselves from the body Jewish. But the date which is now assigned to the epistle would seem to suggest that its object was to counteract the missionary effort which Judaism was making from Rome between the years 80 to 100. This would indicate that there was in Judaism a wonderful recuperative power; it would also show that there must have been something in Judaism, spiritual or otherwise, which appealed to educated men and was able to win adherents to its ranks.

Gnosticism does not come to be discussed in this essay; but it must be mentioned, for it left its influence on Judaism. Gnostic ideas about æons, emanations, classes of God, affected Jews as well as Christians. "To enter into Paradise," they called the search into the realms of Gnosticism, but the dangers consequent on this study were clearly brought out. Ben Zoma and Ben Azzai, who only tasted it, came to an early death. Elisha ben Abuya became a renegade and fell away from Judaism. Akiba alone of those who studied it preserved his mental balance and remained firm to the religion of his fathers. This great man will now occupy our attention: he is the greatest figure in many respects in post-Biblical Judaism, and his influence on the history of his religion is still manifest.

Akiba ben Joseph was born about the year 50 and was put to death about 132. Round his name there has centred such a wealth of legend that it is hard to distinguish facts

---

[1] The word now used is ולמלשינים—"slanderers." *Cf.* article in *J. E.* The question as to Minim is well discussed in R. T. Herford's *Christianity in Talmud and Midrash*, 1903. He fully answers the theory of M. Friedländer, who contends that the Minim never are the Judæo-Christians but Gnostics. *Cf.* also Bacher's review of this book in *J. Q. R.*, vol. xvi.

U

from affectionate imagination. His parents were poor and his origin humble. But to trace his descent, as some do, from Sisera [1] is hardly permissible. This much we know—in his youth he studied little, and it was not till the age of forty that a desire to please his wife made him settle down to the study of the Law. His genius was extraordinary, and in time he became the most distinguished scholar in the schools of Jamnia and Lydda. His teacher was Eliezer ben Hyrcanus, one of the school of Jochanan ben Zakkai. Later, Akiba became head of the College in Bene-Berak, a town five miles from Jaffa. Akiba is said to have taken a prominent part in the Bar-cochba war, but here again we are on no certain ground. We know that he was martyred by the Romans in 132 after languishing for a time in prison. Many legends embodied in the Jewish Liturgy in the prayers for the anniversary of the Temple's fall tell of the heroic Akiba's death, how with his last breath he proclaimed the Jew's unswerving belief—" Hear, O Israel, the Lord our God is one." [2] But we are more concerned with Akiba's teaching and his place in the development of Judaism. It was he who helped to fix the canon of the Jewish Scriptures. While he objected to the canonicity of Ecclesiasticus he was all in favour of receiving Ecclesiastes and the Song of Songs into the canon. His objection to the Apocrypha was directed against Jewish Christians, who drew many of their arguments from that source. But it was in the realms of Halacha that his influence was most pronounced. Broadly speaking, he held the view that the Law was not stationary, but capable of growth and development; the more one searched there the more treasures one would find. I have already referred, when speaking of Jochanan, to the lack of systematic classification and to the necessary difficulty of committing the Laws to memory and handing them down orally from one age to another. Akiba saw the difficulty too plainly. The first thing he did was to systematise the Halachas in such a way as to aid the memory. Thus he divided them into six parts according to

---

[1] *Cf.* article " Akiba " in *J. E.* Cf. *Menachoth,* 29*b.*

[2] See Prayer on the Ten Martyrs read on the 9th of Ab—the anniversary of the destruction of the Temple.

their contents—Sabbath Laws, Marriage Laws, Property, &c. He paved the way for the Mishna of Rabbi Judah, which assumed its present form about the year 200.[1] Mishna, Tosefta, and Midrash were all culled from the Halacha and distinguished one from the other. But Akiba's work went further. The Bible was, generally speaking, as much the accepted guide of the Christian sects as of the Jews. As an intellectual bond uniting Jews together—for they required such a bond in their scattered condition—it was not enough. The nature of the Jew is to adapt himself to his surroundings. Intercourse with Greek philosophy or communion with Gnosticism might make the Jew turn from the path. The fate of Elisha ben Abuya was a terrible example of what might happen. So Akiba enunciated a new system. Beginning with the idea that the Torah is not written as other books, that its language is peculiar to itself, he sought to prove that there is not a letter, a particle, a syllable, a sign but has its meaning and its purpose more significant than one would at first imagine. Here lay a new field for thought, and a new avenue for research was opened up. The immutability of Scripture and its powers of development—two antagonistic ideas—were reconciled. In another department also Akiba was zealous—to preserve the purity of the idea of God, to keep the conception of God free from Gnostic taints or Christian ideas. "In the image of God created He man," says the Bible. Is there a shape of God and is man His image? "Certainly not," said Akiba, "but we must understand the passage in this way—God created man in a definite image. God forbid that we even in poetic expression should speak of an image of God." Or again it says, "No man shall see Me and live." Can this mean that any man can see God if he risks the penalty of death? Certainly not! But the verse means this—no man sees God: neither living being, nor angels, nor holy spirits. Of his sayings, independent of Biblical quotations, the following is one of the most famous—"All is foreseen, yet freedom is given to man." Providence and human free-will, side by side—this has been the stumbling-block of many religions.

---

[1] The Mishna which we have to-day is mainly that of Rabbi Judah.

Some, in order to preserve the supreme perfection of God, tied down man to a being unable to act for himself. But Akiba refused to take this view. Freedom is given, though everything is foreseen. Grasp this point and our knowledge of God is increased and our capacity for piety is widened. These ideas are the very basis of Judaism and they have never been upset. The idea that man can work out his own destiny as long as he keeps along the path of God has never been absent from Judaism. It is a dignified conception of man, and one that exalts him; it comes near to what the writer of the Eighth Psalm conceived man to be—a little lower than the angels.

There is another event of importance that happened at this time. The Greek-speaking Jews of the second century were badly in need of a version of the Bible. The Septuagint no longer satisfied their needs; the alterations that had been made in the text, and the distortions made often to prove points inimical to Judaism, rendered it no longer trustworthy.[1]

There was a proselyte, Aquila, who undertook the task of translating the Bible again. This proselyte became one of the most ardent Jews. Rich in estates, he had received a thorough education in Greek and other philosophy, and had at first joined the Christians; but at the time when Jewish converts in Rome were numerous (Josephus bears witness to their frequency) Aquila became a Jew. Being well versed in Hebrew, he was fitted for the task. Aquila's version is characterised by a strict adherence to the literal Hebrew; he renders the Hebrew word for word with so much caution as to rob the version of any literary worth, and to make the meaning, at times, obscure. To translate Hebrew idioms into equivalent Greek is to render the translation tedious and unreal. Yet the accuracy or ἀκρίβεια of the work made it acceptable to the people, and Aquila did a great service.[2] At the same time the Targum Onkelos, an Aramaic translation,

---

[1] Charges of distorting the text of Scripture were also made against the Jews (*cf.* Justin's *Dialogue*). The charges against Jewish-Christians were that they expunged or introduced words to prove the truth of Christianity.

[2] For a good account of Aquila and his work see F. C. Burkitt, *J. Q. R.*, vol. x. Also his edition of *Aquila on Kings*.

was commenced, though the form in which we have it now does not date from earlier than the fifth century.

Here we can conveniently pause, for henceforth Talmudic or Rabbinic Judaism is the development of the structure of which Jochanan ben Zakkai, Gamaliel, Akiba, to mention no others, are the pillars. For our purpose the reign of Hadrian marks the limit of investigation. This epoch saw all connection between Judaism and Christianity cease; from now Synagogue and Church are two distinct bodies, not two hostile wings of the same house. From this point Rabbinic Judaism advanced and developed. By the year 200 the Mishna of Rabbi Judah was completed, and the field of Jewish activity was further extended. Whatever longing the Jews might have for Palestine it now seemed too uncertain a field for their faith. Babylon once again became the home of the Jewish Renaissance. Here Ezra had arisen, and from here Hillel had gone to Palestine; schools were now organised in Sura, Pumbeditha, and many other places in Babylon, and a new spirit took hold of the teachers. To Palestine the Jew might cast a wistful glance, but here, in Babylon, he found a quiet haven of refuge far from the interference of Rome, and here the river of Judaism could flow on in its course uninterrupted and unimpeded. The Babylonian Gemara or completion,[1] the Rabbinic discussion on the Mishna, was finished by the sixth or seventh century, and the influence of the teachers of the Babylonian schools is still dominant in Judaism. It is not within our scope to estimate the value of the Talmud. Thus much may be said. Only superficiality condemns it. Those who speak lightly of the hair-splitting casuistries of the Rabbis would do well to study the Talmud and reserve their judgement—

> " Errors like straw upon the surface flow,
> Who seeks for pearls must dive below."

Church Councils and the tomes of Church Fathers are not without their threadbare dialectics. The closer the argument the keener the debate, the greater the love for the religion. And the Talmud, embracing the whole code of man's life in

---

[1] Bacher maintains that Gemara means "learning." The root גמר means "to complete" in late Hebrew.

every direction—the whole scheme of Judaism involved therein —can still feed the Jewish mind. " Ponder therein again and again for everything is there," say the Rabbis. It speaks clearer than anything else of the enormous vitality which the religion of the Old Testament displayed. And not only the Jews but the whole civilised world reaps the benefit. Judaism never canonised ignorance; when a Rabbi laid his hands on the head of a disciple he gave him an acknowledgment of learning; knowledge of the Law was the criterion of nobility and the standard of rank. The Bible might not be the heritage of the world to-day if scrupulous care had not been taken to guard its every letter and its every particle.[1] The pedlars and hucksters and dealers in old clothes, as the medieval Jew was painted, trafficked and carried about philosophy and learning and enabled the world to profit by it the remnants of lore they preserved, and clothed the nakedness of the rest of the world. Their work still endures to-day. And as for the Jew, his monotheism is still pure and unassailable. A steadfast belief in God, an intense consciousness of the call of Israel, unswerving faith in the truth of the Prophets, an undying recognition of the mission of the Jew, the never-failing hope that the Messiah will come and gather the outcasts of Israel—on these the Jew still nourishes his spiritual nature. Thus, nearly nineteen centuries after the loss of their Temple, the tribes of the Wandering Foot have preserved their faith and have carried on their mission. Who will say that the curtain has fallen on the last act of the drama? In the future religious history of the world the ancient faith of the Jew will have its part to play. " The Guardian of Israel neither sleepeth nor slumbereth."

[1] For an account of rabbinical aids to exegisis see I. Abrahams' *Cambridge Biblical Essays*, 1909. For the part the Jews played in preserving the text of the Bible *cf.* Reuchlin in *Essays* by S. A. Hirsch (Macmillan, 1905). That Jews contributed in no small way to Luther's work and the Reformation is an idea urged with great force in *The Jewish Review* (Routledge), November 1911, by Dr. D. Pool.

ESSAY X

REVELATION

BY

P. GARDNER-SMITH, B.A.

Formerly Lady Kay Scholar of the College

ANALYSIS

There are two explanations of positive religion, the one purely psychological, the other involving the conception of a Revelation from God.

The necessity of examining our fundamental conceptions of the relationship between God and Man before any satisfactory conclusion can be reached.

I. REVELATION IN GENERAL.

(a) The popular theory of a purely *objective* revelation.
Its presuppositions and its necessary consequences.
Its inadequacy.

(b) The revolt against this view, and the rise of the *subjective* theory.
Its strength and its weakness.

(c) An attempt at reconstruction leading on to—

II. REVELATION IN CHRIST.

The historical fact of the life of Christ and the Christian interpretation of it.

If there was a revelation through Him, it was both subjective and objective at once.

The Incarnation.

III. INSPIRATION.

(a) History of the ecclesiastical doctrine.
Its origin in the theology of Judaism, its adoption and extension in the Christian Church, and its growth and modification in later times.

(b) The doctrine in its modern form.
Criticism of the dogma as—(α) meaningless, (β) unnecessary, (γ) resting upon a false dualism of the human and the Divine.

(c) Conclusion.

ESSAY X

REVELATION

THE foregoing essays have mainly treated of the formation of the sacred books of the Christian Church. Beginning from the Captivity, the endeavour has been made to show how the ancient history and legislation of the Hebrews became the sacred book of the Jewish Church. The rise of Christianity out of the soil of Judaism has been traced, and some account has been given of the different forms which it assumed even in the days of the apostles. Finally, it has been shown how the Synagogue and the Church parted from one another, the one developing into Rabbinic Judaism, the other into Catholic Christianity.

The task which now lies before us is less historical and more strictly theological. The question which must be answered before a volume of Biblical Essays can be complete is the supreme question underlying all the rest—Has man received a revelation from God? The historical study of religion is interesting, as all history is interesting, in disclosing the steps of the ladder of human progress, in enabling us to trace the stages in the gradual unfolding of that mystery of mysteries, the psychical nature of man. But is that all? If it were, religion would be a curiosity for the dealer in antiquities rather than a vital force in the world to-day; it would be an interesting skeleton to be reconstructed by the anthropologist of fragments rescued from the dust-heaps of the past; at the most, it would be an "epiphenomenon" of human progress, a shadow cast by the human mind upon the plane of history, an eternal shadow perhaps, but a shadow still.

We are faced, then, with two possible explanations of religion—the naturalistic, and what we may call the supernaturalistic. Either religion, with all its developments and all its complexities, is an "accident," of which man's nature is the "substance," a necessary accompaniment of his natural endowment, or religion, at least in some cases, is something more, a revelation from without, not merely a process from within.

Perhaps we should not be too hasty in declaring the former view fatal to the reality of religion in general. Even a shadow has to be accounted for; it does not appear unless there is a light behind, and indeed it is chiefly in a consideration of the natural faculties of man that modern arguments for theism find their support. But such a view has never been that of Christianity, and its adoption would profoundly modify our conceptions of the Person of Christ and other fundamental ideas of the faith. We are therefore bound before accepting it to review the whole question with the greatest care, and to see whether it is necessary to travel so far from traditional ideas.

"Theology," says Mr. J. K. Mozley, "must precede Christology. The Old Testament came before the New, Arianism before Nestorianism." [1] And so with the problem before us. Many of the discussions upon the question of the Revelation of God to man are so barren because they rest upon no clear conception of God or of man, and in theology, if not in mathematics, the relation between indeterminates is a hopeless study. We must have some definite idea of God, and of man in relation to Him, before any self-consistent theory of Revelation is possible. The present essay falls naturally into three main divisions. Firstly, we must discuss the problem of Revelation in its widest aspects as determined by our conceptions of God and Man. Secondly, we may consider in what special sense a revelation has been given in the Person of Christ. Thirdly, in the light of conclusions thus reached we shall be able to turn our attention to the question of the Inspiration of Holy Scripture.

If this seems a tiresome and roundabout method, we should remember the admirable maxim of Descartes, "To

---

[1] As regards the Arian controversy, it must be here assumed that it was primarily occupied with the nature of the Godhead rather than with the Divinity of the Logos. In the opinion of Athanasius, the teaching of Arius that the Son is an inferior God leads us back again to polytheism. The Nicene fathers defended the Unity of the Godhead.

make everywhere enumerations so complete, and surveys so wide, that I shall be sure of omitting nothing." [1]   Dr. M'Taggart has remarked upon the difficulty of setting a paper of questions on Philosophy. "There is only one question in Philosophy," he says, "all the rest are but corollaries of the fundamental proposition." It is the same in Theology. Superficiality is the father of controversy, and the only way in which superficiality can be avoided is by beginning at the beginning, and striving to lay our foundations secure before we proceed to the construction of our edifice.

I.—REVELATION IN GENERAL

We may begin by taking the question of Revelation as it presents itself to the unreflective mind. Popular thought is still so thoroughly steeped in a dualism of a semi-deistic type that to it the subject can only appear in one aspect. Man is on earth, and God, if there be a God, is in heaven. Therefore, if man on earth is to have any knowledge of God in heaven it must be derived solely from external revelation at particular times and in particular places. Sometimes Jehovah descends to speak to His people from the Mount, sometimes He appears to His prophets in a vision; but, whatever the circumstances may be, every revelation is regarded as an abnormal event, clearly distinguishable from ordinary human experience. Those who did not stand at the foot of Sinai, and those who have not seen the glory of the Lord in a vision, must rely upon the testimony of the chosen few; the religious man must walk with his head turned backwards, and the last word in determining the creed must be spoken by the historian of the past.[2]

Applied to Christianity, the results of such a theory are obvious and inevitable. In Jesus, it is asserted, we have a

---

[1] Descartes, *Discourse on Method*, sect. ii.

[2] The error of this position lies in its neglect of the present, not in its respect for the past. We can ill afford to neglect God's revelation in bygone ages. In particular, those who regard the revelation in Christ as the supreme revelation of the mind of God must constantly look backwards, but it will be argued later that Christianity does not necessitate a complete surrender of the positive and constructive powers of the human mind in the manner demanded by those who rely solely on objective revelation.

revelation of a strictly objective character; except for a partial revelation to the saints of the Old Testament, the life and teaching of our Lord must be the one and only source of our knowledge of God, and in order that we may be sure that the revelation has been accurately transmitted to us, it is absolutely necessary to suppose that an inspired record of His Words and His Works was left by His contemporaries. As our knowledge of God depends wholly upon the revelation in Christ, so our knowledge of Christ depends wholly upon the inerrancy of Scripture, and any doubt cast upon the historical accuracy of the Bible strikes religion at its centre by robbing us of the assurance that we possess any certain knowledge of God.

No wonder Christian theology of this type has had little use for the doctrine of the Holy Spirit. It is not guidance in the present which is looked for, so much as authority in the past. Yet, granted its premises, the development of the theory is reasonable. If it be true that man cannot have any knowledge of God except that derived from external revelation, then it is clearly of vital importance that a man should be able to place explicit reliance upon his sources of information; for once that confidence is shaken he is cut adrift from all hope of attaining to the truth.

That, of course, is the reason for the distress felt in many pious minds at the progress of the Higher Criticism. It is not so much a dread of the results of such criticism which inspires opposition to the work of critics; many of the sternest opponents of critical study are honestly convinced that nothing can shake what they call the " truth of the Bible." What is really objected to is the attitude of mind which admits the faintest possibility that these priceless records may be fallible; and to the pious Protestant of the old school, to pursue a course of study which entertains such a possibility, seems tantamount to a betrayal of the Faith.

Now every advance in knowledge brings home the fact more clearly that there is no external standard of truth which can be imposed on the individual. The Scriptures are not free from human imperfections. However sympathetic we may be with the old-fashioned believer in his search for some absolute external authority, we must still resist the temptation arbitrarily to create one for his benefit. If the Bible contains elements repugnant to our developed moral consciousness, we can no longer proclaim its every word to have been written by the finger of God, any more than we can accept the formularies of the Church, drawn up by men not all of whom were governed by the Spirit and Word of God, as the complete and final expression of eternal truth. However we may desire it, there exists no "*regula fidei*" which can be accepted by the individual as his infallible authority in matters of belief, and the fact that the external theory of revelation depends upon the existence of such an authority is in itself sufficient to convince us of its inadequacy.

But even if such an authority were forthcoming the gain would be a very questionable one. The purely objective theory of revelation necessitates the imposition of a rigid restraint upon individual thought in accordance with the revealed dogmas embodied in the infallible authority. The intellect revolts at once. If revelation can find no place for reason then reason retaliates by excluding revelation, and there is an immediate collision between theology and philosophy. The mind is not a machine which can be made to run within fixed grooves, and those who have tried to confine philosophic thought within the limits of a series of theological dogmas have only succeeded in robbing philosophy of any value it could ever have. This was the ultimate fate of Scholasticism. And yet the external theory unquestionably demands the disparagement of reason, at least in the religious sphere; *ex hypothesi* God is beyond the reach of unaided human knowledge, and the sooner the philosopher relinquishes the vain attempt to bridge the gulf between heaven and earth the better. So we are left with the eternal conflict between religion and science, a conflict in which each successive encounter ends in the complete or partial discomfiture of "religion."

Historically it is probable that the struggles between religion and science during the last century did more than anything else to expose the poverty of the old ideas concerning

God and man. In view of the triumphs of the rational faculty, men have rebelled against the demand that they should regard reason as profane in its origin and phenomenal in its application. The intellect is felt to be too noble an endowment to be banished from the noblest activities of the human consciousness; clearly religion has no more a right to suppress reason than reason is justified in ignoring religion, and some way must be found of reconciling the two.

The inquirer is therefore led to question the validity of the assumption from which he started; he begins to doubt whether he was justified in taking it for granted that men are wholly dependent upon objective revelation for their knowledge of God. The question is so obvious that it has occurred to the thinking minds of every generation. Jeremiah saw the deficiencies of a covenant in which it was necessary for every man to teach his neighbour and every man his brother, saying, "Know the Lord"; St. Paul admitted that the Gentiles might be a law unto themselves, though they had never heard of Moses and the Prophets; the more liberal of the early Fathers taught that the Greek philosophers had found some truth in their own consciousness independently of the Mosaic revelation; and, during more recent times, we have only to point to the growth of a theory of natural religion to show the unwillingness of religious thinkers to confine the revelation of God to particular times and particular places. The fact is that the whole idea of a revelation solely "*ab extra*" is untenable in that it fails to do justice both to the majesty of God and to the dignity of man. Moreover, the theory is psychologically unsound: it is realised now that if man were by nature "ungodly," no theophany with signs and wonders could teach him to know the Lord; if the imagination of his heart were only evil continually, then he could not be persuaded even though one rose from the dead. The Divine spark must be latent in the human mind if the Spirit of God is to fan it into flame.

The recognition of these simple facts has brought about a revolution in religious thought, the purely objective theory has collapsed like a house of cards, and some new solution of the problem is sought to put in its place.

Modern theism has come to involve the recognition of one fundamental truth, namely, that man does share in some degree in the nature of God. That being so, it can no longer be believed that he is solely dependent upon external revelation for his knowledge of Him from whom His own being is derived. Consequently it must be possible for man to hear the voice of God in the whisperings of his own heart at least as clearly as he can hear it in the thunder on the Mount. Revelation thus becomes no longer an objective communication of Divine truth, but a development of all that is best in man's own consciousness; as Dr. Wilson has expressed it in the *Cambridge Theological Essays*, "We have ceased to think of the sun's rising upon the earth, we know now that it is the earth which turns towards the sun."

The new conception of revelation as subjective in character is hailed at first with delight by the Christian apologist; he has no longer to face difficult questions as to why Revelation in the past should have been confined to so small a portion of the human race, and why it should have ceased completely at a time when to all appearances it is as much needed as ever; he is freed from constant anxiety as the destructive critic throws doubt upon point after point in the records of Revelation in the past; he is delivered from the necessity of giving year by year a fresh scientific demonstration of "the fact of Revelation"; he can face without misgiving the doubter who suggests that Revelation is incomplete and insufficient for modern needs; and so on with nearly all the difficulties which harassed the exponent of the old objective theory. If Revelation is, and always must be, subjective in character, then the variations and deficiencies which exist in historic presentations of the truth depend upon differences in the religious insight of successive generations rather than upon any plan of progressive but defective revelations from God to man.

But the champion of the subjective theory of Revelation has to face other difficulties scarcely less perplexing. He may be able to silence the sceptic, but he has the believer to reckon with, and the believer wants a clear definition of his attitude towards the alleged facts of external revelation which have been regarded in the past as the sole source of religious knowledge. This is the rock upon which attempts to formulate a comprehensive theory of Revelation on a subjective basis have suffered shipwreck in the past. If we are to avoid a similar fate and a new divorce between Religion and Philosophy, we must seek diligently for some *via media* between Supernaturalism and Rationalism to a reasonable religion which lies somewhere beyond them both.

The time has passed when a denial of an objective revelation of statutes and judgements on Mount Sinai would be likely to shock the feelings of the majority of thinking men; for us the centre of gravity of the Old Testament lies no longer in the Law, but in the Prophets, and they are easily comprehended in the subjective scheme. But in the sphere of the New Testament the problem becomes much more pressing. The question really comes to this—If God be present in the reason of man, man must be capable of apprehending Divine truth by the exercise of his own mental powers, as some of the Fathers admitted, with qualifications, in the case of the Greek philosophers; why, then, did God give an external revelation in the Person of Christ? To admit the possibility of such a revelation seems at first sight to sacrifice the whole subjective position; on the other hand to deny it is to sacrifice Christianity, and we are not anxious to do either.

The problem is an old one. The first solution proposed was the obvious suggestion brought forward by Thomas Aquinas and still heard occasionally in theological lecture-rooms, that in the discovery of Dogma Reason can take us up to a certain point and Revelation must do the rest. This theory may be plausible enough at first sight, but a closer scrutiny cannot fail to reveal in it the reintroduction of the fundamental fallacy of the old idea, namely, that an objective revelation is possible, the truth of which provokes no response in the human consciousness, a revelation which is in fact beyond the power of man to grasp. Once that is admitted, there is no reason why any revelation should be comprehensible, and we are back in the old objective theory from which we have already escaped.

No compromise of this kind is possible; we must seek some solution of the difficulty which transcends the underlying dualism instead of confusing its elements.

Lessing faced the problem in his *Education of the Human Race*, in which he regarded all positive religions as successive stages in the education of man's religious consciousness. But although in this scheme Lessing allowed certain concessions to Christianity, his conception of the Person of Christ remained one which no Christian can fail to regard as inadequate. Herder's theory is somewhat similar. He defines Revelation as "the providential guidance of the development of the human mind," and he admits that Christianity marks the highest point to which this development has attained; but, like Lessing, Herder distinguishes sharply between the religion *of* Christ, the worship of God as the Father of man, and the religion *on* Christ, which he describes as the unthinking worship of a human person Jesus. So again with Hegel. He distinguishes three stages in man's religious progress—the nature stage corresponding to man's childhood, the stage of law or beauty (Judaism or Hellenism) corresponding to man's youth, and the final stage, where the pure notion of religion itself becomes phenomenon corresponding to man's full development; this last is Christianity.

Now all these schemes are satisfactory as doing justice to man's rational and religious faculty, but they do not do justice to the unique position of the Person of Christ; they do not make it clear why the Incarnation was necessary in order that man should grow up to maturity; indeed they make belief in the Incarnation extremely difficult. The Christian, when he has read them all, feels that he has not yet reached a solution of his difficulties.

Perhaps, at the risk of being tedious, our safest course is to go back to the beginning, to trace the line of thought which has exercised so supreme a dominion over the religious philosophies of the last two centuries, and to see whether it is possible to remain true to the principles of scientific

x

thought and yet to retain some more satisfying conception of the Person and Work of Christ.

We may take the old view of an external revelation to a profane people as finally overthrown; a revelation which awoke no answering chord in the consciousness of men, would at the most be barren, incomprehensible, and useless. No religious genius ever succeeded in freeing himself from the thoughts and feelings of his age; if he had done so his age would not have listened to his message. "We call that man great," said Bacon, "who thinks and speaks the people's thoughts the best," and however the genius may transcend the conscious ideas of his contemporaries, his work can only become fruitful in so far as it brings to the surface the latent intuitions of his fellow-men. No man ever acted solely on the teaching of another; he must make that teaching his own before it can become a living force in his life, and that is only possible if the intuitions of the genius and of the pupil are ultimately the same.

As with the teaching of the genius, so with the teaching of God; in Revelation the human mind must be a co-operative and conditioning factor, otherwise the revelation is degraded from being an active force to the position of an incomprehensible curiosity.[1] The whole theory of Revelation as the communication to man of dogmatic formularies which he cannot understand is ridiculous, and the sooner it disappears from the pages of popular apologetic the better it will be for the Christianity it is intended to defend. We must not be misunderstood. We have little sympathy with that impertinent dogmatism which throws over at once everything of which the meaning is not immediately clear, we have no brief for the shallow "free-thinking" which sets up its own paltry intelligence as the supreme standard of truth and falsehood, discarding creeds and formularies with

---

[1] This is the fact which is so constantly neglected in the current controversies of the day. It is difficult to conceive what object can be served in getting men to believe a series of propositions which are admittedly beyond the realm of human thought ; but when the further step is taken of inducing them to acquiesce by a public recitation in the consignment to eternal torment of all who do not believe these incomprehensible mysteries, the position becomes not only irrational but profane.

impatient scorn because their deepest meaning is not apparent at a glance; the fact that the dogmas of the Church have survived the lapse of centuries is enough to show that they do conceal real interests of the religious life; only we would plead that it is "the business of the theologian not to enforce their unintelligent recitation, but to interpret to each generation the living and reasonable message which they contain" (Pfleiderer).

So far, then, we have established the fact that a revelation to be conceivable at all must be capable of being grasped and appreciated by the mind of man; it must appeal to his reason, it must stimulate and guide his emotions, it must take hold upon his whole being, otherwise it is useless and unnecessary. But does this mean that it is merely "subjective" in the narrower sense of the term? Does this compel us to conclude that our religious ideas are simply the result of the unaided thought of successive generations of religious men? This is the real point at issue, and we cannot see that we are bound to join the rationalists and give an affirmative reply. For the Pantheist the above suggestion would be open to no very serious objection, since if the mind of man is wholly Divine then of course it may be trusted to discover truth without any fear of serious error. But in this, as in many other cases, experience does not favour the Pantheistic assumption; the judgements of men do err, and therefore they cannot be exclusively controlled by the Divine Wisdom; to all who see in the apparent evil of human nature something more than a negative imperfection, unquestioning reliance upon the deliverances of the unaided human intellect will seem a somewhat hazardous venture. The old dogmatist forgot that men were sons of God, but the Pantheist forgets that they are sons of Adam; the inquirer feels that there is still some guarantee required of "the truth of religion," and he turns once more to the idea of Revelation.

Now it is admitted that history reveals certain men who far transcended their fellows in the comprehension of Divine truth; must we assume that this was due in each case only to a psychological accident, or have we here traces of a

special revelation from a transcendent God ?   No doubt
there is much truth in the former suggestion ; it does require an exceptional ear to hear clearly the still, small voice ;
but surely the still, small voice must be an objective fact
in order that even an exceptional ear may hear it.   Granted
that all men are born of the Spirit of God, the Pantheist
has never been able to explain clearly why some men show
such evident traces of their Divine origin, while others give
little or no indication of a spiritual parentage.   Surely it is
more reasonable to explain religious genius by accepting
in some measure the clear and universal testimony of its
possessors, to believe that Isaiah did have a vision concerning Judah and Jerusalem, and that the Lord did appear to
St. Paul on the road to Damascus.   Does this involve the
abandonment of the subjective principle of Revelation on
which we determined to take our stand ?   Philosophers have
been too ready to assume that it does, forgetting that the
one truth which compelled us to adopt the subjectivist
position was the fact that man must have that in his nature
which renders him capable of receiving an objective revelation.   We do not argue that the subjective theory makes the
objective revelation impossible, but rather that it renders it
necessary.   In the sphere of metaphysics we are constantly
reminded of the danger of separating subject and object, and
of treating either in isolation from its logical complement,
and in dealing with the problem of Revelation we seem liable
to make the same mistake ; a purely objective revelation is
impossible, but a purely subjective revelation is a contradiction in terms.   No doubt man's nature is not without the
Divine spark, so that he can recognise the Voice of God
and attend to its commands.   But the Voice of God must
speak before he can hear it, otherwise what he takes for
the Divine Voice may be no more than the echo of his own
imperfect understanding ; what he thinks is the light of
heaven may be a will-o'-the-wisp leading him into the slough
of delusion and error.

But in whom is the Divine Voice to speak ?   The answer
can only be, in the heart of every man who will listen.
There is no man to whom the Voice from heaven will not

speak, but not to all will it ring with equal sound. "Blessed are the pure in heart," said our Lord, "for they shall see God"; in other words, the purer the heart of the prophet, the deeper will be the revelation which he can convey to his fellow-men.[1] This leads us directly to the second section of our inquiry—the determination of the place of the revelation in Christ in the general scheme of God's revelation to man.

II.—CHRISTOLOGY

WE have seen that it is precisely in the region of Christology that theories of the immanence of the Divine Reason are most unsatisfying. There has been a tendency to represent the revelation in Jesus Christ as merely a stage in the progressive education of the human race, to place Him, as did the Manichæans, in a line with Abraham, Moses, and the rest, and to suggest that the particular stage of development represented by His teaching may be already out-grown. Indeed at this point the ancient heretics were more consistent than many of their modern successors; for when once it has been granted that Christianity is simply a phase in human progress and Christ an embodiment of the enlightenment attained in man's religious consciousness, there seems no reason to suppose that the highest phase was reached two thousand years ago, or that the religious consciousness exhibited in the life and teaching of Christ is the highest to which it is possible to attain. Such an assumption is intrinsically improbable, and Hegel, in describing Christianity as the "absolute religion," is making a somewhat illogical concession to traditional ideas rather than following out the principles of his system.

Now it is conceded by most that in the life and death of Jesus of Nazareth we find an altogether unique phenomenon. We behold One who appeared as a Galilean Peasant of humble origin, who sought no worldly power and who certainly never possessed any, who lived in a remote corner of

---

[1] It should be noted that purity of heart is no more than the conditioning factor on the side of man ; it is still open to us to believe that God *chooses* certain men thus qualified to be the bearers of a special revelation to mankind.

the Roman Empire, who spent His life among Galilean fisher-
men, who was finally tortured and murdered by the malice of
His own countrymen, and who yet left behind Him a society
of men who, solely by reliance on the power of His Personality, were able to change the whole course of the world's
history, to subdue alike the civilisation of the ancient world
and the barbarism of its northern conquerors, and to remain
to-day the greatest power operative in the civilised world.

It is the consideration of facts like these which make
us hesitate in classing Jesus with Moses and Buddha and
Mahomet. No doubt there are many points of similarity
between His life and theirs, between His teaching and that of
the other great men who had helped to bring heaven and
earth nearer together, but when all has been said there remains a difference which demands explanation. Other faiths
are too much religions of the past to become the religions of
the future; Christianity alone displays the capacity of adapting itself to every stage of human progress, and the power of
adapting every stage of human progress to itself.

What is the explanation? Who was this Prophet of
Nazareth? The early followers of Jesus ultimately suggested
an answer; they said that the revealing Logos of God, who had
been immanent throughout the history of the world, finally
became incarnate in the Person of Christ, and the Word was
made flesh and dwelt among us, that in Him alone the Voice
from Heaven was not hushed by the imperfect capacities of
human nature, but in Christ the Divine in all its fulness
was made Human.

This was the conviction in the strength of which the
Christian Church went forth to battle with the world, this
was the dogma which it enshrined in creeds and formularies,
and this has been the philosophy of revelation on which it
has built its theology. Is it true? We cannot prove it; if
we believe it our belief will remain to the end a venture of
faith, but when we consider the unique power of Christianity
in all ages to stimulate and to control, to cheer and to ad-
monish, we can at least insist that our venture is a reasonable
one, that what evidence there is or can be favours the
Christian doctrine.

But further, if there is an objective revelation in the teaching of our Lord, it is not purely objective in the old sense of the term. We may search His teaching in vain for a code of dogmatic theology; even the Fathers at Nicæa, who entertained no doubts as to the historical character of the discourses in the fourth Gospel, had to admit that there was no exact equivalent in Scripture to the test word ὁμοούσιον. He taught His disciples a Prayer, but not a creed; He told them little or nothing of the state of the departed; He demanded faith in Himself, but He gave them no metaphysical instruction as to the nature of the Godhead; what He did was to stir to the depths their own religious consciousness, to draw out all that was noblest in their religion and in their characters, and to leave them with a Spirit who should guide them into all truth. If ever there was a "subjective" revelation it is that of Jesus Christ.

As with the power of Christ, so with the power of His Church. Christianity, whenever it has been taken seriously, has carried with it not only a death unto sin but a new birth unto righteousness; the work of faith in the hearts of men has always been the same, a quickening of all that is best in man's nature and its concentration upon the service of God. And all this is because the revelation Christ provokes so immediate a response in the heart of him who grasps it, because the teaching of Christ is *subjective* in the true sense of the word. It is because we find that Christianity is eminently human that we believe that its Author was pre-eminently Divine.

There is one question more. Why was it necessary for God to give this unique revelation in the Person of His Son? If the question is raised in a captious spirit it is no doubt an impertinence; we have no right to expect a clear insight into all the plans of God, and the revelation in Jesus Christ was doubtless a part of His purpose which we may never completely understand. Nevertheless, we may perhaps catch a glimpse of the significance of this supreme revelation.

This is not the place to discuss the thorny problem of the origin of evil, but only the Pantheist can deny that man is very far from fulfilling the true destiny of his nature. However the theory is stated, the fact of original sin remains unshaken. That being so there is no reason to reject summarily the ecclesiastical doctrine of Redemption, because it has too often been involved with what Dr. Inge calls "immoral theories of forensic transactions between the Persons of the Trinity." Why it should be so we do not know; but the fact remains that man left to himself, without external religious influences, deteriorates. The Divine spark in him is never quenched, but it burns dimly and feebly; the Divine Reason remains in man's nature ready to respond to the quickening influence of a transcendent God, but it is too weak to apprehend God without the light of a special revelation.

How could such a revelation be perfectly given? Surely not by a voice from Sinai, nor by a prophet who himself shared in the spiritual degradation of his race, however far he might transcend the general level; only One could do it, and truly this man was the Son of God—

> "There was no other good enough
> To pay the price of sin,
> He only could unlock the gate
> Of heav'n and let us in."

It is a simple hymn, but it expresses a profound truth. This is what St. Paul meant by his doctrine of the Second Adam; only the "generic man," He who represented human nature as it should be rather than humanity as it is, could become a life-giving Spirit. "As in Adam all die, so in Christ shall all be made alive." In a sense the old dogmatists were right, it was the Fall which made the Atonement necessary; it was the sin of Adam which necessitated a revelation through the Son of God if man were ever to come to a knowledge of the Father; but one thing they too often forgot—that he who was ὁμοούσιος with the Father called Himself the Son of Man.

III.—INSPIRATION

We pass now to the third and last section of this essay, and proceed to inquire what position our views upon the subject of Revelation in general lead us to adopt with regard to the particular question of the Inspiration of the Sacred Scriptures of the Christian Church. It has already been remarked that superficiality is responsible for a good deal of controversy, and one of the most superficial controversies ever waged is that concerning the Inspiration of Scripture. Writers upon the subject nearly all begin from the assumption that a belief in the inspiration of the Bible is an essential element of Christian faith; they do not ask what exactly they mean by Christian faith; they give no accurate definition of Inspiration, and only very seldom do they make any adequate attempt to show the connection between the two. It is our object in the present essay to treat the subject in the widest possible manner, therefore it is to these fundamental questions that we must turn our attention.

(*a*) It is generally easier to estimate the value of that of which we know the origin, and therefore it is important that we bear in mind an outline of the history of the doctrine of Inspiration, both of the origin of such a belief and of the various forms in which it has appeared.

The idea of a collection of books, to which special reverence is due, was derived by the Christian Church from the theology of later Judaism. From the time of Ezra and Nehemiah, who first presented the Mosaic code in its completed form, the very existence of Judaism had been centred in the Law, and it is not surprising that regard for the code gradually passed into a regard for the books in which it was contained. In the case of the Pentateuch the Rabbis developed an extreme view of Inspiration. First it was taught, as later in the Talmud, that Moses had written every word at the dictation of God, then the Alexandrians inferred that this implied the complete suspension of his natural faculties, and, finally, there were those who believed that the Law had been written in heaven and handed to Moses in one volume or in two. One Rabbi found it possible to conceive of God's employing His spare time in the study of the Mosaic code. There is no reason to suppose that these extreme views were shared by the ordinary Jew any more than Professor Cheyne's Jerameelite theories are shared by the ordinary critic, but they serve to show us from whence sprang those ideas concerning the inspiration of written oracles, which have been so prominent a feature in

Christian theology, and to what lengths these ideas were pushed quite apart from Christian influences.

The writings of the prophets were treated with a respect only second to that accorded to the Law, and the miscellaneous literature of the Jews, though only collected into a fixed "canon" at a comparatively late date, was considered sufficiently edifying to be read in public.

It is interesting to note the attitude of the Early Church towards the sacred Scriptures of the Jews. The first generation of Christian believers were Jews first and Christians later, and it was natural that they should retain their reverence for the Old Testament which they had been brought up to regard as the Word of God. Thus the Bible of the Jews became the Bible of the Church, and for many years it had no rival in the esteem of the majority of Christian believers. We say "the majority of Christian believers," for the Old Testament Scriptures did not establish their position in the Church without any protest from the Gentile converts, and it is important that this protest, and the causes from which it arose, be borne in mind. The writers of the New Testament no doubt reflect the opinion of the first century in treating Christianity as the culmination of God's Revelation to the Jews. In this they were right: our Lord came not to destroy, but to fulfil, and in many ways Christianity represents the best elements in Judaism brought to perfection. But the recognition of this fact carried with it a grave danger lest the Synagogue should become the only door to the Church, and Christianity be degraded to the position of a Jewish sect. The Tübingen school of critics have at least performed one service in enabling us to realise how formidable was this danger in the first century; and had it not been for the devotion and energy of St. Paul there is little doubt that the Judaistic party would have gained the day. Through him, however, more liberal views triumphed and Christianity was emancipated from the bonds of Judaism. It was an absolutely necessary step, but the rejection of the Mosaic Code brought about a complete breach between the Synagogue and the Church, and made the Jew henceforth the fiercest enemy of the Christian. In the present connection this mutual hostility between Church and Synagogue is important, because it led to a movement within the Christian society towards a comprehensive denial of the Divine origin of the Old Testament. It culminated in the second century in the teaching of Marcion and of certain Gnostic sects who agreed in representing the God of the Old Testament as distinct from the Supreme Deity revealed under the New Dispensation, and as an inferior or, possibly, evil Being who could be safely disregarded by Christian believers. This was an extreme position, and it is interesting, not because it had the slightest chance of becoming the official view of the Church, but because it is instructive to notice that despite the high regard in which the Jewish Scriptures have generally been held, there have yet been those who thought they could reject *in toto* both Judaism and its books and still remain members of the Christian Church. The leaders of the Church rose in defence of the Old Testament Scriptures; firstly, because they had always been taught to look upon them as inspired, and all Churches are conservative; secondly, because there could be no reasonable doubt that Christ Himself had quoted them with approval; and thirdly, because the early Christians were convinced that the Messiahship of Jesus of Nazareth could be proved by quotation from Old Testament prophecies, and they were not likely to deny the inspiration of those writings which supplied the most trusted weapons they possessed for controversy with the Jews. Thus the extravagances of the Gnostics, far from endangering the position of the Old Testament in the regard of the Church, only served to establish it more firmly, and from the second century onwards we hear no more of any doubts concerning the inspiration of the Jewish Scriptures.

One point, however, is worthy of notice. Whereas the Jews had fixed their attention mainly upon the Law, according only a secondary respect to the prophets, and frankly disregarding the spirit of their writings, the Church, on the other hand, exalted the prophets to the position of supreme importance, and treated the Law as representing a stage of God's revelation to man which had been superseded by the revelation in Christ. It is curious to observe how modern criticism has confirmed this view. There is a wide difference between ancient and modern methods of exegesis, and many of the deductions which the Fathers made from particular passages strike us as simply amazing, yet we have learnt that they were right in finding the centre of gravity of the Old Testament in the prophets and not in the Law, that they were led by a true instinct when they made the prophets the precursors of Jesus Christ.

So far, then, we have seen how and why the Church accepted from Judaism the idea of a collection of sacred writings differentiated from other writings by the Divine nature of their contents. It is not necessary to trace in detail the familiar history of the addition to the Jewish canon of certain other books held in special esteem by the Christian Church. It is sufficient to bear in mind that the recognition of a Christian canon of equal or even greater authority than that of the Jews was the result of a gradual process due in a great measure to the particular circumstances of the time. There was no "New Testament" in the first century. Writings known to proceed from the hand of an apostle were doubtless treated with respect; Clement of Rome refers the Corinthians to the advice of St. Paul on the subject of unity, and Polycarp contrasts his own work with that of Peter or Paul; but if we except one strange and isolated sentence in the Epistle of Barnabas there is no reference to a New Testament book as Scripture before the middle of the second century, and we must go to the very end of the century before we find a New Testament canon placed beside that of the Jews and treated with equal respect. Even then no agreement was reached, and no authoritative list drawn up; it was not until the end of the fourth century that the main body of the Church reached a decision upon the number of books which must be considered inspired, and the canon of the Syriac-speaking Church remained incomplete until the Middle Ages. These are facts which cannot be ignored; they should help us considerably in estimating the relations between the Bible and the Church.

The last point to be considered is the function of the Scriptures in the development of the doctrine of the Church, and this will lead us to an examination of those views of inspiration with which we are familiar at the present day.

The canonisation of the New Testament writings was a process which developed rapidly during the second century. The reason for this is not far to seek. The Church was harassed on every hand by teachers who proclaimed mystical theosophical systems of their own manufacture as representing the true teaching of Christ and His apostles, and although the traditions of the great sees repudiated entirely the fancies of the Gnostics, the Church needed some authority more definite than that of tradition with which to confute the teachers of error. Obviously this authority was best supplied by these writings which had come down from the apostles and their immediate followers. They, if any one, knew the teaching of Christ, and if it could be proved from their writings that they not only knew nothing of æons and pleromas, but repudiated the foundations upon which such conceptions were based, then the orthodox could conclusively refute the claim of the Gnostics to be in sole possession of the Catholic Faith. Thus through conflict with the heretics the Church came to regard the New Testament Scriptures as the invaluable guide and standard for determining the true doctrine of Christianity, and it was but a step from this attitude to the idea we find widespread at the time of the Council of Nicæa that all the essentials of faith are to be found in the pages of those books accepted as canonical, and that no doctrine which cannot be plainly proved therefrom is to be included in the official statement of the Catholic Faith.

This *regulative* function of Scripture has been of the highest importance in the history of the Church, and although it has been profoundly modified in the Roman Church by the admission of "tradition" to a place of authority equal to that of Holy Scripture it has never been formally denied. Even in the Roman Communion until comparatively recently the function of tradition has been supposed to be the interpretation of Scripture rather than its completion, and although no attempt is made to-day to derive Roman dogmatics wholly from the New Testament no Romanist would admit a contradiction between the two. The early Church made the Scriptures the supreme authority in matters of faith, and by an inevitable process of thought came to apply to them the ideas of Inspiration current among the Jews, and inconvenient as this principle proved in the development of medieval doctrine, it was too firmly rooted to be denied, so that the Church had recourse to forced and arbitrary methods of interpretation and suppression of Scripture, rather than to a bold repudiation of the doctrine of its Divine inspiration.

The Reformation made the supremacy of Scripture once more the guiding principle in the life of the Church. The Reformers had had unpleasant experience of the power of tradition to sanction every abomination which the rulers in Rome cared to suggest, and they realised that their only course was to repudiate its authority. This was the work of Luther, the apostle of individual freedom, who, being convinced that Catholicism was inconsistent with the fundamental principles of early Christianity, boldly defied the Pope and proclaimed his right to return to an earlier and purer theology. But one important point must be borne in mind. Luther did not renounce the unthinking worship of the Pope in order to put the unthinking worship of the Bible in its place; no one can accuse Luther of making the Bible his fetish; nothing could be freer than his treatment of many passages in Scripture, and, as every one knows, he called the Epistle of St. James "an epistle of straw."

Unfortunately the Reformers were not all possessed of the genius of Luther, and, moreover, they were in a difficult position. The principle of the complete freedom of the individual is a noble religious theory, but it is a bad principle on which to drill an army. Luther himself did not carry it out consistently, and when the later Reformers stood exposed to the ferocity of the Catholic reaction, they cast around in despair for some firm common principle on which they could fall back, for some bond of union to give their forces the coherence commanded by the authority of the Pope. Like the Church of the second century they turned to the

Scriptures, but in proportion as their need was the more desperate, they made the more desperate use of their authority. Long before, the old rule that the Scriptures contain all things necessary to salvation had been unconsciously inverted and had become the false principle that all things contained in the Scriptures are necessary to salvation, and Calvin, and still more his followers, pressed this principle to its furthest logical conclusion. Every book was equally inspired, every word of it was the very word of God, and in short, the Reformers presented to the world the famous doctrine of the Verbal Inspiration of the Bible.[1]

The rest of the history is familiar enough. During the last century natural science, historical criticism, philosophy, and common sense combined to destroy this belief in the verbal infallibility of the Scriptures; and although to-day there are thousands who still hold the old-fashioned theory, they are not those who have studied the problems it involves or the grounds upon which it rests; for Biblical scholars the doctrine is of merely historical interest.

(*b*) But what is to be put in its place ? That is the question which has occupied the mind of the Church during the last fifty years, and two answers have been suggested.

On the one hand, the special Inspiration of Scripture is denied altogether, and the Bible placed in a line with other religious literature; on the other hand, as much of the old theory is retained as appears possible in the light of modern investigation, and search is made for a new definition of Inspiration which does not preclude the admission of mistakes and inaccuracies among the sacred pages.

The latter answer has been that supplied by the vast majority of students within the Church, and, in England at least, it is practically supreme in liberal circles. The view is ably stated in a large mass of current literature, amongst which mention may be made of works by Dr. Sanday, Dr. Kirkpatrick, the Dean of Westminster, and Dr. Horton, as perhaps the most familiar. It is this view which we will now proceed to examine.

[1] *Cf.* the Swiss *Formula Consensus* of 1675, where the vowel points and accents of the Hebrew text were declared to be inspired.

The widest divergence exists between individual members of the modern school as regards their critical position; some would accept practically the whole of the Bible as it stands, making allowances only for slight inaccuracies in scientific or historical fact, others would abandon most of the Old Testament as a historical authority and treat the New Testament as providing only relative certainty even in those parts retained as comparatively reliable, and yet we find writers of both these extreme schools, and many who occupy an intermediate position, ascribing with the greatest confidence "Inspiration" to the Bible. The Scriptures, they say, contain a Divine and a human element; the human element is due to their human authorship, and is made evident by historical inaccuracies and by crude religious and ethical conceptions reflecting the immature religious consciousness of those who wrote the books; the Divine element is a mysterious "something" rendering the books of the Bible different from all other religious literature, and justifying their inclusion in a canon of Holy Scripture. Thus, to quote Dr. Horton: "Inspiration is a word *sui generis*. It is a term which has only one thing for its content. It is true we use the word in other connections also; for instance, we speak of the *inspiration* of a great action when a man rises above himself; but no one for a moment confuses this use of the word with Inspiration as applied to Scripture." Similarly in the case of great writers, poets, and preachers, "We call them inspired because they see more than we do, not more than we can. They reveal the unobserved to us, but not the unknown or the unknowable."[1]

Dr. Sanday evidently agrees when he says, "It is far better not to ask what an inspired book ought to be, but to content ourselves with the inquiry what this Book, which comes to us as inspired, in fact and reality is."[2]

It appears to us that this theory does not truly represent the results of modern investigation and modern thought, that it is of the nature of a provisional compromise between the old and the new, and that the time has come when it

---

[1] *Inspiration and the Bible*, p. 11. It would be interesting to know what Dr. Horton understands by "a revelation of the unknowable." The contrast between "the unobserved" and "the unknown" is not obvious.

[2] Sanday, *Oracles of God*, p. 36.

must be seriously questioned. The theory seems open to three main objections; two arising from the study of the facts, and one of an *a priori* character.

(*a*) *In view of the phenomena on which it is supposed to rest, the modern theory of Inspiration is meaningless.*

The present-day theologian is ready enough to declare that he believes the Bible to be specially inspired, but the question must be asked, Does this confession amount to anything? Passing over the impropriety of employing so inaccurate an expression as " the Bible" in a scientific inquiry concerning a collection of books which includes the Epistle to the Romans and the Song of Solomon, we must ask for a definite statement of what is meant when this collection is described as divinely inspired.

Let us take one or two examples. The two books of Chronicles appear in the Canon as providing a history of Israel and Judah from the time of David to the Exile. As every student must admit, the work is difficult to rival for the free exercise of the inventive faculty and the deliberate falsification of history in the interests of ecclesiastical tradition. To quote but one passage from Wellhausen's memorable examination of the work of the Chronicler: " See," he says, " what Chronicles has made out of David! The founder of the Kingdom has become the founder of the Temple and the public worship, the king and hero at the head of his companions in arms has become the singer and master of ceremonies at the head of a swarm of Priests and Levites; his clearly cut figure [familiar in the Book of Kings] has become a feeble holy picture, seen through a cloud of incense." [1]

No doubt the picture of the Chronicler is not without interest—very probably many of his misstatements and false pictures are due to what Professor Kennett calls his " powers of inference," combined with his enthusiasm for the religion of his own day, rather than to any deliberate attempt to deceive his readers; but the point is this, how can we possibly describe the work he produced as " inspired " in any intelligible sense of the word? Doubtless he was a

[1] Wellhausen, *Prolegomena*, p. 182.

Y

religious enthusiast; we are not lacking in religious enthusiasts to-day who are only too willing to draw fancy pictures of the early Church as they consider it ought to have been, but we do not include their works in a canon of Scripture, and it is difficult to see why we should do so in the case of their intellectual kinsman merely because he was not a Christian of the twentieth century but a zealous Jew of 300 B.C.

The case of the Chronicler is exceptional, but let us consider such a work as the Book of Isaiah, which is treated by the modern critic with the highest respect; indeed Dr. Sanday argues for the real inspiration of the prophetical books, and thence seems to infer the general inspiration of the Old Testament. No one with a spark of religious appreciation could read the Book of Isaiah without admitting that it contains some of the most inspiring flights of religious rhetoric found in any literature. But this admission does not strictly imply the inspiration of the book itself. Here we pass to our second objection to the current doctrine of Inspiration—namely, that it is

(β) *Unnecessary as an explanation of the facts.* Very many books are *inspiring*, but that acknowledgment does not carry with it the admission that they are *inspired* in the particular ecclesiastical sense. The words of Isaiah are intensely inspiring, but if they were directly inspired how comes it that some of his predictions were never fulfilled? Take as another instance the Synoptic Gospels; the amount of inspiration which they have supplied to the human race is beyond all power of calculation, and yet surely this is not due to any special merit in the composition of the books themselves, but rather to the fact that they report the words of the Son of God. No faithful account of the events in Palestine at the time of which they write could fail to be inspiring, but this by no means implies the "inspiration" of the writers themselves. They, as St. Luke tells us, set about their task in the same way as all other historians, by the collection and criticism of material, and when we bear in mind the frequent contradictions between their respective narratives of the same events, it is difficult to believe that there was any divine interference with their work. "We have come," says Professor Gwatkin, "to look upon the Bible not as a Revelation, but as a record of a Revelation," and may we not add that there is no apparent reason why we should look upon such a record as itself inspired?

Moreover, it is to be observed the doctrine of the inspiration of the books themselves is not only unnecessary but positively mischievous, inasmuch as it places us in a position from which we must either retreat or advance. The upholders of verbal inspiration are perfectly right—an inspired *book* cannot contain mistakes. An inspired writing which misleads is a contradiction in terms, and no amount of protestation from the theologians can make it into a rational and consistent conception. Who can believe in Christianity and not believe that Isaiah, Jeremiah, and St. Paul were guided in their lives and words by the inward light of the Spirit? But between this conviction and a belief in the peculiar inspiration of their surviving writings there is a great gulf fixed.

(γ) We pass to our third objection to the current dogma, viz. *that it implies too sharp a distinction between the human and the divine.* In an earlier part of this essay we endeavoured to show that the supreme revelation of God to man could only consist in exhibition of the divine as human, and of the human as divine in the person of Him who, being of one substance with the Father, called Himself the Son of Man. And how is such a revelation possible if we cling to the popular dualism of God and man? The rigid distinction turns the doctrine of the Incarnation into an incomprehensible puzzle, a combination of contradictions, rather than a truth which is itself the answer to the riddle of existence. And the puzzle is unnecessary. The idea of a fundamental cleavage between the human and the divine belongs to the philosophy of Deism rather than to the theology of the Church; even the Old Testament dignified men with the title of gods, and surely the unity of God and man in Christ is the fundamental conception underlying the theology of the New Testament. If our Lord's teaching concerning the Fatherhood of God, and St. Paul's doctrines of Redemption and Atonement, and St. John's conception of the Incarnation of the pre-existent Logos, and the Church's doctrine of the Holy Spirit, are to be living truths and not irrational speculations, there can be no ultimate separation between the spheres of the human and the divine. Man as we know him is not God, and God as we worship Him must be something more than an abstract deification of humanity. Nevertheless if God is only in heaven, and man only on earth, no legions of angels could suffice to establish a communion of the soul with its Maker. We might explain the life of Christ as a Theophany, but not as an Incarnation; we might be Gnostics or Docetic heretics, but we could not hold the Catholic Faith. Man has fallen far from his high estate, he has never realised the dignity of his nature or fulfilled the lofty destiny of a son of God; but his errors can never wholly obscure his origin, his birthright may be sold but his parentage remains. Humanity at its worst may be contemptible, humanity at its best is still divine. Deep down beneath the sin and degradation of the natural man is the eternal element of divinity which makes it possible for him to rise above his sordid environment, and to follow the Saviour who led the way into the presence of God Himself.

The bearing of these conclusions upon the subject of our present inquiry is obvious. If a certain number of books are placed in a canon by themselves and treated as wholly divine, while all other religious literature is included in the category of the merely human, then we are committed to the unchristian dualism which we have condemned, to an implicit denial of the message of the Incarnation that the divine can be human, and the human can be divine. To call the canonical Scriptures the inspired foundation of the Church, and thence to infer their verbal infallibility is to assign to them that sort of divinity which is incompatible with any union with humanity. It is to insist wholly on the objective character of revelation, and to rob the Bible of its power to be a living force. Christianity, like Judaism under the Rabbis, becomes a Covenant written on stones and not on the tables of the heart. On the other hand, to maintain that unless they are absolutely divine the Scriptures are merely human, is to break the link between the historic Christ and the historic Church. By recognising that the truly human and the divine are not two irreconcilable elements but various manifestations of the same thing, as was shown in the person of Jesus, we can free ourselves from the dilemma.[1]

(c) *Conclusion.* Thus we conclude that the current doctrine of Inspiration is at fault, not because it claims too much, but because it claims too little. The term must be extended, not disused. Inspiration cannot be confined within a narrow period of time. In all ages of the Church men have felt its power, for in a very real sense all Christians must be inspired, else they are not Christians at all. Why then should their writings be considered merely human unless they can be dated before the end of the second century? Of course the writings of the New Testament must always retain an unique place in the esteem of the Christian Church. The immediate followers of our Lord are most likely to have been familiar with His teaching, and the books which they wrote most probably contain the essentials of the Faith uncontaminated and unadorned. Moreover their value is inestimable, not only for their witness to the beliefs of men who lived in the closest intimacy with the Lord Himself, but because they reflect the spiritual enthusiasm of the first century of the Church's history. From a purely spiritual standpoint the literature of the Apostolic age is unsurpassed, therefore throughout all ages the Church has turned for spiritual help to the writings of the Apostles and their immediate successors. It is to be hoped that it will ever continue to do so.

But this admission does not commit us to any hard and

---

[1] A critic objects that the dualism is not really transcended so long as we retain the antithesis of "perfect" and "imperfect." But surely this antithesis is not a "dualism" properly so called. It is a relation of degree, not a difference in kind which alone can constitute a dualism. For example, Bergson represents "matter" and "spirit" as two principles generally opposed, but he escapes an ultimate dualism by supposing both to proceed from an original "super-consciousness," of which "spirit" is a more or less perfect manifestation, and "matter" a kind of bye-product. So in this paper we have endeavoured to represent the divine and the human, not as belonging to two essentially different realms, but as the perfect and the imperfect manifestations of the same ultimate nature.

fast theory of Inspiration as a supernatural phenomenon manifested only in the distant past. Such a theory derives no support from the New Testament writings themselves, and it is untrue to religious experience. On the other hand the extended doctrine of Inspiration is morally helpful and empirically true. The message of the Incarnation was the revelation of the humanity of the divine, the task of the Church is the revelation of the divinity of the human. That task it can never accomplish so long as it confines the working of the divine in man to occasional moments of supernatural inspiration. If the Church and its members are to grow up into the measure of the stature of the fullness of Christ, a consciousness of the abiding presence of the Holy Spirit is a primary necessity. Men must realise that the revelation without is but a means to the revelation within, and when once that fact is grasped it follows that Inspiration is regarded, not as an abnormal affection in the past, but as a necessary state in the present. The Church of the future may respect the past less, but it will value the present more. Surely that is not to be regretted, so long as it worships Him who is not the God of the dead, but of the living.

INDEX

THE END

Printed by BALLANTYNE, HANSON & Co.
Edinburgh & London

Mr. Edward Arnold's List of Theological Books.

Devotional

JESUS SALVATOR MUNDI : Some
Lenten Thoughts on Salvation. By the Rev. J. H. BEIBITZ,
Rector of Shelsley Beauchamp and Shelsley Walsh, Wor-
cester ; late Vice-Principal of the Theological College,
Lichfield. Crown 8vo. 2s. 6d. net.

There are few tasks more important than that of subjecting our ordinary
religious ideas to a thoroughgoing analysis. Only so can they become real
to us, and gain, or regain, the power of directing and moulding our lives.
This little book represents an attempt to fulfil this task in regard to the
fundamental Christian conception of our salvation through and in Jesus
Christ ; in other words, to answer the question in what sense, and by what
means, are we ' saved ' ?

THE SAINTS' APPEAL. By the Rev. S. A.
ALEXANDER, Canon and Treasurer of St. Paul's; Author of
' The Mind of Christ,' etc. Fcap. 8vo. 2s. net.

It is hoped that, while suitable for devotional reading throughout the year,
the book will be found especially helpful as a companion for quiet hours in Lent.
It consists of a selection of the sermons preached by Canon Alexander last year
to very large congregations in St. Paul's Cathedral on Sunday afternoons.
They are an attempt to show the romance and heroism of the Christian life,
to bring the mystical and spiritual side of it into closer touch with ordinary,
practical affairs, and to illustrate in general ways the power and fascination
both of the belief and of the character of those who have endeavoured to live
that higher life under many different conditions of society.

THE CROWN OF THORNS. By the Rev.
A. E. BURN, Vicar of Halifax, Prebendary of Gaia Major
in Lichfield Cathedral; Author of ' An Introduction to the
Creeds and the Te Deum,' etc. Crown 8vo. 2s. 6d. net.

This is a course of meditations for Lent, Holy Week, and Easter, representing the substance of teaching given to many town congregations during
the last ten years.

' Dr. Burn's addresses are full of solid instruction and thoughts which
may foster devotion.'—*Church Times.*

' While the tone is truly devotional, touched here and there with the
secret we call mystical, there is a thought in every sermon for the intellect to
find pleasure in.'—*Expository Times.*

LONDON ; EDWARD ARNOLD, 41 & 43 MADDOX STREET, W.

Scriptural Interpretation and Commentary

AN INTRODUCTION TO THE SYNOPTIC PROBLEM. By the Rev. ERIC REDE BUCKLEY, Vicar of Burley-in-Wharfedale, Proctor in Convocation. Crown 8vo. 5s. net.

This book gives the main results of recent research as to the literary origin and composition of the Gospels of St. Matthew, St. Mark, and St. Luke. A distinctive feature of it is that all the more important passages on which the rguments rest are printed in full in English, thus relieving the reader of the necessity of constant reference to his Bible or Greek Testament. Besides giving a careful explanation of the theories most widely accepted by contemporary critics, the author has stated some alternative theories which seem worthy of consideration.

THE OLD TESTAMENT. By the Rev. H. C. O. LANCHESTER, Rector of Sall. Crown 8vo. 2s. 6d. net.

An attempt to place the general reader in a better position for the intelligent study of the Old Testament. The main results of the Higher Criticism are frankly accepted, and it is recognized that this movement has been fraught with considerable perils to faith ; but the writer endeavours to point out that modern studies have resulted in a broadening, rather than in an evaluation, of a reasonable faith. Some account is given of the historical background of the Old Testament, and of the assistance which recent researches have afforded to the study of it.

THE MIND OF ST. PAUL : As Illustrated by his Second Epistle to the Corinthians. By Canon H. L. GOUDGE, D.D., Principal of Ely Theological College. 2s. 6d. net.

' In a singularly lofty and spiritual book, Dr. Goudge, of Ely, handles with much insight and courage some urgent practical problems. Amidst the flood of small books on theology this one should survive.'—*Church Family Newspaper.*

MIRACLES IN THE NEW TESTAMENT : A Study of Evidence. By the Rev. J. M. THOMPSON, Fellow of Magdalen College, Oxford. Third Impression. Crown 8vo. 3s. 6d. net.

S. PAUL IN THE LIGHT OF MODERN RESEARCH. By the Rev. J. R. COHU, Rector of Aston Clinton, Bucks; sometime Fellow of Jesus College, Oxford. Crown 8vo. 5s. net.

' The treatment in every chapter is profoundly thoughtful, but exceedingly lucid in expression. The book is a real contribution to the literature of divinity.'—*Homiletic Review.*

THE BOOK OF BOOKS: A Study of the Bible. By Canon LONSDALE RAGG, B.D., Rector of Tickencote and Prebendary of Buckden in Lincoln Cathedral. Crown 8vo. Cloth. 5s. net.

' Mr. Ragg's volume is a timely and welcome piece of work. The author is an orthodox High Churchman, whose leanings are fundamentally traditional. His mind, however, is open to new light, and he sees clearly that the old-fashioned view of Scripture can no longer be held in face of the difficulties which modern investigation has brought to light. Yet this has meant no abandonment of his reverence for Scripture, no surrender of the claim which he makes for its uniqueness. His work will be found helpful by many who are conscious that great changes are required, but who are also conscious that the Bible must hold a solitary place in their affection and allegiance.'— *Holborn Review.*

THE SERVANT OF THE LORD. By ROBERT HATCH KENNETT, D.D., Canon of Ely, and Regius Professor of Hebrew in the University of Cambridge. Crown 8vo. 2s. 6d. net.

' Professor Kennett's work is marked by such qualities of originality and acuteness that it is always with expectation that we take up a book or article by him. The present volume contains simply four lectures delivered to the clergy in Cambridge, so that in the main it is a statement designed for educated readers rather than for experts. His results, however, and such indication of processes as can be given are of unusual interest, and his discussion will be found very stimulating.'—*Holborn Review.*

IN OUR TONGUES : Some Hints to Readers of the English Bible. By ROBERT HATCH KENNETT, D.D. Crown 8vo. 3s. 6d. net.

OUTLINES OF THE SYNOPTIC RECORD. By the Rev. BERNARD HUGH BOSANQUET, Vicar of Thames Ditton, and R. A. WENHAM. Crown 8vo. 6s.

The Work of the Clergy

HOW TO DEAL WITH LADS : A Handbook of Church Work. By Canon PETER GREEN. With a Preface by the Right Rev. LORD BISHOP OF GLOUCESTER. Crown 8vo., cloth. 2s. 6d. net.

'We have seldom read a volume of the nature of the present treatise with such unmixed pleasure as we have received from a perusal of Mr. Green's excellent work. There is a freshness about the whole treatment of the subject which is most stimulating.'—*Church Times.*

HOW TO DEAL WITH MEN : A Handbook of Church Work. By the Rev. PETER GREEN, M.A., Canon of Manchester, Rector of Sacred Trinity, Salford. Crown 8vo. 2s. 6d. net.

THE CHURCH AND MODERN PROBLEMS. By the Rev. C. F. GARBETT, M.A., Vicar of Portsea. 3s. 6d. net.

'We can confidently recommend the volume to those who wish to clear their views and see how a well-informed and sympathetic working clergyman boldly and manfully faces hard questions.'—*Church Family Newspaper.*

PREACHERS AND TEACHERS. By JAMES GILLILAND SIMPSON, D.D., Canon of St. Paul's; recently Principal of Leeds Clergy School. 5s. net.

' The whole book may be profitably studied both by preachers and hearers.' —*Church Times.*

THE CLERGY AND SOCIAL SERVICE. Cambridge Lectures on Pastoral Theology. By the Very Rev. W. MOORE EDE, D.D., Dean of Worcester. Crown 8vo., cloth. 2s. 6d. net.

THE ART OF READING AND SPEAKING. By JAMES FLEMING, B.D., late Vicar of St. Michael's, Chester Square, London. Ninth Impression. Crown 8vo., cloth. 3s. 6d.

Ecclesiastical History and Biography

THE PARTING OF THE ROADS:

Studies in the Development of Judaism and Early Christianity. By MEMBERS OF JESUS COLLEGE, CAMBRIDGE. With an Introduction by W. R. INGE, D.D., late Professorial Fellow, now Honorary Fellow of the College and Dean of St. Paul's. Edited by F. J. FOAKES JACKSON, D.D., Fellow and Dean of the College. Demy 8vo. 10s. 6d. net.

THE SPIRIT OF POWER: The Church in

the Early Second Century. By the Rev. ERNEST A. EDGHILL, M.A., B.D., Sub-Warden of the College of St. Saviour in Southwark; Hulsean Lecturer in the University of Cambridge. 5s. net.

THEODORE OF STUDIUM: His Life and

Times. By ALICE GARDNER, Associate and Lecturer of Newnham College, Cambridge. With Illustrations. 10s. 6d. net.

CHURCH AND STATE IN FRANCE

(1300=1907). By ARTHUR GALTON, Vicar of Edenham, and Chaplain to the Earl of Ancaster. 12s. 6d. net.

JERUSALEM UNDER THE HIGH

PRIESTS: Five Lectures on the Period between Nehemiah and the New Testament. By EDWYN BEVAN. 7s. 6d.

'These lectures deserve careful study by everyone interested in the history of how Hellenism and Judaism first came into contact.'—_Cambridge Review._

A MEMOIR OF THE VERY REV.

EDWARD CHARLES WICKHAM, Dean of Lincoln, and formerly Head Master of Wellington College. By Canon LONSDALE RAGG. With Illustrations. 7s. 6d. net.

'A very readable memoir.'—_Spectator._

A SERIES OF SHORT LIVES OF SAINTLY MEN

FRANCIS: THE LITTLE POOR MAN OF ASSISI. By the Hon. and Rev. JAMES ADDERLEY.
With Portrait of St. Francis. 3s. 6d.

MONSIEUR VINCENT: A Short Life of
St. Vincent de Paul. By the same Author. With Portrait.
3s. 6d.

HUGH OF LINCOLN. By CHARLES MARSON,
Vicar of Hambridge, Taunton. With Portrait. 3s. 6d.

Mission Work

EIGHTEEN YEARS IN UGANDA AND EAST AFRICA. By ALFRED R. TUCKER,
D.D., formerly Bishop of Uganda. With Illustrations by
the Author. Cheaper Edition. Crown 8vo. 7s. 6d. net.

'This complete and official episcopal narrative surpasses in interest and
authority all the smaller volumes hitherto published.'—*Times.*

A PARSON IN THE AUSTRALIAN BUSH. By the Rev. C. H. S. MATTHEWS, M.A., late
Vice-Principal of the Brotherhood of the Good Shepherd,
N.S.W. Fully Illustrated. 3s. 6d. net.

Social Work

ACROSS THE BRIDGES: A Study of
Social Life in South London. By ALEXANDER PATERSON.
With Preface by the BISHOP OF SOUTHWARK. New and
Cheaper Edition. Cloth, 2s. net; paper, 1s. net.

LETTERS FROM A SETTLEMENT.
By Miss A. L. HODSON. Illustrated. 4s. 6d. net.

'The letters were well worth publishing, and prove the great good which
is accomplished by a well-organized Settlement.'—*Athenæum.*

MISS LOANE'S BOOKS

'We would not merely recommend, but would urge, their attentive perusal upon all men and women who are concerned with the question of poor relief, and who are sincerely anxious to help the people without harming them.'
—*Spectator*.

THE COMMON GROWTH. By M. LOANE.
Crown 8vo. 6s.

THE QUEEN'S POOR : Life as they find it
in Town and Country. 3s. 6d.

NEIGHBOURS AND FRIENDS. 6s.

AN ENGLISHMAN'S CASTLE. 6s.

Philosophy and Religion

CATHOLICISM AND THE MODERN
MIND: A Contribution to Religious Study and Progress. With a Prefatory Letter to Pope Pius X. By MALCOLM QUIN, Author of 'Aids to Worship,' 'Notes on a Progressive Catholicism,' etc. Crown 8vo. 7s. 6d. net.

FROM RELIGION TO PHILOSOPHY.
By F. M. CORNFORD, Fellow and Lecturer of Trinity College, Cambridge. Demy 8vo. 10s. 6d. net.

Mr. Cornford's theory is that the originators of Greek philosophy did not, as is usually supposed, turn their backs wholly on religion and go direct to their own consciousness and the world around them for data for an explanation of the universe ; but that at the very outset of their investigations they in fact, though unconsciously, took over certain fundamental conceptions—those of Nature, God, and Soul—from the religious system which they believed themselves to have got rid of. In an elaborate and brilliant argument he traces back these conceptions to their roots in the 'collective mind' of primitive pre-religious man, and then, having established his theory, applies it to the explanation of the subsequent history of religious and philosophic thought, on which it throws a flood of new light.

THE FAITH OF AN AVERAGE MAN.
By the Rev. CHARLES H. S. MATTHEWS, M.A., Author of 'A Parson in the Australian Bush,' etc. 3s. 6d. net.

SOME DOGMAS OF RELIGION. By
J. M. E. McTAGGART, Litt.D., Fellow and Lecturer of Trinity
College, Cambridge; Author of 'Studies in the Hegelian
Dialectic,' etc. Demy 8vo. 10s. 6d. net.

**A REPORTED CHANGE OF RE-
LIGION.** By ONYX. 3s. 6d.

SOME PROBLEMS OF EXISTENCE.
By NORMAN PEARSON. Demy 8vo. 7s. 6d. net.

THE DIARY OF A MODERNIST. By
WILLIAM SCOTT PALMER, Author of 'An Agnostic's Progress,' etc. Crown 8vo., cloth. 5s. net.

'It is a reconstructive and creative book; above all, it is a spiritual book,
and it kindles in others that fire of the spirit by which the author has been
illuminated and warmed. It is a long time since we have met with a volume
of its kind which is so suggestive, so truly inspired in thought, so interesting
and attractive in style.'—*Spectator.*

Miscellaneous

A GOODLY FELLOWSHIP : Thoughts in
Prose and Verse from many Sources. Collected by ROSE E.
SELFE. With a Preface by the ARCHBISHOP OF CANTERBURY.
2s. 6d. net.

**THE ROMANCE OF THE HOLY
LAND.** By Dr. CHARLES LEACH, M.P. With numerous
Illustrations. 7s. 6d. net.

PATROLLERS OF PALESTINE. By
the Rev. HASKETT SMITH, M.A., F.R.G.S., Editor of
'Murray's Handbook to Syria and Palestine,' 1902; Author
of 'The Divine Epiphany,' 'Calvary and the Tomb of
Christ,' etc. With Illustrations. Large crown 8vo. 10s. 6d.

LETTERS TO A GODCHILD. By ALICE
GARDNER, Associate and Lecturer of Newnham College,
Cambridge. 2s. 6d. net.

LONDON : EDWARD ARNOLD, 41 & 43 MADDOX STREET, W.